TAKE CHARGE
of
YOUR WRITING

TAKE CHARGE
of
YOUR WRITING

Discovering Writing
Through Self-Assessment

David Daniel
Newbury College

Chris Fauske
Newbury College

Peter Galeno
Newbury College

Debbie Mael
Newbury College

Houghton Mifflin Company
Boston • New York

To Our Students

Senior Sponsoring Editor: Mary Jo Southern
Associate Editor: Kellie Cardone
Senior Project Editor: Fred Burns
Senior Production/Design Coordinator: Sarah Ambrose
Senior Manufacturing Coordinator: Sally Culler
Senior Marketing Manager: Nancy Lyman

Cover design: Dutton & Sherman Design
Cover image: © 1995 Brad Ellis

Acknowledgments for reprinted material appear starting on page 341.

Printed in the U.S.A.

Library of Congress Catalog Card Number: 00-105038

ISBN: 0-618-01181-1

123456789-DOC-04 03 02 01 00

Contents

P À R T   T W O
C H A P T E R   7

C H A P T E R   8

C H A P T E R   9

C H A P T E R   1 0

CHAPTER 11

WRITING THE RESEARCH PAPER   271

PART THREE

YOUR PORTFOLIO: ASSESSING YOUR WRITING   307

ADDENDUM   319

ACKNOWLEDGMENTS   341

INDEX   345

Rhetorical Table of Contents

To the Instructor

Take Charge of Your Writing is built upon the principle that the single most important skill students can learn in a writing course is the ability to assess their own writing. Especially for beginning writers, the ability to assess the strengths and weaknesses of their writing is a critical step in becoming self-aware, confident, and mature writers. With this skill, students can apply the fundamental concepts of writing to improve their mastery of writing and to meet future writing challenges.

The text is grounded in the belief that students are writers, that they have been writers for quite some time, and that they will continue to be writers. Since all students have experience as writers, one of the goals of self-assessment is to elicit their prior knowledge about particular components of the writing process and to use this prior knowledge to prime the students' learning and understanding of the concepts presented within each chapter. Through self-assessment, class content becomes more student-centered because students are given the opportunity to generate and present course concepts and material in a way that is meaningful to them, thus creating opportunities for deeper and more long-lasting learning.

Since a college writing course is viewed as a gateway, the need for students to develop skill in assessing their own work is critical. In such a course, the major challenge facing the college writing instructor is to teach students the writing skills they will need to become successful writers in college and in their chosen careers. The difficulty of meeting the challenge is compounded by the expectation that students can learn what they need to know about writing during the relatively brief span of a semester.

Clearly, teaching students all that they will need to know about the varied and complex process of writing is an impossible goal. However, through self-assessment, students can develop increased self-awareness, insight, and understanding of their own writing process and of their strengths and weaknesses as writers. Through this deeper self-awareness, they will develop skills and habits of writing and thinking that they can use throughout their lives.

Special Features of the Text

The Text

Take Charge of Your Writing is written in a clear and easy-to-read style. The text addresses students directly and encourages their involvement with the text. Activities are designed to encourage collaborative learning and relevant application of the principles presented in the chapters.

The text is designed as a complete writing course. Part One presents the elements of the writing process. This is followed by a section that contains a complete illustration of how one student uses the process to create a paper. Part Two discusses how the writing process might be used for the particular types of writing the student will encounter in college and beyond: Summary, Evaluation, Analysis, Persuasion, and the Research Paper. Part Three presents a complete portfolio assignment based on the principles of self-assessment.

Although the chapter topics are organized in a logical sequence of increasing difficulty, each chapter is designed as a self-contained teaching unit, thus allowing instructors to choose the order in which they present topics.

Self-Assessment

Each chapter begins and ends with a self-assessment. The opening self-assessment introduces students to the major topics presented in the chapter. In addition to introducing the chapter content, it encourages students to assess what they already know about the particular topics discussed in the chapter. Completion of this self-assessment elicits students' prior knowledge, and this establishes a context for learning the concepts in the chapter. Each chapter ends with a self-assessment that encourages students to consider what they have learned from the chapter and how that knowledge might apply to their own writing.

As students complete each self-assessment, they will develop the critical thinking skills of evaluating their assumptions and knowledge about writing. Through the development of their skills of evaluation and their enhanced self-awareness, students will become critical readers of the texts they have created, an important element in their growth as writers.

Activities and Exercises

"Working Alone" and "Working Together" activities are placed at appropriate places throughout the chapters. These writing and thinking exercises are intended to reinforce the specific ideas presented within each chapter. Through peer activities and collaborative learning, students will develop a sensitivity to writing for an audience within the writing community of the classroom. Additional "Suggestions for Writing" are placed at the end of each chapter to reinforce the general concepts presented in the chapter.

Readings

Because reading and writing are such intertwined activities, each chapter ends with a series of readings. Essays, short stories, and poetry are included to expose students to the various ways in which the principles of the chapter might apply to the writing process. The "Topics for Thinking and Writing" at the end of each reading encourage students to become critical readers who are more self-aware as they engage a written text. The inclusion of short stories and poetry provides the added opportunity to develop the skills of literary analysis that students will need in their their subsequent English courses.

The Intermezzo: From Idea to Essay

Since illustration is an important way for students to learn abstract concepts, the text contains a complete illustration of the process a student uses to write a paper—from the initial idea through the final draft. This illustration is designed to help students understand what a typical writing process might look like and thereby more easily visualize their own writing process.

The illustration also demonstrates the importance of self-assessment at key points in the writing process. While completing the "Working Alone" and "Working Together" activities within the *Intermezzo*, students are engaged as peer evaluators of the student-written text as it is being created.

The Portfolio

The Portfolio section is a complete portfolio self-assessment assignment that can be used as the capstone assignment for the course. This multifaceted assignment asks students to assess their understanding and application of the writing principles presented in the course. The goal of the Portfolio section is to encourage students to work independently and to develop the critical thinking skill of self-assessment as they review their own writing. Each piece selected for the portfolio is intended to reinforce key concepts of the writing process. Because students work independently to complete their portfolios, the assignment enables them to recognize that the writing skills and concepts they have learned in this writing course are directly transferable to their other courses and to their lives.

To the Student

Think back to your first memory of writing. Perhaps it was an attempt to express a simple emotion or a simple idea. Perhaps your first effort was a bit more ambitious—a short adventure or mystery story. Chances are, as you wrote those early pieces, you were excited at the prospect of capturing your ideas in written words.

As you progressed through school and took on more responsibility in your personal life, the writing tasks you completed became more complex. Through your experiences of expressing your ideas, you have become more knowledgeable about writing, more aware of the process you use to write, and more familiar with various forms writing can take.

You now have considerable experience as a writer. You *are* a writer. You have been a writer for some time, and you will continue to be a writer. As you progress through college and your chosen career, you will continue to develop your skills as a writer.

You already know a lot about the fundamentally important elements of writing, and you can use what you already know to evaluate, or self-assess, your own writing. Self-assessment is perhaps the most important skill of a thoughtful writer. It will enable you to succeed in this course and, more importantly, to develop your writing skills throughout your personal and professional life.

Acknowledgments

Many people were helpful as we undertook the task of writing this textbook. We are grateful to the staff at Houghton Mifflin—Claudine Bellanton, Fred Burns, Kellie Cardone, Maureen Duffy, Nancy Lyman, and Mary Jo Southern—for their expertise. We also want to thank Jane Gentry, our colleague; Janet Hiyashi, our research librarian; and Jyl Deering, who provided a student's eye. For their valuable editorial advice, we owe a special thanks to Maggie Barbieri, Vici Casana, and Pamela Getz.

Thank you to our reviewers and colleagues at other institutions: Kathleen Aguero, Pine Manor College, Massachusetts; Joyce Rain Anderson, University of New Hampshire; David Cappella, Wabash College, Indiana; John and Susan Ford, Delta State University, Mississippi; Judy Galbraith, Paradise Valley Community College, Arizona; Andrea Halpin Leary, Loyola University, Maryland; Bernard C. McKenna, Barry University, Florida; Arthur Seamans, Point Loma College, California; Timothy Trask, Massasoit Community College, Massachusetts. Chris Fauske would also like to acknowledge the support and encouragement of Robert J. Connors (1951–2000) who was an excellent teacher and patient friend.

We would also like to thank the following reviewers who contributed constructive suggestions for *Take Charge of Your Writing*: Ellen H. Bell, Manatee Community College, Florida; Marlys A. Cordoba, College of the Siskiyous, California; John J. Covolo, Lakeland Community College, Ohio; Valerie Hennen, Gateway Technical College, Wisconsin; David Lang, Golden Gate University, California; Patricia Licklider, John Jay College of Criminal Justice–CUNY; Jim Murphy, Southern Illinois University–Edwardsville; Richard Pepp, Massasoit Community College, Massachusetts; Kathleen Rice, Ivy Tech State College, Indiana; Carolyn Russell, Rio Hondo College, California.

Thank you to the publishers and authors whose works are included here.

Finally, to our families—Stephanie and Alexandra Daniel, Cara Connors and Connor Fauske, Laura Pascale, and Tom and Michelle Mandino—our loving appreciation for their patience and support.

TAKE CHARGE
of
YOUR WRITING

Chapter

1

Self-Assessment: Who Are You as a Writer?

YOU HAVE BEEN A WRITER.
YOU ARE A WRITER.
YOU WILL CONTINUE TO BE A WRITER.

Y ou are a writer.

You have been writing for a long time. In fact, you probably remember the first time you scribbled your name on a birthday card and proudly block-printed the words *thank you* on a note to a grandparent. In elementary school, you wrote reports about trees and dinosaurs and narrated stories about your summer vacations. In middle school, you passed notes to classmates and wrote book reports for the teacher.

In high school, the reports turned into longer research papers, and you composed essays for college applications. You may even have written poems for a special someone in your life. In college you may be asked to complete a variety of writing assignments ranging from essays to research papers, from summaries to analyses, from lab reports to journal entries, and from case histories to business letters. You might also need to write a letter to the housing director asking for a roommate change or to send an email to the computer support person requesting information about how to download assignments for your online course.

In the work world, you will write evaluations of employees, recommendations for colleagues, proposals for new projects, case history notes, letters to clients, advertising pamphlets, and summaries of business meetings. In your personal life, you may need to write a note to your child's teacher expressing concern about a recent test grade or to send an email to the phone company disputing a charge on your bill. Perhaps you will write a letter to the editor about a local issue which greatly concerns you. You may even continue to write poems to a new special someone.

As you can see, you have been writing, and you will continue to write for a long time. In many ways, writing has become second nature to you. Therefore, a writing course in college is the one course to which you bring much background experience and knowledge. Thinking about applying this experience and assessing this knowledge will help you to better understand your writing identity, your writing **process**, your writing needs, and your writing goals as you continue to grow and evolve. **Learning about yourself as a writer, and adding to that self-awareness, is the key to lifelong writing success**. You can begin this evolution through self-assessment, discovering and building upon what you already know.

What Is Self-Assessment?

Self-assessment is **you** thinking about and evaluating your actions.

Since you were young, you have done some type of self-assessment. You've compared your running and jumping skills to your friends', judged your appearance against others', critiqued a meal that you prepared, measured your skills in math or science. By using observation, reflection, and comparison, you gained insight and information about your performance, your strengths, and the areas in which you needed to grow. The more you thought about what you were doing, the more you realized what you already knew, what you still needed to learn, and where you might need some guidance. These self-evaluations have led you to develop plans for the improvement and growth of your skills.

Just as you did with other skills, you will be applying observation, reflection, and comparison—but now specifically to your writing through self-assessment. Self-assessment will help you to draw on past experiences as you evaluate and critique your writing, your writing process, your writing strengths and weaknesses, your writing needs, and your writing's effectiveness. Throughout this text, you will be asked to assess your current knowledge of writing and to practice some aspects of writing. From there, you will assess what you still need to learn and will continue to practice becoming a stronger, more successful writer in all areas of your life.

Working Alone: In a journal, keep a list of the types of writing you do during the next week. Set up the list in three columns labeled "type of writing," "purpose of writing," and "audience for writing." At the end of the week, write a paragraph summarizing what you have noticed about your writing. This is a good activity to continue throughout the course.

Self-Assessment: The Development of Your Writing Profile

This first chapter's **self-assessment** asks you to think about your experiences as a writer, your understanding of what your writing is like, and your writing goals for this course and for the future. You will be developing your **writing profile**, which you will revisit throughout the semester.

WRITING EXPERIENCES

Complete the checklist and the following statements.

1. Here are some of the kinds of writing I have done, in and out of school, during the past year. (Check those that apply.)

essays about literature	summaries
book reports	persuasive essays
emails for work or to friends	definitions
journal entries	diaries
personal narratives	descriptions
short stories	songs
speeches for special occasions	poems
research papers and reports	newspaper articles
job applications	letters to friends
letters for business purposes	postcards
notes to a teacher	thank-you notes

2. Of the items on my list, I most liked writing _____ and _____ because

3. I least enjoyed writing _____ and _____ because

4. When I am given a writing assignment, I usually follow this process:

5. I think that the strongest aspects of my writing are

6. I think that the area of my writing needing the most work is

7. The types of writing that I will probably do in my college courses are _____; in my possible career, _____; in my personal life, _____.

8. My writing goals for this composition course are

9. My thoughts and concerns as I begin this course are

In each chapter of this text, you will see a box at the end of the opening self-assessment and another at the end of the chapter. The first box asks you to list what you already know about some aspect of writing and what you hope to learn. The second box asks you to summarize what you have learned from working through the material in the chapter. These boxes will serve as quick review snapshots showing where you were in your writing, where you are now, and where you want to go.

What I know about my writing:	What I want to know about my writing:

Working Alone: Write a paragraph about what kind of writer you are and what kind of writer you would like to be.

Working Together: Exchange self-assessments with a classmate. What common themes do you share?

By completing this self-assessment, you have begun to explore and discover what you already know about writing. You have specifically discussed your writing experiences, your writing successes, and your writing goals. In the box provided, you have listed some things you know about writing. How have you come to know those things? Perhaps you have learned about them through thinking about and reading your own writing and the writing of others. While doing this reading, you have probably been formulating some general ideas of what writing is. This next exercise takes you from "you as writer" to "writing in general."

Working Alone: Complete the following statements:

I am a writer who _____

_____.

When I write, I _____

_____.

Writers _____

_____.

Writing involves _____

_____.

To write means to _____

_____.

Working Together: With a classmate, take a few minutes and list the different kinds of writing you do. Then look at your lists. What do they reveal?

Part One of this text is divided into six chapters which explore writing, the decisions writers need to make, and the ways in which writers go about writing. The following statements preview the upcoming chapters by introducing you to ideas about writing. As you read through the list, think about those statements which correspond to your ideas about writing.

What Is Writing?

Writing is communicating with an audience.
Writing is purposeful.
Writing is an active, dynamic process.
Writing comes in many forms.
Writing is thinking, learning, decision making, and problem solving.

Working Together: With a partner, look through the sections of a newspaper. What types of writing do you see? What are the purposes of these types? Who are their audiences?

Working Alone: Visit a campus office. Interview an employee about the types of writing he/she does as part of the job. Then write a paragraph summarizing the interview.

Writing Is Communicating with an Audience

And all the while you are writing away, editing, revising, trying new leads, new endings, until finally, at some point, you want some feedback. You want other people to read it. You want to know what they think. We are social animals, and we are trying to communicate with others of our species.

Anne Lamott

Each time you have written, you've had something that you wanted to communicate to someone. You have been a risk taker who has displayed a piece of yourself for public view. You've thought about your readers or **audience**: their likes, their attitudes, and their interests. You've wanted your words to be read because you've wanted to be understood by others.

As you review the checklist in your self-assessment, you probably will realize that you have written for a variety of audiences. The poem that you composed was for a special audience; that research paper was for a more general audience. Knowing your audience is an essential aspect of writing. In each writing situation, you make choices about the words that you use, the formality and informality of the language and form, the ideas that you present, and the length of your piece—all from what you have learned about your audience.

Working Alone:

1. Look back at question 2 of your self-assessment. Whom were you writing for in each example? What did you know about these audiences? How did you find out about them? How did what you learned about your audience influence your writing?
2. Write a paragraph discussing what you know about audience.

Writing Is Purposeful

> I wrote this book because it was one of the major missing American biographies. Another reason for writing this biography is there are many people who have no knowledge of DuBois because he became a virtual un-person. . . .
>
> David Levering Lewis

> Writers write to influence their readers, their preachers, their auditors, but always, at bottom, to be more themselves.
>
> Aldous Huxley

Each time you have written, you have had some purpose in mind, some goal you have wanted to achieve. You have wanted your audience to react to your text with certain thoughts and feelings. You have had reasons for putting those words to paper in that particular order.

From your checklist, you can see that your purposes were varied. You wrote applications so that you could get hired and emails to exchange quick information. You drafted speeches to entertain audiences. Perhaps you wanted to convince your audience of your views with facts and humor; thus, you were writing to inform, to persuade, and to entertain. Just as having a sense of your audience affected the way in which you wrote your piece, the purposes you had in mind also influenced your writing decisions.

Working Alone:

1. Write a paragraph that discusses what you know about the role of purpose in writing.

2. Once again, look at your self-assessment checklist. What were the purposes of three of the pieces of writing? How did each purpose affect your writing? Did you successfully achieve your purpose?

Working Together: With a peer, look at a campus bulletin board. Write down the purposes behind each type of announcement or sign posted there. Then write a paragraph which summarizes your discoveries about purpose.

Writing Is an Active, Dynamic Process

> When I write, everything is visual, as brilliantly as if it were on a lit stage. And I talk out the lines as I write. When I was in Rome, my landlady thought I was demented. She told [my friend], "Oh, Mr. Williams has lost his mind! He stalks about his room, talking out loud!" [My friend] said, "Oh, he's just writing."
>
> Tennessee Williams

There are some useful strategies you may use during the phase before you actually begin to write, **prewriting.** Like Tennessee Williams, you may be the type of writer who likes to talk out your ideas before you commit them to paper. Maybe you need to **brainstorm** all your thoughts on scratch paper or to jot notes in a journal. You may have discovered that exchanging ideas with a friend best helps you come up with writing topics. Perhaps you like to organize your ideas by using some type of graphic such as a **tree, pyramid,** or **map**. Or are you the type of writer who likes to **freewrite** about anything that comes to mind?

Working Together: Working with a peer, discuss the prewriting strategies you used when you wrote some of the pieces listed on your self-assessment. Did the audience or purpose of the pieces affect your decision about whether to prewrite?

Working Alone:

1. Write a paragraph discussing whether or not prewriting has been helpful to you.

2. Write a paragraph discussing what you know about prewriting.

Whatever initial strategies you have used, you should realize that you are always thinking and making decisions when you write. You may revisit your initial brainstorm, or you may only brainstorm from one item on the list and discard the rest. You are continuously thinking about what you know about your topic, what you hope to learn, and what you wish to convey to others. You realize that writing, from the very start, is an active, dynamic process.

After you've considered your audience and purpose and have gathered your ideas, it's time to write the piece.

Your decisions will help to determine the number of drafts that you will write. For the email to your friend, often one draft is all you'll do. For the memo to your boss, maybe a recheck of your wording and sentences is called for. For your college essay, writing multiple drafts is advisable.

You may have found that you have your own process for drafting and redrafting. If you compose at the computer, perhaps you write three lines, stop and read, and revise as you go along. Or you may write out as much as you can, print out a copy, and then take a pen to the draft for further notations. Maybe working from an outline is helpful for keeping your writing organized. Sometimes you may find that you like to put the piece aside and come back to it later when you're refreshed. Perhaps you need to write in longhand on yellow tablet paper before you sit down at the keyboard to compose your second draft.

You have probably discovered that you usually keep some of your initial draft but toss out the rest. It's useful to consider the process of writing as actually writing, reading, thinking, rewriting, deleting, adding, reading, thinking, rewriting, deleting, adding . . . until you've got it right.

Working Together: As members of a small group, ask each other: Did any of the pieces that you checked in your self-assessment require you to draft? Did you choose to draft any of the pieces? Did drafting improve the effectiveness of your work?

Working Alone: Write a paragraph describing what you do when you rewrite a paper.

No matter what process you use, you probably realize that writing is active and dynamic. This is the *recursive* nature of writing. Tornado-like, it loops back on itself, spirals upward and downward, scoops up what's best from the first version, leaves behind what doesn't work, and moves on as you continue to discover what you want to say and how best to say it.

Throughout this course, you will be thinking and learning about the active process that you use in writing. You will examine what parts of the process work best for you and what aspects you may wish to modify or enhance. In so doing, you will grow as a writer. There's no magic formula for this process, but there are habits you can learn and use. Whatever process you employ and however much experience you have, remember that your writing can always improve. This book will help.

Working Together: With a partner, share something that you have learned to do better through practice. How might the idea of practice apply to writing?

Writing Takes Many Forms

As you saw in the self-assessment, you can write long, involved research papers or short emails. You can write a quick poem to a special friend or a paper detailing the reasons why you are pursuing higher education. It is useful to think of form as the package in which your writing is delivered—and there are many packages or forms of writing. You may be asked to **summarize, evaluate, analyze, argue a point,** or **research** a topic, and each of these forms might come in a different package.

Perhaps the most common form required in college, and one which can accomplish all of the tasks previously listed, is the *essay*. Essays have three main components: introductions, bodies, and conclusions. These components are guided by a controlling idea, or **thesis statement**. Essays and the theses which drive them can also be presented in many forms. Some essays use the art of persuasion to deliver the main idea. Some create comparisons and contrasts to drive home their points while others teach how to do something. The form that you choose will be based on decisions you make about your audience and your purpose.

One form of writing which is often used in a college English course is *narrative*. Because this form is frequently an effective way to start an essay, learning more about the narrative is useful at this point.

Narrative: When you go home after a day at school or work, and someone asks, "How was your day?" you might simply answer, "Fine" and let it go at that. Or you might say, "Let me tell you what happened to me today . . . ," and you're off and running, telling a story.

Storytelling, or *narrative*, is one of the most fundamental kinds of writing. As you previously learned, you will find that much of what you write in college will be in the nonfiction essay form. For your purposes, therefore, narrative can be very useful for making a point, illustrating ideas, exploring an experience, or creating interest for your audience.

A familiar form of essay is the **personal narrative**. In this kind of writing, you use events from your own life—often from your past—dramatizing them in various ways to bring them alive again and to give your reader a chance to share the experience.

A personal narrative works best when the story is told to make a point that other people can relate to or appreciate. If you write of an experience that taught you something, helped you discover something about yourself or others, or changed your life in some way, it will usually have some drama—even trauma—connected with it. This might be an encounter with someone, an incident, or some other occurrence that had an impact on you. Of course, not every little thing that happens to you would work as the subject of an effective personal narrative, but some will, and those can lead you to produce some very strong writing.

A personal narrative is almost always written in the first person—*I*. Although this isn't a requirement, it is a logical way to do it. Since the story you're telling is most likely an experience that you've had firsthand and that taught you something, writing about it in the first person gives your essay a sense of reality and can make it easy for your reader to identify with it.

The personal narrative should focus on a particular incident or experience. The summer after seventh grade, for instance, might have been a time of important growth and wonderful memories, but it probably wouldn't make a good subject for a personal narrative because it's not specific enough. The topic encompasses several months and numerous events. A better topic would be a specific experience that you had during that summer.

Working Alone: Think about an incident from your past—the meeting of a wonderful new friend, perhaps, or a serious conflict that strained your relationship with a parent, the death of your dog, or the time you took a dare and jumped into a quarry. Would the incident make a good topic for a personal narrative? Why? Write a brief summary of what you would say.

Working Together: With several classmates, discuss experiences that you've each had and determine which ones might be effective topics for personal narrative essays.

Regardless of the form your essay takes, however, the one thing which should remain constant as you write is your continuing habit of self-assessment.

Working Alone:

1. Looking again at the opening self-assessment, what are some of the forms that your writing has taken?
2. Write a paragraph discussing what you think you would need to include in a persuasive essay.
3. Write a paragraph discussing what you might do to write an effective introduction which would draw your reader into your piece.

Writing Is Thinking, Learning, Decision-making, and Problem-solving

> Writing is no trouble: you just jot down ideas as they occur to you. The jotting down is simplicity itself—it is the occurring which is difficult.
>
> Stephen Leacock

Regardless of your audience, purpose, process, or form, writing requires you to use a variety of thinking skills. You use your memory and imagination to come up with ideas to write about; you use your skills of perception and your senses to add details that make the reader see, hear, taste, smell, and feel what you're writing about. You employ your skills of response, analysis, summary, and evaluation as you research, organize, categorize, classify, narrate, and present your ideas. You are continuously making decisions as you choose the right words, organization, details, and tone.

The writing task may be viewed as a problem to be solved, one to which you bring these many critical thinking skills. In writing, you delve into areas you wish to explore, and in doing so, you deepen your knowledge. By writing, you refine your thoughts, clarify your points, and expand upon them. By writing, you can truly assess your understanding of what you are learning as you explore and make meaning.

Working Together: With a peer, look back at your self-assessment: Which writings called on you to use memory? For which did you rely more on your emotional responses? Which required sensory observations? Which writings asked that you use problem-solving techniques? Which writings required that you do some research?

Working Alone:

1. Search online for information about any one of the authors quoted in this chapter. In one paragraph, summarize your findings.
2. Write a one-paragraph summary of a chapter from a textbook. In a second paragraph, discuss how summarizing the chapter helped you to learn the material.

As a writer who engages in this dynamic, communicative, purposeful, varied, and thoughtful act of writing, the most important skill you will use is self-assessment, the key to lifelong writing success!

Suggestions for Writing

1. Review the work you have already done for this chapter and write a history of yourself as a writer. Consider these questions: What kinds of writing have you done? What was the purpose of each type of writing? Who was your audience?
2. Among writers it is often said that "easy writing makes hard reading; hard writing makes easy reading." What does this statement mean to you? Which part of the statement describes your writing? Why?

READINGS

THE QUARRY
DAVID DANIEL

I stood on the Chair, looking down between my feet to the water far below.

I don't know who first called it the Chair. I'm sure it had been called that long before my friends and I ever set foot on it in the summer of my fourteenth year. The name fit. The Chair was a tall rock formation in an old granite quarry where we would sometimes go to swim.

The quarry was an appealing place. Long abandoned, filled with cool water, hidden away, it gave promise of adventure. Just the simple act of getting there required that we hitchhike or walk several miles, and then we had to blaze a trail through the woods. But perhaps most alluring of all was that it was forbidden, possessed of a quality of danger that lurked there. This had to do with the sheer rock walls and calm green surface of the water, hiding whatever might lie below in its 100-foot depth.

The quarry was almost exclusively the domain of adolescent boys. In all the times I went there, I can rarely remember seeing girls, and they were usually with their older boyfriends. Although we never would have said so at the time, the quarry was a kind of proving ground for manhood.

At the quarry there were various heights to jump from, starting with the baby-ish two- and four-footers, a variety of more challenging spots in the 10- to 30-foot range, where we spent most of the time…and then the Chair.

Just the simple act of swimming in the quarry gave us bragging rights, but to jump from the Chair, that was special. Only the most daring kids would climb there, making the ascent through sharp rocks to reach the top. On any given day this might happen one or two times total. I never knew anyone to jump more than twice on a given day.

I had never jumped from it. And then, toward the end of the summer, know-ing that sooner or later my turn would come, I found myself climbing the rocks to the Chair. I stood there, looking down. My stomach felt feather-light and my heart was dancing in my chest. If there had been a way out other than straight below me, I'd have grabbed it. But there wasn't. The other kids had stopped what they'd been doing and now stood looking up.

So what made me hesitate? The plunge could only take a second or two, after all. Was it fear of falling? Of hitting the water wrong? Or even a nagging idea that with that impact I might go so deep I'd get snagged on some tree limb or other menace lurking beneath the water and drown? But that was crazy, the quarry was too deep.

No, it was something else which held me there, on the brink, in that summer of my fourteenth year.

"Come on, Dave! Let's go!" My friends' voices sounded small from up this high. I didn't look at them. I could make out the whisper of cars speeding along the dis-tant Route 3, and I wished I were in one of those cars…

"Time's wasting…" someone called.

Wasting? Why? It wasn't like the diving board at some public pool; no one else was waiting in line behind me. I stood alone.

But time was wasting. There was no way out.

Drawing a slow breath, gritting my teeth against my terror…

"Dave." Other, older voices break my reverie.

I glance up from the river to see my two grown friends standing there, a short distance above me. My impulse is to scramble up there where they stand on the river bank, ten feet or so up. It wasn't high, certainly not the Chair, but still, I hes-itate, asking myself: Why go?

Jim and Terry are going to jump. The swimming hole is practically in Jim's backyard, and we're his guests today. Terry has a new girlfriend to impress, sit-ting over there with my wife and Jim's, the three women dangling their legs in the water. I'm 30 now. I have nothing to prove. I have a wife who loves me. Who do I have to show off for? And what if I get hurt, sprain an ankle or something? I prob-ably won't get hurt, but so what? Why take a chance? For what?

I took a little hop out into thin air. I remember the sensation of falling. Of plunging into the green water of the quarry. Of kicking elatedly back to the surface and the sunshine and the happy shouts of my friends. I'd jumped from the Chair. I'd do it again one more time that summer, shortly before school began. I never did it again after that, and after a while, I never went to the quarry again.

"*Dave*," my friends call down from the river bank. "Come on."

Shielding my eyes, I look up at them: two not-quite-grown-up men standing on the river bank. "No, thanks," I say. "Go for it. I'm enjoying myself right here."

Topics for Thinking and Writing

1. How many experiences is the author writing about here? How does he link them?
2. Some effective ways of dramatizing writing include using concrete details, appealing to the senses, using dialogue, and using action words to convey activity. Point to specific instances of each of these in "The Quarry."
3. Although there isn't a clear statement of thesis (as there often should be in an essay), you nevertheless get a feeling that this personal narrative is somehow "about" something. What are some of the ideas that come to mind?
4. Write brief answers to the following questions: What power does the quarry hold over the young males in the essay? Why was it important for the narrator finally to jump from the Chair? Why doesn't he go back to the quarry much after that summer? Why doesn't he jump years later when he's swimming in the river with friends? What has he learned about himself by the time of the second experience?
5. Examine a time in your own life when you had to deal with peer pressure. In a short personal narrative, recreate the situation and show how you dealt with it.

POLAROIDS
ANNE LAMOTT

Writing a first draft is very much like watching a Polaroid develop. You can't—and, in fact, you're not supposed to—know exactly what the picture is going to look like until it has finished developing. First you just point at what has your attention and take the picture. In the last chapter, for instance, what had my attention were the contents of my lunch bag. But as the picture developed, I found I had a really clear image of the boy against the fence. Or maybe *your* Polaroid was supposed to be a picture of that boy against the fence, and you didn't notice until the last minute that a family was standing a few feet away from him. Now, maybe it's his family, or the family of one of the kids in his class, but at any rate these people are going to be in the photograph, too. Then the film emerges from the camera with a grayish green murkiness that gradually becomes clearer and clearer, and finally you see the husband and wife holding their baby with two children standing beside them. And at first it all seems very sweet, but then the shadows begin to appear, and then you start to see the animal tragedy, the baboons baring their teeth. And then you see a flash of bright red flowers in the bottom left quadrant that you didn't even know were in the picture when you took it, and these flowers evoke a time or a memory that moves you mysteriously. And finally, as the portrait comes into focus, you begin to notice all the props surrounding these people, and you begin to understand how props define us and comfort us, and show us what we value and what we need, and who we think we are.

You couldn't have had any way of knowing what this piece of work would look like when you first started. You just knew that there was something about these people that compelled you, and you stayed with that something long enough for it to show you what it was about.

Watch this Polaroid develop:

Six or seven years ago I was asked to write an article on the Special Olympics. I had been going to the local event for years, partly because a couple of friends of mine compete. Also, I love sports, and I love to watch athletes, special or otherwise. So I showed up this time with a great deal of interest but no real sense of what the finished article might look like.

Things tend to go very, very slowly at the Special Olympics. It is not like trying to cover the Preakness. Still, it has its own exhilaration, and I cheered and took notes all morning.

The last track-and-field event before lunch was a twenty-five-yard race run by some unusually handicapped runners and walkers, many of whom seemed completely confused. They lumped and careened along, one man making a snail-slow break for the stands, one heading out toward the steps where the winners receive their medals; both of them were shepherded back. The race took just about forever. And here it was nearly noon and we were all so hungry. Finally, though, everyone crossed over the line, and those of us in the stands got up to go—when we noticed that way down the track, four or five yards from the starting line, was another runner.

She was a girl of about sixteen with a normal-looking face above a wracked and emaciated body. She was on metal crutches, and she was just plugging along, one tiny step after another, moving one crutch forward two or thee inches, then moving a leg, then moving the other crutch two or three inches, then moving the other leg. It was just excruciating. Plus, I was starving to death. Inside I was going, Come On, come on, come on, swabbing at my forehead with anxiety, while she kept taking these two- or three-inch steps forward. What felt like four hours later, she crossed the finish line, and you could see that she was absolutely stoked, in a shy, girlish way.

A tall African American man with no front teeth fell into step with me as I left the bleachers to go look for some lunch. He tugged on the sleeve of my sweater, and I looked up at him, and he handed me a Polaroid someone had taken of him and his friends that day. "Look at us," he said. His speech was difficult to understand, thick and slow as a warped record. His two friends in the picture had Down's syndrome. All three of them looked extremely pleased with themselves. I admired the picture and then handed it back to him. He stopped, so I stopped, too. He pointed to his own image. "That," he said, "is one cool man."

And this was the image from which an article began forming, although I could not have told you exactly what the piece would end up being about. I just knew that something had started to emerge.

After lunch I wandered over to the auditorium, where it turned out a men's basketball game was in progress. The African American man with no front teeth was the star of the game. You could tell that he was because even though no one had made a basket yet, his teammates almost always passed him the ball. Even the people on the *other* team passed him the ball a lot. In lieu of any scoring, the men stampeded in slow motion up and down the court, dribbling the ball thunderously. I had never heard such a loud game. It was all sort of crazily beautiful. I imagined describing the game for my article and then for my students: the loudness, the joy. I kept replaying the scene of the girl on crutches making her way up the track to the finish line—and all of a sudden my article began to appear out of the grayish green murk. And I could see that it was about tragedy transformed over the years into joy. It was about the beauty of sheer effort. I could see it almost as clearly as I could the photograph of that one cool man and his two friends.

The auditorium bleachers were packed. Then a few minutes later, still with no score on the board, the tall black man dribbled slowly from one end of the court to the other, and heaved the ball up into the air, and it dropped into the basket. The crowd roared, and all the men on both teams looked up wide-eyed at the hoop, as if it had just burst into flames.

You would have loved it, I tell my students. You would have felt like you could write all day.

Topics for Thinking and Writing

1. Chapter 1 describes writing as "an active, dynamic process." Citing specific examples, show how this statement fits Lamott's discussion of writing.
2. Who is the audience for Lamott's essay? Why? What does her essay suggest about her understanding of her audience?
3. Lamott says that she "could not have told you exactly what the piece was going to be about." Write a paragraph about when you have had a similar feeling about a writing assignment.
4. Imagine that you are Anne Lamott and have been asked to write a self-assessment paragraph describing your writing process. Then write the paragraph.

DIGGING
SEAMUS HEANEY

Between my finger and my thumb
The squat pen rests; snug as a gun.

Under my window, a clean rasping sound
When the spade sinks into gravelly ground.
5   My father, digging, I look down.

Till his straining rump among the flowerbeds
Bends low, comes up twenty years away
Stooping in rhythm through potato drills
Where he was digging.

10   The coarse boot nestled on the lug, the shaft
Against the inside knee was levered firmly.
He rooted out tall tops, buried the bright edge deep
To scatter new potatoes that we picked
Loving their cool hardness in our hands.

15   By God, the old man could handle a spade.
Just like his old man.

My grandfather cut more turf in a day
Than any other man on Toner's bog.
Once I carried him milk in a bottle
20   Corked sloppily with paper. He straightened up
To drink it, then fell to right away.

Nicking and slicing neatly, heaving sods
Over his shoulder, going down and down
For the good turf. Digging.

25   The cold smell of potato mould, the squelch and slap
Of soggy peat, the curt cuts of an edge
Through living roots awaken in my head.
But I've no spade to follow men like them.

Between my finger and thumb
30   The squat pen rests.
I'll dig with it.

Topics for Thinking and Writing

1. Citing specific lines, show how digging potatoes and writing might be similar.
2. What does the comparison tell us about the narrator's view of writing and the writing process?
3. Write a paragraph discussing the characteristics a writer must have as implied by the narrator of the poem.
4. Write a short essay comparing writing to some physical activity with which you are familiar.

THE THOUGHT FOX
TED HUGHES

I imagine this midnight moment's forest:
Something else is alive
Beside the clock's loneliness
And this blank page where my fingers move.

5   Through the window I see no star:
     Something more near
     Though deeper within darkness
     Is entering the loneliness:

     Cold, delicately as the dark snow,
10   A Fox's nose touches twig, leaf;
     Two eyes serve a movement, that now
     And again now, and now, and now

     Sets near prints into the snow
     Between trees, and warily a lame
15   Shadow lags by stump and in hollow
     Of a body that is bold to come

     Across clearings, an eye,
     A widening deepening greenness,
     Brilliantly, concentratedly,
20   Coming about its own business

     Till, with a sudden sharp hot stink of fox
     It enters the dark hole of the head.
     The window is starless till; the clock ticks,
     The page is printed

Topics for Thinking and Writing

1. This poem "seems" to be about the writing process; cite words and lines that suggest this.
2. What is the significance of the fox in the poem? What might it represent to the poet?
3. Write a paragraph in which you use some animal or bird to represent some aspect of yourself as a writer.
4. Write a short essay comparing what Hughes has to say about writing with what Seamus Heaney says about it in "Digging."

SPIN
TIM O'BRIEN

The war wasn't all terror and violence. Sometimes things could almost get sweet. For instance, I remember a little boy with a plastic leg. I remember how he hopped over to Azar and asked for a chocolate bar—"GI number one," the kid said—and Azar laughed and handed over the chocolate. When the boy hopped away, Azar clucked his tongue and said, "War's a bitch." He shook his head sadly. "One leg, for Chrissake. Some poor fucker ran out of ammo."

I remember Mitchell Sanders sitting quietly in the shade of an old banyan tree. He was using a thumbnail to pry off the body lice, working slowly, carefully depositing the lice in a blue USO envelope. His eyes were tired. It had been a long two weeks in the brush. After an hour or so he sealed up the envelope, wrote FREE in the upper right-hand corner, and addressed it to his draft board in Ohio.

On occasions the war was like a Ping-Pong ball. You could put fancy spin on it, you could make it dance.

I remember Norman Bowker and Henry Dobbins playing checkers every evening before dark. It was a ritual for them. They would dig a foxhole and get the board out and play long, silent games as the sky went from pink to purple. The rest of us would sometimes stop by to watch. There was something restful about it, something orderly and reassuring. There were red checkers and black checkers. The playing field was laid out in a strict grid, no tunnels or mountains or jungles. You knew where you stood. You knew the score. The pieces were out on the board, the enemy was visible, you could watch the tactics unfolding into larger strategies. There was a winner and a loser. There were rules.

I'm forty-three years old, and a writer now, and the war has been over for a long while. Much of it is hard to remember. I sit at this typewriter and stare through my words and watch Kiowa sinking into the deep muck of a shit field, or Curt Lemon hanging in pieces from a tree, and as I write about these things, the remembering is turned into a kind of rehappening. Kiowa yells at me. Curt Lemon steps from the shade into bright sunlight, his face brown and shining, and then he soars into a tree. The bad stuff never stops happening: it lives in its own dimension, replaying itself over and over.

But the war wasn't all that way.

Like when Ted Lavender went too heavy on the tranquilizers. "How's the war today?" somebody would say, and Ted Lavender would give a soft, spacey smile and say, "Mellow, man. We got ourselves a nice mellow war today."

And like the time we enlisted an old poppa-san to guide us through the mine fields out on the Batangan Peninsula. The old guy walked with a limp, slow and stooped over, but he knew where the safe spots were and where you had to be careful and where even if you were careful you could end up like popcorn. He had a tightrope walker's feel for the land beneath him—its surface tension, the give and take of things. Each morning we'd form up in a long column, the old poppa-san out front, and for the whole day we'd troop along after him, tracing his footsteps, playing an exact and ruthless game of follow the leader. Rat Kiley made up a rhyme that caught on, and we'd all be chanting it together: *Step out of line, hit a mine; follow the dink, you're in the pink.* All around us, the place was littered with Bouncing Betties and Toe Poppers and booby-trapped artillery rounds, but in those five days on the Batangan Peninsula nobody got hurt. We all learned to love the old man.

It was a sad scene when the choppers came to take us away. Jimmy Cross gave the old poppa-san a hug. Mitchell Sanders and Lee Strunk loaded him up with boxes of C-rations.

There were actually tears in the old guy's eyes.

"Follow dink," he said to each of us, "you go pink."

If you weren't humping, you were waiting. I remember the monotony. Digging foxholes. Slapping mosquitoes. The sun and the heat and the endless paddies. Even in the deep bush, where you could die any number of ways, the war was nakedly and aggressively boring. But it was a strange boredom. It was boredom with a twist, the kind of boredom that caused stomach disorders. You'd be sitting at the top of a high hill, the flat paddies stretching out below, and the day would be calm and hot and utterly vacant, and you'd feel the boredom dripping inside you like a leaky faucet, except it wasn't water, it was a sort of acid, and with each little droplet you'd feel the stuff eating away at important organs. You'd try to relax. You'd uncurl your fists and let your thoughts go. Well, you'd think, this isn't so bad. And right then you'd hear gunfire behind you and your nuts would fly up into your throat and you'd be squealing pig squeals. That kind of boredom.

I feel guilty sometimes. Forty-three years old and I'm still writing war stories. My daughter Kathleen tells me it's an obsession, that I should write about a little girl who finds a million dollars and spends it all on a Shetland pony. In a way, I guess, she's right: I should forget it. But the thing about remembering is that you don't forget. You take your material where you find it, which is in your life, at the intersection of past and present. The memory-traffic feeds into a rotary up in your head, where it goes in circles for a while, then pretty soon imagination flows in and the traffic merges and shoots off down a thousand different streets. As a writer, all you can do is pick a street and go for the ride, putting things down as they come at you. That's the real obsession. All those stories.

Not bloody stories, necessarily. Happy stories, too, and even a few peace stories.

Here's a quick peace story:

A guy goes AWOL. Shacks up in Danang with a Red Cross nurse. It's a great time—the nurse loves him to death—the guy gets whatever he wants whenever he wants it. The war's over, he thinks. Just nookie and new angles. But then one day he rejoins his unit in the bush. Can't wait to get back into action. Finally one of his buddies asks what happened with the nurse, why so hot for combat, and the guy says, "All that peace, man, it felt so good it *hurt*. I want to hurt it *back*."

I remember Mitchell Sanders smiling as he told me that story. Most of it he made up, I'm sure, but even so it gave me a quick truth-goose. Because it's all relative. You're pinned down in some filthy hellhole of a paddy, getting your ass delivered to kingdom come, but then for a few seconds everything goes quiet and you look up and see the sun and a few puffy white clouds, and the immense serenity flashes against your eyeballs—the whole world gets rearranged—and even though you're pinned down by a war you never felt more at peace.

What sticks to memory, often, are those odd little fragments that have no beginning and no end:

Norman Bowker lying on his back one night, watching the stars, then whispering to me, "I'll tell you something, O'Brien. If I could have one wish, anything, I'd wish for my dad to write me a letter and say it's okay if I don't win any medals. That's all my old man talks about, nothing else. How he can't wait to see my goddamn medals."

Or Kiowa teaching a rain dance to Rat Kiley and Dave Jensen, the three of them whooping and leaping around barefoot while a bunch of villagers looked on with a mixture of fascination and giggly horror. Afterward, Rat said, "So where's the rain?" and Kiowa said, "The earth is slow, but the buffalo is patient," and Rat thought about it and said, "Yeah, but where's the *rain*?"

Or Ted Lavender adopting an orphan puppy—feeding it from a plastic spoon and carrying it in his rucksack until the day Azar strapped it to a Claymore antipersonnel mine and squeezed the firing device.

The average age in our platoon, I'd guess, was nineteen or twenty, and as a consequence things often took on a curiously playful atmosphere, like a sporting event at some exotic reform school. The competition could be lethal, yet there was a childlike exuberance to it all, lots of pranks and horseplay. Like when Azar blew away Ted Lavender's puppy. "What's everybody so upset about?" Azar said. "I mean, Christ, I'm just a *boy*."

I remember these things, too.

The damp, fungal scent of an empty body bag.

A quarter moon rising over the nighttime paddies.

Henry Dobbins sitting in the twilight, sewing on his new buck-sergeant stripes, quietly singing, "A tisket, a tasket, a green and yellow basket."

A field of elephant grass weighted with wind, bowing under the stir of a helicopter's blades, the grass dark and servile, bending low, but then rising straight again when the chopper went away.

A red clay trail outside the village of My Khe.

A hand grenade.

A slim, dead, dainty young man of about twenty.

Kiowa saying, "No choice, Tim. What else could you do?"

Kiowa saying, "Right?"

Kiowa saying, "Talk to me."

Forty-three years old, and the war occurred half a lifetime ago, and yet the remembering makes it now. And sometimes remembering will lead to a story, which makes it forever. That's what stories are for. Stories are for joining the past to the future. Stories are for those late hours in the night when you can't remember how you got from where you were to where you are. Stories are for eternity, when memory is erased, when there is nothing to remember except the story.

Topics for Thinking and Writing

1. In this chapter from O'Brien's book about the Vietnam war, *The Things They Carried*, the narrator tells us the purposes of stories in the last paragraph. First,

what are some of those purposes? Second, how does the writer demonstrate those purposes throughout the chapter?

2. Chapter 1 in this textbook describes writing as taking "many forms." What forms of writing do you see in this excerpt by O'Brien? What do you think O'Brien is telling us about stories and writing through his use of these forms?

3. Look closely at one of the ministories the narrator tells in the chapter. What do you notice about the choice of words, the sentence structure, and the images? What effects do you think these choices have on the audience? Write a paragraph summarizing your findings.

4. Write a paragraph describing what you observe about O'Brien's writing style.

5. What is the purpose of this chapter of O'Brien's book?

Self-Assessment

Reread your self-assessment from the beginning of this chapter.

What would I change?

Why?

What do I now know about writing?

Audience: Who Is Your Reader?

"HOW YA DOIN'?"
"HELLO."
"GOOD MORNING."

When you write, you write for someone.

Assume that you have become ill, and the doctor told you to stay home and rest. As a result, you have to miss an important class, miss a day at work, and cancel plans to go to a concert with your friend. How would you write notes or emails to your teacher, your boss, and your friend explaining your predicament?

Although the purpose, or reason, for writing in the three situations is basically the same, the **audience** in each case differs. Because of this situation, each note requires a different approach and a different use of language and style for you to successfully convey the message.

For example, in your note to your professor or your boss, it's unlikely that you would begin with the greeting "How ya doin'?" Those notes probably require more formal greetings such as "Hello" or "Good morning." However, "How ya doin'?" would probably be just fine in a note to your friend.

Because your relationship to your friend is closer and less formal than your relationship to your professor or your boss, your style would most likely be informal or casual. You probably wouldn't think too much about the correctness of the words and sentences you would choose to express your ideas. You might use language with your friend that would be inappropriate to use with your teacher or your boss. Your relationship to them is more formal, so you would choose words and plan sentences more carefully to reflect that.

In Chapter 1, you developed a profile of yourself as a writer and identified the types of writing you have done and may currently be doing. Each of those pieces was written with a particular audience in mind, and this audience influenced how you expressed your ideas.

Self-Assessment

As you will see in the following chapters, writing is a complex and dynamic process. Basic to this process are defining your audience and identifying your purpose for writing. In this chapter you will explore the role that your reader plays in your writing. Chapter 3 deals with purpose.

Whenever you write, you do so with a specific audience in mind. Sometimes this might be an individual—such as the close friend or your boss in the previous example. At other times, your audience might be a group such as your fellow students or members of an online chat group. Each writing situation varies, and your communication will succeed in part by how well you imagine your audience and adapt your language to its knowledge and expectations.

ADAPTING MY WRITING TO MY AUDIENCE

1. Listed below are three significant pieces of writing that I have completed in the past year. (You might discuss job or college applications, letters for work, assignments for class, or letters home. Describe your audience for each piece.)

Piece of Writing	Audience

2. My audience influenced my choice of words and writing style in one of these pieces in the following ways:

3. My audience influenced the examples and details that I used to explain my ideas in this piece. Here's how:

4. In general, here are some ways I think my audience might influence the presentation or organization I choose for the final version of a piece of my writing:

5. Some audiences for which I expect to write in college and in my professional life include:

What do I know about audience?	What do I need to know about audience?

Working Alone: Write a paragraph discussing what you know about audience.

Your Reader

Who Is Your Reader?

A good starting point for all of your writing is to identify and analyze your reader. Your relationship to the reader is important because it is one of the factors that establishes a framework for the exchange of ideas from you to your reader.

When you are speaking, you automatically adapt to your audience because you can see and/or hear your listeners' reactions to what you are saying. When you're writing, however, your relationship to your audience is more complex because you have to imagine your reader.

As you write, it is important to consider how your audience might influence the way you choose to express your ideas. In order for your writing to be understood and your ideas accepted, you should analyze your reader's background and adapt your language and writing style accordingly. Because readers' knowledge, expectations, and needs will vary, it is helpful to use some of the following general characteristics as a guide to knowing your audience.

Audience Characteristics Checklist

age	political background
education	relationship to writer
profession	hobbies or interests
gender	knowledge of the topic
religion	attitude toward the topic
nationality	attitude toward the writer

Of course, you can consider other specific audience characteristics, but these are good starting points for developing a profile of the person who will be reading your writing. Thinking about these characteristics will give you an idea of what you can expect your reader to know—and need to know—about your topic. This, in turn, will help you determine the language, style, and format you should use so that your reader will understand and accept your ideas.

Working Alone: Select an advertisement in a magazine. What do you find in its use of language, ideas, and images that indicate its target audience?

Read the following passages, thinking about the type of reader the writer imagined. Using the audience characteristics checklist as a guide, describe the audience for each piece. What assumptions does the writer make about the reader's vocabulary and knowledge of the subject? How do these assumptions influence the writer's use of language?

Research shows clearly that parents' conversations with babies are extremely important to the infants' development. The Harvard Preschool Project, a longitudinal study conducted at Harvard University, observed the contacts between parents and their infants that occurred naturally in the families' own homes. At various intervals, the infants were assessed for both intelligence and social skills. When the assessments were correlated with the results of home observations, one result stood out clearly: the most intellectually and socially competent infants had parents who directed large amounts of language at them. The most competent babies received about twice as much language as the least competent in this study did.

The previous passage is from a textbook on child and adolescent development. Notice that the writer uses words like *longitudinal*, *assessments*, and *correlated*. Note, too, the long sentences. If this passage were rewritten for an audience of parents rather than academics, it might read like this:

Have you ever watched a parent talking to her baby? She asks questions and talks about her day at work, the weather, what's for supper—anything she has on her mind. And watch the infant. He stops his arm-waving and leg-stretching to attentively listen and politely responds with a "bababababa" of his own. Crazy? Absolutely not! In fact, psychologists tell us that this parent is helping to increase her baby's thinking and social skills. The baby appears to be wired to "know" how to take turns, how to really listen—how to engage in the polite rules of conversation and to "feed" on language. The well-fed baby makes the best listener. So pour out your heart to that child. It's never too early to start exposing infants to a good diet of language!

Notice how this passage uses everyday words and expressions and many shorter sentences. Can you find other differences that suggest that the writers of the two passages had different audiences in mind?

When you write, you often make similar adjustments to your audience's expectations and knowledge of the subject. Likewise, as the two passages show, the nature of your relationship to the audience influences your level of formality or informality. Remember the difference between "How ya doin'?" and "Good morning."

What Is Your Relationship to Your Reader?

The "distance" between you and your reader is important because it tells you how to present, or "dress," your ideas for your reader. Just as shorts and a T-shirt would be inappropriate clothing for a formal party, so, too, might it be inappropriate to present your ideas in a way that goes against your reader's expectations or understanding of the subject.

All writing is built on communicating ideas. This communication is your fundamental goal whenever you sit down to write. Many factors influence whether you reach that goal, but the general relationship you establish with your audience is an important basis for the exchange of ideas from writer to reader. Each writing situation is different. In some situations you may be writing for audiences who are close to you, such as friends or coworkers. In other situations you may be writing for an audience that is more distant or removed from you, such as your boss, a bank loan officer, or a total stranger.

Once you have determined your relationship to your reader, it is important to consider specific ways to adapt your writing so that your reader will understand and accept what you have to say.

Adapting Your Writing Style to Your Audience

Just as your presentation of yourself through your choice of clothing, hair style, makeup and jewelry constitutes your personal **style**, so, too, can your writing have style. Style in writing is the conscious selection of words and sentences to express an idea.

As the previous examples illustrated, when you communicate an idea, you often have a choice of ways—or styles—of doing so. To a certain extent, the style you choose is determined by the "distance," or relationship, between you and your audience. One of the significant ways in which distance can influence your style is in the level of **formality** you use to express your ideas.

Formality in language generally refers to the degree to which you follow the rules of writing and the precision of your vocabulary, sentence structure, and grammar. Both purpose and audience influence the level of formality. Depending on the audience, some writing situations require strict adherence to these rules while other situations allow for more casual treatment.

The following chart illustrates some of the ways in which formality may influence your writing.

	Formal	Informal
Word Choice	Standard English and precise meaning	Slang and imprecise usage
Sentences	Long sentences Complex structures Variety	Short sentences Simple structures Less variety
Punctuation	Accurate punctuation	Punctuation less important
Paragraph Structure	Attention to paragraphs	Little attention to paragraphs
Appearance	Attention to appearance	Appearance less important

Working Together: With a peer, discuss ways in which your writing might be influenced by the formality, or distance, of your relationship to your reader. Imagine various readers such as a parent, a best friend, or an anonymous person in a business office.

Adapting Words

Another element of style is word choice. In addition to the overall formality of your writing, one of the ways you should adapt your writing to your audience is in the words you choose to convey your ideas. Your word choice should consider not only your relationship to your reader but also your reader's expectations and knowledge of the subject.

Words are the building blocks for all of your writing. They are the fundamental element in creating the appropriate level of formality for each writing situation. In general, the more precisely you follow the dictionary definitions of the words you use, the more formal your writing will be. The more you use slang and contractions (*can't, she's, they'll,* etc.), the less formal your writing will be.

Working Alone:

1. Find an article in a special interest magazine (*Golf Digest, Surfer, PC World,* and so on). Identify words and phrases that you believe could only be understood by people who share the interest.
2. Take one paragraph from the article you have found and rewrite it so that it could be understood by a general audience.

There are many ways in which your audience might influence your word choice. For example, suppose you have been asked to write a paper on some aspect of computers for your computer science course. Since the audience for this paper will be your computer science teacher and perhaps your fellow computer science students, you could fully expect this audience to know the language of computers. You could also assume that this audience would know such specialized terms as *meg, RAM, main frame,* and *server,* so you would not need to provide definitions or examples to explain what these words mean.

On the other hand, if your English composition teacher asks you to submit an analytical essay on computer science, you might anticipate that this audience would be less familiar with the specialized terms. As a result, you might wisely choose to explain such terms as *mega* and *RAM* when you use them. By doing so, you would be anticipating the needs of your reader and adapting your language to meet those needs, thereby increasing the likelihood of your reader's understanding your ideas.

Word choice is also important because of the effect your words will have on the reader. Words can be powerful vehicles for communicating ideas and feelings because they express meaning in literal and emotional ways. For example, the expressions *old person* and *senior citizen* have similar dictionary, or **denotative,** meanings. However, as you know, the words have very different emotional suggestions, or **connotative** meanings. Because of the differences in the suggested meanings of words, it is also important to consider the effect that your word choice will have on your audience and to choose words that are appropriate for the reader. You wouldn't advertise a restaurant by saying it catered to "old people" because your audience might find such an expression emotionally offensive.

Finally, word choice is important because as you write, you have many options for expressing the same idea. Think of all of the words—or **synonyms**—that are available in English to express "being happy." *Cheerful, delighted, glad, thrilled, stoked,* and *ecstatic* are just some of the choices you have. Each word describes a slightly different kind of being happy or represents the language of a certain subculture; *stoked,* for instance, is a word some surfers use. Because of these variations, one word might be more appropriate than another because it better expresses a meaning for your particular audience.

Working Alone:

1. Examine a chapter in one of your textbooks. Identify specific words and sentences that are subject related. Does the writer explain the terms or assume that the reader understands them? Why?
2. List some of the common technical terms used in your favorite sport or hobby. Choose three words from your list and write an explanation of them for someone who is unfamiliar with the sport or hobby.
3. Choose less formal words for *terminate, procure, utilize, melancholy,* and *altered.*
4. Choose less offensive synonyms for *skinny, cheap, old-aged, used,* and *slaughter.*

Adapting Sentences

Remember the old definition of a sentence that you probably learned early in your schooling? *A sentence is a group of words expressing a complete thought.* When you write, you connect words together to build sentences, which are the basic units for creating meaning. As you create meaning with sentences, you also establish a level of formality for your writing. In general, longer, accurately punctuated sentences create a formal writing style. Short, loosely punctuated sentences and groups of words that aren't sentences (**fragments**) create an informal writing style. Just as with choosing words, the way in which you build your sentences has a great deal to do with who will be reading them.

Imagine for a moment that you have opened a children's book. What type of sentences do you expect to read? In what ways are the sentences in the children's book different from those you find in a college textbook? In what way does the audience influence the way in which the writer builds sentences (and chooses words) to convey meaning in each of these books?

Obviously, the sentences differ in their complexity, length, and variety. In both cases the writer adapts the structure of the sentences so that the reader will understand the meaning. The writer of a college textbook assumes that an audience of college students has the ability to read and understand complex, varied sentences whereas the writer of a children's book believes that an audience of children has the ability to read and understand simple, short, repetitive sentences. Thus, sentence complexity, length, and variety—like the choice of words—are fundamental aspects that you can adapt so that your reader will understand and be interested in what you have to say.

Working Together: Read the following excerpts. Then, with a peer, discuss what conclusions you can draw about the audience for each. Explain.

> A little more than a hundred years ago, a group of artists in France called the Impressionists experimented in their paintings with how they saw the world around them. One famous impressionist was Auguste Renoir, who painted a picture of a young girl with a watering can. He painted a quick impression of the girl and her surroundings as they appeared at that particular moment in time.

> Impressionism was a movement in painting originating in France in the 1860s. The artists involved were not a formal body, but to varying degrees they shared related

outlooks and techniques, and they grouped together for the sake of exhibiting. Renoir was one of the greatest of the Impressionists. The weighty and somber style of his early canvasses gave way to light-filled scenes built up in characteristically Impressionistic brush strokes.

Working Alone: You have contracted the flu, and you have to stay in bed. Write an email to your friend telling her that you will have to cancel plans for tomorrow night. Then write an email to your professor explaining that you are sick and that you would like her to send you assignments for the next two classes.

Adapting Ideas

The ideas you choose to write about—or "talking points"—are also an important way of adapting your writing to your reader. Obviously, you want to write about ideas in such a way that your audience will find them interesting. Since the fundamental aim of most writing is to be read, your chances of achieving this goal increase if the reader is interested in what you have to say. As a writer, your job is to grab your reader's attention and keep it as you develop your ideas. One way of doing this is to focus on ideas that the reader wants to read, that the reader finds interesting, that the reader will understand, or that the reader needs to learn more about.

Let's say that you have been given an assignment to write an article on new compact-disc recordings for the college newspaper. Since this is a student newspaper, you know that your primary audience will be college students. Although students' musical tastes vary dramatically, you know that most college students are interested in the latest popular music releases. Few, if any, students would be interested in the latest recording of Franz Schubert's "Trout Quintet" or *Boxcar Willy's Greatest Hits*. Because you want your article to be read, you decide to adapt it to your audience's interests and to focus on the latest rock and hip-hop releases.

You can see that adapting talking points is important in your writing. That is, it's important when choosing a topic or focus for your writing. However, it is also important when selecting the details, reasons, and examples you will use to develop the topic.

When planning your article on the latest rock and hip-hop releases, you might assume that your audience is interested in the political messages of the lyrics, so you could include specific examples of lyrics with political content to develop your ideas. By doing so, you can make your point and also keep your audience interested. On the other hand, since few people have a deep knowledge of musical composition, you might decide that any discussion of chord progression would not interest your audience, so you would omit this from your article.

Working Together:

1. With a classmate, describe the type of language you use in a specialized course of study (an astronomy course, for example, or an introduction to web page design). Identify at least ten specialized terms that you would assume students in this field of study should know.

2. Working in a group, choose two textbooks: one from a science course and one from a humanities course. How are the language and format of each text adapted for the audience? What assumptions does the writer of the text make about the audience?

Hop the Fence

A good strategy in adapting your writing to your audience is to "**hop the fence.**" This means imagining the writing situation from the point of view of the reader, not from your point of view as the writer. As the writer, you already know what you want to communicate to the reader. Hopping the fence will help you find the right words, express the right ideas, choose the right details, and assume the right style. When you hop the fence successfully, your reader will not only understand what you are trying to communicate but will also be open to your ideas. After all, isn't that the ultimate goal of all good writers?

Working Alone: Complete the Audience Profile Box for a piece of your writing. You may choose a piece from this class, from another class, or from your personal or professional life.

Audience Profile Box

Based on your reading of this chapter, respond to the following:

Describe your reader.

What ideas or information do you want to convey?

How do you want your reader to respond?

What reasons, ideas, or examples can you use to get your reader to respond?

How much does the reader already know about your topic?

What are your reader's expectations?

Suggestions for Writing

1. Write a description of your college campus for someone who has never seen it. Then write a description for someone who has seen it.
2. Write directions to your house for someone who lives far away. Then write directions for someone who lives in your town.
3. Write an article on adapting to college life for the student newspaper at your former high school.
4. Write the definition of a complicated process or term in your major area of study. Assume that your reader knows nothing about the subject.
5. Write an email to a friend in another country describing your favorite American TV show.

READINGS

BLACK MEN AND PUBLIC SPACE
BRENT STAPLES

1   My first victim was a woman—white, well dressed, probably in her early twenties. I came upon her late one evening on a deserted street in Hyde Park, a relatively affluent neighborhood in an otherwise mean, impoverished section of Chicago. As I swung onto the avenue behind her, there seemed to be a discreet, uninflammatory distance between us. Not so. She cast back a worried glance. To her, the youngish black man—a broad six feet two inches with a beard and billowing hair, both hands shoved into the pockets of a bulky military jacket—seemed menacingly close. After a few more quick glimpses, she picked up her pace and was soon running in earnest. Within seconds she disappeared into a cross street.

2   That was more than a decade ago. I was twenty-two years old, a graduate student newly arrived at the University of Chicago. It was in the echo of that terrified woman's footfalls that I first began to know the unwieldy inheritance I'd come into—the ability to alter public space in ugly ways. It was clear that she thought herself the quarry of a mugger, a rapist, or worse. Suffering a bout of insomnia, however, I was stalking sleep, not defenseless wayfarers. As a softy who is scarcely able to take a knife to a raw chicken—let alone hold it to a person's throat—I was surprised, embarrassed, and dismayed all at once. Her flight made me feel like an accomplice in tyranny. It also made it clear that I was indistinguishable from the muggers who occasionally seeped into the area from the surrounding ghetto. That first encounter, and those that followed, signified that a vast, unnerving gulf lay between nighttime pedestrians—particularly women—and me. And I soon gathered that being perceived as dangerous is a hazard in itself. I only needed to turn a corner into a dicey situation, or crowd some frightened, armed person in a foyer somewhere, or make an errant move after being pulled over by a policeman. Where fear and weapons meet—and they often do in urban America—there is always the possibility of death.

3   In that first year, my first away from my hometown, I was to become thoroughly familiar with the language of fear. At dark, shadowy intersections in Chicago, I could cross in front of a car stopped at a traffic light and elicit the *thunk, thunk, thunk, thunk* of the driver—black, white, male, or female—hammering down the door locks. On less traveled streets after dark, I grew accustomed to but never comfortable with people who crossed to the other side of the street rather than pass me. Then there were the standard unpleasantries with police, doormen, bouncers, cab drivers, and others whose business it is to screen out troublesome individuals *before* there is any nastiness.

4   I moved to New York nearly two years ago and I have remained an avid night walker. In central Manhattan, the near-constant crowd cover minimizes tense one-

on-one street encounters. Elsewhere—visiting friends in SoHo, where sidewalks are narrow and tightly spaced buildings shut out the sky—things can get very taut indeed.

5   Black men have a firm place in New York mugging literature. Norman Podhoretz in his famed (or infamous) 1963 essay, "My Negro Problem—And Ours," recalls growing up in terror of black males; they "were tougher than we were, more ruthless," he writes—and as an adult on the Upper West Side of Manhattan, he continues, he cannot constrain his nervousness when he meets black men on certain streets. Similarly, a decade later, the essayist and novelist Edward Hoagland extols a New York where once "Negro bitterness bore down mainly on other Negroes." Where some see mere panhandlers, Hoagland sees "a mugger who is clearly screwing up his nerve to do more than just *ask* for money." But Hoagland has "the New Yorker's quick-hunch posture for broken-field maneuvering," and the bad guy swerves away.

6   I often witness that "hunch posture," from women after dark on the warren-like streets of Brooklyn where I live. They seem to set their faces on neutral and, with their purse straps strung across their chests bandolier style, they forge ahead as though bracing themselves against being tackled. I understand, of course, that the danger they perceive is not a hallucination. Women are particularly vulnerable to street violence, and young black males are drastically overrepresented among the perpetrators of that violence. Yet these truths are no solace against the kind of alienation that comes of being ever the suspect, against being set apart, a fearsome entity with whom pedestrians avoid making eye contact.

7   It is not altogether clear to me how I reached the ripe old age of twenty-two without being conscious of the lethality nighttime pedestrians attributed to me. Perhaps it was because in Chester, Pennsylvania, the small, angry industrial town where I came of age in the 1960s, I was scarcely noticeable against a backdrop of gang warfare, street knifings, and murders. I grew up one of the good boys, had perhaps a half-dozen fist fights. In retrospect, my shyness of combat has clear sources.

8   Many things go into the making of a young thug. One of those things is the consummation of the male romance with the power to intimidate. An infant discovers that random flailings send the baby bottle flying out of the crib and crashing to the floor. Delighted, the joyful babe repeats those motions again and again, seeking to duplicate the feat. Just so, I recall the points at which some of my boyhood friends were finally seduced by the perception of themselves as tough guys. When a mark cowered and surrendered his money without resistance, myth and reality merged—and paid off. It is, after all, only manly to embrace the power to frighten and intimidate. We, as men, are not supposed to give an inch of our lane on the highway; we are to seize the fighter's edge in work and in play and even in love; we are to be valiant in the face of hostile forces.

9   Unfortunately, poor and powerless young men seem to take all this nonsense literally. As a boy, I saw countless tough guys locked away; I have since buried several, too. They were babies, really—a teenage cousin, a brother of twenty-two, a childhood friend in his mid-twenties—all gone down in episodes of bravado played out in the streets. I came to doubt the virtues of intimidation early on. I chose, perhaps even unconsciously, to remain a shadow—timid, but a survivor.

10   The fearsomeness mistakenly attributed to me in public places often has a perilous flavor. The most frightening of these confusions occurred in the late 1970s and early 1980s when I worked as a journalist in Chicago. One day, rushing into the office of a magazine I was writing for with a deadline story in hand, I was mistaken for a burglar. The office manager called security and, with an ad hoc posse, pursued me through the labyrinthine halls, nearly to my editor's door. I had no way of proving who I was. I could only move briskly toward the company of someone who knew me.

11   Another time I was on assignment for a local paper and killing time before an interview. I entered a jewelry store on the city's affluent Near North Side. The proprietor excused herself and returned with an enormous red Doberman pinscher straining at the end of a leash. She stood, the dog extended toward me, silent to my questions, her eyes bulging nearly out of her head. I took a cursory look around, nodded, and bade her good night. Relatively speaking, however, I never fared as badly as another black male journalist. He went to nearby Waukegan, Illinois, a couple of summers ago to work on a story about a murderer who was born there. Mistaking the reporter for the killer, police hauled him from his car at gunpoint and but for his press credentials would probably have tried to book him. Such episodes are not uncommon. Black men trade tales like this all the time.

12   In "My Negro Problem—And Ours," Podhoretz writes that the hatred he feels for blacks makes itself known to him through a variety of avenues—one being his discomfort with that "special brand of paranoid touchiness" to which he says blacks are prone. No doubt he is speaking here of black men. In time, I learned to smother the rage I felt at so often being taken for a criminal. Not to do so would surely have led to madness—via that special "paranoid touchiness" that so annoyed Podhoretz at the time he wrote the essay.

13   I began to take precautions to make myself less threatening. I move about with care, particularly late in the evening. I give a wide berth to nervous people on subway platforms during the wee hours, particularly when I have exchanged business clothes for jeans. If I happen to be entering a building behind some people who appear skittish, I may walk by, letting them clear the lobby before I return, so as not to seem to be following them. I have been calm and extremely congenial on those rare occasions when I've been pulled over by the police.

14   And on late-evening constitutionals along streets less traveled by, I employ what has proved to be an excellent tension-reducing measure: I whistle melodies from Beethoven and Vivaldi and the more popular classical composers. Even steely New Yorkers hunching toward nighttime destinations seem to relax, and occasionally they even join in the tune. Virtually everybody seems to sense that a mugger wouldn't be warbling bright, sunny selections from Vivaldi's *Four Seasons*. It is my equivalent of the cowbell that hikers wear when they know they are in bear country.

Topics for Thinking and Writing

1. Describe Staples's audience. Is he writing for a general or a specific audience? Support your claim with specific references to his word choice and examples.
2. Why does Staples use the word *victim* in the opening paragraph? What does the word mean? Who are some of the victims in this essay?

3. Look at Staples's references to geographic locations. What assumptions does he make about his audience's knowledge of these places? Are there any places he refers to that you don't know of? How important are these geographic references to Staples's point?
4. Staples's essay describes how people misjudge him because of his appearance. Write a description of a time when you were misjudged because of the way you looked. Assume that your audience has had the same experience that you did.

HOW WE LISTEN TO MUSIC
AARON COPLAND

We all listen to music according to our separate capacities. But, for the sake of analysis, the whole listening process may become clearer if we break it up into its component parts, so to speak. In a certain sense we all listen to music on three separate planes. For lack of a better terminology, one might name these: (1) the sensuous plane, (2) the expressive plane, (3) the sheerly musical plane. The only advantage to be gained from mechanically splitting up the listening process into these hypothetical planes is the clearer view to be had of the way in which we listen.

The simplest way of listening to music is to listen for the sheer pleasure of the musical sound itself. That is the sensuous plane. It is the plane on which we hear music without thinking, without considering it in any way. One turns on the radio while doing something else and absent-mindedly bathes in the sound. A kind of brainless but attractive state of mind is engendered by the mere sound appeal of the music.

You may be sitting in a room reading this book. Imagine one note struck on the piano. Immediately that one note is enough to change the atmosphere of the room—providing that the sound element in music is expressive quality of a theme or, similarly, an entire piece of music. And if it is a great work of art, don't expect it to mean exactly the same thing to you each time you return to it.

Themes or pieces need not express only one emotion, of course. Take such a theme as the first main one of the *Ninth Symphony*, for example. It is clearly made up of different elements. It does not say only one thing. Yet anyone hearing it immediately gets a feeling of strength, a feeling of power. It isn't a power that comes simply because the theme is played loudly. It is a power inherent in the theme itself. The extraordinary strength and vigor of the theme results in the listener's receiving an impression that a forceful statement has been made. But one should never try to boil it down to "the fateful hammer of life," etc. That is where the trouble begins. The musician, in his exasperation, says it means nothing but the notes themselves, whereas the nonprofessional is only too anxious to hang on to any explanation that gives him the illusion of getting closer to the music's meaning.

Now, perhaps, the reader will know better what I mean when I say that music does have an expressive meaning but that we cannot say in so many words what that meaning is.

The third plane on which music exists is the sheerly musical plane. Besides the pleasurable sound of music and the expressive feeling that it gives off, music does exist in terms of the notes themselves and of their manipulation. Most listeners are not sufficiently conscious of this third plane....

Professional musicians, on the other hand, are, if anything, too conscious of the mere notes themselves. They often fall into the error of becoming so engrossed with their arpeggios and staccatos that they forget the deeper aspects of the music they are performing. But from the layman's standpoint, it is not so much a matter of getting over bad habits on the sheerly musical plane as of increasing one's awareness of what is going on, in so far as the notes are concerned.

When the man in the street listens to the "notes themselves" with any degree of concentration, he is most likely to make some mention of the melody. Either he hears a pretty melody or he does not, and he generally lets it go at that. Rhythm is likely to gain his attention next, particularly if it seems exciting. But harmony and tone color are generally taken for granted, if they are thought of consciously at all. As for music's having a definite form of some kind, that idea seems never to have occurred to him.

It is very important for all of us to become more alive to music on its sheerly musical plane. After all, an actual musical material is being used. The intelligent listener must be prepared to increase his awareness of the musical material and what happens to it. He must hear the melodies, the rhythms, the harmonies, the tone colors in a more conscious fashion. But above all he must, in order to follow the line of the composer's thought, know something of the principles of musical form. Listening to all of these elements is listening on the sheerly musical plane.

Let me repeat that I have split up mechanically the three separate planes on which we listen merely for the sake of greater clarity. Actually, we never listen on one or the other of these planes. What we do is to correlate them—listening in all three ways at the same time. It takes no mental effort, for we do it instinctively.

Perhaps an analogy with what happens to us when we visit the theater will make this instinctive correlation clearer. In the theater, you are aware of the actors and actresses, costumes and sets, sounds and movements. All these give one the sense that the theater is a pleasant place to be in. They constitute the sensuous plane in our theatrical reactions.

The expressive plane in the theater would be derived from the feeling that you get from what is happening on the stage. You are moved to pity, excitement, or gayety. It is this general feeling, generated aside from the particular words being spoken, a certain emotional something which exists on the stage, that is analogous to the expressive quality in music.

The plot and plot development is equivalent to our sheerly musical plane. The playwright creates and develops a character in just the same way that a composer creates and develops a theme. According to the degree of your awareness of the way in which the artist in either field handles his material, you will become a more intelligent listener.

It is easy enough to see that the theatergoer never is conscious of any of these elements separately. He is aware of them all at the same time. The same is true of music listening. We simultaneously and without thinking listen on all three planes.

In a sense, the ideal listener is both inside and outside the music at the same moment, judging it and enjoying it, wishing it would go one way and watching it go another—almost like the composer at the moment he composes it; because in order to write his music, the composer must also be inside and outside his music, carried away by it and yet coldly critical of it. A subjective and objective attitude is implied in both creating and listening to music.

What the reader should strive for, then, is a more *active* kind of listening. Whether you listen to Mozart or Duke Ellington, you can deepen your understanding of music only by being a more conscious and aware listener—not someone who is just listening, but someone who is listening *for* something.

Topics for Thinking and Writing

1. Describe the audience for Copland's essay. Support your description by pointing to specific words, phrases, and ideas that Copland assumes his audience will understand.
2. What assumptions does Copland make about his audience's knowledge and experiences listening to music? How do these assumptions influence his writing?
3. Do you agree with Copland? In what way is your experience of listening to music similar to or different from that described by Copland?
4. Using a type of music that you like, rewrite Copland's essay for a different audience. Use language, details, and examples that are appropriate for your audience.
5. Analyze your rewrite from topic 4. Identify any expectations and assumptions you made about your audience's interest in and knowledge of your subject.

THE TIMES THEY ARE A-CHANGIN'
BOB DYLAN

Come gather 'round people
Wherever you roam

And admit that the waters
Around you have grown
5   And accept it that soon
You'll be drenched to the bone.
If your time to you
Is worth savin'
Then you better start swimmin'
10 Or you'll sink like a stone
For the times they are a-changin'.

Come writers and critics
Who prophesize with your pen

And keep your eyes wide
15 The chance won't come again
And don't speak too soon
For the wheel's still in spin
And there's no tellin' who
That it's namin'.
20 For the loser now
Will be later to win
For the times they are a-changin'.

Come senators, congressmen
Please heed the call
25 Don't stand in the doorway
Don't block up the hall
For he that gets hurt
Will be he who has stalled
There's a battle outside
30 And it is ragin'.
It'll soon shake your windows
And rattle your walls
For the times they are a-changin'.

Come mothers and fathers
35 Throughout the land
And don't criticize
What you can't understand
Your sons and your daughters
Are beyond your command
40 Your old road is
Rapidly agin'.
Please get out of the new one
If you can't lend your hand
For the times they are a-changin'.

45 The line it is drawn
The curse it is cast
The slow one now
Will later be fast
As the present now
50 Will later be past
The order is
Rapidly fadin'.

And the first one now
Will later be last
For the times they are a-changin'.

Topics for Thinking and Writing

1. Describe the general audience Dylan is addressing in this song. What general message does Dylan want to convey to this audience?
2. In stanzas 2, 3, and 4, Dylan addresses three specific audiences. How is the general message of the song adapted to each specific audience?
3. Rewrite each stanza of the song in two or three sentences. Keep the same audience in mind and try to keep as many of the original ideas as you can. Combine your sentences into a letter that you would address to this imaginary audience.
4. "The Times They Are A-Changin'" is usually thought of as a song of social protest from the 1960s. Identify some current social issues that are addressed in a recent popular song. Write a description of the social issues and the way in which the song addresses the issues. Describe the segment of society that the issues affect. How are the language and ideas of the song adapted to this audience?

DREAM DEFERRED
LANGSTON HUGHES

What happens to a dream deferred?

Does it dry up
like a raisin in the sun?
Or fester like a sore—
5   And then run?
Does it stink like rotten meat?
Or crust and sugar over—
like a syrupy sweet?

Maybe it just sags
10   like a heavy load.

Or does it explode?

Topics for Thinking and Writing

1. Who do you think is the audience for this poem? How can you tell?
2. What response does the speaker hope to generate among that audience?
3. Which words do you think are most important for establishing the mood of this poem?
4. Write a brief account of why you think this poem is so short. Would it be more effective if it contained specific examples of what the author is writing about?
5. Write a short essay about your own frustrations while waiting for one particular event to happen.

GIRL
JAMAICA KINCAID

Wash the white clothes on Monday and put them on the stone heap; wash the color clothes on Tuesday and put them on the clothesline to dry; don't walk barehead in the hot sun; cook pumpkin fritters in very hot sweet oil; soak your little clothes right after you take them off; when buying cotton to make yourself a nice blouse, be sure that it doesn't have gum on it, because that way it won't hold up well after a wash; soak salt fish overnight before you cook it; is it true that you sing benna in Sunday School?; always eat your food in such a way that it won't turn someone else's stomach; on Sundays try to walk like a lady and not like the slut you are so bent on becoming; don't sing benna in Sunday School; you mustn't speak to wharf-rat boys, not even to give directions; don't eat fruits on the street—flies will follow you; *but I don't sing benna on Sundays at all and never in Sunday school;* this is how to sew on a button; this is how to make a buttonhole for the button you have just sewed on; this is how to hem a dress when you see the hem coming down and so to prevent yourself from looking like the slut I know you are so bent on becoming; this is how you iron your father's khaki shirt so that it doesn't have a crease; this is how you iron your father's khaki pants so that they don't have a crease; this is how you grow okra—far from the house, because okra tree harbors red ants; when you are growing dasheen, make sure it gets plenty of water or else it makes your throat itch when you are eating it; this is how you sweep a corner; this is how you sweep a whole house; this is how you sweep a yard; this is how you smile to someone you don't like very much; this is how you smile to someone you don't like at all; this is how you smile to someone you like completely; this is how you set a table for tea; this is how you set a table for dinner; this is how you set a table for lunch; this is how you set a table for breakfast; this is how to behave in the presence of men who don't know you very well, and this way they won't recognize immediately the slut I have warned you against becoming; be sure to wash every day, even if it is with your own spit; don't squat down to play marbles—you are not a boy, you know; don't pick people's flowers—you might catch something; don't throw stones at blackbirds, because it might not be a blackbird at all; this is how to make a bread pudding; this is how to make doukona; this is how to make pepper pot; this is how to make a good medicine for a cold; this is how to make a good medicine to throw away a child before it even becomes a child; this is how to catch a fish; this is how to throw back a fish you don't like, and that way something bad won't fall on you; this is how to bully a man; this is how a man bullies you; this is how to love a man, and if this doesn't work there are other ways, and if they don't work don't feel too bad about giving up; this is how to spit up in the air if you feel like it, and this is how to move quick so that it doesn't fall on you; this is how to make ends meet; always squeeze bread to make sure it's fresh; *but what if the baker won't let me feel the bread?;* you mean to say that after all you are really going to be the kind of woman who the baker won't let near the bread?

Topics for Thinking and Writing

1. Describe the primary speaker. Is the speaker addressing a general or a specific audience? Describe the audience.
2. Jamaica Kincaid grew up in the West Indies. Identify specific words and phrases that are directly related to her cultural heritage. What assumptions does she make about her readers' understanding of this culture?
3. When you were young, you were probably given advice by an older person similar to that given in "Girl." Write a brief explanation of one of the pieces of advice you were told. Explain why you rejected or accepted the advice.
4. Write a letter to a young person who has asked for your advice on a particular subject such as dating, alcohol, clothing, or education.
5. Using "Girl" as a model, write a piece called "Boy" addressed to a young teenage boy. Draw on your own cultural background to develop ideas for your piece.

Self-Assessment

Reread the self-assessment which you completed at the beginning of this chapter.

What would I change?

Why?

What have I learned about the role of the audience in writing?

Purpose: Why Are You Writing?

A MACK TRUCK
A TREK MOUNTAIN BIKE
A FERRARI TESTAROSA

Each of these vehicles is designed with a specific use in mind. The Ferrari is sleek, fast, and expensive. It would be a great choice if you wanted to get somewhere quickly—and in style. However, if you had to pick up and move a grand piano along the way, the Ferrari wouldn't meet the demands of the task because it wasn't designed with that purpose in mind.

The Trek bike, likewise, would not be anyone's first choice for moving a piano or taking a special friend on a date. However, unlike either the Ferrari or the Mack truck, it would be the perfect vehicle for spending a weekend on trails in the woods. You would use the Mack truck to move the piano but perhaps not to take a quick spin down the interstate. Each vehicle has its own strengths and weaknesses, not due to the quality of its construction but due to the purpose for which it was designed.

Similarly, different types of writing are designed for specific purposes. Just as selecting the Ferrari for moving a piano would be the wrong choice, making the wrong choices in writing can also result in not achieving your goal or being misunderstood.

In Chapter 1, you explored your profile as a writer and identified the types of writing you have done. In each of the examples you discussed there—whether a book report, a note to a teacher, or an essay for a college application—you were writing with a specific aim in mind. You conveyed information to your **audience** because you wanted something to happen. You wanted your reader to do something with the information. Because whenever you write, you are attempting to influence your audience in some way, an important element of all writing is **purpose**.

Working Together: Think of a folktale, fairy tale, or myth from your culture. Share it with a classmate and discuss the tale's purpose.

Self-Assessment

As you will see in this chapter, determining your purpose, or *why* you are writing, is basic to all writing. Every time you write, you do so with a specific purpose in mind, and your purpose influences many of the decisions you make about what you are writing. For example, you probably wouldn't be concerned about grammar and style if you were writing to a friend describing what you did last weekend. If you were writing an essay for class on the same topic, however, grammar and style would be very important. Similarly, you wouldn't take a typed shopping list to the supermarket when a handwritten list would suit your needs. The choices you make depend on the reason why you are writing. In all instances, the reason why you are writing influences how you express your ideas.

You already know many things about the importance of purpose in writing. This self-assessment will help you explore what you already know and the ways in which purpose might influence the decisions you make when you write.

What Do I Write?

1. On the following list, I have placed a checkmark beside the kinds of writing I have done during the past few months.

shopping list	research paper	job application
report	bank check	email for school
postcard	email for work	letter to a friend
email to a stranger	letter to a business	poem or a song
college application	essay for a class	newspaper editorial
love note	posting to a listserv	short story
memo	book report	novel

2. I have checked off some of the purposes I have had for my writing:

Purpose	Audience	Example of Writing
Persuade		
Inform		
Entertain		
Analyze		
Summarize		
Argue		
Compare		
Remind		

Take notes

Evaluate

Define

Describe

3. I think that some of the purposes for which I will write in college are

What do I know about purpose in writing?	What will I need to know to better understand purpose in writing?

Working Alone:

1. Write a paragraph discussing how purpose might affect language choice, style, and the format of writing.
2. Look at one piece of writing which you are working on for another course. What is the purpose of the piece? Choose another purpose and rewrite the introduction.
   A. What specific word changes have you made? Why?
   B. Has your sentence length differed?
   C. Has your organization of the examples changed?
   D. Have you altered the details in the content?

Why Are You Writing?

In order for your writing to be understood by your reader, it is important to ask yourself these questions:

Why am I writing this piece?
and
What writing decisions do I need to make to achieve my purpose?

Assume, for example, that an acquaintance of yours has had a minor car accident. You might retell the story of the accident to one of your friends by simply stating the facts and letting him decide for himself who was at fault. But you might decide to tell another friend about the accident in order to illustrate the importance of wearing a seat belt while driving. In this case, you would concentrate on the part in which the police report stated that if the driver had been wearing a seat belt, she would not have had to be treated in the emergency room for facial cuts. Because of the purpose of the story, you would concentrate on the after-effects of the accident rather than on its cause. In a third case, you might want to highlight your friend's bad luck as a driver, so you would choose to concentrate on the fact that this was her third accident in one year rather than on the details of this specific accident.

Working Alone: Write a brief introduction for a paper about the accident previously described. Your introduction should fit one of the purposes and audiences mentioned.

In the previous self-assessment, you saw that people can have many specific purposes in writing. In your personal life, in college, and in your future career, you will find that most writing can be grouped into three broad categories of purpose: to **inform**, to **persuade**, or to **entertain**.

To **inform** means to write with the primary purpose of conveying information to the reader. Some common examples of writing to inform are an explanatory essay, a news article, a press release, answers to essay exam questions, and an analysis of a procedure.

To **persuade** means to write to convey information to the reader in a way that attempts to influence the reader's thinking or attitude. Some common examples of writing to persuade are an argumentative essay, a newspaper editorial, an advertisement in a magazine, a movie review, a letter requesting a donation, a sales letter, and a political flyer.

To **entertain** means to write to provide information that is intended to divert or amuse. Some common examples of writing to entertain are a joke, a song, a humorous anecdote, a satire or parody, and a detective novel.

To further understand how purpose influences your writing, imagine a series of newspaper articles based on a record-breaking drought in the West. There might be a front-page story, editorials, and articles in the living and science sections. All of these stories would, in some sense, be about the drought, and all would target the same audience of readers, but each would likely have a different purpose.

These writings might include the following:

Informative: Articles on the front page and in the science section about how to conserve water during the drought, facts and figures illustrating the drought's effects on the local economy, and an explanatory essay on the meteorological causes of the drought

Persuasive: Editorials chastising local officials for neglecting to plan for drought relief, essays calling for long-range conservation policies, letters to the editor, and analyses suggesting a relationship between the drought and global warming

Entertaining: Articles in the living section recollecting old-timers' experiences with past droughts, and features about how local families are dealing with the drought on a day-to-day basis as they struggle to conserve water and save their livestock.

Working Together: With a partner, read a front-page article in a newspaper. Then turn to the editorial section and read a related story on the same topic. Discuss how the pieces differ in language, organization, format, style, and so on. For what other purposes might stories be written about this topic?

Of course, this is not to say that all writing fits neatly into these three categories of purpose. Sometimes you will write with multiple purposes in mind. For example, you might begin an essay by telling a humorous story to entertain your reader and to create interest in your ideas. You might then follow with facts to inform your reader about the topic. You might conclude by stating an opinion and encouraging your reader to accept your view.

Through the use of ongoing self-assessment and the experience you gain by writing, you will become adept at determining purpose.

Working Together: With a partner, visit one of the following offices on campus: career placement, athletics, financial aid, admissions, or health services. Gather publications from the office. Then discuss the purpose of each publication and how that purpose influences the publication's style, language, and format.

Purpose and Language

Informative Writing

Each of the previously mentioned purposes—to inform, persuade, or entertain—will result in writing that has certain characteristics. For example, because **informative writing** has as its primary purpose conveying information to the reader, it needs to be clear, logical, and precise. Its tone will tend to be straightforward and formal, the main idea will be expressed in the beginning of the passage, there will be few action verbs, and the words used will tend to be factual instead of emotional.

Example

Freud believed that the personality is divided into three separate entities: the id, the ego, and the superego. Each entity has its particular role in governing and guiding human behavior. The id, present at birth, is associated with impulses and biological drives. It operates on the pleasure principle. Its goal is to fulfill its needs without regard for the consequences of that fulfillment. Next to develop is the ego, which operates on the reality principle. Its job is to hold off the id's impulses until a safe and appropriate mode of fulfillment is available. Also, the ego gives the individual realistic information about the environment. Last to develop is the superego, which operates on the morality principle. The superego's chief component is the conscience, which consists of the internalized values of the caregivers and the surrounding culture. The function of the superego is to help the individual determine what is morally right and wrong.

Analysis: As you can see from this example of informative writing, the main idea about Freud's personality components is stated in the first sentence. Each component is then more fully explained as the paragraph is developed. The explanations repeat key terms: *operating principle* and *goal*. Transition words—used between the terms *next, also,* and *last*—help to indicate clearly and precisely the progression of the components. The tone is direct and straightforward. You could quickly outline the passage:

 I. Freud's Personality Components
   A. Id
      1. Pleasure principle
      2. Goal: to fulfill biological needs
   B. Ego
      1. Reality principle
      2. Goal: to hold off the id's impulses, to sort reality
   C. Superego
      1. Morality principle
      2. Goal: to determine right and wrong

Persuasive Writing

The purpose of persuasive writing is to convince the reader to accept the writer's viewpoint. Its main point is followed by supporting evidence in the order of each example's power to persuade. It often uses colorful, emotional words. Repetition of key words may be used to reinforce the arguments being made. Persuasive writing may begin with a striking anecdote, a controversial question, a bold opinion, or a startling statistic. The goal is to quickly and emphatically draw the reader in.

Example

> The brutal truth is that the bulk of the white people in America never had any interest in educating black people, except as this could serve white purposes. It is not the black child's language that is in question, it is not his language that is despised: It is his experience. A child cannot be taught by anyone who despises him, and a child cannot afford to be fooled. A child cannot be taught by anyone whose demand, essentially, is the child repudiate his experience, and all that gives him sustenance, and enter a limbo in which he will no longer be black, and in which he knows that he can never become white. Black people have lost too many black children that way.
>
> James Baldwin

Analysis: In this example Baldwin uses powerful, emotive words such as *brutal, demand, repudiate, limbo, lost,* and *never*. The points are reinforced by the repetition of the words *a child cannot* and *despised*. Each of these words or phrasings has emotional appeal and is capable of evoking strong feelings and images. Of particular persuasive importance is the author's connection of the words *truth, brutality, children,* and *education*.

Working Alone: Write a paragraph persuading your instructor that your most recent piece of writing deserves a good grade.

Working Together: With a peer, review three or four ads from a newspaper or magazine. Make a list of the ads' words and images which have strong emotional appeal.

Entertaining Writing

The purpose of entertaining writing is to amuse readers (making them laugh, cry, feel sentimental, frightened, and so on). Informal language, variety in sentence patterns and organization, strong active verbs, and exaggerations often mark entertaining writing. Because the writer wants to close the distance between herself and the reader, she may use the pronouns *I* or *you*.

Example

> The men in my family are known for their fast driving. Uncle Josh could have wallpapered a room with the speeding tickets he'd accumulated over the years. Of the five brothers in the family business, at least one, at any given time, was "retired" from driving for a while, courtesy of the Law. My dad, the oldest of the "boys," was the worst. So bad, in fact, that after twenty-five years of slamming on the brakes on the passenger's side of the car, my mother took a stand. Or rather, she took a new seat. She moved herself to the back, never to return to her husband's side.
>
> One Sunday, my dad was, once again, pulled over for going "just a little bit too fast." The State Trooper approached the window. Dad already had his license and registration waiting.

"Officer, of course, he drives too fast. Why do you think I always sit in the back seat?"

The Trooper paused, then pushed the license and registration back through the window.

"Mister, with a wife like that, you don't need a ticket from me."

And, thus, an example of mercy tempering justice …

Analysis: In this example of entertaining writing, the author makes the reader feel close by using the words *my*, *Mom*, and *Dad*. She heightens the humor by exaggeration—wallpapered a room—and the use of irony—"retired." The image of the wife slamming on the brakes on the passenger side is sure to strike a chord with some readers. Notice the use of dialogue, the variety in sentence length, and the informal structure signaled by the word *Or* beginning a sentence and the sentence fragment which ends the piece.

Strategy

Mapping

One way to think about informative, persuasive, and entertaining writing is to imagine them as maps. For example, journalists might use the pyramid to guide them when writing an informative piece. It looks like this:

These questions are the building blocks of an informative piece of writing. Most important to the reader is the information at the top of the pyramid. In this case the story will begin by telling the reader who did what, where they did it, when and why, and, finally, how it was done. Rearranging the order of the building blocks will allow you to alter the priority of the information you are giving the reader.

Working Together: Working in pairs, rearrange the order of the information in the front-page news article that you discussed earlier (see page 47). How does the new organizational pattern affect the purpose of the piece?

Once a writer has created a map for any piece of writing, all that remains to be done is to fill in the details. Using the pyramid map for the story on the drought in the West, for example, a writer would take the following information and create a particular structure for an **informative** piece of writing:

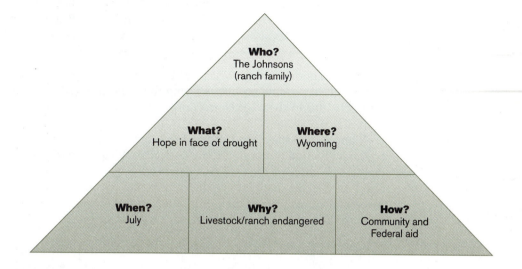

The resulting piece of writing could begin something like this:

The Johnsons, who face the prospect of losing their family cattle ranch in this rural part of Wyoming because of the severe drought, are discovering that they have friends to rely on for support.

The remainder of the story would then go on to develop as many of the points as the writer thinks the audience needs to know. The general structure of the writing, however, has been established right from the very start by thinking about purpose.

A map for a **persuasive** piece of writing might look like this:

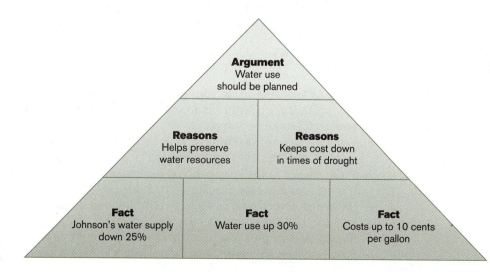

The resulting piece of writing could begin something like this:

The current drought in Wyoming helps demonstrate the need for better planning and use of existing water resources. Such planning would help ranching families should another drought ever affect this region again. Better planning would help ensure that there were sufficient water reserves during a drought and would help keep costs from rising during such water shortages.

The remainder of the story would then go on to support these arguments by looking at the specific problems facing the Johnson family as they struggle to get enough water to their cattle and to pay the rising bills associated with such increased use of water.

Mapping the third kind of writing, entertaining writing, very much depends on the individual writer and topic. Indeed, one strength of entertaining writing is that it does not meet the traditional expectations of how an essay should be structured. In fact, the flexibility of the rules is one reason why it is so hard to write a successful comic piece. Often, it is much easier to produce strong writing if you have specific guidelines to follow.

Note: Maps used to organize writing do not necessarily have to follow a pyramid pattern. They can follow any geometric pattern. Nor is a map essential for planning a piece of writing. These are simply useful ways to **think** about writing.

Working Alone:

1. Choose a topic of interest to you. Then choose a purpose for writing about the topic. Create a map for organizing your writing about the topic that will showcase your purpose.
2. Complete the following purpose profile:
   A. My general topic is
   B. My audience is
   C. My purpose for writing this piece is
   D. I would like to make the following points to achieve my purpose:

Suggestions for Writing

1. Write an anecdote about your grandfather to be read at his seventy-fifth birthday party. Your purpose is to entertain your audience with examples of his wonderful sense of humor.
2. Write a letter to the editor of your local newspaper that addresses a campus issue which concerns or excites you.
3. Write a letter to the special needs department of your child's school advocating for additional services for your child.
4. Write a review of a film you have recently seen. Your goal is to convince your friends to see (or not to see) the film.
5. Summarize, in prose form, a chapter from one of your textbooks. Your purpose is to provide your study group with a guide for the upcoming exam.

6. Write a letter to the dean of your college in which you argue that the administration should or should not abolish this course.

7. Write a paragraph in which you identify what your ideal car (or other vehicle) would be. Focus on the purposes that car would serve.

READINGɾ

THE GREATEɾT PERɾON-HOLE COVER DEBATE: A MODEɾT PROPOɾAL FOR ANYONE WHO THINKɾ THE WORD "HE" Iɾ JUɾT PLAIN EAɾIER ...
LINDSY VAN GELDER

1   I wasn't looking for trouble. What I was looking for, actually, was a little tourist information to help me plan a camping trip to New England.

2   But there it was, on the first page of the 1979 edition of the State of Vermont *Digest of Fish and Game Laws and Regulations:* a special message of welcome from one Edward F. Kehoe, commissioner of the Vermont Fish and Game Department, to the reader and would-be camper, *i.e.*, me.

3   This person (*i.e.*, me) is called "the sportsman."

4   "We have no 'sportswomen, sportspersons, sportsboys, or sportsgirls,'" Commissioner Kehoe hastened to explain, obviously anticipating that some of us sportsfeminists might feel a bit overlooked. "But," he added, "we are pleased to report that we do have many great sportsmen who are women, as well as young people of both sexes."

5   It's just that the Fish and Game Department is trying to keep things "simple and forthright" and to respect "long-standing tradition." And anyway, we really ought to be flattered, "sportsman" being "a meaningful title being earned by a special kind of dedicated man, woman, or young person, as opposed to just any hunter, fisherman, or trapper."

6   I have heard this particular line of reasoning before. In fact, I've heard it so often that I've come to think of it as The Great Person-Hole Cover Debate, since gender-neutral manholes are invariably brought into the argument as evidence of the lengths to which humorless, Newspeak-spouting feminists will go to destroy their mother tongue.

7   Consternation about woman-handling the language comes from all sides. Sexual conservatives who see the feminist movement as a unisex plot and who long for the good olde days of *vive la différence,* when men were men and women were women, nonetheless do not rally behind the notion that the term "mankind" excludes women.

8   But most of the people who choke on expressions like "spokesperson" aren't right-wing misogynists, and this is what troubles me. Like the undoubtedly well-meaning folks at the Vermont Fish and Game Department, they tend to reassure you right up front that they're only trying to keep things "simple" and to follow "tradition," and that some of their best men are women, anyway.

9   Usually they wind up warning you, with great sincerity, that you're jeopardizing the worthy cause of women's rights by focusing on "trivial" side issues. I would like to know how anything that gets people so defensive and resistant can possibly be called "trivial," whatever else it might be.

10   The English language is alive and constantly changing. Progress—both scientific and social—is reflected in our language, or should be.

11   Not too long ago, there was a product called "flesh-colored" Band-Aids. The flesh in question was colored Caucasian. Once the civil rights movement pointed out the racism inherent in the name, it was dropped. I cannot imagine reading a thoughtful, well-intentioned company policy statement explaining that while the Band-Aids would continue to be called "flesh-colored" for old time's sake, black and brown people would now be considered honorary whites and were perfectly welcome to use them.

12   Most sensitive people manage to describe our national religious traditions as "Judeo-Christian," even though it takes a few seconds longer to say than "Christian." So why is it such a hardship to say "he or she" instead of "he"?

13   I have a modest proposal for anyone who maintains that "he" is just plain easier: since "he" has been the style for several centuries now—and since it really includes everybody anyway, right?—it seems only fair to give "she" a turn. Instead of having to ponder over the intricacies of, say, "Congressman" versus "Congress person" versus "Representative," we can simplify things by calling them all "Congresswoman."

14   Other clarifications will follow: "a woman's home is her castle ..." "a giant step for all womankind".... "all women are created equal".... "Fisherwoman's Wharf." ...

15   And don't be upset by the business letter that begins "Dear Madam," fellas. It means you, too.

Topics for Thinking and Writing

1. What do you think is Van Gelder's purpose (or purposes) in writing this essay? What words and phrases does she use to convey her purpose?
2. In Van Gelder's title, she addresses a specific audience. Who is the intended audience of this piece? What writing decisions do you think Van Gelder has made to reach this audience?
3. Van Gelder says that the English language is "alive and constantly changing." What recent examples of changes in language have you noticed? Write a paragraph discussing some of these changes and the reasons why you think they have occurred.
4. Write a one-paragraph response to Van Gelder's argument that her concerns are not trivial.

5. Think about your own decisions about gender use in language when you speak or write. How closely do you pay attention to this issue when you are writing? How closely do you think you should consider this issue? Write a two-paragraph answer to these questions.

LAST RITES FOR INDIAN DEAD
SUZAN SHOWN HARJO

1   What if museums, universities, and government agencies could put your dead relatives on display or keep them in boxes to be cut up and otherwise studied? What if you believed that the spirits of the dead could not rest until their human remains were placed in a sacred area?

2   The ordinary American would say there ought to be a law—and there is, for ordinary Americans. The problem for American Indians is that there are too many laws of the kind that make us the archaeological property of the United States and too few of the kind that protect us from such insults.

3   Some of my own Cheyenne relatives' skulls are in the Smithsonian Institution today, along with those of at least 4500 other Indian people who were violated in the 1800s by the U.S. Army for an "Indian Cranial Study." It wasn't enough that these unarmed Cheyenne people were mowed down by the cavalry at the infamous Sand Creek massacre; many were decapitated and their heads shipped to Washington as freight. (The Army Medical Museum's collection is now in the Smithsonian.) Some had been exhumed only hours after being buried. Imagine their grieving families' reaction on finding their loved ones disinterred and headless.

4   Some targets of the Army's study were killed in noncombat situations and beheaded immediately. The officer's account of the decapitation of the Apache chief Mangas Coloradas in 1863 shows the pseudoscientific nature of the exercise. "I weighed the brain and measured the skull," the good doctor wrote, "and found that while the skull was smaller, the brain was larger than that of Daniel Webster."

5   These journal accounts exist in excruciating detail, yet missing are any records of overall comparisons, conclusions or final reports of the Army study. Since it is unlike the Army not to leave a paper trail, one must wonder about the motive for its collection.

6   The total Indian body count in the Smithsonian collection is more than 19,000, and it is not the largest in the country. It is not inconceivable that the 1.5 million of us living today are outnumbered by our dead stored in museums, educational institutions, federal agencies, state historical societies and private collections. The Indian people are further dehumanized by being exhibited alongside the mastodons and dinosaurs and other extinct creatures.

7   Where we have buried our dead in peace, more often than not the sites have been desecrated. For more than 200 years, relic hunting has been a popular pursuit. Lately, the market in Indian artifacts has brought this abhorrent activity to a fever pitch in some areas. And when scavengers come upon Indian burial sites,

everything found becomes fair game, including sacred burial offerings, teeth and skeletal remains.

8   One unusually well-publicized example of Indian grave desecration occurred two years ago in a western Kentucky field known as Slack Farm, the site of an Indian village five centuries ago. Ten men—one with a business card stating "Have Shovel, Will Travel"—paid the landowner $10,000 to lease digging rights between planting seasons. They dug extensively on the 40-acre farm, rummaging through an estimated 650 graves, collecting burial goods, tools and ceremonial items. Skeletons were strewn about like litter.

9   What motivates people to do something like this? Financial gain is the first answer. Indian relic-collecting has become a multimillion-dollar industry. The price tag on a bead necklace can easily top $1000; rare pieces fetch tens of thousands.

10   And it is not just collectors of the macabre who pay for skeletal remains. Scientists say that these deceased Indians are needed for research that someday could benefit the health and welfare of living Indians. But just how many dead Indians must they examine? Nineteen thousand?

11   There is doubt as to whether permanent curation of our dead really benefits Indians. Dr. Emery A. Johnson, former assistant surgeon general, recently observed, "I am not aware of any current medical diagnostic or treatment procedure that has been derived from research on such skeletal remains. Nor am I aware of any during the 34 years that I have been involved in American Indian ... health care."

12   Indian remains are still being collected for racial biological studies. While the intentions may be honorable, the ethics of using human remains this way without the full consent of relatives must be questioned.

13   Some relief for Indian people has come on the state level. Almost half of the states, including California, have passed laws protecting Indian burial sites and restricting the sale of Indian bones, burial offerings and other sacred items. Representative Charles E. Bennett (D-Fla.) and Sen. John McCain (R-Ariz.) have introduced bills that are a good start in invoking the federal government's protection. However, no legislation has attacked the problem head-on by imposing stiff penalties at the marketplace, or by changing laws that make dead Indians the nation's property.

14   Some universities—notably Stanford, Nebraska, Minnesota and Seattle—have returned, or agreed to return, Indian human remains; it is fitting that institutions of higher education should lead the way.

15   Congress is now deciding what to do with the government's extensive collection of Indian human remains and associated funerary objects. The secretary of the Smithsonian, Robert McC. Adams, has been valiantly attempting to apply modern ethics to yesterday's excesses. This week, he announced that the Smithsonian would conduct an inventory and return all Indian skeletal remains that could be identified with specific tribes or living kin.

16   But there remains a reluctance generally among collectors of Indian remains to take action of a scope that would have a quantitative impact and a healing quality. If they will not act on their own—and it is highly unlikely that they will—then Congress must act.

17   The country must recognize that the bodies of dead American Indian people are not artifacts to be bought and sold as collectors' items. It is not appropriate to

store tens of thousands of our ancestors for possible future research. They are our family. They deserve to be returned to their sacred burial grounds and given a chance to rest.

18   The plunder of our people's graves has gone on too long. Let us rebury our dead and remove this shameful past from America's future.

Topics for Thinking and Writing

1. What is Harjo's purpose in writing the essay? How does she expect her audience to react?
2. Point out specific examples that Harjo uses to achieve her purpose. How might you categorize the examples? Which examples seem most effective to you? Why?
3. Outline the essay. Why do you think Harjo has chosen to organize the essay as she has? Does the organization affect the purpose of the essay?
4. Think of an issue on campus which you believe calls for some change. Write a three hundred-word essay which ends with a call to action. Model the essay on Harjo's format for this piece.

THE SACRED
STEPHEN DUNN

After the teacher asked if anyone had
      a sacred place
and the students fidgeted and shrank

in their chairs, the most serious of them all
5   said it was his car,
being in it alone, his tape deck playing

things he'd chosen, and others knew the truth
      had been spoken
and began speaking about their rooms,

10   their hiding places, but the car kept coming up,
      the car in motion,

music filling it, and sometimes one other person

who understood the bright altar of the dashboard
      and how far away
15   a car could take him from the need

to speak, or to answer, the key
      in having a key
and putting it in, and going.

Topics for Thinking and Writing

1. Explain the reaction of the students in the poem when given the assignment to write about the sacred.
2. What does the "most serious" student mean when he begins to talk about his car? Why is his car a sacred place for him?
3. How would you define a *sacred place*?
4. Give some examples of language in the poem that connects to the idea of "sacred."
5. Write a paragraph about a recent classroom discussion that really got you interested in a topic. What was the topic? What made the discussion interesting? What ideas did you contribute?
6. Write an essay about one of your sacred places.

DULCE ET DECORUM EST
WILFRED OWEN

Bent double, like old beggars under sacks,
Knock-kneed, coughing like hags, we cursed through sludge,
Til on the haunting flares we turned our backs
And toward our distant rest began to trudge.
Men marched asleep. Many had lost their boots
But limped on, blood-shod. All went lame; all blind;
Drunk with fatigue; deaf even to the hoots
Of tired, outstripped Five-Nines* that dropped behind.

Gas! Gas! Quick boys!—An ecstasy of fumbling ,
Fitting the clumsy helmets just in time;
But someone still was yelling out and stumbling
And flound'ring like a man in fire or lime …
Dim, through the misty panes and thick green light,
As under a green sea, I saw him drowning.
In all my dreams, before my helpless sight,
He plunges at me, guttering, choking, drowning.

If in some smothering dreams you too could pace
Behind the wagon that we flung him in,
And watch the white eyes writhing in his face,
His hanging face, like a devil's sick of sin;
If you could hear, at every jolt, the blood
Come gargling from the froth-corrupted lungs,
Obscene as cancer, bitter at the cud
Of vile, incurable sores on innocent tongues,—

*gas-shells

My friend, you would not tell with such high zest
To children ardent for some desperate glory,
The old Lie: Dulce et decorum est
Pro patria mori.*

Topics for Thinking and Writing

1. What do you think is the purpose of Owen's poem?
2. Using specific words from the poem, discuss how Owen achieves his purpose.
3. Freewrite your response to the poem.
4. Look at each stanza in the poem. What is the purpose of each?
5. How does the poem's purpose influence its organization?
6. Write an essay in which you connect this poem to other images of war that you've seen in other writings or in films. Do they share the same purpose? Why or why not?

THE LESSON
TONI CADE BAMBARA

Back in the days when everyone was old and stupid or young and foolish and me and Sugar were the only ones just right, this lady moved on our block with nappy hair and proper speech and no makeup. And quite naturally we laughed at her, laughed the way we did at the junk man who went about his business like he was some big-time president and his sorry-ass horse his secretary. And we kinda hated her too, hated the way we did the winos who cluttered up our parks and pissed on our handball walls and stank up our hallways and stairs so you couldn't halfway play hide-and-seek without a goddamn gas mask. Miss Moore was her name. The only woman on the block with no first name. And she was black as hell, cept for her feet, which were fish-white and spooky. And she was always planning these boring-ass things for us to do, us being my cousin, mostly, who lived on the block cause we all moved North the same time and to the same apartment then spread out gradual to breathe. And our parents would yank our heads into some kinda shape and crisp up our clothes so we'd be presentable for travel with Miss Moore, who always looked like she was going to church, though she never did. Which is just one of the things the grownups talked about when they talked behind her back like a dog. But when she came calling with some sachet she'd sewed up or some gingerbread she'd made or some book, why then they'd all be too embarrassed to turn her down and we'd get handed over all spruced up. She'd been to college and said it was only right that she should take responsibility for the young ones' education, and she not even related by marriage or blood. So they'd go for it. Specially Aunt Gretchen. She was the main gofer in the family. You got some ole dumb shit foolishness you want somebody to go for, you

---

* "It is sweet and fitting to die for one's country."

send for Aunt Gretchen. She been screwed into the go-along for so long, it's a blood-deep natural thing with her. Which is how she got saddled with me and Sugar and Junior in the first place while our mothers were in a la-de-da apartment up the block having a good ole time.

So this one day Miss Moore rounds us all up at the mailbox and it's puredee hot and she's knockin herself out about arithmetic. And school suppose to let up in summer I heard, but she don't never let up. And the starch in my pinafore scratching the shit outta me and I'm really hating this nappy-head bitch and her goddamn college degree. I'd much rather go to the pool or to the show where it's cool. So me and Sugar leaning on the mailbox being surly, which is a Miss Moore word. And Flyboy checking out what everybody brought for lunch. And Fat Butt already wasting his peanut-butter-and-jelly sandwich like the pig he is. And Junebug punchin on Q.T.'s arm for potato chips. And Rosie Giraffe shifting from one hip to the other waiting for somebody to step on her foot or ask her if she from Georgia so she can kick ass, preferably Mercedes'. And Miss Moore asking us do we know what money is, like we a bunch of retards. I mean real money, she say, like it's only poker chips or monopoly papers we lay on the grocer. So right away I'm tired of this and say so. And would much rather snatch Sugar and go to the Sunset and terrorize the West Indian kids and take their hair ribbons and their money too. And Miss Moore files that remark away for the next week's lesson on brotherhood, I can tell. And finally I say we oughta get to the subway cause it's cooler and besides we might meet some cute boys. Sugar done swiped her mama's lipstick, so we ready.

So we heading down the street and she's boring us silly about what things cost and what our parents make and how much goes for rent and how money ain't divided up right in this country. And then she gets to the part about we all poor and live in the slums, which I don't feature. And I'm ready to speak on that, but she steps out in the street and hails two cabs just like that. Then she hustles half the crew in with her and hands me a five-dollar bill and tells me to calculate 10 percent tip for the driver. And we're off. Me and Sugar and Junebug and Flyboy hangin out the window and hollering to everybody, putting lipstick on each other cause Flyboy a faggot anyway, and making farts with our sweaty armpits. But I'm mostly trying to figure how to spend this money. But they all fascinated with the meter ticking and Junebug starts laying bets as to how much it'll read when Flyboy can't hold his breath no more. Then Sugar lays bets as to how much it'll be when we get there. So I'm stuck. Don't nobody want to go for my plan, which is to jump out at the next light and run off to the first bar-b-que we can find. Then the driver tells us to get the hell out cause we there already. And the meter reads eighty-five cents. And I'm stalling to figure out the tip and Sugar say give him a dime. And I decide he don't need it bad as I do, so later for him. But then he tries to take off with Junebug foot still in the door so we talk about his mama something ferocious. Then we check out that we on Fifth Avenue and everybody dressed up in stockings. One lady in a fur coat, hot as it is. White folks crazy.

"This is the place," Miss Moore say, presenting it to us in the voice she uses at the museum. "Let's look in the windows before we go in."

"Can we steal?" Sugar asks very serious like she's getting the ground rules squared away before she plays. "I beg your pardon," say Miss Moore, and we fall out. So she leads us around the windows of the toy store and me and Sugar screamin, "This is mine, that's mine, I gotta have that, that was made for me, I was born for that," till Big Butt drowns us out.

"Hey, I'm goin to buy that there."

"That there? You don't even know what it is, stupid."

"I do so," he say punchin on Rosie Giraffe. "It's a microscope."

"Whatcha gonna do with a microscope, fool?"

"Look at things."

"Like what, Ronald?" ask Miss Moore. And Big Butt ain't got the first notion. So here go Miss Moore gabbing about the thousands of bacteria in a drop of water and the somethinorother in a speck of blood and the million and one living things in the air around us is invisible to the naked eye. And what she say that for? Junebug go to town on that "naked" and we rolling. Then Miss Moore ask what it cost. So we all jam into the window smudgin it up and the price tag say $300. So then she ask how long'd take for Big Butt and Junebug to save up their allowances. "Too long," I say. "Yeh," adds Sugar, "outgrown it by that time." And Miss Moore say no, you never outgrow learning instruments. "Why, even medical students and interns and," blah, blah, blah. And we ready to choke Big Butt for bringing it up in the first damn place.

"This here costs four hundred eighty dollars," says Rosie Giraffe. So we pile up all over her to see what she pointin out. My eyes tell me it's a chunk of glass cracked with something heavy, and different color inks dripped into the splits, then the whole thing put into a oven or something. But for $480 it don't make sense.

"That's a paperweight made of semi-precious stones fused together under tremendous pressure," she explains slowly, with her hands doing the mining and all the factory work.

"So what's a paperweight?" asks Rosie Giraffe.

"To weigh paper with, dumbbell," say Flyboy, the wise man from the East.

"Not exactly," say Miss Moore, which is what she say when you warm or way off too. "It's to weigh paper down so it won't scatter and make your desk untidy." So right away me and Sugar curtsy to each other and then to Mercedes who is more the tidy type.

"We don't keep paper on top of the desk in my class," say Junebug, figuring Miss Moore crazy or lyin one.

"At home, then," she say. "Don't you have a calendar and pencil case and a blotter and a letter-opener on your desk at home where you do your homework?" And she know damn well what our homes look like cause she nosys around in them every chance she gets.

"I don't even have a desk," say Junebug. "Do we?"

"No. And I don't get no homework neither," says Big Butt.

"And I don't even have a home," say Flyboy like he do at school to keep the white folks off his back and sorry for him. Send this poor kid to camp posters, is his speciality.

"I do," says Mercedes. "I have a box of stationery on my desk and a picture of my cat. My godmother bought the stationery and the desk. There's a big rose on each sheet and the envelopes smell like roses."

"Who wants to know about your smelly-ass stationery," say Rosie Giraffe fore I can get my two cents in.

"It's important to have a work area all your own so that ..."

"Will you look at this sailboat, please," say Flyboy, cuttin her off and pointin to the thing like it was his. So once again we tumble all over each other to gaze at this magnificent thing in the toy store which is just big enough to maybe sail two kittens across the pond if you strap them to the posts tight. We all start reciting the price tag like we in assembly. "Handcrafted sailboat of fiberglass at one thousand one hundred ninety-five dollars."

"Unbelievable," I hear myself say and am really stunned. I read it again for myself just in case the group recitation put me in a trance. Same thing. For some reason this pisses me off. We look at Miss Moore and she lookin at us, waiting for I dunno what.

"Who'd pay all that when you can buy a sailboat set for a quarter at Pop's, a tube of glue for a dime, and a ball of string for eight cents? It must have a motor and a whole lot else besides," I say. "My sailboat cost me about fifty cents."

"But will it take water?" say Mercedes with her smart ass.

"Took mine to Alley Pond Park once," say Flyboy. "String broke. Lost it. Pity."

"Sailed mine in Central Park and it keeled over and sank. Had to ask my father for another dollar."

"And you got the strap," laugh Big Butt. "The jerk didn't even have a string on it. My old man wailed on his behind."

Little Q.T. was staring hard at the sailboat and you could see he wanted it bad. But he too little and somebody'd just take it from him. So what the hell. "This boat for kids, Miss Moore?

"Parents silly to buy something like that just to get all broke up," say Rosie Giraffe.

"That much money it should last forever," I figure.

"My father'd buy it for me if I wanted it."

"Your father, my ass," say Rosie Giraffe getting a chance to finally push Mercedes.

"Must be rich people shop here," say Q.T.

"You are a very bright boy," say Flyboy. "What was your first clue?" And he rap him on the head with the back of his knuckles, since Q.T. the only one he could get away with. Though Q.T. liable to come up behind you years later and get his licks in when you half expect it.

"What I want to know is," I says to Miss Moore though I never talk to her, I wouldn't give the bitch that satisfaction, "is how much a real boat costs? I figure a thousand'd get you a yacht any day."

"Why don't you check that out," she says, "and report back to the group?" Which really pains my ass. If you gonna mess up a perfectly good swim day least you could do is have some answers. "Let's go in," she say like she got something up her sleeve. Only she don't lead the way. So me and Sugar turn the corner to where the entrance is, but when we get there I kinda hang back. Not that I'm scared, what's there to be afraid of, just a toy store. But I feel funny, shame. But what I got to be shamed about? Got as much right to go in as anybody. But somehow I can't seem to get hold of the door, so I step away for Sugar to lead. But she hangs back too. And

I look at her and she looks at me and this is ridiculous. I mean, damn, I have never ever been shy about doing nothing or going nowhere. But then Mercedes steps up and then Rosie Giraffe and Big Butt crowd in behind and shove, and next thing we all stuffed into the doorway with only Mercedes squeezing past us, smoothing out her jumper and walking right down the aisle. Then the rest of us tumble in like a glued-together jigsaw done all wrong. And people lookin at us. And it's like the time me and Sugar crashed into the Catholic church on a dare. But once we got in there and everything so hushed and holy and the candles and the bowin and the handkerchiefs on all the drooping heads, I just couldn't go through with the plan. Which was for me to run up to the altar and do a tap dance while Sugar played the nose flute and messed around in the holy water. And Sugar kept givin me the elbow. Then later teased me so bad I tied her up in the shower and turned it on and locked her in. And she'd be there till this day if Aunt Gretchen hadn't finally figured I was lyin about the boarder takin a shower.

Same thing in the store. We all walkin on tiptoe and hardly touchin the games and puzzles and things. And I watched Miss Moore who is steady watchin us like she waitin for a sign. Like Mama Drewery watches the sky and sniffs the air and takes note of just how much slant is in the bird formation. Then me and Sugar bump smack into each other, so busy gazing at the toys, specially the sailboat. But we don't laugh and go into our fat-lady bump-stomach routine. We just stare at that price tag. Then Sugar run a finger over the whole boat. And I'm jealous and want to hit her. Maybe not her, but I sure want to punch somebody in the mouth.

"Watcha bring us here for, Miss Moore?"

"You sound angry, Sylvia. Are you mad about something?" Givin me one of them grins like she tellin a grown-up joke that never turns out to be funny. And she's lookin very closely at me like maybe she planning to do my portrait from memory. I'm mad, but I won't give her that satisfaction. So I slouch around the store bein very bored and say, "Let's go."

Me and Sugar at the back of the train watchin the tracks whizzin by large then small then getting gobbled up in the dark. I'm thinkin about this tricky toy I saw in the store. A clown that somersaults on a bar then does chin-ups just cause you yank lightly at his leg. Cost $35. I could see me askin my mother for a $35 birthday clown. "You wanna who that costs what?" she'd say, cocking her head to the side to get a better view of the hole in my head. Thirty-five dollars could buy new bunk beds for Junior and Gretchen's boy. Thirty-five dollars and the whole household could go visit Granddaddy Nelson in the country. Thirty-five dollars would pay for the rent and the piano bill too. Who are these people that spend that much for performing clowns and $1000 for toy sailboats? What kinda work they do and how they live and how come we ain't in on it? Where we are is who we are, Miss Moore always pointin out. But it don't necessarily have to be that way, she always adds then waits for somebody to say that poor people have to wake up and demand their share of the pie and don't none of us know what kind of pie she talking about in the first damn place. But she ain't so smart cause I still got her four dollars from the taxi and she sure ain't gettin it. Messin up my day with this shit. Sugar nudges me in my pocket and winks.

Miss Moore lines us up in front of the mailbox where we started from, seem like years ago, and I got a headache for thinkin so hard. And we lean all over each other so we can hold up under the draggy-ass lecture she always finishes us off with at the end before we thank her for borin us to tears. But she just looks at us like she readin tea leaves. Finally she say, "Well, what did you think of F.A.O. Schwarz?"

Rosie Giraffe mumbles, "White folks crazy."

"I'd like to go there again when I get my birthday money," says Mercedes, and we shove her out the pack so she has to lean on the mailbox by herself.

"I'd like a shower. Tiring day," say Flyboy.

Then Sugar surprises me by sayin, "You know, Miss Moore, I don't think all of us here put together eat in a year what that sailboat costs." And Miss Moore lights up like somebody goosed her. "And?" she say, urging Sugar on. Only I'm standin on her foot so she don't continue.

"Imagine for a minute what kind of society it is in which some people can spend on a toy what it would cost to feed a family of six or seven. What do you think?"

"I think," say Sugar pushing me off her feet like she never done before, cause I whip her ass in a minute, "that this is not much of a democracy if you ask me. Equal chance to pursue happiness means an equal crack at the dough, don't it?" Miss Moore is beside herself and I am disgusted with Sugar's treachery. So I stand on her foot one more time to see if she'll shove me. She shuts up, and Miss Moore looks at me, sorrowfully I'm thinkin. And somethin weird is goin on, I can feel it in my chest.

"Anybody else learn anything today?" lookin dead at me. I walk away and Sugar has to run to catch up and don't even seem to notice when I shrug her arm off my shoulder.

"Well, we got four dollars anyway," she says.

"Uh hunh."

"We could go to Hascombs and get half a chocolate layer and then go to the Sunset and still have plenty money for potato chips and ice cream sodas."

"Un hunh."

"Race you to Hascombs," she say.

We start down the block and she gets ahead which is O.K. by me cause I'm going to the West End and then over to the Drive to think this day through. She can run if she want to and even run faster. But ain't nobody gonna beat me at nuthin.

Topics for Thinking and Writing

1. What is the purpose of Miss Moore's lesson? What does she want the children to learn?
2. Write a paragraph describing the experiences Miss Moore gives the children.
3. What writing choices does Bambara make that help to create a tone that's both serious and entertaining? Give specific examples of these choices.
4. Miss Moore does most of her teaching by giving the children experiences. Imagine that Miss Moore has decided to "teach" the lesson through a lecture. Write a 250-word version of that lecture.

Self-Assessment

Reread the self-assessment at the beginning of this chapter. Then answer the following questions.

What would I change?

Why?

What have I learned about purpose in writing?

Prewriting: Exploring and Discovering Ideas

4

NULLA DIES SINE LINEA [NEVER A DAY WITHOUT A LINE]

—HORACE

WRITING ... IS LIKE DRIVING AT NIGHT WITH YOUR LIGHTS ON. YOU CAN ONLY SEE SEVERAL FEET IN FRONT OF YOU, BUT YOU CAN MAKE THE WHOLE TRIP LIKE THAT.

—E. L. DOCTOROW

THAT ISN'T WRITING; IT'S TYPEWRITING!

—TRUMAN CAPOTE

You can probably think of times in your life when you knew the "rules" but following them was difficult. For example, when you were young, you may have been shown how to ride a bicycle or how to tie shoelaces, but actually doing either of these activities by yourself took a lot of practice. Many people can still remember the scraped knees and bruised shins that came from falling off a bike, even though they realized that all they had to do was to keep their balance.

Writing is like this, but the bruises aren't real, and, as in learning to ride a bike, you possess the skills required to write effectively—and you can continue to develop these skills to become a more effective writer.

As you discovered in Chapter 1, you already have experience as a writer. You are already developing writing habits that you came up with on your own, habits that suit you. The Latin poet Horace believed that in order to become a good writer, it is important to write something every day, even if only a single line. Stephen King calls this flexing your writing muscles. You have your own habits, but you will improve as a writer only if you evaluate and understand how you work and why. Once you do understand, you can begin to devise strategies to help your writing become even stronger.

Writing takes shape as it happens. When you drive at night, the road beyond the headlight beams is invisible, and it is often not possible to see past the next stretch of road, but you still have faith that the road exists beyond the headlights. Taking it bit by bit is sufficient to get you to your destination. As a writer, you will develop faith that if you begin the journey and take it step by step, you will be able to complete it. This is what is meant by the writing **process**.

What separates good writing from merely adequate writing is not better spelling but rather powerful examples, skillful wording, and compelling organization. Part of ensuring that your organization and examples are effective comes from understanding your audience and your purpose. In order to really think about how to use the tools of writing effectively, however, you must have some understanding of the process of writing that works best for you.

In general, most writers would agree that the writing process is divided into three parts: **prewriting, writing,** and **rewriting**. These, in turn, involve a series of steps, steps which lead to discoveries of exactly what it is you want to say and how you want to say it.

Throughout the writing process, you have to be willing to stop, evaluate, and try again. In the first three chapters, you thought about what you have written in the past, why you write, and for whom you write. In this chapter and the next two, you will think about *how* you write. You will learn some important strategies and acquire some useful tools for implementing them. If you apply these to your writing, you will discover that you can grow as a writer. But remember, as Truman Capote—the gifted author of *In Cold Blood* and *Breakfast at Tiffany's*—recognized, filling a page is not the same as writing. Anyone can type. You can use what you already know about writing, and what you will learn, to become a *writer*—not just someone who fills the page with words.

Working Alone: Below is a list of words or phrases that describe various aspects of the writing process. For each word or phrase, assign a number from 1 to 10 to describe the importance you place on that step. Ten indicates the highest importance; one equals the least.

Finding a topic

Determining what to say about the topic

Gathering examples

Getting the title right

Organizing the paragraphs

Outlining

Paragraphing

Peer reviewing

Planning

Proofreading

Researching

Revising

Selecting the layout and design

Spell checking

Understanding your main idea/thesis

A. Look at the aspects with the highest numbers. Why do you place the most emphasis on them?
B. Why do you place the least emphasis on those aspects of your writing with low scores?
C. What do these numbers reveal about the importance you place on preparing yourself before you begin writing?

Self-Assessment

What do you do when you have to write something? For most writers, the process does not begin with simply sitting down and starting to write any more than riding a bike or tying shoelaces did. First, it is important to decide what you want to say, how you want to say it, and to whom you want to say it. It is also necessary to think of the structure you will need, the examples you will use, and the language that will express your ideas. The following are some questions that ask you to think about how you go about making these decisions before you start writing. In other words, how do you **prewrite**?

1. Before I start writing, I think about

2. Before I start writing, I take the following steps:

3. For two recent pieces of writing, my first action before I started was
   A. Piece one:

   B. Piece two:

4. Once I had done that, I then
   A. Piece one:

B. Piece two:

What do I know about my prewriting process?	What will I need to know to make my prewriting process more effective?

Prewriting Techniques

If you've ever looked at brain-wave patterns—or even just sat quietly and paid attention to your mental activity for a few minutes—you've probably been struck by how the mind is an ever-flowing river of thoughts, images, and perceptions. You've probably also experienced the frustration that sometimes comes when you are asked to write an essay—or almost any other kind of writing—and you have to find something to write about. From amid that constant mental flow, how do you choose a **topic**? And, having chosen one, how do you discover what you know, what you need to know, and what you should write?

A very powerful way to help answer these questions is to prewrite.

As its name suggests, you prewrite before you begin drafting. Luckily, the various ways of determining what to write about, what you know, and what you need to know will also help you begin drafting your work when the time comes to write. Although this stage of the process is useful for any kind of writing which you might do, it is especially valuable for the kinds of writing which you are most likely to do in college—that is, for assignments requiring you to write **essays**. There will be more about the essay in later chapters, but for now it's sufficient to look at prewriting as a valuable first stage of any writing journey.

Most writing is "about" something—that is, there is a topic which you set out to explore, prove, examine, or explain. You've no doubt discovered, however, that finding a topic is often difficult. And even then, having a topic and knowing what you want to say about it and how to say it are very different things. That journey—from topic to finished piece of writing—is the writing process.

The first step in prewriting is to find and explore a topic and to discover how you feel, to determine what you think, and to decide what you want to say about it. There are habits common to most writers and certain proven techniques that can help almost any writer get started on the path of exploration and discovery. Each of the following is a method of prewriting. These techniques are common and effective ways to find a topic, to learn what you already know about your topic, and to discover what you still have to find out.

Keeping a Journal

Do you keep a journal? The list of writers who do is long. They find it valuable to have a place to record things—all sorts of things: images, ideas, dreams, fragments of overheard conversations, books read, movies seen, thumbnail sketches of people, lists of titles, names for characters, *anything*. **There are no rules about keeping a journal**.

If you've ever cleaned out a kitchen-sink drain, you may have found that there's a little "trap" in there designed to catch things and prevent them from going down the pipes. A journal is like that: a trap which can catch things before they flow out of your mind and you forget them. This is especially true for details, which can help you recall emotions after the events that aroused them have faded. And although a journal is valuable to keep for many reasons, it can certainly be a prewriting tool. When the time comes for finding writing topics, your journal can be your private stock.

If you've never kept a journal, this may be a good time to start. Again, there are no rules, but here are a few suggestions:

- Use any sort of book you want, from an inexpensive pocket notebook to a fancy journal. The key is not the package but what you put in it.
- Keep the journal handy.
- Date each entry.
- Write regularly. As with many things in life, the more you do it, the easier it gets.

What follows is a journal entry written when the author's dog was old and injured, and he was forced to make some decisions. Note that although he writes in units of thought, he isn't overly concerned with sentence structure. His main goal is to capture details and feelings.

> 10/14 Took Tess to the vet and learned she's got a broken hip. She can hobble but vet says it'll mean six weeks of being laid up and then, at her age, arthritis will set in. She's in pain and old. Made the hard decision that it's time to put her to sleep. I told him I want to be with her. He said they don't allow owners to be there. I said, "you don't understand, this dog has been with me for 15 years," and he said, "sorry, state laws, etc." Upset, I left. But Tess has been in pain. I talked with S and we decided to take Tess to Maine. If she's going to have to die, I have to be with her, that's all there is to it.

Working Alone: Take a journal entry of your own and write a paragraph. How is the paragraph a more "finished" piece of work than the entry?

Brainstorming

Whereas journaling is a way of scooping out a part of the non-stop river that runs through your head, *brainstorming* is letting the river flow right out onto the paper. The technique is simple and is exactly what its name suggests: a quick recording of everything you can think of relating to a topic. You can start with a brainstorm as a means of establishing what you know about a topic.

Here are some questions writers commonly ask themselves to get started on a brainstorm:

1. What can I write about?
2. What do I know something about?
3. What things do I like?
4. What would I like to learn more about?
5. What would make an interesting topic?

To work well, a brainstorm should not be edited. You should not stop to evaluate your writing as you record all of the ideas that "storm" into your mind about the topic. Later, you can use the brainstorm to help you draft the outline of the essay, but for now it's essential that you *not* edit your work. Keep going for as long as possible. Many people find that their most creative ideas come toward the end of a brainstorm.

Imagine that you have been asked to write an essay about popular music. For a start, you decide to brainstorm about your favorite band. A typical brainstorm might look like this:

> Athens, GA. *Green* comes out on Election Day 1984. Michael Stipe. IRS. REM. Breakout indie band. *Fables of the Reconstruction*. Peter Buck. "Radio Free Europe." Mike Mills. Multimillion dollar, five-album deal with Warner. Natalie Merchant. "Rockville." End of the World. "Ignoreland." Bill Berry. REM covered by Great Big Sea, and others. Indigo Girls. Mike Mills. Lyrics mumbled. "Losing My Religion." College radio stations. *Automatic for the People*. Video as part of image. "Stand."

As you can see, when you brainstorm, ideas tend to spill out randomly, but you shouldn't worry about putting them in order.

Working Alone: Create a brainstorm on a topic of your choice that might be appropriate for a short paper.

Freewriting

Freewriting is just what its name suggests: writing as much as you can on the subject without worrying about any of the "rules" of writing or logic. Once again, you should not edit yourself; just let whatever comes to mind flow out onto the paper. Some of this will seem like nonsense, but that's all right; that's what freewriting is. It's important to keep writing when your mind goes blank. Sooner or later, it will get back onto the topic. One way to keep writing is to just write something such as "blah blah" or "My mind's blank, my mind's blank" until you get back on topic. So if you were freewriting about REM, you might produce a passage that begins like this:

> A long time ago I'm not sure when exactly a band from Athens Georgia began to get some airplay on college radio stations. They had a cool name that was one of the first things anybody noticed about them—REM. Their first song to get any decent sort of airplay was "Radio Free Europe" and like many of the early REM songs its

lyrics were just about impossible to decipher blah blah blah later the lead singer, Michael Stipe would say that one reason the lyrics were mumbled was because he did not actually know what he was singing but this became a trademark of the band perhaps best heard on the early singles "Rockville" and "Radio Free Europe" and acknowledged by the album title "Murmur." Later, the lyrics got easier to hear but no easier to understand. What was "Losing My Religion" about? Blah blah something in here about *Murmur*, was it their first album? I think so. Does it mean anything that they had early titles like *Murmur* and *Fables of the Reconstruction* as if you could not be sure that what they were singing about was really what they meant? How about that line they use in a couple of songs (which ones? "Religion" and at least one other) "I think I thought"? What does it mean that the singer is not even sure what he was thinking? And what exactly was the "sidewinder" which "sleeps tonight" (in what song)? The videos were strange ("Stand") [And so on until you have run out of things to say.]

As you can see, freewriting can be fun and an effective way of opening yourself up to the possibilities contained within a topic. Like the brainstorm, there are no "rules" other than to let the words flow.

Working Alone: Freewrite on a topic that you think would be a good choice for a short paper. You may want to use the same topic that you used for the previous brainstorm exercise.

Working Together: Read your freewrite to a partner (or to the class); then have your partner (or other members of your class) read hers. Make no judgments— "good" "bad," etc.—but discuss any seeds for ideas that emerge from the freewriting. Discuss how these might be turned into paragraphs or essays.

Ghostwriting

Ghostwriting requires a computer. Turn the contrast on the screen all the way up or down and then just start writing. You won't be able to see the words on the screen until you readjust the contrast, but that's the idea. With this method, you also can't edit yourself. Ghostwriting is similar to freewriting, but you might find it easier to do since when you can't see the words, you are less concerned about whether the prewriting makes sense. This situation frees you to concentrate more on content and to not focus on grammar and structure.

Branching/Treeing

Branching or *treeing* is similar to brainstorming but is a little more organized in its initial stages. For this method, you make a note of the first main idea you think of and then pursue that idea to see where it goes. If after you complete one "branch," there is still more to say, then you can start a second branch, and a third, and so on until all of your ideas have been recorded. For a branching activity on REM, you might produce something like this:

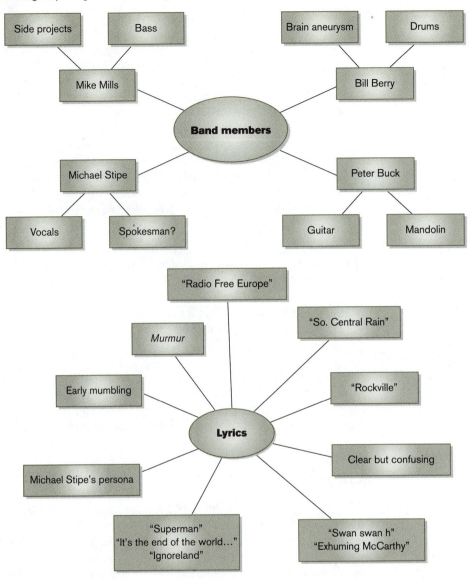

Working Alone:

1. Of the prewriting techniques previously mentioned (journal writing, brainstorming, freewriting, ghostwriting, branching/treeing), which have you used before? Are there other techniques that you use?
2. Write a brief explanation of what you consider the strengths of each technique.

Organizing Your Prewriting

Remember, prewriting is a means to an end, a way of helping you to determine what you actually want to say about your topic. After completing your prewriting, you have to *organize* the result. You've had your "editor" shut off; now it's time to switch it on.

In earlier chapters you thought about audience and purpose; this chapter is where you now apply those ideas to the *particular* task at hand. Knowing your purpose and your audience will help you to determine how you should organize your initial thoughts.

Purpose and Audience

As you look back at your freewriting, you might realize that you are primarily interested in the lyrics that REM uses and the ways in which they have changed over time. You think this approach might provide a clue to explain why the band has been popular for so long. On the other hand, you could arrange your brainstorm to focus on how REM was the first band that really succeeded in moving from college radio station airplay to the mainstream. This approach might lead to an essay that looks at how REM paved the way for the "alternative" rock movement. In each of these instances, you can see how you might move from a broad topic—REM—to focusing on what you actually want to say about that topic.

The decisions you make about the way to arrange your prewriting will depend on your purpose for writing and your audience. For example, if you were writing about REM for a literature class, your audience would probably be interested in the song lyrics, so you would develop your ideas to focus on this aspect of the band's work. But if you were writing an essay about marketing, your audience might be more interested in how REM influenced record labels' marketing strategies, so you would develop your ideas to focus on the business strategies that shaped the band's career.

Now that you have started organizing your initial thoughts, you will quickly discover that you don't need everything that you have written down. Does it matter that REM started playing in Athens, Georgia? If not, you can leave that information out.

You still haven't started an essay, but you now have a plan. You've moved beyond simply having a broad subject area—music—and have explored a topic— REM. Take a look at the REM brainstorm on page 72. Having first thought about what you want to say, you have arranged the ideas you jotted down into some sort of order and have deleted those points you don't think help this *particular* essay. Now your brainstorm looks something like this:

> ~~Athens, GA. Green comes out on election day 1984.~~ REM. Michael Stipe. Peter Buck. Mike Mills. Bill Berry. Break-out indie band. Lyrics mumbled. <u>Fables of the Reconstruction.</u> <u>Reckoning.</u> <u>Murmur.</u> College radio stations. "Radio Free Europe." "Rockville." "Ignoreland." Multimillion, five-album deal with Warner. ~~Natalie Merchant. End of the World. REM covered by Great Big Sea, and others. Indigo Girls.~~ "Stand." "Losing my religion." <u>Automatic for the People.</u> ~~Video as part of image.~~

Even at this early stage, you can see that this is beginning to look like a plan for an essay organized to discuss the band, its members, and their role as one of the first successful mass market alternative rock bands. The writer will talk about the early albums and the airplay the band got on college radio stations. This will lead to a discussion of a few of the early singles and then to the record contract with Warner that the writer is arguing changed forever the meaning of "alternative" rock band. After this, the essay will discuss some of the singles and albums which followed the band's move to Warner. You can see from this analysis that an important early step in the writing process is finding your topic.

Working Alone: Write a brief description of the possible audience and purposes for one of the topics you explored in one of the previous prewriting exercises.

Discovering the Main Idea

Most essays you write will require a **thesis statement**—a statement of the main idea or the point that you are discussing and why it is important. Toward the end of prewriting, it is useful to check whether you have a working thesis. Here, for example, are some possible working theses which might have emerged from the previous prewriting:

- REM has always had a political slant to its work.
- Michael Stipe might have begun mumbling the lyrics to REM songs because he sometimes forgot them, but this device quickly became an ironic comment on the emptiness of much contemporary lyric writing.
- For a band which presented itself as very modern and interested in the music of the moment, REM took big risks early on when it released the album *Fables of the Reconstruction.*

Again, working theses grow out of prewriting. Whatever your initial thesis, bear in mind that you will probably refine it later. You may even change it altogether. But before you can begin writing, you must have a sense of what your point is and why you want to make it. The thesis for the REM essay will likely argue that in the history of modern rock music, REM is one of the most important bands because it made it possible for the range of current alternative rock acts to get recording contracts and airplay. The proof for this argument will be found as the writer develops examples, examples initially identified during prewriting.

Notice, by the way, that this essay does not discuss whether or not the writer likes REM. Very often, your essay will not be about your personal likes and dislikes but rather about matters of fact and evidence. Prewriting can help you discover and establish facts and examples to use in any essay.

Working Alone: Look back at your prewriting and your description of your audience and purpose. Develop some possible working theses for the topic which you have chosen for your essay.

Evaluating a Main Idea

At this stage of the writing process, many writers find it helpful to evaluate the information they already have and to check the decisions they have made. For example, after arranging her brainstorm, the writer of the essay about REM realizes that she clearly knows much more about the early band than about its current identity. At least, that is what the brainstorm suggests; it is top-heavy with ideas about the band's early years. The writer probably needs to learn more about the band's current music. You will find that this is often the case. You will see gaps in the ideas that you initially generated on a topic.

A good way to evaluate the information you've produced for your essay is to complete this box:

Working thesis: _____

What I know about the topic that supports my thesis:

What I still need to learn about the topic to support my thesis:

The difference between the two columns is important. In the first, you record information that you are *certain* you have correct. In the second, you record information that you *think* is correct but that you should check just in case, and you record gaps in your knowledge that you need to fill. To return to REM, you might enter Michael Stipe's name in the first column—you know that he is the lead singer of the band—but you might put *"Murmur,* first album" in the second column—you *think* it was the band's first album but decide it's best to check.

Working Alone: Using a working thesis you have developed, complete a box similar to the previous example, illustrating what you know and what you want to know about the topic. Based on this box, what do you think the focus of your essay on the topic will be?

As you can see, one topic can produce a variety of possibilities. You never have to worry about whether your topic has been written about before. If you take the time, your essay will be unique to you.

The Unseen Starting Point

Just as Memorial Day is considered the "unofficial" start of summer, prewriting is the unofficial or unseen part of many writers' work. But it is, in one sense, the most important part. If you do not prewrite, you will begin a journey in the dark with no map to guide you. Eventually, you may arrive at your conclusion, but along the way you are likely to make wrong turns. You may end up using so many inappropriate examples and missing so many appropriate ones that your reader will not be convinced that you know why you are making whatever point you are trying to make. Gaining your readers' interest and trust is important. Prewriting helps you get to the point more quickly, more efficiently, and more persuasively.

While prewriting may seem like an insignificant step in the process, you'll discover that it helps you produce *writing* instead of typewriting.

Suggestions for Writing

1. Select an assignment that you will have to write later this semester for a course other than English. For this assignment, complete any two of the prewriting strategies discussed at the beginning of this chapter. Which of your prewrites will you develop into an essay for this assignment? Why?
2. Go to a web page of an organization that interests you. If you were asked to improve the page, what prewriting strategy would you use to plan your changes? Why?
3. Find an editorial or opinion piece in a newspaper or magazine. Imagine that you are writing an opposing point of view on the same topic. Prewrite for the article you would write. What major points does your prewrite reveal?
4. Identify a "hot button" student issue—campus parking, safety, or student government, for example—and prewrite a letter to the college president requesting that something be done about the problem.
5. Using a journal entry (or any brainstorm or freewrite) you have produced, write the opening paragraph of what might become an essay.

READINGS

Here is an essay that evolved from several journal entries, one of which you previously saw in this chapter's section on keeping a journal. That entry and another entry have been reprinted here, along with the essay.

10/14 Took Tess to the vet and learned she's got a broken hip. She can hobble but vet says it'll mean six weeks of being laid up and then, at her age, arthritis will set in. She's in pain and old. Made the hard decision that it's time to put her to sleep. I told him I want to be with her. He said they don't allow owners to be there. I said, "you don't understand, this dog has been with me for 15 years," and he said, "sorry, state laws, etc." Upset, I left. But Tess has been in pain. I talked with S and we decided to take Tess to Maine. If she's going to have to die, I have to be with her, that's all there is to it.

10/16 Went to my parents' place in Maine. I called vet and told the woman what I wanted, she said fine, and we set a time for me to come in. So it was sealed: I had a few more hours. I took Tess swimming, which she enjoyed. I held her. When the time came, my dad and I went. Details: my hands shaking. Wanting to cry. The vet's quiet competence. Tess's soft weight as we took her back for burial. Feeling so alone. My dad clipping a rose. In October afternoon, S and I drove home under the weight of sorrow.

Although the entries could have led to essays on several topics (a personal tribute to a beloved pet, the bond between pets and their owners, the difference between city vets and country vets, the question of euthanasia), the writer returned to them years later for a different purpose. When his father died, the writer wanted to memorialize him in some way, so he used the entries as the basis for the following brief essay.

OCTOBER BURIAL
DAVID DANIEL

For my father 1919—1993

I only know that summer sang in me
A little while, that in me sings no more.
    —Edna St. Vincent Millay

We brought Tess on her last trip, to Maine, let her see the woods, smell the earth, drink the lake. I carried her down the steep dirt road, then up, her own walk a broken-hipped hobble on three legs. My Dad and I dug a hole in the stony soil. I called a vet and set up a time. The woman told me in an apologetic tone: We don't have a crematorium. I said I want to take her with me.

We ate, talked, my Dad and I poked among old gravestones in the woods, a premeditation on mortality. We saw a snake. Tess lay in the cool October grass. And then it was time. No more stalling the inevitable.

Stephanie and my Mother waited. We drove there, my Dad and I with Tess. I said to the woman, let's take care of the money right now, knowing I wouldn't be able to later. With trembling hands I paid. $12.50. Cheap. But this was rural Maine. Then, weak-kneed, I waited, scrubbing Tess's head. Dad, lost, gazed out at the yellow afternoon.

The vet came in, a graying young man, friendly and serious of purpose. We held Tess as the needle went in beneath her shaggy coat. She seemed to rise for a moment with an energy of new youth, then lay on her side. I remembered Frost's line: Little, less, nothing. I peered in her eyes, clouded now, beyond me.

"Is she dead?" I asked the vet.

"Yes. The twitching in her feet is just muscular contractions."

Wrapped in a heavy plastic sack, she was put in my car. As we climbed in I had a spooky instant of hearing her collar tags jingle. I glanced back at the bag, then remembered—her collar was on the front floor. Dad's foot had kicked it.

We drove with tears in our eyes and memories, Dad bringing them up, the time Tess did this, did that, rolled in dead fish, got her teeth caught in a wire fence … recollections I'd already gone over in my mind and with Stephanie that morning, but welcome again in Dad's telling.

The burial party: my folks, Stephanie, me carrying the loose, still-warm weight as I'd carried her up the road hours before. No words, or what brief phrases there were, offered in choked voices. And we put her in. We shoveled in the stony Maine soil we had shoveled out earlier.

Then we went back toward the house, retracing our way across the autumn-deep field, and Dad, more comfortable with actions than words, clipped a flower and handed it to me. "A red rose for love," he said.

I walked back up alone, breaking down for the first time, feeling the pain of crying carve my face. I laid the flower down on the turned earth. Later, in separate cars, we drove through the heartbroken beauty of the October afternoon and talked of love and death.

Topics for Thinking and Writing

1. What changes has the author made from journal entries to essay?
2. How would you characterize the language of the piece? What effects do the word choices and sentence lengths achieve? Cite some examples.
3. Comment on the use of the lines from the Edna St. Vincent Millay poem.
4. Write a short essay of your own in which you explore the death of a pet.

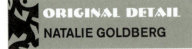

ORIGINAL DETAIL
NATALIE GOLDBERG

Though this is a short chapter, it is an important one: *use original detail in your writing.* Life is so rich, if you can write down the real details of the way things were and are, you hardly need anything else. Even if you transplant the beveled windows, slow-rotating Rheingold sign, Wise potato chip rack, and tall red stools from the Aero Tavern that you drank in in New York into a bar in a story in another state and time, the story will have authenticity and groundedness. "Oh, no, that bar was on Long Island, I can't put it in New Jersey"—yes, you can. You don't have to be rigid about original detail. The imagination is capable of detail transplants, but using the details you actually know and have seen will give your writing believability and truthfulness. It creates a good solid foundation from which you can build.

Naturally, if you have just been to New Orleans in the dripping August heat and have sucked the fat out of the heads of crayfish at the Magnolia Bar on Charles Street, you can't have the thick-wristed character in your story in Cleveland on a January night doing the same thing at his local bar. It won't work, unless, of course, you are moving into surrealism, where all boundaries begin to melt.

Be awake to the details around you, but don't be self-conscious. "Okay. I'm at a wedding. The bride has on blue. The groom is wearing a red carnation. They are serving chopped liver on doilies." Relax, enjoy the wedding, be present with an open heart. You will naturally take in your environment, and later, sitting at your desk, you will be able to recall just how it was dancing with the bride's redheaded mother, seeing the bit of red lipstick smeared on her front tooth when she smiled, and smelling her perfume mixed with perspiration.

Topics for Thinking and Writing

1. What does Goldberg mean when she talks about transplanting details?
2. What are some things you do to give your writing "believability and truthfulness"?

3. Go on a short "field trip" around campus, just looking, listening, inhaling the aromas, and generally absorbing details. Then go back to your room or class-room and start jotting down as many sensory details as you can recall.
4. Write a paragraph in which you use some of the details you've gathered.

THE WRITER
RICHARD WILBUR

In her room at the prow of the house
Where light breaks, and the windows are tossed with linden,
My daughter is writing a story.

I pause in the stairwell, hearing
5 From her shut door a commotion of typewriter-keys
Like a chain hauled over a gunwale.

Young as she is, the stuff
Of her life is a great cargo, and some of it heavy:
I wish her a lucky passage.

10 But now it is she who pauses,
As if to reject my thought and its easy figure.
A stillness greatens, in which

The whole house seems to be thinking,
And then she is at it again with a bunched clamor
15 Of strokes, and again is silent.

I remember the dazed starling
Which was trapped in that very room, two years ago;
How we stole in, lifted a sash

And retreated, not to affright it;
20 And how for a helpless hour, through the crack of the door,
We watched the sleek, wild, dark

And iridescent creature
Batter against the brilliance, drop like a glove
To the hard floor, or the desk-top.

25 And wait then, humped and bloody,
For the wits to try it again; and how our spirits
Rose when, suddenly sure,

It lifted off from a chair-back,
Beating a smooth course for the right window
30 And clearing the sill of the world.

It is always a matter, my darling,
Of life or death, as I had forgotten. I wish
What I wished you before, but harder.

Topics for Thinking and Writing

1. The title of the poem is "The Writer." To whom in the poem does the title refer?
2. To what does the speaker of the poem compare the writer? What words, images, or phrases support the metaphor or comparison?
3. What steps in the writing process does the speaker of the poem describe? What images does he use to describe these steps?
4. Write a short paragraph describing the relationship between the father and daughter in the poem. Use lines from the poem to support your description.
5. First, complete this comparison: To write is like _____." Next, write a short poem about writing, using the metaphor you have created.
6. Write an essay describing your writing habits. What kind of space do you need? What "tools" of the writing trade do you need to have near you?

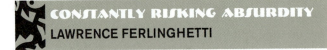

CONSTANTLY RISKING ABSURDITY
LAWRENCE FERLINGHETTI

Constantly risking absurdity
                              and death
            whenever he performs
                        above the heads
5   of his audience
        the poet like an acrobat
                        climbs on rime
                              to a high wire of his own making
        and balancing on eyebeams
10   above a sea of faces
                        to the other side of day
                performing entrechats
                        and sleight-of-foot tricks
        and other high theatrics
15   and all without mistaking
                any thing
                        for what it may not be
        For he's the super realist
                        who must perforce perceive
20   taut truth
                        before the taking of each stance or step
        in his supposed advance
                        toward that still higher perch

where Beauty stands and waits
25   with gravity
                                to start her death-defying leap
     And he
             a little charleychaplin man
                     who may or may not catch
30   her fair eternal form
                     spreadeagled in the empty air
        of existence

Topics for Thinking and Writing

1. How does this poem illustrate the beginning of the writing process?
2. What are some of the emotions experienced by the central character of the poem?
3. Compare the feelings you experience when doing something difficult with those expressed in the poem.
4. Write a brief passage explaining how you would feel watching the activities described in the poem.
5. Assess your own writing process from beginning to end. How does it mirror the ideas in the poem? How does it differ?

NO ONE'S A MYSTERY
ELIZABETH TALLENT

For my eighteenth birthday Jack gave me a five-year diary with a latch and a little key, light as a dime. I was sitting beside him scratching at the lock, which didn't seem to want to work, when he thought he saw his wife's Cadillac in the distance, coming toward us. He pushed me down onto the dirty floor of the pickup and kept one hand on my head while I inhaled the musk of his cigarettes in the dashboard ashtray and sang along with Roseanne Cash on the tape deck. We'd been drinking tequila and the bottle was between his legs, resting up against his crotch, where the seam of his Levi's was bleached linen-white, though the Levi's were nearly new. I don't know why his Levi's always bleached like that, along the seams and at the knees. In a curve of cloth his zipper glinted, gold.

"It's her," he said. "She keeps the lights on in the daytime. I can't think of a single habit in a woman that irritates me more than that." When he saw that I was going to stay still he took his hand from my head and ran it through his own dark hair.

"Why does she?" I said.

"She thinks it's safer. Why does she need to be safer? She's driving exactly fifty-five miles an hour. She believes in those signs: 'Speed Monitored by Aircraft.' It doesn't matter that you can look up and see that the sky is empty."

5   "She'll see your lips move, Jack. She'll know you're talking to someone."

"She'll think I'm singing along with the radio."

He didn't lift his head, just raised the fingers in salute while the pressure of his palm steadied the wheel, and I heard the Cadillac honk twice, musically; he was driving easily eighty miles an hour. I studied his boots. The elk heads stitched into the leather were bearded with frayed thread, the toes were scuffed, and there was a compact wedge of muddy manure between the heel and the sole—the same boots he'd been wearing for the two years I'd known him. On the tape deck Rosanne Cash sang, "Nobody's into me, no one's a mystery."

"Do you think she's getting famous because of who her daddy is or for herself?" Jack said.

"There are about a hundred pop tops on the floor, did you know that? Some little kid could cut a bare foot on one of these, Jack."

10   "No little kids get into this truck except for you."

"How come you let it get so dirty?"

"'How come,'" he mocked. "You even sound like a kid. You can get back into the seat now, if you want. She's not going to look over her shoulder and see you."

"How do you know?"

"I just know," he said. "Like I know I'm going to get meat loaf for supper. It's in the air. Like I know what you'll be writing in that diary."

15   "What will I be writing?" I knelt on my side of the seat and craned around to look at the butterfly of dust printed on my jeans. Outside the window Wyoming was dazzling in the heat. The wheat was fawn and yellow and parted smoothly by the thin dirt road. I could smell the water in the irrigation ditches hidden in the wheat.

"Tonight you'll write, 'I love Jack. This is my birthday present from him. I can't imagine anybody loving anybody more than I love Jack.'"

"I can't."

"In a year you'll write, 'I wonder what I ever really saw in Jack. I wonder why I spent so many days just riding around in his pickup. It's true he taught me something about sex. It's true there wasn't ever much else to do in Cheyenne.'"

"I won't write that."

20   "In two years you'll write, 'I wonder what that old guy's name was, the one with the curly hair and the filthy dirty pickup truck and time on his hands.'"

"I won't write that."

"No?"

"Tonight I'll write, 'I love Jack. This is my birthday present from him. I can't imagine anybody loving anybody more than I love Jack.'"

"No, you can't," he said. "You can't imagine it."

25   "In a year I'll write, 'Jack should be home any minute now. The table's set—my grandmother's linen and her old silver and the yellow candles left over from the wedding—but I don't know if I can wait until after the trout à la Navarra to make love to him.'"

"It must have been a fast divorce."

"In two years I'll write, 'Jack should be home by now. Little Jack is hungry for his supper. He said his first word today besides "Mama" and "Papa." He said "kaka."'"

Jack laughed. "He was probably trying to finger-paint with kaka on the bathroom wall when you heard him say it."

"In three years I'll write, 'My nipples are a little sore from nursing Eliza Rosamund.'"

30   "Rosamund. Every little girl should have a middle name she hates."

"'Her breath smells like vanilla and her eyes are just Jack's color of blue.'"

"That's nice," Jack said.

"So, which one do you like?"

"I like yours," he said. "But I believe mine."

"It doesn't matter. I believe mine."

"Not in your heart of hearts, you don't."

"You're wrong."

"I'm not wrong," he said. "And her breath would smell like your milk, and it's kind of bittersweet smell, if you want to know the truth."

Topics for Thinking and Writing

1. How would you describe Jack? What specific details do you find in the story to support your description?
2. What purpose does the five-year diary serve in the story? What does the characters' discussion about the diary reveal about their attitudes towards their relationship?
3. Reread the imaginary entries that the characters say the girl will write in the diary. Write a brief explanation of how you believe their relationship will progress from this point on. How is your description similar to or different from theirs?

Self-Assessment

Reread the self-assessment that opens this chapter.

What would I change?

Why?

What have I learned about prewriting?

5

Writing: Developing and Expressing an Idea

A WALK TO THE CORNER STORE
A MARATHON
A HIKE ACROSS THE COUNTRY

There is an old saying that a journey of ten thousand miles begins at your feet. Writing is like that journey. As you saw in Chapter 4, most writing journeys begin with prewriting. Once you have selected a topic or an idea, you continue the journey.

As the three examples above illustrate, there are all kinds of journeys; so, too, does writing take many forms. A glance at your self-assessment in Chapter 1 will remind you of how many different forms of writing you have done, are doing, and will do. These range from personal letters to short stories, essays, and lengthy research papers. As different as these forms may be, however, all of them share things in common. They all have a purpose, an intended audience, and demonstrate an effective use of language—and most require prewriting.

A walk to the corner store, a marathon, and a hike across America likewise share things. Each, for example, requires some preparation and, some thinking about the journey and the destination. A walk to the store probably will need relatively little preparation—perhaps a shopping list, certainly some money, and, depending on the weather and time of day, some particular clothing. A marathon and a cross country trek will need a great deal more advance planning and training, most of it very specific to the journey. Stride and pace may vary as well, from speed walk to saunter. So, too, will your prewriting vary, depending upon what you intend to write. Regardless of your chosen form, however—whether essay, business letter, or research paper—once you've done your prewriting, you are ready to write.

Self-Assessment

Remember the image used in Chapter 4 about a mind being an ever-flowing river of mental activity? Through prewriting, you have dipped into that river and come up with a topic to write about. Now that you have discovered a topic, what do you do next? The following are some questions to help you identify the process you have established for yourself. You will find that these questions take into account the difference between what you would do if you had unlimited time for writing and what you actually do in the "real" world, where there are limits on your time. Think about the questions and as you respond, remember that there are no right or wrong answers.

1. Now that I've discovered a topic through prewriting, before I start writing, I think about

2. My first step when I write is

3. When I am writing, I go from beginning to end without worrying about the details until later./I worry about each sentence and detail as I go along. (Cross out sentence that doesn't apply.) Other (describe)

4. I think I am finished writing when

5. The part of the writing process that I find most helpful is

6. The part of the writing process that I find most difficult is

What do I know about the writing process?	What do I need to learn?

Working Together: Share your self-assessment with a classmate. How are your writing processes similar? Different?

Working Alone: Dostoyevsky, the great Russian novelist, wrote, "Taking a new step, uttering a new word is what people fear most." Using this idea, write a paragraph about what you find most "fearful" about the writing process.

The Essay

Again reviewing the self-assessment you did in Chapter 1, you realize that you have done (and will do) many different kinds of writing. One of the most common—and varied—forms of writing is the **essay**.

Consider, for example, the differences among a film review in a local newspaper, a *Cosmopolitan* article on finding the perfect mate, and a feature in *Sports Illustrated* about the greatest heavyweight boxers of all time. Each of these would differ from the others in purpose, style, and target audience; yet each could still be called an essay.

You will find that many of your college writing assignments call for essays. In simple terms, an essay is a system of focusing and organizing ideas. As such, it is a very durable and useful vehicle for all kinds of writing assignments.

Working Alone: As you respond to the following questions, consider what you already know about this time-proven written form; then read on to learn more.

1. For what classes and assignments have you written essays?

2. What have some of these essays been about?

3. How would you define the term *essay*?

4. What would you identify as the parts of an essay?

5. What is the purpose of a thesis statement?

6. What role does an introduction play?

7. What is the purpose of a conclusion?

8. Why does an essay contain details and examples?

What Is an Essay?

When the French writer Montaigne—considered one of the founding fathers of the personal essay—was experimenting with ways to write down his ideas, there was no known form for what he was doing. Writing to a friend, he explained, "Here's what I'm trying to do." The French word *essayer* ("to try") became the English word *essay*. It is good to keep this idea of "trying" in mind because it acknowledges that this is what you are doing when you write, especially in a first draft. You are trying out ideas, and although you may not yet know what form your writing will finally take, you will be using the basic elements of an essay.

For example, an essay has a beginning, a middle, and an end. It has some kind of purpose and an awareness of its audience. The movement in an essay is most often from the general to the specific: from some sort of broad **thesis statement** to a more precise development or demonstration of this statement through supporting details. An essay attempts to make a point and frequently ends with a rephrasing of the thesis statement. It has a logical flow of ideas, bears a title, and may have characters.

But an effective essay is more than just these parts. You probably know the ancient story of the elephant and the blind men. In this tale, six blind men are asked to describe an elephant based upon the way in which they experience it. The first man feels the animal's side and reports that an elephant is like a wall. A second takes hold of its tail and likens the animal to a piece of rope. A third, feeling a leg, declares that an elephant is like a tree trunk, and so on. The point is that our perception of a thing is selective, based upon our own limited experience, while the thing is often much more than just its parts.

An essay is like that, more than merely the sum of its parts—but it is useful, nevertheless, to understand what the parts of an essay are.

What Are the Parts of an Essay?

> *Thesis statement*
> *Introduction*
> *Body*
> *Conclusion*

What Is a Thesis Statement?

Chapter 4 shows you ways of prewriting to discover topics and ideas to write about. The structure of an essay requires that you move from a topic to a statement about that topic and then on to supporting ideas. However, even after you've sufficiently narrowed your topic and gained focus on it, it is sometimes necessary to experiment and to try out several versions of precisely what it is you want to say. At other times, you may be assigned a topic by your instructor. In either case, once you have a topic, the next step in the writing journey is to develop a **thesis**.

In the simplest terms, *a thesis statement is a sentence which expresses your main idea.* It clearly establishes what you are trying to say, show, or prove about your topic. The thesis statement is useful for you as the writer because by stating what it is that your piece of writing wants "to do," it gives you a guide for how best to accomplish that. It is also important for your audience because it gets your readers thinking about what it is you're attempting to convey and prepares them to receive it.

To return once more to an example on the subject of music, consider this thesis statement:

> With his album *What's Going On?* Marvin Gaye leaped from being a singer of pop songs to an artist with a deep political vision.

Based upon this sentence, it is clear what the writer is going to attempt to show with his essay. By serving as a guide, this thesis statement will keep the writer focused on one particular artist (Gaye), one particular work (*What's Going On?*), and one main idea (that this album reveals a serious political agenda.) Furthermore, the statement reminds the writer what kinds of evidence and examples (song titles, lyrics, dates, and so on) will be needed to make the case. Finally, the thesis gives the reader a good idea of what the essay will be about.

Most often, when writing an essay, you'll find it helpful to place your thesis statement near the beginning, where it announces your intention. This isn't a strict rule, but, generally speaking, you'll find it a good idea to keep in mind. By clearly stating right up front what you intend to do, you'll be helping both yourself and your reader.

Later, as you gain experience as a writer, you may find that there will be times when you choose to state your thesis farther along in the essay. At other times, it might not be stated at all—simply hinted at or implied—although if you choose this option, you will still need to clarify what your essay is about.

Whatever the case—whether it's stated at the beginning, later, or merely implied—you will want a thesis. Without one, it's very difficult to write an essay.

With one, however, the way is clear, and as in the journey of a thousand miles (or the walk to the corner store), it's time to take the first step.

Working Alone: Look back at the previous paragraph beginning with the words *Most often*. What is the paragraph's thesis? How do you know?

Hints for Crafting a Thesis Statement

When developing a thesis statement for your essay, you may find it helpful to use some of the strategies that you used in prewriting to discover a topic. At other times, you might simply express an idea about your topic which you feel you can demonstrate or prove to your reader. However you do it, keep in mind that the thesis should matter. That is, it should be something that you can—and want to—demonstrate, prove, or convince your reader is valid.

You should avoid any statement that is self-evident or merely a matter of opinion that can't be proven. For example, the sentence "REM is a great band" would make a poor thesis statement because it is purely an expression of personal taste and impossible to prove. Likewise, a flat statement of fact—"REM comes from Athens, Georgia"—makes a poor thesis statement. This sentence needs nothing more, and so it won't lend itself to an essay.

This doesn't mean, however, that you can't explore ideas that grow out of a statement of fact. For instance, you might have some notion that because its members come from Georgia, REM shares certain traits with other bands from that state. You may have noted similarities as you listened to and thought about the band's music, and now you wish to set about sharing and proving your ideas. You will still need to state your topic precisely as a thesis so that both you (the writer) and your reader can benefit.

Finally, make sure that you have a sufficiently narrow focus on your topic that will allow you to say something interesting and meaningful (as well as provable) about it. Avoid drafting a statement that is so broad that it can't be convincingly written about in the length assigned for your essay. It would be a mistake, for example, to adopt a thesis statement such as "World War II was one of the major events of the twentieth century." Although this statement is true, once you've said it, where can you possibly go with the idea in an essay? This is the subject of volumes. You will find that you're far more likely to stray in the direction of being too broad rather than too narrow. It's probably virtually impossible to have a topic that is too narrow.

Working Alone:

1. Read the following statements. Which would make strong theses? Which are weak? Why?
    A. Whereas football may be more popular in the United States, soccer is more popular worldwide.
    B. Although soccer is the most popular sport worldwide, it will never surpass the popularity of football in the United States.

    C. Most college classes have some type of attendance policy.

    D. Attendance policies in college classes should be abolished.

2. Write a paragraph explaining the characteristics of a good thesis statement.

Working Together: While working with a writing partner, each of you should list five potential thesis statements that you might want to develop into essays. Then review each other's list. Based on what you know, which of the proposed statements show promise? Which fail for any of the reasons listed previously (too broad, strictly factual, and so on)? How might they be reworked to make good thesis statements?

For Openers: What Is an Introduction?

Have you ever strolled along a carnival midway and heard a barker crying, "Hurry, hurry, step right up!"? With such a come-on, it's nearly impossible to resist having a look. A good introduction works like that: it's a way of drawing interest to what you have to offer. As the name suggests, an introduction is the beginning part of an essay and serves to introduce what follows. Usually, it comes right after your thesis statement and may even include your thesis statement. And like the thesis statement, a good introduction helps you, the writer, focus on your topic and also brings your reader into the piece of writing.

These are some questions you need to answer about your introduction (and indeed, about each part of your essay):

What do you want it to do?

How will it do that?

Will it interest your reader?

Working Alone: Consider the previous paragraph (the one beginning "Have you ever strolled …"). How does it serve as an introduction? What topic does it introduce?

Hints for Effective Openers

Not every topic you write about will be of interest to your readers (or even to you, for that matter, especially if you are given a topic for an assignment). Nevertheless, one of your tasks—and challenges—as a writer is to try to make your writing as interesting as possible. Your thesis statement and your introduction are particularly important in this effort.

Writers of fiction often talk about the "hook," an opening line that reaches out and grabs a reader, pulling her into the story. Herman Melville accomplishes this in *Moby-Dick* with his three-word opening sentence: "Call me Ishmael." Stephen King begins his novella *The Body* with "The most important things are the hardest things to say."

As a form of writing, an essay is working toward a different purpose than a piece of fiction (or an email or a research paper), but it's still important that you interest your reader as quickly as possible. Effective beginnings can help you do this.

You might think of the beginning of your essays as "icebreakers," those openers people use at parties or in other social situations to get conversations started with strangers. Here are some ways you can craft your beginnings to simultaneously introduce your topic and grab your reader's attention:

1. *Ask a question.*
"What are the hottest new summer movies?" "Why is the antidepressant Prozac getting so much attention?" "Why is Pete Sampras the best tennis player of all time?" "Where are the next big scientific discoveries going to occur?" "When is the best time to teach children how to use computers?"

By opening with a question, you can often create interest in the topic and also suggest what is to follow.

2. *Tell a story.*

> When Tess was fifteen years old—a good age for a dog—it became clear to me that she was nearing the end of her life. The vet confirmed this, telling me I could leave her with him, and he would take care of what needed to be done. But the thought of all those years together, and Tess's unfailing loyalty to me, made me realize I could not simply hand her over to someone else. No, I knew that if she needed to be put down, I had to be part of the process.

In our childhood, we learn the magic of a story that begins with "Once upon a time." Because all readers are drawn to stories, using a short anecdote can be a powerful way to open an essay. The anecdote serves to draw your readers in, keeping them reading as they seek to learn what happened next.

If you do use this approach, be sure that the story is brief and that it has a connection to the topic you are writing about. The previous example about Tess, for instance, might be a fine way to open an essay about taking more control over one's life, or about the importance of the relationships one forms with pets, or how one learns to deal with death. Whatever the case, it's important that the anecdote be relevant to the thesis of your essay.

3. *Making a surprising statement.*
"Only 10 percent of the population can be considered to be in their *right* minds." (This might introduce an essay on left-handedness and the right side of the brain.)

"By the time you have finished reading this statement, the human population of this planet will have increased by ten."

"The greatest scientific achievement of the twentieth century took place without anyone even being aware that it had happened."

By opening with a surprising—or even shocking—statement, you can heighten your reader's interest in what you have to say about your topic.

4. *Use statistics.*

"If you're under thirty, you may well live to be a hundred. A survey of current research on aging reveals that of people now in their twenties, one out of five can expect to reach the century mark."

As an opener, the use of statistics can be another effective way of creating interest in your topic and encouraging your audience to read on.

Each of these techniques—using statistics, making a surprising statement, telling a story, and asking a question—is like the carnival barker's cry, designed to draw your reader into what follows. These are some of your options, but there are also many other ways to begin an essay, so you should base your choices on what you think will most effectively serve your purpose. As you've been discovering, writing is a craft, and you are learning to be a craftsman. As you continue to practice and develop your craft, you are acquiring tools. These tools are options—just as a master mechanic or carpenter goes to a tool chest and selects from the many tools there, so, too, can you as a writer select from among a variety of writing strategies.

Once you've effectively done that, it's time to get on with developing your essay.

Working Together: With a partner, develop some interesting openers for two of the thesis statements you drafted in the previous section.

Body Building: How Do You Explain Your Main Idea?

After you have written a thesis statement and an introduction, you come to the main part of your essay. Sometimes this is referred to as the **body**. The purpose of this section of the essay—which contains the bulk of your writing—is to fully develop your thesis or main idea by using examples, providing details, giving reasons, or offering proof for your reader.

If the thesis of your essay is to make the case that Billie Jean King was the best tennis player of all time, then the body of your essay will be devoted to providing reasons that support your assertion. If you plan to discuss the invention of the computer as the most important scientific breakthrough of the century, you will present strong reasons for your choice. No matter whether you are writing about REM, the world's population and its impact on the environment, professional football, Prozac, or any other topic, the body of your essay will be the place where you sell your reader on your idea.

To assess the main part of your essay, ask yourself if it has

- **Sufficient evidence or proof**
- **Concrete examples or reasons**
- **A connection to the thesis**
- **A logical order**

Goodbyes: What Is a Conclusion?

Since an essay has a thesis, an introduction, and a body, it also needs a conclusion. Generally, this will be a summing up, a tying together of the pieces of what you have written. Often it will entail reasserting your thesis statement, one final way to plant firmly in the mind of your reader the point you have set out to make. In writing your conclusion, you are providing a sense of completion or resolution. You have answered the questions, made your case, and now, in effect, you are turning it over to your audience to accept or reject.

A Note of Caution: Because your conclusion is about closure, make certain that you don't introduce any *new* ideas at this point. New ideas belong in beginnings, not endings.

A Word About Titles

Just as you probably wouldn't buy a CD or book without a title, so, too, are you unlikely to interest a reader in a piece of writing that has no title or that has a vague or dull-sounding one.

A title is usually a reader's first exposure to your essay, even before your thesis statement or introduction. For this reason, a well-chosen title can get your reader interested before he or she reads another word. So what constitutes a good title?

Think about essays or stories (or movies, poems, novels, or record albums) whose titles you like. Why do you like them? What makes them effective? The answers to these questions may simply be that the titles interest you personally and that they seem appropriate for the work.

Another element of a title can be the use of a subtitle to suggest the thesis of a piece. For instance, the essay title "With a Little Help from Mozart," while interesting, could be amplified to "With a Little Help from Mozart: Using Classical Music to Raise Your Math Scores." This version gives the reader a better sense of what the essay is about.

In the same way in which you brainstormed or freewrote ideas during your prewriting, you can use similar methods to find a good title. Or perhaps you keep a list of good titles in your journal. Sometimes a title will suggest itself as you are writing or come from a phrase or word you've used in the essay. Remember, you don't have to have a title before you start to write; often one will occur to you after you've finished an assignment. The point to remember is that you need a good title. For the brief amount of time spent finding one, the reward can be great.

Working Alone: Go through the list of titles in a collection of short stories or poems or on a CD. Based upon the titles, write brief summaries of what you think the works are about.

Working Together: With a partner, look at the readings at the end of this chapter and consider the effectiveness of their titles.

Bringing It All Together

An old piece of advice that is sometimes offered to someone making a speech is *"Tell 'em what you want to tell 'em. Tell 'em. Tell 'em what you told 'em."* This is an oversimplification, obviously—anyone who has given a speech knows that it is hard work—but as a bare-bones description of the speech process—or of writing an essay—it is helpful to keep in mind.

As you've been discovering, improving as a writer is a valuable goal and one that you can achieve. Again, there is no magic formula for doing this. Master educator John Holt says, "We learn to do something by doing it; there is no other way." Becoming a better writer requires writing more, having your writing critiqued by others, reading the writing of others, and continuing the habit of thinking about your own writing.

The good news is that it can be done.

As you write, you will discover what each particular essay (or other piece of writing) needs to look like. But you can only discover your essay's structure by trying it out. You have thought about your thesis statement, your introduction, the examples and evidence you will be using, and the order in which you want to present your ideas. Now it's time to write the first draft. This is your first attempt at organizing your ideas in a clear and logical order. It is important to understand that what you are writing at this stage is a first draft. Writing, as you saw in Chapter 1, is a recursive process, one that loops back upon itself. You cannot begin making changes until you have a draft to work on, however.

You have already done a lot of work before starting to write a draft, and you will do a lot of work once you've finished that draft, so be good to yourself. Get everything down without worrying about whether it is perfect—or even very good. With revision, the topic of the next chapter, the draft will get better.

It is helpful to recall, as we discussed in Chapter 4, that writing is a process. There is prewriting, the stage in which you think about what you want to write and take measures to generate ideas. There is writing, the stage in which you take your ideas and begin to assemble them into some meaningful whole. And finally, there is rewriting.

Remember that a piece of writing won't be perfect the first time, and you shouldn't expect it to be. Writing gets better as you go back over it, examining it yourself or with the help of peers and instructors and making thoughtful changes. F. Scott Fitzgerald, who is known for the beauty of his language and his skill in constructing stories and novels such as *The Great Gatsby* and *Tender Is the Night*, said that the art of his writing was the art of rewriting. Chapter 6 will help you to master this important step of the writing process.

Working Together: With a writing peer, exchange essays you have written and identify the parts of each other's work. Ask yourself these questions:

1. Is there a thesis statement? What is it?
2. Where is the introduction? Put brackets around it.
3. How many paragraphs are there? What purpose does each serve?
4. What examples, details, reasons, or proofs does the writer present?

5. Does the essay have a conclusion?
6. Is the title a good one? Why?

Suggestions for Writing

1. Using one of the thesis statements you came up with earlier (perhaps as part of a peer activity), write an introductory paragraph.
2. As part of a writing assignment for one of your other classes, write a draft and use this chapter as a checklist of its parts. Think of the essay as a whole but check to see that you've included each of the components: title, thesis statement, introduction, body, and conclusion.
3. Look back at the prewriting you did at the end of Chapter 4. Use it to develop a first draft of an essay

READINGS

IN FOOTBALL SEASON
JOHN UPDIKE

Do you remember a fragrance girls acquire in autumn? As you walk beside them after school, they tighten their arms about their books and bend their heads forward to give a more flattering attention to your words, and in the little intimate area thus formed, carved into the clear air by an implicit crescent, there is a complex fragrance woven of tobacco, powder, lipstick, rinsed hair, and that perhaps imaginary and certainly elusive scent that wool, whether in the lapels of a jacket or the nap of a sweater, seems to yield when the cloudless fall sky like the blue bell of a vacuum lifts toward itself the glad exhalations of all things. This fragrance, so faint and flirtatious on those afternoon walks through the dry leaves, would be banked a thousandfold and lie heavy as the perfume of a flower shop on the dark slope of the stadium when, Friday nights, we played football in the city.

"We"—we the school. A suburban school, we rented for some of our home games the stadium of a college in the city of Alton three miles away. My father, a teacher, was active in the Olinger High athletic department, and I, waiting for him beside half-open doors of varnished wood and frosted glass, overheard arguments and felt the wind of the worries that accompanied this bold and at that time unprecedented decision. Later, many of the other county high schools followed our lead; for the decision was vindicated. The stadium each Friday night when we played was filled. Not only students and parents came but spectators unconnected with either school, and the money left over when the stadium rent was paid supported our entire athletic program. I remember the smell of the grass crushed by footsteps behind the end zones. The smell was more vivid than that of a meadow, and in the blue electric glare the green vibrated as if excited, like a child, by being allowed up late. I remember my father taking tickets at the far corner of the wall, wedged into a tiny wooden booth that made him seem somewhat magical, like a troll. And of course I remember the way we, the students, with all of our jealousies and antipathies and deformities, would be—beauty and boob, sexpot and grind—crushed together like flowers pressed to yield to the black sky a concentrated homage, an incense, of cosmetics, cigarette smoke, warmed wool, hot dogs, and the tang, both animal and metallic, of clean hair. In a hoarse olfactory shout, these odors ascended. A dense haze gathered along the ceiling of brightness at the upper limit of the arc lights, whose glare blotted out the stars and made the sky seem romantically void and ultimately near, like the death that now and then stopped and plucked one of us out of a crumpled automobile. If we went to the back row and stood on the bench there, we could look over the stone lip of the stadium down into the houses of the city, and feel the cold November air like the black presence of the ocean beyond the rail of a ship; and when we left after the game and from the hushed residential streets of this part of the city saw behind us a great vessel steaming with light, the arches of the colonnades blazing like portholes, the stadium seemed a great ship sinking and we the survivors of a celebrated disaster.

To keep our courage up, we sang songs, usually the same song, the one whose primal verse runs,

Oh, you can't get to Heaven
   (*Oh, you can't get to Heaven*)
In a rocking chair,
   (*In a rocking chair*)
'Cause the Lord don't want
   (*'Cause the Lord don't want*)
No lazy people there!
   (*No lazy people there!*)

And then repeated, double time. It was a song for eternity; when we ran out of verses, I would make them up:

Oh, you can't get to Heaven
   (*Oh, you can't get to Heaven*)
In Smokey's Ford
   (*In Smokey's Ford*)
'Cause the cylin*ders*
   (*'Cause the cylin*ders)
Have to be rebored.
   (*Have to be rebored.*)

Down through the nice residential section, on through the not-so-nice and the shopping district, past dark churches where stained-glass windows, facing inward, warned us with left-handed blessings, down Buchanan Street to the Running Horse Bridge, across the bridge, and two miles out the pike we walked. My invention would become reckless:

Oh, you can't get to Heaven
    (*Oh, you can't get to Heaven*)
In a motel bed
    (*In a motel bed*)
'Cause the sky is blue
    (*'Cause the sky is blue*)
And the sheets are red.
    (*And the sheets are red.*)

Few of us had a license to drive and fewer still had visited a motel. We were at that innocent age, on the borderline of sixteen, when damnation seems a delicious promise. There was Mary Louise Hornberger, who was tall and held herself with such upright and defiant poise that she was Mother in both our class plays, and Alma Bidding, with her hook nose and her smug smile caricatured in cerise lipstick, and Joanne Hardt, whose father was a typesetter, and Marilyn Wenrich, who had a gray front tooth and in study hall liked to have the small of her back scratched, and Nanette Seifert, with her button nose and black wet eyes and peach-down cheeks framed in the white fur frilling the blue hood of her parka. And there were boys, Henny Gring, Leo Horst, Hawley Peters, Jack Lillijedahl, myself. Sometimes these, sometimes less or more. Once there was Billy Trupp on crutches. Billy played football and, though only a sophomore, had made the varsity that year, until he broke his ankle. He was dull and dogged and liked Alma, and she with her painted smile led him on lovingly. We offered for his sake to take the trolley, but he had already refused a car ride back to Olinger, and obstinately walked with us, loping his heavy body along on the crutches, his lifted foot a boulder of plaster. His heroism infected us all; we taunted the cold stars with song, one mile, two miles, three miles. How slowly we went! With what a luxurious sense of waste did we abuse this stretch of time! For as children we had lived in a tight world of ticking clocks and punctual bells, where every minute was an admonition to thrift and where tardiness, to a child running late down a street with his panicked stomach burning, seemed the most mysterious and awful of sins. Now, turning the corner into adulthood, we found time to be instead a black immensity endlessly supplied, like the wind.

We would arrive in Olinger after the drugstores, which had kept open for the first waves of people returning from the game, were shut. Except for the street lights, the town was dark like a town in a fable. We scattered, each escorting a girl to her door; and there, perhaps, for a moment, you bowed your face into that silent crescent of fragrance, and tasted it, and let it bite into you indelibly. The other day, in a town far from Olinger, I passed on the sidewalk two girls utterly unknown to me and half my age, and sensed, very faintly, that flavor from far-off carried in their bent arms like a bouquet. And I seemed, continuing to walk, to sink into a chasm deeper than the one inverted above us on those Friday nights during football season.

For after seeing the girl home, I would stride through the hushed streets, where the rustling leaves seemed torn scraps scattered in the wake of the game, and go to Mr. Lloyd Stephens' house. There, looking in the little square window of his front storm door, I could see down a dark hall into the lit kitchen where Mr. Stephens and my father and Mr. Jesse Honneger were counting money around a worn porcelain table. Stephens, a local contractor, was the school-board treasurer, and Honneger, who taught social science, the chairman of the high-school athletic department. They were still counting; the silver stacks slipped and glinted among their fingers and the gold of beer stood in cylinders beside their hairy wrists. Their sleeves were rolled up and smoke like a fourth presence, wings spread, hung over their heads. They were still counting, so it was all right. I was not late. We lived ten miles away, and I could not go home until my father was ready. Some nights it took until midnight. I would knock and pull open the storm door and push open the real door and it would be warm in the contractor's hall. I would accept a glass of ginger ale and sit in the kitchen with the men until they were done. It was late, very late, but I was not blamed; it was permitted. Silently counting and expertly tamping the coins into little cylindrical wrappers of colored paper, the men ordered and consecrated this realm of night into which my days had never extended before. The hour or more behind me, which I had spent so wastefully, in walking when a trolley would have been swifter, and so wickedly, in blasphemy and lust, was past and forgiven me; it had been necessary; it was permitted.

Now I peek into windows and open doors and do not find that air of permission. It has fled the world. Girls walk by me carrying their invisible bouquets from fields still steeped in grace, and I look up in the manner of one who follows with his eyes the passage of a hearse, and remembers what pierces him.

Topics for Thinking and Writing

1. Is there a thesis statement in this essay? If so, underline it. Put brackets around the introduction. Does each of these parts of the essay do its intended job?
2. Updike asks us to use our senses (sight, smell, hearing, and so on) often as we read this essay. List some of the sensory images he uses. Copy some into your journal. Make lists of five of your own images for each of the five senses.
3. Although he is writing about high school experiences, the author uses language which is at times difficult and demanding. Why do you think he does this? Write down some examples of words and expressions that he uses. Then check their meanings in your dictionary.
4. How would you characterize the tone of this essay? What emotions does the writer get us to feel? Give some examples.
5. In your journal or elsewhere, freewrite about a particular moment of your past, perhaps something from high school or earlier. Write down as many specific details as you can recall.
6. One of the themes of "In Football Season" is the contrast between youth and growing older. Using material gathered in topic 4, write an essay in which you look back at an experience and contrast your perceptions of it then with what you understand about it now.

WRITING DRAFTS
RICHARD MARIUS

1   Finally the moment comes when you sit down to begin your first draft. It is always a good idea at the start to list the points you want to cover. A list is not as elaborate as a formal outline. In writing your first list, don't bother to set items down in the order of importance. List your main points and trust your mind to organize them. You will probably make one list, study it, make another, study it, and perhaps make another. You can organize each list more completely than the last. This preliminary process may save you hours of starting and stopping.

2   Write with your list outline in front of you. Once you begin to write, commit yourself to the task at hand. Do not get up until you have written for an hour. Write your thoughts quickly. Let one sentence give you an idea to develop in the next. Organization, grammar, spelling, and even clarity of sentences are not nearly as important as getting the first draft together. No matter how desperate you feel, keep going.

3   Always keep your mind open to new ideas that pop into your head as you write. Let your list outline help you, but don't become a slave to it. Writers often start an essay with one topic in mind only to discover that another pushes the first one aside as they work. Ideas you had not even thought of before you began to write may pile onto your paper, and five or six pages into your first draft you may realize that you are going to write about something you did not imagine when you started.

4   If such a revelation comes, be grateful and accept it. But don't immediately tear up or erase your draft and start all over again. Make yourself keep on writing, developing these new ideas as they come. If you suddenly start all over again, you may break the train of thought that has given you the new topic. Let your thoughts follow your new thesis, sailing on that tack until the wind changes.

5   When you have said everything you can say in this draft, print it out if you are working on a computer. Get up from your desk and go sit in a chair somewhere else to read it without correcting anything. Then put it aside, preferably overnight. If possible, read your rough draft just before you go to sleep. Many psychological tests have shown that our minds organize and create while we sleep if we pack them full before bedtime. Study a draft just before sleep, and you may discover new ideas in the morning.

6   Be willing to make radical changes in your second draft. If your thesis changed while you were writing your first draft, you will base your second draft on this new subject. Even if your thesis has not changed, you may need to shift paragraphs around, eliminate paragraphs, or add new ones. Inexperienced writers often suppose that revising a paper means changing only a word or two or adding a sentence or two. This kind of editing is part of the writing process, but it is not the most important part. The most important part of rewriting is a willingness to turn the paper upside down, to shake out of it those ideas that interest you most, to set them in a form where they will interest the reader, too.

7   I mentioned earlier that some writers cut up their first drafts with a pair of scissors. They toss some paragraphs into the trash; others they paste up with rubber cement in the order that seems most logical and coherent. Afterward they type the whole thing through again, smoothing out the transitions, adding new mate-

rial, getting new ideas as they work. The translation of the first draft into the second nearly always involves radical cutting and shifting around. Now and then you may firmly fix the order of your thoughts in your first draft, but I find that the order of my essays is seldom established until the second draft.

8   With the advent of computers the shifting around of parts of the essays has become easy. We can cut and paste electronically with a few strokes of the keyboard. We can also make back-up copies of our earlier drafts so we can go back to them if we wish. But as I said earlier, computers do not remove from us the necessity to think hard about revising.

9   Always be firm enough with yourself to cut out thoughts or stories that have nothing to do with your thesis, even if they are interesting. Cutting is the supreme test of a writer. You may create a smashing paragraph or sentence only to discover later that it does not help you make your point. You may develop six or seven examples to illustrate a point and discover you need only one.

10   Now and then you may digress a little. If you digress too often or too far, readers will not follow you unless your facts, your thoughts, and your style are so compelling that they are somehow driven to follow you. Not many writers can pull such digressions off, and most editors will cut out the digressions even when they are interesting. In our hurried and harried time, most readers get impatient with the rambling scenic route. They want to take the most direct way to their destination. To appeal to most of them, you must cut things that do not apply to your main argument.

11   In your third draft, you can sharpen sentences, add information here and there, cut some things, and attend to other details to heighten the force of your writing. In the third draft, writing becomes a lot of fun (for most of us). By then you have usually decided what you want to say. You can now play a bit, finding just the right word, choosing just the right sentence form, compressing here, expanding there.

12   I find it helpful to put a printed draft down beside my keyboard and type the whole thing through again as a final draft, letting all the words run through my mind and fingers one more time rather than merely deleting and inserting on the computer screen. I wrote four drafts of the first edition of this book; I have preserved the final draft of that edition on computer diskettes. But I am writing this draft by propping the first edition up here beside me and typing it all over again. By comparing the first draft and the second draft, one can see how many changes I have made, most of them unforeseen until I sat down here to work.

13   I have outlined here my own writing process. It works for me. You must find the process that works for you. It may be different from mine. A friend tells me that his writing process consists of writing a sentence, agonizing over it, walking around the room, thinking, sitting, down, and writing the next sentence. He does not revise very much. I think it unnecessarily painful to bleed out prose that way, but he bleeds out enough to write what he needs to write. Several of my friends tell me they cannot compose at a typewriter; they must first write with a pencil on a yellow pad. These are the people most likely to cut up their drafts with scissors and paste them together in a different form. They also tend to be older. Most young writers are learning to compose at a keyboard, and they cannot imagine another way to write. Neither can I—though on occasion yet I go back to my pencil for pages at a time.

14   The main thing is to keep at it. B. F. Skinner has pointed out that if you write only fifty words a night, you will produce a good-sized book every two or three years. That's not a bad record for any writer. William Faulkner outlined the plot of his Nobel Prize-winning novel *A Fable* on a wall inside his house near Oxford, Mississippi. You can see it there to this day. Once he got the outline on the wall, he sat down with his typewriter and wrote, following the outline to the end. If writing an outline on a kitchen wall does the trick for you, do it. You can always repaint the wall if you must.

15   Think of writing as a process making its way toward a product—sometimes painfully. Don't imagine you must know everything you are going to say before you begin. Don't demean yourself and insult your readers by letting your first draft be your final draft. Don't imagine that writing is easy or that you can do it without spending time on it. And don't let anything stand in your way of doing it. Let your house get messy. Leave your magazines unread and your mail unanswered. Put off getting up for a drink of water or a cup of tea. (Never mix alcohol with your writing; true, lots of writers have become alcoholics, but it has not helped their writing.) Don't make a telephone call. Don't straighten up your desk. Sit down and write. And write, and write, and write.

Topics for Thinking and Writing

1. The first sentence of Marius's essay is "Finally the moment comes when you sit down to write your first draft." What does this sentence suggest to you about the author's view of the writing process?
2. Marius advises writers to draft at least three times. What does he see as the function of each draft?
3. Implicit in Marius's essay are some of the frustrations a writer may experience as she drafts and revises the drafts. What are some of those frustrations? Which of those frustrations have you experienced as a writer? How did you handle them?
4. Write a short essay about how you go about writing an essay. What have you discovered about your process? What parts of the writing process have been successful for you?
5. Interview three classmates about their writing processes. Write a short essay discussing what you learned from your interviews.

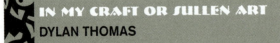

IN MY CRAFT OR SULLEN ART
DYLAN THOMAS

In my craft or sullen art
Exercised in the still night
When only the moon rages
And the lovers lie abed
With all their griefs in their arms,
I labour by singing light
Not for ambition or bread

Or the strut and trade of charms
On the ivory stages
But for the common wages
Of their most secret heart.

Not for the proud man apart
From the raging moon I write
On these spindrift pages
Nor for the towering dead
With their nightingales and psalms
But for the lovers, their arms
Round the griefs of the ages
Who pay no praise or wages
Nor heed my craft or art.

Topics for Thinking and Writing

1. What does Thomas mean by his "craft" and "sullen art"?
2. What are some examples of it? (Examine the intricate rhyme scheme that he uses.)
3. What does he say is his "purpose" in writing? What do you think his purpose really is?
4. Write a short essay in which you examine your own "craft or sullen art."

FOR THE YOUNG WHO WANT TO
MARGE PIERCY

Talent is what they say
you have after the novel
is published and favorably
reviewed. Beforehand what
you have is a tedious
delusion, a hobby like knitting.

Work is what you have done
after the play is produced
and the audience claps.
Before that friends keep asking
when you are planning to go
out and get a job.

Genius is what they know you
had after the third volume
of remarkable poems. Earlier
they accuse you of withdrawing,
ask why you don't have a baby,
call you a bum.

The reason people want M.F.A.'s,
take workshops with fancy names
when all you can really
learn is a few techniques,
typing instructions and somebody else's mannerisms

is that every artist lacks
a license to hang on the wall
like your optician, your vet
proving you may be a clumsy sadist
whose fillings fall into the stew
but you're certified a dentist.

The real writer is one
who really writes. Talent
is an invention like phlogiston
after the fact of fire.
Work is its own cure. You have to
like it better than being loved.

Topics for Thinking and Writing

1. Marge Piercy defines *talent, work,* and *genius* in this poem before she defines a *real writer*. Paraphrase (write out in your own words) her definitions of these terms and show their relationship to "one who really writes."
2. What is Piercy's thesis in the poem? Where does she place the thesis? Does the placement seem effective?
3. What does Piercy say about the relationship between writing and having one's writing read/seen by a public audience? What do her statements suggest about the relationship between writer and audience?
4. Piercy suggests that writing differs from other professions. What specific examples does Piercy provide to show these differences? How do would-be writers try to make up for the differences?
5. Think about your potential career choice or choice of a major in college. Write a short essay defining the key personality traits or behaviors you think you will need to be successful in this career or major.
6. Read the short essay you have written for topic 5. Then write a paragraph evaluating the effectiveness of your examples.

PATTERN FOR SURVIVAL
RICHARD MATHESON

And they stood beneath the crystal towers, beneath the polished heights which, like scintillant mirrors, caught rosy sunset on their faces until their city was one vivid, coruscated blush.

Ras slipped an arm about the waist of his beloved.

"Happy?" he inquired, in a tender voice.

"Oh, yes," she breathed. "Here in our beautiful city where there is peace and happiness for all, how could I be anything but happy?"

Sunset cast its roseate benediction upon their soft embrace.

The End

The clatter ceased. His hands curled in like blossoms and his eyes fell shut. The prose was wine. It trickled on the taste buds of his mind, a dizzying potion. I've done it again, he recognized, by George in heaven, I've done it again.

Satisfaction towed him out to sea. He went down for the third time beneath its happy drag. Surfacing then, reborn, he estimated wordage, addressed envelope, slid in manuscript, weighed total, affixed stamps and sealed. Another brief submergence in the waters of delight, then up withal and to the mailbox.

It was almost twelve as Richard Allen Shaggley hobbled down the quiet street in his shabby overcoat. He had to hurry or he'd miss the pick-up and he mustn't do that. *Ras And The City of Crystal* was too superlative to wait another day. He wanted it to reach the editor immediately. It was a certain sale.

Circuiting the giant, pipe-strewn hole (When, in the name of heaven would they finish repairing that blasted sewer?) he limped on hurriedly, envelope clutched in rigid finger, heart a turmoil of vibration.

Noon. He reached the mailbox and cast about anxious glances for the postman. No sign of him. A sigh of pleasure and relief escaped his chapped lips. Face aglow, Richard Allen Shaggley listened to the envelope thump gently on the bottom of the mailbox.

The happy author shuffled off, coughing.

Al's legs were bothering him again. He shambled up the quiet street, teeth gritted slightly, leather sack pulling down his weary shoulder. Getting old, he thought, haven't got the drive any more. Rheumatism in the legs. Bad; makes it hard to do the route.

At twelve fifteen, he reached the dark green mailbox and drew the keys from his pocket. Stooping, with a groan, he opened up the box and drew out its contents.

A smiling eased his pain-tensed face; he nodded once. Another yarn by Shaggley. Probably be snatched up right way. The man could really write.

Rising with a grunt, Al slid the envelope into his sack, relocked the mailbox, then trudged off, still smiling to himself. Makes a man proud, he thought, carrying his stories; even if my legs do hurt.

Al was a Shaggley fan.

When Rick arrived from lunch a little after three that afternoon, there was a note from his secretary on the desk.

New ms. from Shaggley just arrived, it read. *Beautiful job. Don't forget R.A. wants to see it when you're through. S.*

Delight cast illumination across the editor's hatchet face. By George in heaven, this was manna from what had threatened to be a fruitless afternoon. Lips drawn back in what, for him, was smiling, he dropped into his leather chair, restrained emphatic finger twitchings for the blue pencil (No need of it for a Shaggley yarn!)

and plucked the envelope from the cracked glass surface of his desk. By George, a Shaggley story; what luck! R.A. would beam.

He sank into the cushion, instantly absorbed in the opening nuance of the tale. A tremor of transport palsied outer sense. Breathless, he plunged on into the story depths. *What balance, what delineation!* How the man could write. Distractedly, he brushed plaster dust off his pin-stripe sleeve.

As he read, the wind picked up again, fluttering his straw-like hair, buffeting like tepid wings against his brow. Unconsciously, he raised his hand and traced a delicate finger along the scar which trailed like vivid thread across his cheek and lower temple.

The wind grew stronger. It moaned by pretzeled I-beams and scattered brown-edged papers on the soggy rug. Rick stirred restlessly and stabbed a glance at the gaping fissure in the wall (When, in the name of heaven, would they finish those repairs?), then returned, joy renewed, to Shaggley's manuscript.

Finishing at last, he fingered away a tear of bittersweetness and depressed an intercom key.

"Another check for Shaggley," he ordered, then tossed the snapped-off key across his shoulder.

At three-thirty, he brought the manuscript to R.A.'s office and left it there.

At four, the publisher laughed and cried over it, gnarled fingers rubbing at the scabrous bald patch on his head.

Old hunchbacked Dick Allen set type for Shaggley's story that very afternoon, vision blurred by happy tears beneath his eyeshade, liquid coughing unheard above the busy clatter of his machine.

The story hit the stand a little after six. The scar-faced dealer shifted on his tired legs as he read it over six times before, reluctantly, offering it for sale.

At half past six, the little bald-patched man came hobbling down the street. A hard day's work, a well-earned rest, he thought, stopping at the corner newsstand for some reading matter.

He gasped. By George in heaven, a new Shaggley story! What luck!

The only copy too. He left a quarter for the dealer who wasn't there at the moment.

He took the story home, shambling by skeletal ruins (Strange, those burned buildings hadn't been replaced yet), reading as he went.

He finished the story before arriving home. Over supper, he read it once again, shaking his lumpy head at the marvel of its impact, the unbreakable magic of its workmanship. It inspires, he thought.

But not thought. Now was the time for putting things away: the cover on the typewriter, the shabby overcoat, threadbare pin-stripe, eye-shade, mailman's cap and leather sack all in their proper places.

He was asleep by ten, dreaming about mushrooms. And, in the morning, wondering once again why those first observers had not described the cloud as more like a toadstool.

By six A.M. Shaggley, breakfasted, was at the typewriter.

This is the story, he wrote, *of how Ras met the beautiful priestess of Shagilee and she fell in love with him.*

Topics for Thinking and Writing

1. Write a paragraph exploring what you think is going on in this story.
2. When the fictional author in the story, Richard Allen Shaggley, writes, who is his audience? What is his purpose?
3. Why doesn't Shaggley rewrite his work? Why doesn't the editor, Rick, edit Shaggley's story? Do you think that Matheson revised and edited *his* story?
4. What are some elements that repeat themselves in the story? Why?
5. What is the significance of the story's title? How does it tie in with the ending?
6. Matheson suggests that one purpose of writing is to give order to a sometimes chaotic world and to offer hope. With this in mind, and looking at what Elayne Rapping (p. 137 in the *Intermezzo*) says about writing being a way of "discovering what you know" and of "owning" a subject, write your own statement about the role writing plays in *your* life.

Self-Assessment

Reread your responses to the self-assessment at the beginning of this chapter and respond to the following questions:

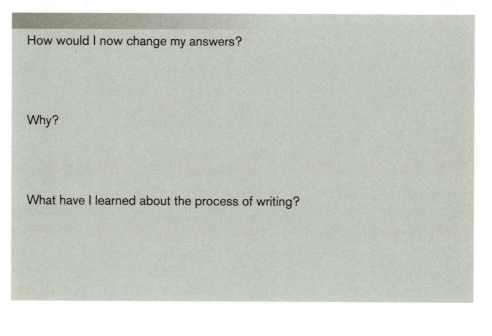

How would I now change my answers?

Why?

What have I learned about the process of writing?

Rewriting: Revising and Editing

6

CATERPILLAR
CHRYSALIS
BUTTERFLY

Sometimes it takes a while for the true nature of an object to develop. Although the first phase may appear impressive, there can be a still more impressive object waiting to be born. A caterpillar can appear beautiful, but its beauty is nothing when compared with that of the butterfly it will become. What makes the butterfly even more remarkable is that it is so different from the caterpillar as which it began life.

Even the middle stage, the chrysalis, has its own charm, though this is not a stage which anyone would describe as perfection. Nonetheless, the chrysalis is what makes the butterfly possible. Each stage of the process, the caterpillar and the chrysalis, is judged by the beauty of the finished product, the butterfly.

It is just the same with the writing process. After the first draft has been written, there is much still to be done. You might like what you have written. You might be able to see beauty and charm in it, but once you understand the process, you will always know that there is an even better piece of writing waiting to be born.

Just as the caterpillar turns into a butterfly only after passing through the middle stage of the chrysalis, so also does your writing need to pass through a stage at which it might no longer look as good as it did when you finished the first draft. After all your work is done, however, if you did it well, your final draft will be a butterfly when compared to the caterpillar of your first draft.

This process is rewriting.

Rewriting: "Writing Again"

One of the biggest hurdles in rewriting is recognizing that the first draft is not what you will end up with. A first draft is one possible way of looking at something. As you rewrite, you are trying to find ways to express ideas differently and better. You will stop and decide which version works best. That's the one you'll want to keep.

Over time, you will develop one of your most important skills as a writer, anticipating the questions of your readers. Readers often have questions about what they are reading that they would like to ask the writer, but they cannot do so because the writer is not there to answer such questions. When you rewrite your essay, you are trying to predict your readers' questions and to answer them. An important part of rewriting is "fence hopping," switching roles and looking at your work as a reader would.

Self-Assessment

What do you do when you rewrite? For most writers, the process begins with rereading what they have written. After that, the paths that writers take vary considerably. All writers agree, however, that rewriting is about more than just correcting spelling and grammar. Rewriting is a much larger exercise: the testing of your best ideas against your reader's expectations. Rewriting turns your caterpillar into a butterfly. The following are some questions that ask you to think about how you go about making the decisions that will reshape your work so that it will become the best it can be. In other words, how do you rewrite?

In responding to these questions, try to probe yourself to find out *why* you do certain things.

1. The things that I find most valuable to do when I rewrite are

2. Who else typically reads my first draft? Why?

3. When I am rewriting, I use my prewriting notes to

4. The part of rewriting I find easiest to do is

5. The part I find most difficult to do is

6. As I think about a piece of writing I've recently completed, I realize that what changed the most was

7. The most significant change that I made in rewriting this piece was

How do I rewrite?	What can I do to make my rewriting process more effective?

Working Alone: Write a paragraph about the way in which you rewrite.

Visualizing Rewriting

If you wish to visualize rewriting, it may be helpful to picture the swirling funnel of a tornado, narrow at the bottom and wide at the top.

First Draft

The base of the funnel could represent your first draft. It won't get completely lost in the rewrite, but it will grow and become something else. As a second draft develops, it will collect some material that you omitted from the first draft or had not even thought about and will discard some other material along the way.

Perhaps the most difficult rewriting skill is to visualize your own writing in the form that the audience will read it. Since what you have just written is still fresh in your mind, it's hard to step outside of your role as a writer and imagine your work from the reader's point of view. Because of this difficulty, you are likely to read over and accept many of your writing's flaws and are less likely to detect its weaknesses. However, your readers will approach your writing with a fresh outlook. They are more likely to see the errors and weaknesses immediately.

It is also hard to visualize your own writing from the point of view of the reader because as the writer, you have a personal stake in what you have just created. In a very real way, your writing represents *you*, or one important aspect of you, and so you are less likely to be objective. The majority of your readers, on the other hand, will have no such personal stake in what you've written. For them, your writing is not personal, and they are free to evaluate and respond to what you have written with an objective, unbiased eye.

This is the same objectivity that effective writers achieve as they reread their own work. In fact, in many ways it would be more accurate to refer to such people not as effective writers but as effective *re*writers. Part of their success as writers comes from the objectivity with which they approach their own work. Like them, you, too, have experienced this type of objectivity if you have reread an old work that you once considered a "masterpiece" only to find the errors and flaws that you didn't see after you had just finished writing it.

You can usually gain an advantage by putting some time between drafts of what you write. Once you have written a first draft, set it aside for a time—the longer the better—before returning to work on a second version. You may not reread your work with the eye of a total stranger, but you will be able to see it more clearly for what it is, warts and all. Ray Bradbury, who is acclaimed for writing superb tales like *Fahrenheit 451* and *The Martian Chronicles*, used to set aside each piece of his work for a whole calendar year before returning to it for rewriting. Obviously, this won't work for your assignments, which frequently have short deadlines, but whenever possible give yourself some time between drafts. If this means not putting off assignments and starting them sooner, that can only make you a stronger student. Instead of having the deadline be a ticking clock, make time your friend.

The key to becoming a successful rewriter is to first become an active reader of your own work.

Active Reading

- Read aloud.
- Read and imagine that you're hearing the piece for the first time.
- Read with your intended audience and purpose in mind.
- Read to find your thesis.

- Read to see if your introduction draws you (and others) in.
- Read for logical organization and presentation of ideas.
- Read for fresh and expressive wording and interesting sensory images.

Working Alone: Reread aloud a piece of writing that you wrote last semester or last year. Mark sentences that you think are unclear and/or passages that you'd like to change. How has the time which has elapsed since you first wrote the piece influenced your view of it now?

Although visualizing your writing from a reader's point of view is fundamental to creating a good piece of writing, there are other important elements of rewriting. As you have seen in previous chapters, most writing tasks can be broken down into parts. As you work on early drafts moving towards completion of the final copy, it helps to evaluate the parts of the draft that you have already produced, to connect the parts, and to refine the parts.

Evaluating the Parts of the Essay

As you saw in Chapter 5, an essay—in fact, most writing—consists of a thesis, an introduction, a body, and a conclusion. Because these are likely to be the most important elements in the piece you are working on, as you reread your writing, it is useful to evaluate each of these parts for clarity and effectiveness.

The Thesis Statement

The thesis statement presents the main idea of the essay. It provides your audience with a guide to what they can expect from the rest of the piece. As you learned in Chapter 5, the thesis is not a statement of fact, but, rather, is a statement of interpretation. In most writing the thesis is placed near the beginning of the piece. When you begin your evaluation process, ask yourself these questions about your thesis:

Can my thesis be easily discovered?
Is my thesis clearly stated?
Is my thesis more than a statement of fact?
Do I have only one thesis in the piece?

If your answer to any of the previous questions is *No*, then you will want to begin your rewriting with a reworking of your thesis. You can begin this reworking by reviewing your purpose and by looking at the **Hints for Thesis Statements** in Chapter 5.

Working Alone: Underline the thesis statement of the draft which you are working on. Does it fit the criteria for a good thesis? If not, brainstorm some new theses for your essay.

The Introduction

Introductions create interest in your topic for your readers. Your introduction serves two goals:

1. It tells the audience the main idea of your essay.
2. It entices them to read on.

To meet the first goal, your introduction should move from a general statement about your topic to your specific thesis. Although the thesis statement can appear anywhere, most good writers state their thesis early. Look at the following brief introductions. Which seems to better meet this first goal? Why?

> America was built on the idea of individual liberty. The Founding Fathers recognized that each person had the right to express an opinion. Therefore, it is important that the governing board of the college have a student representative to express the opinions of the student body.

> A college community consists of many stakeholders: trustees, alumni, administrators, staff, faculty, and students. When major decisions need to be made that will affect the direction and status of the college, it's essential that input about these decisions be gathered from all corners of the campus. Therefore, student representation on college committees is vital to the well-being of the institution.

Working Alone: Review your introduction for a draft of an essay you are working on. Is the opening related to your specific topic? Do the sentences move from the general to the more specific?

To meet the second goal—enticing a reader—review the **Hints About Introductions** in Chapter 5. Which of these introduction strategies have you used to engage your reader? Have you used an amusing anecdote? A surprising statistic? A startling fact? A dramatic question? Are the facts you have used well connected to your thesis? Why did you choose your particular option? Did you experiment with other options?

Working Alone: Read the following brief introductions. Which of the two attracts your attention better? Why?

> Romantic love can be thought of as a universal feeling. Most people have described themselves as being in love at some time. But there are many definitions of love, and love can come in many forms. In order to have a successful love relationship, both of the involved people should share a mutual understanding of what they mean by the word *love*.

> *Romantic love*—what do you think of when you hear these words? The crush you had on the brown-eyed boy in the seventh-grade classroom? The "running-across-a-field-of-daisies-into-open-arms" love of a Hollywood movie? The love celebrated by your grandparents at their fiftieth wedding anniversary? It's not easy to define romantic love, but it does seem true that couples who have success in love share a common understanding of the meaning of these words.

Working Together: Give a completed draft of an essay—minus the introduction—to a peer. Then have your classmate write what she thinks the introduction would have been. Next, pass the draft, again without the introduction, to a third reader. Have the third reader also write an opening. Compare your original introduction with the two new introductions you now have. What are the differences? Which of the three is most likely to draw in a reader?

The Body

Since the body has to develop the main idea of your paper, you may need to significantly revise it once you have revised either your introduction or your thesis. One of the best ways to start thinking about this rewriting is to go back to your prewriting. Check through everything you had decided to leave out. Did you make the right decisions? The easiest way to answer this question is to try to use the material you omitted. If you have to struggle to incorporate it, or if it makes no sense when you include it in your second draft, you probably did the right thing by leaving it out. But if you can easily fit the information into your essay, you should probably think about including it.

Another problem you may discover is that you need more examples. Now you have an opportunity to revisit one of the prewriting techniques you used in Chapter 4. What additional examples will support your idea? You can also ask yourself if your examples are specific and factual, and whether they are connected in the best possible order to your thesis.

Working Alone: Look at the body of a draft you have written. Circle your examples. Are they specific? Are they factual?

The Conclusion

As you saw in Chapter 5, the conclusion ties together the parts of your writing. Check your conclusion. Have you summed up your points? Have you ended, perhaps, with another related anecdote? Most importantly, have you made sure that you haven't introduced a totally new idea (which would mean that you would need to write a different essay)?

Connecting the Parts of the Essay

In many ways, writing is like creating a complicated map of your ideas. As you rewrite, you try to make the map easier for your audience to follow. Here are two ways of guiding your readers:

1. Providing information in a logical order
2. Providing signposts or transitions to signal what you are trying to express

These two methods are particularly important in the body of the essay.

Order

To a certain extent, the order of an essay will be determined by its thesis. For example, if you were writing about a trip across the Midwest, you might order the paragraphs in the body by describing states and towns you traversed from east to west. If you were writing about second-hand smoke and its dangers, you might organize your information from the least significant fact to the most significant evidence. If you were writing about the historical causes of the Great Depression, you might present your information in a chronological order, perhaps starting with the stock market collapse in 1929 and moving through the thirties. No matter what method you use to develop your essay, your readers must be able to follow the logical development of your ideas from your introduction to your conclusion. Readers must be able to anticipate what will follow next in your essay after reading the idea previously presented.

Working Alone:

1. To help you determine whether there's a logical order to the presentation of ideas in your essay, write a brief summary of each paragraph in the left-hand margin. Explain why the parts of the essay are organized in this order. (If you can't easily do this, you may have to consider using another order.)
2. Print out a copy of your essay and cut it up so that each paragraph is on a separate page. Then ask a classmate to reconstruct your essay in what she assumes is the logical order. Is the order of the returned paragraphs the same as in your original? If not, what does this suggest about the order of your draft and the changes you might want to make?

Working Together: Read a line of your essay. Then ask a classmate to predict what will logically follow from that line. Does the prediction hold true?

You may decide to move a paragraph from the middle of your essay closer to the end. However, there may be more than one place to which you can move a paragraph. You will need to determine the right locations for such changes by deciding which best suit your thesis and purpose.

Transitions

To give your writing a smooth and logical flow, you need to make clear connections between ideas. This connecting is done by means of **transitions**, which may be words or phrases that indicate a relationship, repeated key words, or pronouns. Using transitions is perhaps the easiest and most effective way to help the reader see the connections among the ideas on a page. Transitions also indicate the relationships among the supporting ideas and their relationship, ultimately, to the thesis statement.

Look at this skeleton structure of a paragraph:

The first _____. The second _____.
In addition, _____. Lastly, _____.

Although you don't know the content of the paragraph, you can see that the transitional words signal a relationship between ideas. In the following paragraph you can see the relationships made clear.

The first factor to consider when choosing an elective is to identify your reason for taking the elective. Is it to learn something of interest that's completely outside of your major? Is it to complement your major field of study? Is it to find a course that will ease your load of difficult courses in your major? The second factor to consider is your schedule. Which elective will best fit into your time constraints? In addition, you may want to check out a course syllabus to see what the course requires for work. Lastly, you might ask around to learn about the professor's reputation before you register.

> ### Some Common Transition Words and Phrases
>
> as a result, besides, consequently, for example, finally, furthermore, however, in addition to, in conclusion, in other words, likewise, meanwhile, moreover, nevertheless, on the other hand, similarly, subsequently, whereas

Key Words

Another way to guide your readers is to provide them with key word transitions or phrases which will remind them of the main idea you're developing. One of the ways in which you can provide such patterns is to repeat key words related to your topic. Reread the paragraphs throughout this section (**Connecting the Parts of the Essay**). Notice that the key word *transition* is frequently repeated. This repetition reinforces the section's main idea for the reader.

Perfecting Your Writing: Revising and Editing

Imagine that you've just washed and dried your car. It's clean, and it looks good. Now it's time to go to work on the details—polishing chrome, applying wax, cleaning glass—to make it really shine. Similarly, once you've reviewed the parts of your essay and the connections among the parts, and you're satisfied that they support your thesis statement and have a logical flow, you can begin the work of rewriting.

Rewriting consists of two activities: **revising** and **editing**. When you revise, you are making *significant* changes to your work. These might include rewording your thesis to reflect more precisely what you are trying to do and finding stronger examples to support your thesis. You should think about word choice, sentence structure, and the accuracy of facts and details. You may rewrite your conclusion so that it has greater impact. In other words, revising is much more than merely "fixing" minor mechanical and spelling errors that your instructor points out to you. Editing, on the other hand, means addressing those matters of spelling, punctuation, and mechanics.

Both revising and editing are important for perfecting your writing. It is important to remember that the word *essay* means "to try." In rewriting you are trying out new words and new constructions which will add clarity and expressiveness to your work.

Two Rewriting Hints: In Chapter 2, when learning about audience, you were asked to "hop the fence"—that is, to imagine yourself as the reader while you wrote. Assuming that point of view can again be helpful as you prepare to rewrite. Forget that you wrote the piece; approach it with fresh eyes, as though you were encountering it for the first time. This technique will help you evaluate it for strengths and weaknesses.

Secondly, read your writing aloud. This method will enable you to hear your work and determine how it sounds to your inner ear.

Words

Your word choice should reflect your knowledge of your audience. How will your audience respond to the words they read in your essay? What will the words "say" to them? Will they understand the words? Will they be able to picture your ideas from your word choices?

You should avoid using empty words and hollow phrases that convey little or nothing, and, in fact, actually detract from your ideas. Check your draft to see if you've used any of the following common empty words. If you ban them from your papers, you will find that you are immediately forced to come up with better, stronger alternatives.

Some common "empty words"

nice	really
happy	awesome
interesting	different
very	thing
stuff	cool

Even the abbreviation *etc.*, if used just to avoid thinking about further details or points you want to make, can be empty.

Working Together: Exchange drafts with a classmate. Then circle the empty words in each other's drafts. Reexchange your drafts and replace the circled words with stronger choices or eliminate them entirely. Then discuss your choices.

You should also assess your draft to ensure that you have used the best word to convey your point. Think about word *connotation*. Check a thesaurus and dictionary for shades of meaning to find the most accurate words for your writing.

A Note of Caution: When changing words, don't automatically use a bigger or more obscure word—or one that "sounds" intelligent. If the smaller, more common word is adequate or clearer, stay with it. Changing "there was a *small* crack in the cup" to "there was a *diminutive* crack" isn't an improvement.

Finally, stronger writing uses concrete, specific words more often than abstract, general words. Contrast, for example, these passages:

The tennis match was really interesting because I'd never been to one before. It's really a different game, and I learned a lot of things about it.

Watching the tennis match was a new experience. I was fascinated to learn the meanings of terms such as *ace, love,* and *overhead smash.*

Also, whenever you can, choose words that will create sense images for your reader, words that will make your reader see, hear, smell, taste, or feel what you are attempting to say. *"The stick-figure old man tottered along the street"* is more vivid than *"The skinny old man walked down the street."*

Sentence Structure

Just as you ordered your paragraphs to convey your meaning, you will also want to ensure that your sentences make sense and logically follow each other. Think of your sentences as building blocks: the first supports the second, the second adds to the first and supports the third, and so on. The transitions between sentences help to cement the relationships between the ideas.

Next, you can refine your draft by checking for sentence variety. Have you varied both the length and the construction of your sentences? Do too many of them begin with the same words or word patterns? Do you have a combination of simple and complex sentences? Have you written most of your sentences in the **active voice** instead of in the **passive voice**?

In the previous section, you checked for and eliminated empty words. Here you will eliminate empty phrases such as "there is" and "it is." These phrases, known as *expletive constructions,* generally add nothing to the meaning of your writing. Often you will find that the stronger sentence opener comes *after* these phrases.

Working Together: Exchange drafts with a classmate and circle any sentences which use "there is" and "it is" (and their plural forms). If more than two or three expletive constructions are used, try to rewrite the sentences.

The previous exercise is just one activity for making your sentences more concise. As often as you can, prune your sentences of any unnecessary words or phrases. Ask yourself, again and again: "Why is this particular word or phrase in my sentence? What is its purpose? Do I need it to convincingly and expressively relate my idea?" If the answer to this last question is *no,* then get out those "shears" and clip away.

Editing for Accuracy

Throughout this chapter you have spent much time evaluating your draft(s). You may feel satisfied and think that your writing is just about ready to be submitted. But you still have one last step: You must check and recheck your piece for accuracy. This final stage is editing. Remember that when you present a piece of your writing, you are presenting a piece of yourself. You will be judged on it, so you should make it appear as polished as possible. Here's a quick checklist of editing functions:

- *Check for spelling errors.* If you are using a spell checker on a computer, remember that it will not catch all errors. *Read* a paper draft, too. You can also have a friend read your draft.
- *Check for grammar and punctuation errors.* Consult a handbook or one of the many grammar resources on the Web. Use a friend, a teacher, or the writing lab to enlist another pair of eyes.
- *Check for missing words.* The best strategy is to read your piece aloud. You can catch many editing errors this way.

Working Together: With a partner, revise and edit a draft of a paper on which you are currently working.

Working Alone: Find an article in a professional journal in a field in which you are interested. Imagine that you have been asked to rewrite the article. How would you go about performing this task? What are three major changes you would make when rewriting the article. Why?

Some Final Words on Rewriting

Again, think of yourself as the reader. Read your work aloud. Think about what the reader would expect next. Is this what happens? If not, will the reader get confused? If so, is the piece too predictable? If the answer to any of these questions is *yes*, then you need to make changes. As you listen to yourself, always remember one thing: If you are confused, your readers will be confused. Therefore, you will need to make changes—to rewrite your piece.

All of the strategies discussed in this chapter work together. You do not have to pick only one to use. Use as many as you have time to employ. During the time while you are revising, think of the image of the funnel cloud. Once material has become caught up in the swirling cloud, it moves around, changing its location yet remaining a part of the whole. Occasionally, something gets hurled out of the cloud, but the spiral helps to keep all the parts of the cloud together. Revising your work is much the same. Content may move around. New ideas will be gathered into your writing, and sometimes you'll throw out ideas you no longer want. Most writers do not simply take the first draft and produce a second draft. They start with the first draft and make changes, discarding some ideas and keeping others; then they write the second draft (and very often a third, a fourth, and more).

Keep all the comments you receive on your draft. Keep all the ideas and notes you have made. Try them out again until you are satisfied and then write that second draft. If your second draft is really rewritten rather than just edited, you'll be able to point to at least two or three substantive changes—paragraphs that have shifted position, ideas that have been added, examples that have been deleted, introductions or conclusions that have been changed, or transitions that have been made stronger.

Working Alone: Look again at the draft of the paper you revised with your peer. Write a short but complete answer to each of these questions:

1. The most important changes that I made between the first and second draft were

2. As I thought about rewriting this essay, what I learned about audience and purpose was

3. As a result of what I learned about audience and purpose, the most important change I made was

4. As I worked on the second draft, I realized that the idea I still most needed to explain clearly was

5. Some of the sentences and words that I changed were

The Secret to Rewriting

There is no magic formula for rewriting. Repeat what you have done until you run out of time or until you are no longer making significant changes. Some excellent writers go through this process dozens of times. Dean Koontz, whose novels of suspense have sold millions of copies, says he puts in eighty-hour work weeks, with much of that time spent rewriting. At the very least, most writing needs to go through three or four drafts before it becomes really strong.

Suggestions for Writing

1. Rewrite a draft of one of your essays.
2. Take one of the poems from the readings that follow and rewrite it as an essay.
3. Choose one of the following essays and rewrite it as a story or a poem.
4. As you read the following selections, think about the decisions the writers must have made to achieve their final drafts. What else could they have said about their subjects? Why do they begin and end their writing as they do? What information might they have left out? Why?

READINGS

TWO PAST MIDNIGHT
STEPHEN KING

A Note on "Secret Window, Secret Garden"

I'm one of those people who believe that life is a series of cycles—wheels within wheels, some meshing with others, some spinning alone, but all of them performing some finite, repeating function. I like that abstract image of life as something like an efficient factory machine, probably because actual life, up close and personal, seems so messy and strange. It's nice to be able to pull away every once in awhile and say, "There's a pattern there after all! I'm not sure what it means, but by God, I see it!"

All of these wheels seem to finish their cycles at roughly the same time, and when they do—about every twenty years would be my guess—we go through a time when we end things. Psychologists have even lifted a parliamentary term to describe this phenomenon—they call it cloture.

I'm forty-two now, and as I look back over the last four years of my life I can see all sorts of cloture. It's as apparent in my work as anywhere else. In *It*, I took an outrageous amount of space to finish talking about children and the wide perceptions which light their interior lives. Next year I intend to publish the last Castle Rock novel, *Needful Things* (the last story in this volume, "The Sun Dog," forms a prologue to that novel). And this story is, I think, the last story about writers and writing and the strange no man's land which exists between what's real and what's make-believe. I believe a good many of my long-time readers, who have borne my fascinations with this subject patiently, will be glad to hear that.

A few years ago I published a novel called *Misery* which tried, at least in part, to illustrate the powerful hold fiction can achieve over the reader. Last year I published *The Dark Half*, where I tried to explore the converse: the powerful hold fiction can achieve over the writer. While that book was between drafts, I started to think that there might be a way to tell both stories at the same time by approaching some of the plot elements of *The Dark Half* from a totally different angle. Writing, it seems to me, is a secret act—as secret as dreaming—and that was one aspect of this strange and dangerous craft I had never thought about much.

I knew that writers have from time to time revised old works—John Fowles did it with *The Magus*, and I have done it myself with *The Stand*—but revision was not what I had in mind. What I wanted to do was to take familiar elements and put them together in an entirely new way. This I had tried to do at least once before, restructuring and updating the basic elements of Bram Stoker's *Dracula* to create *'Salem's Lot*, and I was fairly comfortable with the idea.

One day in the late fall of 1987, while these things were tumbling around in my head, I stopped in the laundry room of our house to drop a dirty shirt into the washing machine. Our laundry room is a small, narrow alcove on the second floor. I disposed of the shirt and then stepped over to one of the room's two windows. It was casual curiosity, no more. We've been living in the same house for eleven or twelve years now, but I had never taken a good hard look out this particular window before. The reason is perfectly simple; set at floor level, mostly hidden behind the drier, half blocked by baskets of mending, it's a hard window to look out of.

I squeezed in, nevertheless, and looked out. That window looks down on a little brick-paved alcove between the house and the attached sunporch. It's an area I see just about every day … but the *angle* was new. My wife had set half a dozen pots out there, so the plants could take a little of the early-November sun, I suppose, and the result was a charming little garden which only I could see. The phrase which occurred to me was, of course, the title of this story. It seemed to me as good a metaphor as any for what writers—especially writers of fantasy—do with their days and nights. Sitting down at the typewriter or picking up a pencil is a physical act; the spiritual analogue is looking out of an almost forgotten window, a window which offers a common view from an entirely different angle … an angle which renders the common extraordinary. The writer's job is to gaze through that window and report on what he sees.

But sometimes windows break. I think that, more than anything else, is the concern of this story: what happens to the wide-eyed observer when the window between reality and unreality breaks and the glass begins to fly?

Topics for Thinking and Writing

1. In this short introduction to a longer work of fiction, King talks about writers revising old works. What are some examples of this?
2. According to King, what is the writer's job? Do you agree with him? What might you add to what he says?
3. Referring to some of King's work (or that of Shakespeare, Poe, or any other writer whose work you know), cite some ideas that the author uses often in his writing.
4. King talks about how an idea for a story was born. Using a piece of your own writing, write a paragraph discussing where your idea came from and what you did with it.

REVISING
DONALD HALL

1   Almost all writers, almost all the time, need to revise. We need to revise because spontaneity is never adequate. Writing that is merely emotional release for the writer becomes emotional chaos for the reader. Even when we write as quickly as our hand can move, we slide into emotional falsity, into cliché or other static. And we make leaps by private association that leave our prose unclear. And we often omit steps in thinking or use a step that we later recognize as bad logic. Sometimes we overexplain the obvious. Or we include irrelevant detail. First drafts re-

main first drafts. They are the material that we must shape, a marble block that the critical brain chisels into form. We must shape this material in order to pass it from mind to mind; we shape our material into a form that allows other people to receive it. This shaping often requires us, in revising, to reorganize whole paragraphs, both the order of sentences and the sentences themselves. We must drop sentences and clauses that do not belong; we must expand or supply others necessary to a paragraph's development. Often we must revise the order of paragraphs; often we must write new paragraphs to provide coherent and orderly progress.

2   Good writing is an intricate interweaving of inspiration and discipline. A student may need one strand more than the other. Most of us continually need to remember both sides of writing: *we must invent, and we must revise*. In these double acts, invention and revision, we are inventing and revising not just our prose style but our knowledge of ourselves and of the people around us. When Confucius recommended "Make it new," he told us to live what Socrates called "the examined life." It was a moral position. By our language, we shall know ourselves—not once and for all, by a breakthrough, but continually, all our lives. Therefore, the necessity to write well arises from the need to understand and to discriminate, to be genuine and to avoid what is not genuine, in ourselves and in others. By understanding what our words reveal, we can understand ourselves; by changing these words until we arrive at our own voices, we change ourselves; by arriving at our own voices, we are able to speak to others and be heard.

Themes and Revisions

3   On the first day of class, the assignment was to write for twenty minutes on the topic "How I Came to College." Here is an impromptu theme by Jim Beck.

> Education is of paramount importance to today's youth. No one can underestimate the importance of higher education. It makes us well-rounded individuals and we must realize that all work and no play is not the way to go about it, but studies is the most important part, without a doubt. Therefore I decided when I was young that I would go to college and applied myself to studies in high school so that I would be admitted. I was admitted last winter and my family was very happy as was I. Coming here has been a disappointment so far because people are not very friendly to freshmen and everyone has their own clique and the whole place is too big. But I expect that it will get better soon and I will achieve my goal of a higher education and being a well-rounded person.

4   Repetition at the end of the impromptu gives it some unity. When Jim says that "people are not very friendly to freshmen," the reader glimpses Jim Beck and his feelings. But through most of the paragraph, the writer is not being himself. You can tell that he is not being himself because he is sounding like so many other people. Doubtless he thinks that he writes for a teacher who wants to hear this sort of language. Really, he makes contact with no audience at all. Jim is assembling an impromptu from the cliché collection in the why-I-want-to-go-to-college box. When he says *paramount importance*, does he really know what *paramount* means? Does he mean that *today's youth* is genuinely different from yesterday's or tomor-

row's? And how far into history does *today* extend? What does *well-rounded* mean? Why say *individual* instead of *person* or *people*? *Importance* is vague, and saying it twice makes it vaguer. In the sentence of complaint, where the reader briefly senses an actual writer, Jim would have done better to *show* his loneliness in an anecdote, instead of just *telling* us about it. Showing makes contact; telling avoids it.

5   Later in the term, when he had a free theme, Jim wrote an essay which was not so much a revision of his impromptu as a new start and which *really* told how he came to college.

The Race to College
Jim Beck

It's horrible now, and I don't know if it will get any better. The only people who pay attention to me are the people who are trying to beat me out for the track team. My roommate is stoned all day and gets A's on his papers anyway. I hate him because he hates me because I'm a jock. My classes are boring lectures and the sections are taught by graduate students who pick on the students because the professors pick on them.

But I remember wanting to come here so bad! Nobody from Hammerton named Beck had ever been to college. Everybody knew the Becks were stupid. This went for my father, who never got through high school, and for my grandfather, who died before I was born, and who was the town drunk. It went for my two older brothers who went bad, as they say in Hammerton. Steve got a dishonorable discharge from the Marines and he works on a farm outside town and gets drunk on Fridays and Saturdays. Curt stole a car and did time at Jackson and nobody has heard from him since. My sister had a three-month baby and the town liked to talk about that.

I was different. Everybody told me I was. My mother told me I wasn't a Beck. My father told me I was going to bring back the family's good name. (I never knew it had one.) In grammar school the teachers all told me how much better I was than my brothers. By the time I was in sixth grade my father and the school Principal were talking about the University.

My father isn't really dumb. Sometimes people look dumb because it's expected of them. He's worked at the same grocery for twenty years, I guess. Now that I made it to the University, he wants to be called Manager, because he's the only man there besides Mr. Roberts who owns it. (The rest of the help are—is?—kids who bag and an old lady cashier.) When I went back for a weekend everybody treated me as if I won the Olympics.

I said the Principal and my father were talking about my going to the University. All through junior high I said I didn't want to go. I was scared. No Beck could do that. Bad things kept happening to my family. My father had an accident and to-talled the car and lost his license and for a year we didn't have a car at all. He had to walk home two miles every night pushing a basket of groceries. When I said I would quit school and get a job, everybody jumped on me.

It wasn't that I was an A student. It was just that I tried hard at everything I did. I got B's mostly. Now with B's, the counsellors kept telling me, I could be admitted to the University, but I wouldn't get a scholarship. I needed mostly A's for that, and then when I got to the University I would lose the scholarship if I couldn't keep the grades up. Then my brother Steve, who was a pretty good athlete once, suggested athletics.

I was too skinny for football, too short for basketball, I could barely swim and my school didn't have a swimming team anyway. There is one sport you can practice with no money and no equipment. I started to run when I was in my last year of junior high. It felt good right away. I ran to and from school. I went over to the high school and did laps. The high school coach noticed me and asked me to go out the next year. Running long distances hurts a lot. Sometimes you get a stitch in your left side and suddenly it shifts to your right side. I didn't exactly mind the pain. I studied it. I studied it in order to go to the University, the way I studied everything else.

In my Senior year I was all-state and held two high-school records (600 and half-mile) and I had an athletic scholarship to the University. Now I am here, the first Beck to make it. I don't know why I'm here or why I ran so hard or where I go from here. Now that I am here, the race to get here seems pointless. Nothing in my classes interests me. I study, just as I did before, in order to pass the course or even get a good grade. I run to win, but what am I running for? I will never be a great runner. Sometimes when I cannot sleep I imagine packing my bags and going back to Hammerton. But I can't do that. They would say, "He's a Beck, all right."

6   Jim's essay has the two most important features of good writing: it has unity, which means the focus, the point, the coming together of many details; and it has the voice of a real person speaking out of experience with a minimum of tired phrases, of borrowed clothing. It has discipline, and it has feeling. Although Jim is discouraged and feels aimless and melancholy, his mind has made an enormous stride toward knowing and being able to present itself. He revised, using his own experience in his own language. *And* he was disciplined; he used tighter sentence structure, and he found a narrative structure that contained and shaped his thought. Therefore he made contact with his readers.

7   This revision was the product of much hard work, of which only a portion went to the actual revision. Jim's daily writing—with which he struggled at first and which he later enjoyed—was a source of improvement. He began to find his own, unpompous voice. He also revised other essays after reading his teacher's comments, and after discussing these comments in conferences. Jim Beck also talked with his English teacher during office hours, and thought about his writing and his ideas while he ran cross-country in the autumn of his freshman year.

Topics for Thinking and Writing

1. Reread the first two paragraphs of the essay. Outline the major reasons Hall presents for the need to revise. Which two of these reasons most apply to your own writing?
2. In paragraph 4, Hall evaluates Jim Beck's impromptu writing on the topic "How I Came to College." What major criticisms does Hall have of Beck's first effort?

3. Read Beck's reworking of the original idea in the essay "The Race to College." In what ways is this a stronger piece of writing? Point to specific details and examples that you think are effective. Why do you consider them effective?
4. Assume that you had to rewrite another draft of the essay "The Race to College." Describe how you would revise Beck's draft to make it even stronger.
5. Write for fifteen minutes on some aspect of your college experience. Then spend an additional fifteen minutes revising your first draft. Next, write a brief paragraph explaining the changes you have made and what those changes reveal about your writing and the revision process.

THE AUTHOR TO HER BOOK
ANNE BRADSTREET

Thou ill-formed offspring of my feeble brain,
Who after birth didst by my side remain,
Till snatched from thence by friends, less wise than true.
Who thee abroad, exposed to public view,
5 Made thee in rags, halting to th' press to trudge.
Where errors were not lessened (all may judge).
At thy return my blushing was not small,
My rambling brat (in print) should mother call,
I cast thee by as one unfit for light,
10 Thy visage was so irksome in my sight;
Yet being mine own, at length affection would
Thy blemishes amend, if so I could:
I washed thy face, but more defects I saw,
And rubbing off a spot still made a flaw.
15 I stretched thy joints to make thee even feet,
Yet still thou run'st more hobbling than is meet;
In better dress to trim thee was my mind,
But nought save homespun cloth i' th' house I find.
In this array 'mongst vulgars may'st thou roam.
20 In critic's hands beware thou dost not come,
And take thy way where yet thou art not known
If for thy father asked, say thou hadst none;
And for thy mother, she alas is poor.
Which caused her thus to send thee out of door.

Topics for Thinking and Writing

1. Bradstreet describes her book as if it is a child to which she has given birth. What words and phrases does she use which support this metaphor or comparison?
2. The poet also suggests that her "child" or book was sent out to be read by an audience before it was ready. What is still "so irksome" to her about the book in

its current form? What aspects of "revision" would Bradstreet still like to make to this child of hers? Which lines suggest these aspects of revision to you?

3. Write a short paper using a metaphor or simile for a piece of writing which you have drafted but think is still incomplete. You might use one of the following metaphors or similes to develop the comparison:

My draft of my paper is like a meal not fully cooked.

My draft of my paper is like a baseball game in the fifth inning.

My draft of my paper is like a sketch of a portrait.

My draft of my paper is like the first day of a vacation.

My draft of my paper is how I am at the start of my education.

My draft of my paper is how I am at 7 a.m.

4. Write a short paper discussing a time when you handed in a paper which you knew needed more work. Describe your feelings about the paper as you submitted it to your teacher.

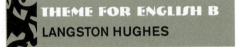

THEME FOR ENGLISH B
LANGSTON HUGHES

The instructor said,

> *Go home and write*
> *A page tonight.*
> *And let that page come out of you—*
5 > *Then, it will be true.*

I wonder if it's that simple?
I am twenty-two, colored, born in Winston-Salem.
I went to school there, then Durham, then here
to this college on the hill above Harlem.
10 I am the only colored student in my class.
The steps from the hill lead down into Harlem,
through a park, then I cross St. Nicholas,
Eighth Avenue, Seventh, and I come to the Y,
the Harlem Branch Y, where I take the elevator
15 up to my room, sit down, and write this page:

It's not easy to know what is true for you or me
at twenty-two, my age. But I guess I'm what
I feel and see and hear, Harlem, I hear you:
hear you, hear me—we two—you, me, talk on this page.
20 (I hear New York, too.) Me—who?
Well, I like to eat, sleep, drink, and be in love.
I like to work, read, learn, and understand life.
I like a pipe for a Christmas present,
or records—Bessie, bop, or Bach.

25 I guess being colored doesn't make me *not* like
the same things other folks like who are other races.
Being me, it will not be white.
But it will be
a part of you, instructor.

30 You are white—
yet a part of me, as I am a part of you.
That's American.
Sometimes perhaps you don't want to be a part of me.
Nor do I often want to be a part of you.

35 But we are, that's true!
As I learn from you,
I guess you learn from me—
although you're older—and white—
and somewhat more free.

40 This is my page for English B.

Topics for Thinking and Writing

1. What does Hughes's poem reveal about his writing process and his feelings about writing?
2. Explain the last line of the poem. How does it relate to the instructor's assignment stated in the opening of the poem?
3. Based on what he reveals about himself in this poem, write a profile of the poet. Include the details he mentions in the poem and some details that you think are implied but are not specifically stated.
4. Research a brief biography of Langston Hughes. Rewrite your profile of the poet which was your response to topic 3. Base your rewrite on the material that you discovered during your research.

THE STOLEN PARTY
LILIANA HEKER

1 As soon as she arrived she went straight to the kitchen to see if the monkey was there. It was: what a relief! She wouldn't have liked to admit that her mother had been right. *Monkeys at a birthday?* her mother had sneered. *Get away with you, be-lieving any nonsense you're told!* She was cross, but not because of the monkey, the girl thought; it's just because of the party.

2 "I don't like you going," she told her. "It's a rich people's party."

3 "Rich people go to Heaven too," said the girl, who studied religion at school.

4 "Get away with Heaven," said the mother. "The problem with you, young lady, is that you like to fart higher than your ass."

5 The girl didn't approve of the way her mother spoke. She was barely nine, and one of the best in her class.

6 "I'm going because I've been invited," she said. "And I've been invited because Luciana is my friend. So there."

7   "Ah, yes, your friend," her mother grumbled. She paused. "Listen, Rosaura," she said at last. "That one's not your friend. You know what you are to them? The maid's daughter, that's what."

8   Rosaura blinked hard: she wasn't going to cry. Then she yelled: "Shut up! You know nothing about being friends!"

9   Every afternoon she used to go to Luciana's house and they would both finish their homework while Rosaura's mother did the cleaning. They had their tea in the kitchen and they told each other secrets. Rosaura loved everything in the big house, and she also loved the people who lived there.

10   "I'm going because it will be the most lovely party in the whole world, Luciana told me it would. There will be a magician, and he will bring a monkey and everything."

11   The mother swung around to take a good look at her child, and pompously put her hands on her hips.

12   "Monkeys at a birthday?" she said. "Get away with you, believing any nonsense you're told!"

13   Rosaura was deeply offended. She thought it unfair of her mother to accuse other people of being liars simply because they were rich. Rosaura too wanted to be rich, of course. If one day she managed to live in a beautiful Palace, would her mother stop loving her? She felt very sad. She wanted to go to that party more than anything else in the world.

14   "I'll die if I don't go," she whispered, almost without moving her lips.

15   And she wasn't sure whether she had been heard, but on the morning of the party she discovered that her mother had starched her Christmas dress. And in the afternoon, after washing her hair, her mother rinsed it in apple vinegar so that it would be all nice and shiny. Before going out, Rosaura admired herself in the mirror, with her white dress and glossy hair, and thought she looked terribly pretty.

16   Señora Ines also seemed to notice. As soon as she saw her, she said:

17   "How lovely you look today, Rosaura."

18   Rosaura gave her starched skirt a slight toss with her hands and walked into the party with a firm step. She said hello to Luciana and asked about the monkey. Luciana put on a secretive look and whispered into Rosaura's ear: "He's in the kitchen. But don't tell anyone, because it's a surprise."

19   Rosaura wanted to make sure. Carefully she entered the kitchen and there she saw it: deep in thought, inside its cage. It looked so funny that the girl stood there for a while, watching it, and later, every so often, she would slip out of the party unseen and go and admire it. Rosaura was the only one allowed into the kitchen. Señora Ines had said: "You yes, but not the others, they're much too boisterous, they might break something." Rosaura had never broken anything. She even managed the jug of orange juice, carrying it from the kitchen into the dining room. She held it carefully and didn't spill a single drop. And Señora Ines had said: "Are you sure you can manage a jug as big as that?" Of course she could manage. She wasn't a butterfingers, like the others. Like that blonde girl with the bow in her hair. As soon as she saw Rosaura, the girl with the bow had said:

20   "And you? Who are you?"

21   "I'm a friend of Luciana," said Rosaura.

22   "No," said the girl with the bow, "you are not a friend of Luciana because I'm her cousin and I know all her friends. And I don't know you."

23   "So what," said Rosaura. "I come here every afternoon with my mother and we do our homework together."

24   "You and your mother do your homework together?" asked the girl, laughing.

25   "I and Luciana do our homework together," said Rosaura, very seriously.

26   The girl with the bow shrugged her shoulders.

27   "That's not being friends," she said. "Do you go to school together?"

28   "No."

29   "So where do you know her from?" said the girl, getting impatient.

30   Rosaura remembered her mother's words perfectly. She took a deep breath.

31   "I'm the daughter of the employee," she said.

32   Her mother had said very clearly: "If someone asks, you say you're the daughter of the employee; that's all." She also told her to add: "And proud of it." But Rosaura thought that never in her life would she dare say something of the sort.

33   "What employee?" said the girl with the bow. "Employee in a shop?"

34   "No," said Rosaura angrily. "My mother doesn't sell anything in any shop, so there."

35   "So how come she's an employee?" said the girl with the bow.

36   Just then Señora Ines arrived saying *Shh, shh,* and asked Rosaura if she wouldn't mind helping serve out the hotdogs, as she knew the house so much better than the others.

37   "See?" said Rosaura to the girl with the bow, and when no one was looking she kicked her in the shin.

38   Apart from the girl with the bow, all the others were delighted. The one she liked best was Luciana, with her golden birthday crown; and then the boys. Rosaura won the sack race, and nobody managed to catch her when they played tag. When they split into two teams to play charades, all the boys wanted her for their side. Rosaura felt she had never been so happy in all her life.

39   But the best was still to come. The best came after Luciana blew out the candles. First the cake. Señora Ines had asked her to help pass the cake around, and Rosaura had enjoyed the task immensely, because everyone called out to her, shouting "Me, me!" Rosaura remembered a story in which there was a queen who had the power of life or death over her subjects. She had always loved that, having the power of life or death. To Luciana and the boys she gave the largest pieces, and to the girl with the bow she gave a slice so thin one could see through it.

40   After the cake came the magician, tall and bony, with a fine red cape. A true magician: he could untie handkerchiefs by blowing on them and make a chain with links that had no openings. He could guess what cards were pulled out from a pack, and the monkey was his assistant. He called the monkey "partner." "Let's see here, partner," he would say, "turn over a card." And, "Don't run away, partner: time to work now."

41   The final trick was wonderful. One of the children had to hold the monkey in his arms and the magician said he would make him disappear.

42   "What, the boy?" they all shouted.

43   "No, the monkey!" shouted back the magician.

44   Rosaura thought that this was truly the most amusing party in the whole world.

45   The magician asked a small fat boy to come and help, but the small fat boy got frightened almost at once and dropped the monkey on the floor. The magician

picked him up carefully, whispered something in his ear, and the monkey nodded almost as if he understood.

46   "You mustn't be so unmanly, my friend," the magician said to the fat boy.

47   "What's unmanly?" said the fat boy.

48   The magician turned around as if to look for spies.

49   "A sissy," said the magician. "Go sit down."

50   Then he stared at all the faces, one by one. Rosaura felt her heart tremble.

51   "You with the Spanish eyes," said the magician. And everyone saw that he was pointing at her.

52   She wasn't afraid. Neither holding the monkey, nor when the magician made him vanish; not even when, at the end, the magician flung his red cape over Rosaura's head and uttered a few magic words … and the monkey reappeared, chattering happily, in her arms. The children clapped furiously. And before Rosaura returned to her seat, the magician said:

53   "Thank you very much, my little countess."

54   She was so pleased with the compliment that a while later, when her mother came to fetch her, that was the first thing she told her.

55   "I helped the magician and he said to me, 'Thank you very much, my little countess.'"

56   It was strange because up to then Rosaura had thought that she was angry with her mother. All along Rosaura had imagined that she would say to her: "See that the monkey wasn't a lie?" But instead she was so thrilled that she told her mother all about the wonderful magician.

57   Her mother tapped her on the head and said: "So now we're a countess!"

58   But one could see that she was beaming.

59   And now they both stood in the entrance, because a moment ago Señora Ines, smiling, had said: "Please wait here a second."

60   Her mother suddenly seemed worried.

61   "What is it?" she asked Rosaura.

62   "What is what?" said Rosaura. "It's nothing; she just wants to get the presents for those who are leaving, see?"

63   She pointed at the fat boy and at a girl with pigtails who were also waiting there, next to their mothers. And she explained about the presents. She knew, because she had been watching those who left before her. When one of the girls was about to leave, Señora Ines would give her a bracelet. When a boy left, Señora Ines gave him a yo-yo. Rosaura preferred the yo-yo because it sparkled, but she didn't mention that to her mother. Her mother might have said: "So why don't you ask for one, you blockhead?" That's what her mother was like. Rosaura didn't feel like explaining that she'd be horribly ashamed to be the odd one out. Instead she said:

64   "I was the best-behaved at the party."

65   And she said no more because Señora Ines came out into the hall with two bags, one pink and one blue.

66   First she went up to the fat boy, gave him a yo-yo out of the blue bag, and the fat boy left with his mother. Then she went up to the girl and gave her a bracelet out of the pink bag, and the girl with the pigtails left as well.

67   Finally she came up to Rosaura and her mother. She had a big smile on her face and Rosaura liked that. Señora Ines looked down at her, then looked up at her mother, and then said something that made Rosaura proud:

68   "What a marvelous daughter you have, Herminia."

69   For an instant, Rosaura thought that she'd give her two presents: the bracelet and the yo-yo. Señora Ines bent down as if about to look for something. Rosaura also leaned forward, stretching out her arm. But she never completed the movement.

70   Señora Ines didn't look in the pink bag. Nor did she look in the blue bag. Instead she rummaged in her purse. In her hand appeared two bills.

71   "You really and truly earned this," she said handing them over. "Thank you for all your help, my pet."

72   Rosaura felt her arms stiffen, stick close to her body, and then she noticed her mother's hand on her shoulder. Instinctively she pressed herself against her mother's body. That was all. Except her eyes. Rosaura's eyes had a cold, clear look that fixed itself on Señora Ines's face.

Topics for Thinking and Writing

1. Explain the title of the story. How do your perceptions of the title's meaning and significance change as you read the story?
2. Discuss the role of social class in this story. What point do you think the author is making about how class influences behavior?
3. Freewrite for twenty minutes on a childhood experience that was particularly embarrassing or upsetting.
4. Consider your response to topic 3 a first draft for an essay. Rewrite this draft and develop the idea into a complete essay.

Self-Assessment

Reread the self-assessment that opens this chapter. Then answer the following questions.

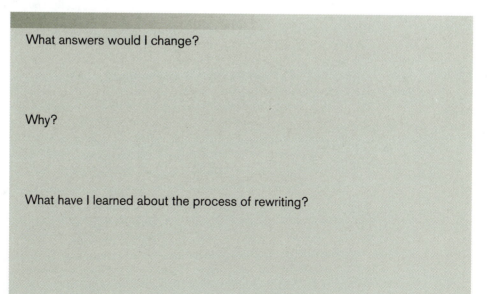

What answers would I change?

Why?

What have I learned about the process of rewriting?

Review your writing profile from Chapter 1. Rewrite it in light of what you've been thinking and learning about writing since then.

A Final Word

If you have reached this point, congratulations! In *Take Charge of Your Writing*, you have been engaged in the challenge of finding and crafting language that can express the subtle nature of your ideas and feelings. Rewriting is one important aspect of this process. As you "re-envision," change, and rewrite your work, you are assessing your abilities as a writer. By producing writing that will appeal to your audience and will achieve your purpose, you are developing one of the most important skills that you can possess. However, the task doesn't end here. Writing is a skill that you will need all of your life, and self-assessment is an ongoing process of thinking about your writing.

Whenever you engage the written word, you use the tool of assessment. Thoughtful writers self-assess their writing constantly—not only when they are creating their own work but also when they are reading other writers' work. Good writers are good, in part, because they pay attention to how other writers use language and try to incorporate what they regard as good into their own writing.

Self-assessment is the single most important habit you can develop as a writer because it is one that you will use for the rest of your life. Long after you have finished this course, have graduated from college, and have forgotten much of what you discussed in your classes, you can continue to develop as a writer through self-assessment.

The next part of this book builds upon what you have been doing in Chapters 1 through 6. Write on.

INTERMEZZO

FROM IDEA TO ESSAY

Intermezzo is a term applied in music to a short movement separating the major sections of a lengthy piece of work. It suggests a breather, a chance to see where you are. Here it is used to provide a pause between Parts 1 and 2 of this book to give you an opportunity to see where you are as a writer and to observe close up the writing process in action.

As you've learned in the first six chapters of this book, writing is a process that includes **prewriting, writing**, and **rewriting**. Put another way, the writing process is exploring an idea, discovering what you have to say about the idea, and refining the ways in which you express the idea. Essayist Elayne Rapping puts it this way: "Writing is a way of figuring out who you are and what you think. If you can't explain it, you don't really own it." Of course, each writer has an individual approach to writing; what works for one won't necessarily work for another.

What follows is an example of how one student writer uses the writing process to respond to a writing assignment in her English class. In this *intermezzo* you will see a writer in action as she discovers an idea, creates a draft essay, and, through rewriting, refines that draft to produce a finished essay. Along the way, she uses many of the techniques discussed in the first six chapters and receives advice on developing her ideas from her peers and her instructor.

Self-assessment is an important technique that the writer uses. As she explores, discovers, and refines her ideas, she stops working at key places to ask questions, to solve writing problems, and to evaluate her progress. This ongoing self-assessment enables her to "own" her ideas, as Rapping would say. As a by-product, it also helps her to understand her writing process so that she will be able to approach future writing assignments with confidence and skill.

As you read through this section, ask yourself how you might have responded differently. Imagine yourself as the student's writing peer. What advice would you offer to help her improve her essay? There are also exercises throughout this section that ask you to respond to the writer's development of her ideas. Taking the time to do these will help you strengthen your own writing process.

The Assignment

Here is the assignment that was given by the student's instructor:

> Using the writing and self-assessment strategies that have been discussed in the first six chapters of the text, write a five- to seven-hundred-word essay on a topic of your choice. As you begin to identify a topic, define your audience and purpose. Maintain a complete record of the process you use to develop your idea.

What follows are the notes and writing that the student produced in response to the assignment.

Sample Student Writing Process and Essay, Michele Mandino

BRAINSTORM

What can I write about?

What do I know something about?

What are the things I like?

What would I like to know more about?

the beach	movies
volleyball	music
basketball	Woodstock III
college b'ball	food
tennis	sweets
Martina Hingis	Thanksgiving
Pete Sampras	Thanksgiving dinner
travelling	holiday treats
camping	meeting new people
trail biking	Italian food
women's soccer	lasagna
The Super Bowl	chocolate
going to concerts	dark chocolate
dancing	hot chocolate
jogging	chocolate addiction
video games	chocolate gifts

Which do I think might make interesting or unusual topics?

My camping trip on the Appalachian Trail
My experiences at Woodstock III
Video games and violence
My chocolate addiction
The Super Bowl and what it tells us about America

JOURNAL ENTRY

Thursday, October 10.

I see from your brainstorm and your journal entry that you're considering chocolate as a topic for your essay. Why not do another brainstorm—on chocolate this time?

Last night I went out with some people I met on campus during the first week of school. There were six of us—Bob, Sarah, Masuka (sp?), Julliana, Justine and I. The night started out at a Mexican restaurant where we all met. The food was good, and it was cheap, a good spot to go back to. I really liked the meal, especially this dish I had called Chicken with Mole Sauce. The sauce was the thing because it was made with chocolate. Sounded weird to me, but I had to try it because I couldn't believe that they put chocolate on top of chicken. Not only that—it was also served with chili peppers. The dish tasted a lot better than it sounded. The sauce wasn't too sweet, and the chilies gave it just the right kick. Another item I can add to the list of things I love with chocolate.

After dinner we went to some club on Pearl St. that Bob knew about where there was a sorry guy playing some excuse for folk music. Maybe he thinks it's sexy, but he was just a lonely guy and his guitar. Maybe if he stopped playing, he'd have more friends. I never did understand why people like all those folk songs about love gone bad or some other depressing subject. Anyway, we still had a good time because Justine and Julliana seemed to have an endless supply of jokes and stories, and Masuka got us dancing. Got back home late.

BRAINSTORM ON TOPIC

Chocolate

Why is choc. so popular?
Everybody loves it.
There's a type of choc. for almost everyone.
chocolate desserts
hot chocolate
a main dinner course?
chocolate and Mexico
a chocolate kiss
Death by chocolate/eat chocolate, die happy
eat chocolate, live forever
Swiss chocolate
chocolate as a gift of love
chocolate sauces
sweet chocolate

bitter chocolate

the time I ate baking choc. YUK!

the mystique of chocolate

melts in your mouth

chocolate-covered cherries

white chocolate

Easter eggs

Christmas chocolate

Valentine's Day

the gift of love

Where did it come from?

milk chocolate

an energy food?

chocolate Girl Scout cookies

picks you up when you're down

Working Alone

1. How has this writer used prewriting strategies to identify an idea to develop into an essay?
2. What other prewriting strategies might the writer have used? Add ten more topics to the brainstorm on chocolate.

Self-Assessment

AUDIENCE PROFILE

Describe the reader.

My teacher will be a reader for this essay, along with my fellow students. My fellow students are typical college students—male, female, age 18–30, etc.

What ideas or information do I want to convey?

I'll present some general information about chocolate. I want to use examples and details that I think the audience will find interesting … and that I'll find interesting, too.

How do I want my readers to respond?

I want them to be interested in what I have to say. I'd also like them to think that my essay is funny in places, that it's not too serious but is informative and worth the read.

What reasons or examples can I use to get my readers to respond?

Use the Mexican food example from my journal. Give examples of different types of chocolate. Ask the readers questions to try to keep their interest. Start off the essay by stating something to attract their attention.

How much do my readers already know about the topic?

Everybody is familiar with chocolate. Everyone has tasted it, and most people like it, but I doubt that they know its history.

What are my readers' expectations?

My teacher is expecting a well-written essay of at least five hundred words. He'll want to see a good introduction with a thesis statement and a good use of details in the body of the essay to explain the thesis. My classmates will want an interesting topic. They should be more sympathetic because they have the same assignment.

How will my readers react?

I hope that they'll be interested in what I have to say. I will consider this essay successful if I can get them to laugh while they are reading it. I would also consider it successful if I can tell them something they didn't know before they started reading.

Working Alone

1. Describe at least one other potential audience for this essay.
2. How might the addition of this audience influence the way in which the essay is developed?

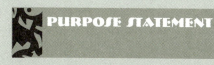
PURPOSE STATEMENT

This is a good start. But you'll want to have more focus & be clearer about what you intend your essay to do.

My purpose is to write an essay of about five hundred words. The essay's basic purpose is to be informative. Since my topic is chocolate, I'm not planning on writing a serious paper. I think I want to write a paper that will tell the reader something new and interesting. I also hope to present a few ideas that are strange or funny.

Working Alone: Assume that you are writing this essay to persuade or to entertain. What are some possible ideas you might use to develop the essay? How might these different purposes influence the way in which you write the essay?

Possible ideas for a persuasive essay:

Possible ideas for an entertaining essay:

FREEWRITE

ON CHOCOLATE

Good details

Where'd chocolate come from? OK, this idea came out of my head, but I mean where did chocolate come from originally? I think it was one of those foods Columbus discovered in America. I remember reading that chocolate, the potato, and the tomato were some of the new foods they brought back from the New World. Boy, what a boring place the world would be without them, especially chocolate. I'll take a bar of chocolate over a boiled potato any day. Who wouldn't? A lot of people say that they're addicted to chocolate. I know that people say it about me, and maybe I am. I could eat it almost every day, actually I do, hmmm. How did I get to love chocolate so much? I've always loved chocolate for as long as I can remember.... My first strong memory is when I was a kid and my dad would buy us a chocolate Easter egg on Easter Sunday. I can remember my excitement peeling off the foil and seeing the perfect shape of the egg underneath. It was almost too good to break open, but it didn't stay whole for long. Me and my brother would compare our eggs and protect the last piece and maybe even save it to be eaten much later, kind of like a contest between us to see who still had some at the end...

"

You might want to check on this.

As I grew up, I discovered there was more to the world of chocolate, like last week I went to a Mexican restaurant where they served chocolate as the main course, on chicken and enchiladas. That's my kind of cooking. I think that sauce was called a mole sauce but I'm not too sure exactly what it is.

Chocolate is kind of an international food though. I bet you could go anywhere in the world and find some kind of chocolate because people eat it everywhere. One time my cousin came to visit and he didn't speak English too well and I opened a box of chocolates and almost right away it was like he became my best friend. That's another good thing about chocolate, it helps break the ice between people like that time with my cousin. Show me a person that doesn't like chocolate and I'll show you a person with no taste—we don't want chocolate with good

"

taste, Charlie, we want chocolate that tastes good! Maybe they should keep a huge open box at the U.N. then maybe there wouldn't be so many problems in the world. What else can you say about chocolate? I don't know. I'm stuck.... OK, one time I ate so much when I was a kid that I think I got sick on it. But even that didn't turn my stomach. It took me a while but I got over it and then I just began eating it again. Some people might say a chocolate addiction is bad, but it could be worse. There's a lot of good things you can say about chocolate. It's a great energy food. It really picks you up when you're down, and not just physically, it gives your spirit a boost too. It's comfort food for me and a lot of other people feel that same way, and it's never too expensive.

You've come up with some strong ideas & details here.

Once I went to a restaurant and they had this dessert called Death by Chocolate. Had to try it. I think that was probably the best dessert I ever had. It was like four or five different kinds of chocolate. Chocolate on chocolate with chocolate covered by more chocolate—sounds kind of gross writing it like that, but it was excellent!! What a way to go! At least I'd die happy.

Self-Assessment

POSSIBLE THESES

What are some possible theses that I could develop into an essay?

Possible theses:

1. Everybody loves chocolate because it's a unique food that tastes great and can pick you up when you are down.
   Self-assessment: Too vague and general

2. Chocolate was discovered in America by Columbus.
   Self-assessment: Too specific. What else is there to say? Plus I'd have to do research to be sure it's true.

3. Chocolate is a unique food that helps the body and comforts the spirit.
   Self-assessment: This one has possibilities, but I'd have to do research to learn how chocolate helps the body.

4. Why do so many people like chocolate?
   Self-assessment: Too general

5. Everybody likes chocolate because it comes in so many varieties and has such unique flavors.
   Self-assessment: Duh. Not very interesting. Too general and obvious.

6. For me, I love chocolate because there are so many varieties to choose from, it has a complex and delicious taste, and there is something special about the mystery of what happens when you bite into a creamy, smooth piece of chocolate.

Self-assessment: This could work. It states an opinion, and it has three ideas (varieties, taste, and mystery) that I could develop in the body of the essay.

7. Dark chocolate is the best kind of chocolate because it has a complex taste, goes well with other ingredients, and can be put to many uses.
Self-assessment: Not bad. It states an opinion, and I could write about the foods it goes with and how it can be used.

8. Although there are many types of chocolate, true chocolate lovers know that there is really only one kind—dark chocolate—because it has a complex taste, goes well with other additives, and has a variety of uses.
Self-assessment: This is a little better. It states an opinion. It's fairly specific, but I could write about taste, additives, and uses—although I'm not sure what I would say about additives, and this thesis only discusses dark chocolate. Research needed. Limited?

Working Alone:

1. Develop two other possible theses the writer might use for this topic.
2. Look back at your ideas for writing an essay with the purpose of persuading or entertaining your audience. Write two theses that you might use for an essay with each of these purposes.

Self-Assessment

WORKING THESIS

Better — It's more focused and specific. These are elements you can explore and develop using details from your journal and your freewrite.

For me, I love chocolate because there are so <u>many kinds to choose from</u>. It has a <u>complex and delicious taste</u>, and there is something about <u>the mystery of</u> what happens when you bite into a creamy, smooth piece of chocolate.

What I know about the topic that supports my thesis:

I love it.

It gives energy.

Several types

Swiss, Italian, Belgian are best.

Used in cooking

Sweet and bitter

Light and dark

Hot choc. drink

Melts in your mouth

Valentine's gift

What I still need to learn about the topic to support my thesis:

Check the origin.

How is it made?

Find out about Mexican mole sauce.

What type of plant does it come from?

What are some famous chocolates?

Ask some people about the topic.

FIRST DRAFT

CHOCOLATE

You do a good job
of getting your
ideas into your
opening. I like the
question you
start with.
Can you leave out
the "I"?
"
(ditto marks)

Good.

Again. Try to
leave yourself out
of it.

Your ¶s have
good topic sen-
tences.
The body should
explain and sup-
port your thesis.

"

"

What makes chocolate so appealing? There's probably a different answer to this for every person who loves chocolate. Some people might say they like it because of its taste. I bet other people would say they don't know why they like it; they just do. For me, I love chocolate because there are so many kinds to choose from, it has a complex and delicious taste, and there is something mysterious that happens when you bite into a creamy, smooth piece of chocolate. How do you like your chocolate? Liquid or solid? Bitter or sweet? Chocolate is like no other food.

There are so many different varieties of chocolate. Chocolate comes in liquid or solid, and then there's the kind that is something in between, like chocolate pudding. Hot chocolate is great on a cold winter day. Some people drink hot chocolate the way they drink tea or coffee. They have to have it every day. I know that one of my favorite things is a hot fudge sundae with chocolate ice cream. When I was in high school, I think I ate one almost every day after school. One time I went to a Mexican restaurant, and they had chicken with a chocolate sauce called mole. I remembered the name of the sauce because I thought that it was so cool.

When I think of chocolate, I think of it in solid form. In my opinion most people probably feel the same way that I do. It really is the best way to eat chocolate. When it's solid, you can feel the chocolate melting on your tongue and the taste gradually filling every part of your mouth.

Probably the most famous shape that chocolate comes in is the Easter egg. Maybe it's my imagination, but for some reason the shape and the chocolate seem to be made for each other. The reason I believe this is so is because there's nothing like unwrapping a chocolate egg and taking that first bite. What would Valentine's Day be without chocolate? If chocolate hearts aren't as popular as roses are on Valentine's Day, they are very close. Christmas is another holiday when chocolates are popular. I bet kids have fun biting off the heads of chocolate Santas.

But the real reason to eat chocolate is not because of its shape but because of its taste. Nothing compares with how your mouth feels when you put a piece of chocolate in it. Nothing compares with the feeling of the way chocolate melts in your mouth. It starts out slow and then spreads to the rest of your taste buds. I can't describe the way chocolate turns from a solid form into a liquid form as it spreads over your mouth.

Then there are the different tastes of different types of chocolate. If you have a sweet tooth, there is extra sweet chocolate. If you like it on the light side, there is the smooth taste of milk chocolate. The real serious chocolate is dark chocolate. This is where you can tell the true chocolate lover from just the average chocolate lover. People who know chocolate prefer dark chocolate over other kinds of chocolate because it seems to have a perfect balance of sweet and bitter taste. When I was young, I used to eat milk chocolate, but now I like dark chocolate better. Don't get me wrong. I wouldn't turn my nose up at a piece of milk chocolate, either.

I think that chocolate is mysterious. It's like no other food. Young people and old like chocolate because there's something exciting about opening up a fresh box of chocolates; that's why we use it for so many special occasions and especially for gifts like at Valentine's. Can you imagine getting excited about the potato the way people get excited about chocolate? What did you get for Christmas? Oh, I got a five-pound bag of potatoes doesn't cut it the way a two-pound box of chocolates does.

Everybody loves to eat chocolate. It's probably the one international food. People who don't speak the same language can agree on liking chocolate. One time my cousin who didn't speak English came to visit from Italy and we couldn't talk to each other too well because of the language problem but as soon as I opened up a box of chocolates it was like he was my best friend, so I think that if you put people who speak different languages in a room with a box of chocolates, they'll instantly have something in common. Maybe if they used it at the U.N., it would help to bring peace to the world. Chocolate goes beyond your country and languages and it helps to communicate when words can't.

It doesn't matter who you are or where you come from. Chocolate will find you. It's an inexpensive pleasure that everyone can afford to indulge in. Everyone has a chocolate lover inside of them. Some people control it more than others.

This can use some work — it should sum up and echo ideas you've introduced earlier. Conclusion — Tie your idea together … work on this.

Self-Assessment

FIRST DRAFT

1. The strongest parts of my essay are

I think I have a good working thesis, but I need to make it a little clearer. I have some good examples to explain or support my thesis. I also like the basic topic of the essay and some of the details.

2. The weakest parts of my essay are

I'm rambling, just putting down ideas without giving enough thought to where they should go. My introduction and conclusion are a bit confusing. I'm not sure I know how to get started, and then once I get started, I don't know how to stop.

3. Three strong examples that support my main idea are

I like the example about the Mexican food. I think it's interesting and unusual. I also like my examples about using chocolate on Christmas and on Valentine's Day. The third example that I like is the one about my cousin who couldn't speak English coming to visit.

4. I think I need to work on the following parts of my essay:

The beginning and ending for sure. I think that some parts of the body of the essay are confusing. When I read it out loud, parts of it don't sound right. I want to choose my examples and not just put in everything.

I'm sure I need to work on my grammar and spelling as well. My paper doesn't really have a title. I called it "Chocolate," but that's too vague.

Working Alone: Complete the following peer review sheet of the rough draft as though you were the writer's classmate.

PEER REVIEW FOR FIRST DRAFT

Name of writer: _____   Title of essay: _____

Peer reviewer's name: _____

Completely answer all questions. Unless it's obvious, each answer should be at least one full paragraph.

1. The thesis of the essay is

2. The main examples used to support the thesis are

3. The strongest example is _____ because

4. After reading this essay, the main thing I have learned is

5. Three questions or suggestions that I have for the author are (Explain why these questions or suggestions are important for the essay's development):

Self-Assessment

REWRITE OF WORKING THESIS

This is tight and to the point!

Many people love chocolate because of its countless varieties, its satisfying taste, and its mystique.

BRAINSTORM OF POSSIBLE TITLES

"Eat Chocolate, Die Happy"

"The Things I Love About Chocolate"

"Chocolate: The Food of Love and Friendship"

"Confessions of a Chocolate Lover"

"Why I Love Chocolate"

"Chocolate: Its Variety and Mystery"

"The Special Language of Chocolate"

"The Mysterious Language of Chocolate"

"Chocolate: The International Food"

SECOND DRAFT

THE MYSTERIOUS LANGUAGE OF CHOCOLATE

This intro is more interesting.

Swiss. Italian. Belgian. Chocolate. It comes in different colors, endless varieties, and almost every imaginable shape. Today it's a food we almost take for granted. We use it to celebrate special occasions like birthdays and holidays, to declare our love on Valentine's Day, and to eat as the exclamation point at the end of a special meal. What makes chocolate so appealing?

Strong thesis. Nice use of your question to set up your thesis.

Although there are probably as many answers as there are chocolate lovers, most people would agree that so many people love chocolate because of its countless varieties, its satisfying taste, and its unique mystique.

Whatever your taste, you are sure to find a variety of chocolate to fit the occasion. What could be better than hot chocolate on a cold winter's day—or on any day, for that matter? Today, hot chocolate is the most common liquid form of this delicious substance, but lovers of soft or liquid chocolate can also enjoy it in chocolate syrups and hot fudges. Those who can't get enough of the liquid variety

This body is well-detailed & very specific. You do a good job incorporating your ideas & details.

can satisfy their addiction with a main course—a dish called *Pollo con Mole Negro*. This Mexican recipe uses a chocolate mole sauce served over chicken. Those who still can't get enough can finish off their meal with a bowl of chocolate mousse or pudding.

However, most chocolate lovers enjoy their pleasure in solid form, and even here, there seems to be an endless variety. The list includes milk chocolate, dark chocolate, sweet chocolate, bitter chocolate, and white chocolate, which true chocolate lovers know isn't really chocolate at all. To add to the pleasurable confusion, chocolate comes in almost every imaginable shape and size. There is bite size for those who think they only want one bite, and then there's the five-pound bar for those with bigger appetites. On Valentine's Day chocolate lovers exchange chocolate-shaped hearts. At Christmas even Grinches enjoy biting off the heads of chocolate Santas. What would Easter be without the chocolate Easter egg? For some reason, the egg shape and the chocolate just seem to be made for each other.

Although shape and variety are important, the true pleasure of chocolate is in the taste. Nothing compares with the way chocolate melts in your mouth. It starts out slowly and then seems to spread to all of your taste buds at once. The way solid chocolate turns into a creamy liquid as it bathes the front and back of your mouth is indescribable.

There is a chocolate taste for almost everyone. Those with a very sweet tooth can choose their chocolate extra sweet. Others prefer their chocolate on the light side and opt for the smooth, sweet taste of milk chocolate. Most mature, or serious, chocolate lovers prefer their chocolate dark. This is the chocolate of chocolates because it provides a perfect balance of sweet and bitter tastes. Dark chocolate has a richness of taste and texture like that of no other chocolate.

Good transitions.

To add to all of this, chocolate has a mystique like that of no other food. Aside from its taste, for the young and old alike there is something special about chocolate. We use it for so many occasions because no other food provides a thrill like the gift of chocolate does. Can you think of any other food that you would like to receive as a gift? The potato is wonderful, but a gift of a five-pound bag of potatoes doesn't possess the same mystique that a five-pound box of chocolates does.

Part of the mystique of chocolate is that everybody loves it. You will never hear anyone say that she hates chocolate. People from almost every part of the world understand and love chocolate. Put two people who speak different languages in a room, give them a box of chocolates, and they will instantly have something in common that they can talk about and share. Its mystique can bring people together and communicate where words are insufficient.

Very effective summing up!

It doesn't matter if you are Swiss, Italian, Belgian, or any other nationality, for that matter. You can find a chocolate variety and flavor that speaks your language, and chocolate can likewise find the chocolate lover inside every person.

Self-Assessment

FINAL DRAFT

Reread your essay and review the process that you used to complete this assignment. Assess your work by completing the following statements:

1. The parts of the process that I found most valuable for completing this assignment were

I liked brainstorming because it helped me explore many topics and ideas very quickly. Brainstorming was also good for helping me write the first draft. Once I had a first draft, I was able to work with it to make the essay better.

2. The parts of the process that I found most difficult were

Going through all of my prewriting and trying to find a topic that I could write about. I had a hard time deciding exactly what I wanted to say about the topic, but once I did, it was not bad. Writing the introduction was also difficult. It was hard to organize my ideas so that the introduction began smoothly.

3. The most important changes that I made while progressing from my first draft to this draft were

I cut out needless things (especially in the first few paragraphs) and organized my examples better. I went from a rambling draft of 832 words to a more organized essay of 690 words. As my instructor keeps telling us, "More isn't necessarily better. Make each word and sentence count."

4. If I were given an opportunity to write this paper again, I would do the following things differently:

I think I would finish the first draft sooner. I discovered that once I have a draft to work with, I can begin to see how the ideas in the paper will come together. This helps me to get my ideas organized. Also, I can work on my sentences and paragraphs to make them clearer, etc.

We have observed one student's response to an assignment, taken through the various steps of the writing process from prewriting to rewriting. Hopefully, this *intermezzo* has given you an opportunity to pause and assess where you are with your own writing. Your efforts will look different from those of this student—no two writers work in exactly the same way—but many of the steps that you follow will be similar. Remember the advice given elsewhere in this book: **Hard writing results in easy reading**.

For your review, here are some things you'll want to do as you write:

1. Pick a topic about which you can say something interesting and meaningful.
2. Use prewriting strategies (brainstorming, freewriting, and so on) to help you develop ideas about your topic. These prewriting strategies can be used both before and after you find a topic.
3. State your topic in the form of a thesis statement which clearly expresses what you intend to demonstrate in your essay.
4. Have a strong introduction which gets your reader's attention and creates interest in what you have to say.
5. Organize your essay in some logical fashion.
6. Provide adequate details and examples to illustrate and support your thesis.
7. Have a strong conclusion.
8. Revise your work to create a clearer and more polished piece of writing.

Chapter

7

Summaries: Condensing Original Material

DESCRIPTION WRITTEN TO A FRIEND
LECTURE NOTES
AN ESSAY

Your friend is thinking about enrolling in an art history course for the spring semester. You are currently taking the course. She asks you to tell her what the course is about, what kinds of assignments the teacher gives, and how much time, on average, you have to study for the course.

You attend your art history class. The day's lecture is on the beginning of the Renaissance in fifteenth-century Florence. The lecturer presents a detailed overview of the important events and artists of the period. He tells an interesting story about how Michaelangelo got his nose broken in a fist fight. As you take notes, you focus on what you believe are the significant facts and ideas of the period and any additional information that might be on the final exam.

The day of your art history final arrives. You are ready. You have studied your lecture notes and have summarized important sections of the text. The first question on the exam asks you to outline the major events of the early Renaissance and to choose three significant works that reflect the artistic ideals of the period.

In each of these situations, you are creating a summary, or condensing a body of information and restating it in your own words. You are not analyzing or evaluating the information, nor are you responding to the information with a personal opinion. You are briefly retelling or outlining the information. As the previous examples illustrate, the presentation of a summary depends on the **purpose** and the **audience** of the piece.

When you are describing the course to your friend, the purpose is not formal; you might be very casual about the information you choose to include and the way in which you decide to present it. When you are summarizing the lecture, you are the audience for the notes, and the purpose is to learn the subject and to perform well on the test. You probably wouldn't be concerned about your grammar, style, and spelling, but you would be very concerned about accurately capturing and remembering the information and doing well on the exam. When you take the exam, you are very aware of your lecturer as the audience. Therefore, you pick three works that your lecturer has mentioned as being important, works he expects you to know about. You also choose your words and sentences more carefully.

Working Together: With a partner, summarize a movie or sporting event. Write down the way in which you organized your thoughts as you summarized the plot or the progression of the game.

Working Alone: Summarize the responsibilities you had on a job you have held.

Self-Assessment

Summary is a basic technique that you use every day because it is a quick way to remember and relay information. You use summary when your boss asks you to write a progress report on how the day's sales have gone, when your roommate asks you to tell her what happened at the last student council meeting, when you tell a friend about your child's typical morning at the local daycare center, when you make a mental note of the events reported on the television news, or when you write about the difficulties you have experienced with your new computer. You try to be objective in each of these situations, stating the facts rather than your evaluation of or your response to them. This self-assessment asks you to think about what you know about summaries.

1. I have written these types of summaries for school, work, or personal situations:

2. The purpose and audience affects my writing of a summary in these ways:

3. I think that summaries might be useful for completing research projects because

4. When I finish writing a summary, I check to make sure that I have accurately summarized the information by

What I know about writing summaries:	What I want to know about writing summaries:

Working Alone: Write a paragraph discussing what you know about writing summaries and how you think summary writing will be helpful to you in your college career.

What Is a Summary?

A summary is a condensed restatement of the main ideas and essential information of another piece of communication. Summaries can take many forms; they can be oral or written; they can be formal or informal. This chapter focuses on the types of written summaries you might be asked to write in college.

As with most other forms of writing, your audience and your purpose for writing a summary are the two most significant factors to consider as you go about the task. A summary of a textbook chapter that you would write for your instructor might differ from a summary of the same chapter that you would write for a classmate. A summary of a section of a book used in a research paper may differ from a summary of that same section written for your own class notes.

This last example points out another major distinction in the way in which you write a summary. Summaries may be private or public. If the intended use is private—that is, only you will read the summary—you have more freedom when deciding what type of information to include in the summary. On the other hand, public summaries, those to be read by others, will require that you think about your reader's expectations as you choose ideas and details to include in your writing.

Summaries are versatile, useful, and efficient means of learning, recording, and conveying information. The following are some of the primary purposes for writing summaries:

- To demonstrate what you know about a topic
- To condense information which can be used as a study guide for a course or as a section of a research paper

- To help you connect new material to old
- To preview what will be detailed in a longer paper. This specialized type of summary is called an **Abstract** and is often found at the beginning of articles in professional journals
- To help you reduce complex ideas and complex language into meaningful segments of information to be studied

Working Together: Which of the previous purposes would you categorize as private or public writing? Which would you categorize as both?

Working Alone: Write a paragraph explaining the purpose of one summary which you have recently written.

Regardless of its purpose, summary writing requires that you do the following:

1. Find the **topic** of the original piece, determine its **main idea,** and pick out the **essential information**.
2. Write in a neutral, **objective** tone, presenting the original author's facts and ideas, not your opinions of those facts or ideas.
3. Restate or rewrite the ideas, primarily in your **own words**.

Finding the Topic

The topic is the *subject matter* of the piece of writing. It can usually be stated in one word or in a short phrase. You can find the topic by

- Reading the title. Does the title tell you what the topic is?
- Reading the opening paragraph. Is the topic clearly expressed in a thesis statement?
- Reading through the text. What key words are repeated? What subject is the piece primarily about?

You can use a graphic organizer, which will help you keep track of your discovery of the topic and its relationship both to the main ideas and to other essential information. The following organizer is shaped like the letter *T*.

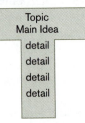

As you read the following passage, think about the topic, the main idea, and the essential details. Then notice how the "T" organizational pattern is used to keep track of the key information. Eventually, the information in the graphic can be turned into a written summary of the passage.

DIFFERENT WORLDf OF WORDf
DEBORAH TANNEN

Even if they grow up in the same neighborhood, on the same block, or in the same house, <u>girls and boys grow up in different worlds of words</u>. Others <u>talk</u> to them differently and expect and accept different ways of talking from them. Most important, children learn how to <u>talk</u>, how to have conversations, not only from their parents, but from their <u>peers</u>. After all, if their parents have a foreign or regional accent, children do not emulate it; they learn to <u>speak</u> with the pronunciation of the region where they grow up. Anthropologists Daniel Maltz and Ruth Borker summarize research showing that <u>boys and girls</u> have very different <u>ways of talking</u> to their friends. Although they often play together, <u>boys and girls</u> spend most of their time playing in same-sex groups. And, although some of the activities they play at are similar, their favorite games are different, and <u>their ways of using language</u> in their games are separated by a world of difference.

Boys tend to play outside, in large groups that are hierarchically structured. Their groups have a leader who tells others what to do and how to do it, and who resists doing what other boys propose. It is by giving orders and making them stick that high status is negotiated. Another way boys achieve status is to take center stage by telling stories and jokes, and by sidetracking or challenging the stories or jokes of others. Boys' games have winners and losers and elaborate systems of rules that are frequently the subject of arguments. Finally, boys are frequently heard to boast of their skill and argue about who is best at what.

Girls, on the other hand, play in small groups or in pairs; the center of a girl's social life is a best friend. Within the group, intimacy is the key: Differentiation is measured by relative closeness. In their most frequent games, such as jump rope and hopscotch, everyone gets a turn. Many of their activities (such as playing house) do not have winners or losers. Though some girls are certainly more skilled than others, girls are expected not to boast about it, or show that they think they are better than the others. Girls don't give orders; they express their preferences as suggestions, and suggestions are likely to be accepted. Whereas boys say, "Gimme that!" and "Get outta here!" girls say, "Let's do this" or "How about doing that?" Anything else is put down as "bossy." They don't grab center stage—they don't want it—so they don't challenge each other directly. And much of the time, they simply sit together and talk. Girls are not accustomed to jockeying for status in an obvious way; they are more concerned that they be liked.

You discovered the main idea in the previous excerpt by looking at the repetition of words and phrases in the introduction. Those words are underlined. The topic is then listed in the first line of the graphic organizer. It is in the form of a short phrase.

Using the T organizer results in this:

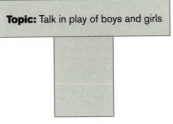

Working Alone: Read an article assigned for another class or from a magazine that interests you. Begin constructing a T organizer of the article by listing its topic on the first line.

Finding the Main Idea or Thesis

The *main idea* is the point about the topic that the writer considers most significant. It is what the author wants us to know about the topic. Once you have found the topic, you are ready to determine the main idea or thesis about the topic. When you write a formal summary, you want to convey to the reader that main idea. Some authors thoughtfully place the main idea in the first or last sentence of the introduction. Others state the main idea in the title. However, some readings require a little more detective work to discover the main idea. You may have to read the piece several times before the gist of it is clear to you.

To find the main idea:

- Look at the end of the introduction. Quite often this is where you will find the main idea explicitly stated in the form of a **thesis statement**. Remember that a thesis statement is not a statement of fact but rather suggests an opinion or an analysis that will be supported by the body of the paper.
- Decide if the rest of the information in the reading adds details which develop, support, contrast, define, prove, or illustrate the sentence. If your answer is *yes*, you have found the main idea. If it's *no*, you may have an *implied main idea*. In this case, you can't continue to search for that one sentence. You will have to answer the question "What is the most important thing I should know about this topic after I finish reading this piece?" You may be able to discover the implied main idea by listing statements about the topic. Do a number of them appear to support an idea that's not specifically stated? Can you put this idea into words? If you can, you have found your implied thesis.

 DIFFERENT WORLDS OF WORDS
DEBORAH TANNEN

Even if they grow up in the same neighborhood, on the same block, or in the same house, *girls and boys grow up different worlds of words*. Others *talk* to them differently and expect and accept different ways of *talking* from them. Most important, children learn how to *talk*, how to have conversations, not only from their parents, but from their peers. After all, if their parents have a foreign or regional accent, children do not emulate it; they learn to *speak* with the pronunciation of the region where they grow up. Anthropologists Daniel Maltz and Ruth Borker summarize research showing that *boys and girls* have very different *ways of talking* to their friends. Although they often play together, *boys and girls* spend most of their time playing in same-sex groups. And, **although some of the activities they play at are similar, their favorite games are different, and their ways of using language in their games are separated by a world of difference.**

In this passage the main idea or thesis is conveniently placed at the end of the introduction. It is printed in boldface type. The rest of the passage elaborates on this main idea with specific, concrete details.

The main idea or thesis is added to the second line on the T organizer:

Topic: Talk in play of boys and girls

Main idea/thesis: Their favorite games are different, and their ways of using language in their games are separated by a world of difference.

Working Alone: Summarize how you go about finding the main idea in a difficult piece of writing. *Reminder*: Your goal is to find the one sentence that will help you achieve the overall goal of understanding the reading.

The final step in completing the T-organizer is to decide which of those details would be essential in a summary of the passage.

Finding the Essential Information

Once you have found the main idea, you are ready to look for the reasons, details, and examples which support it. Because you want to keep your summary brief, you should include only those details which are essential for summarizing the main idea. You will need to determine which are necessary details that the author uses to explain or prove the main idea and which are unnecessary details that add description but are not essential. One example of an essential supporting detail might be statistics used by the author. You would include these statistics in your summary.

Writers frequently give clues to help you recognize quickly what they consider necessary information about their pieces. Often, particularly in textbooks or scholarly articles, key facts are printed in bold or italicized type, bulleted, item- ized, or underlined. Sometimes the important information is repeated or restated throughout the chapter. At other times, you may find the significant details in the topic sentences of each paragraph. Writers also use transition words such as *in ad- dition, moreover,* or *as a result* to indicate important information. You may also see important information conveniently summarized in boxes or restated in the conclusion.

DIFFERENT WORLDS OF WORDS
DEBORAH TANNEN

Even if they grow up in the same neighborhood, on the same block, or in the same house, **girls and boys grow up in different worlds of words**. Others **talk** to them differently and expect and accept different ways of **talking** from them. Most important, children learn how to **talk**, how to have conversations, not only from their parents, but from their peers. After all, if their parents have a foreign or regional accent, children do not emulate it; they learn to **speak** with the pronunciation of the region where they grow up. Anthropologists Daniel Maltz and Ruth Borker summarize research showing that **boys and girls** have very different **ways of talking** to their friends. Although they often play together, **boys and girls** spend most of their time playing in same-sex groups. And, **although some of the activities they play at are similar, their favorite games are different, and their ways of using language in their games are separated by a world of difference.**

Boys tend to play outside, in **large groups** that are **hierarchically structured**. Their groups have a **leader who tells others** what to do and how to do it, and who resists doing what other boys propose. It is by **giving orders** and making them stick that high status is negotiated. Another way boys achieve status is to take **center stage by telling stories and jokes**, and by sidetracking or challenging the stories or jokes of others. Boys' games have **winners and losers** and elaborate systems of rules that are frequently the **subject of arguments**. Finally, boys are frequently heard **to boast of** their skill and argue about who is best at what.

Girls, on the other hand, play in **small groups or in pairs**; the center of a girl's social life is a best friend. Within the group, **intimacy** is the key: Differentiation is measured by relative closeness. In their most frequent games, such as jump rope and hopscotch, everyone gets a turn. Many of their activities (such as playing house) **do not have winners or losers**. Though some girls are certainly more skilled than others, girls are **expected not to boast** about it, or show that they think they are better than the others. Girls **don't give orders**; they express their preferences as **suggestions**, and suggestions are likely to be accepted. Whereas boys say, "Gimme that!" and "Get outta here!", girls say, "Let's do this" or "How about doing that?" Anything else is put down as "bossy." They **don't grab center stage**—they don't want it—so they don't challenge each other directly. And much of the time, they **simply sit together and talk**. Girls **are not accustomed to jockeying for status** in an obvious way; they are more concerned that they be liked.

In the previous passage, the essential details are the specifics which elaborate on the differences in play and talk between boys and girls. They have been underlined and bolded and then added—in shortened versions—to the stem of the T organizer.

Topic: Play and talk in boys and girls

Main idea/thesis: Their favorite games are different, and their ways of using language in their games are separated by a world of difference.

Detail: Boys—large groups

Detail: Boys—hierarchy

Detail: Boys—giving orders

Detail: Boys—center stage

Detail: Boys—competition

Detail: Boys—arguments

Detail: Boys—boasting

Detail: Girls—small groups

Detail: Girls—intimacy

Detail: Girls—no boasts, no orders, no center stage, no status

Detail: Girls—cooperation

Detail: Girls—sit together and talk

The completed T organizer can now be used as an outline for the written summary. It can be applied to the forms of summary called the "nutshell" and the "line-by-line" discussed later in this chapter. As an outline, it can also serve as a study guide for a chapter.

Working Together: With a classmate, write a list of the clues used in this chapter to signal essential information.

Working Alone:

1. Write a summary of a web site you have recently used for a research project. Focus on the site's essential details.
2. Read a piece of your writing for this class or another. Then write a brief paragraph discussing how you have signaled your reader about the piece's main ideas and essential information.

Writing with Objectivity

Summaries require that you put aside your critical eye and report only on the purpose of the text. Your varied audiences want to know what the *authors* you have read *have to say* about a topic, not what you *think* about what they have to say. (That's **evaluative** writing, which is discussed in Chapter 8). If your audience is your professor, she wants to be certain that you have accurately understood the assigned material. If your audience is your student peers, they might want to know if it will be useful for them to read the whole article.

Therefore, when you write a summary, you have to be faithful to the author's view. You have to write with an objective, neutral tone. You can achieve objectivity by omitting your own bias and carefully selecting words and ideas.

For example, if you were to write a summary based on the passage about the talk of children, you would not include anecdotes from your own life which would either support or negate the writer's ideas about children's play. Nor would you express your opinions about the validity of those ideas. The T organizer will help you to stay objective as you write your summary because it focuses on the passage's topic, main idea, and essential details.

Working Together: Read the following passages. Then decide which of the two is an objective summary of this chapter's discussion of main ideas.

Finding the main idea is hard because sometimes writers confuse the reader by hiding the main idea. It would be a lot easier if all authors would spell out their main idea somewhere near the beginning of an essay. Unfortunately, many don't do that, although they probably should. Therefore, the reader has to spend an enormous amount of time searching for clues about the main idea. She can first try to list any statements about the topic, but this might not always work.

Finding the main idea in an essay often requires a two-step process. First, the reader has to identify the essay's topic. Second, the reader has to determine what is the most important idea about the topic. Sometimes this essential idea, also known as the thesis statement, is located at the end of the essay's introduction. If this is the case, the thesis is explicit. If, however, the main idea is not found in one sentence, it is called an "implied" thesis. There are strategies to help the reader find both the essay's topic and its main idea.

The first passage expresses the summary writer's opinion about the topic. The writer uses words which are considered "value-laden"; that is, they relate a personal opinion, an emotional response, or an evaluation of the topic. Therefore, the first passage is not an objective summary of the points raised in the reading.

In the second passage, the tone is matter-of-fact. The key ideas of the text are expressed in neutral language. Your job in writing a summary is to use words that reflect the author's opinions, not your own.

Working Together: With a classmate, read two letters to the editor in the op-ed section of a newspaper. Then pick out those words which can be considered value-laden.

Working Alone: Find a movie review from the newspaper or from an Internet site such as E-online. Then rewrite the review to make it an objective summary of the movie.

Using Your Own Words

Although you are capturing the original writer's ideas in your summary, you should develop the summary mostly in your own words. You can ensure that you have used your own words and that you fully understand the reading by follow-ing this technique: Read the original text, taking notes on the main idea. Place the original out of sight. Then write your summary. Lastly, reread the original to make sure that you have been faithful to the author's work.

Working Alone: Read the essay in the *Intermezzo* on pages 149–150. Then put the essay aside and write a summary of it.

On occasion, you may want to "spice up" your summary with a particularly catchy quotation from a work. If you decide that you want to use words, phrases, or longer passages from the original, you will have to put quotation marks around the author's words. You will also need to cite the source of the informa-tion and to reference it to indicate that you have taken the words directly from the text. Check with your instructor for the preferred documentation form.

Working Alone: Reread your summary of the essay on chocolate from the *Inter-mezzo* (pp. 149–150). Then add two quotations from the original essay to your summary.

How to Write a Summary

Writing a summary requires that you keep in mind the main ideas and the essen-tial information of the original text. Since a summary is a condensed version of the original text, a helpful "rule" is to use the ratio *one-quarter to one whole*. That is, your summary's length should be about one-fourth of the original piece's length.

You can use a number of techniques to write a summary. However, remember that the technique that you use and the details that you include will depend on your purpose and your audience. Here are three common summary-writing tech-niques:

- The nutshell summary
- The line-by-line summary
- The outline

The Nutshell Summary: The *nutshell summary* conveys the essence of the original "in a nutshell." That is, you compact the original into a condensed form that ex-presses the work's essential meaning. Follow these steps when you are writing a nutshell summary:

1. Read the passage several times. Take notes as you are reading.
2. Answer the question "What point is the author making about the topic of the passage?"
3. State the point in your own words. This statement will become the main idea of your summary.
4. Continue to build your summary by adding to it—in your own words—the essential details of the original work. You can make sure that you have used

your own words by placing the original out of reach while you are writing your summary.

Working Alone: Write a fifty-word nutshell summary of a paper you are writing for this class or another class.

The Line-by-Line Summary: In the *line-by-line summary*, you begin by writing a one-sentence summary, in your own words, of each paragraph of the original text. You then combine these sentences into paragraphs, adding the appropriate transitions. Your first sentence will often be a one-line summary of the main idea, along with the author's name and the title of the original piece. This technique works particularly well with material that is dense and contains a lot of technical language.

The line-by-line summary can also be used when you want your summary to be an outline of the original work. Instead of writing in paragraph form, you will use an outline form. For the outline you may decide to shorten the sentences into one to three-word phrases.

The Outline Summary: The outline summary seeks to capture the main idea and examples of a piece of writing as quickly and concisely as possible. It takes its name from the fact that the finished product looks like a list. Most outline summaries begin with a brief sentence summarizing the main idea of the piece. After that, record the key examples as briefly as you can. As you read through the piece you are summarizing, make a note of each principle or example as it occurs. You want to limit these notes to as few words as possible.

Once you have read the piece and recorded the principle ideas and examples, simply list them in the order in which they occur, and you have your summary. In short, you are recreating, as best you can, the author's original outline.

Working Alone: Write a line-by-line summary or an outline summary of a paper that you are working on for this class or another class.

The following are examples of a nutshell, a line-by-line, and an outline summary of the excerpt "Different Worlds of Words."

Nutshell Summary

Boy talk significantly differs from girl talk. One of the most common settings in which these differences can be observed is the world of play. Boys, who most often play in large groups, emphasize winning. Girls, playing in small groups or in pairs, emphasize closeness with each other. Boys will vie for leadership positions by taking center stage and by giving orders to others. Girls, on the other hand, offer suggestions to others but shy away from taking charge. Boys argue about who's best at what skill while girls avoid bragging about skills. Rather than trying to establish high status in the group through language, girls use talk to be liked by their peers.

Line-by-Line Summary

In "Different Worlds of Words," Deborah Tannen writes that boy talk significantly differs from girl talk, particularly in peer groups. Boys learn to give orders to others, to argue about the rules of the games they play, and to tell stories and jokes in order to establish leadership in the group. The goal of their play is to "win." Girls, however, aim for closeness in small groups and in pairs. They do not brag or give orders, but rather give suggestions about what games to play. The goal of their play is to be "liked."

Outline Summary: Main Idea: Boy talk differs significantly from girl talk, particularly in play.

I. Boys
    a. Play in large groups
    b. Status is the goal.
    c. Competitive
    d. Boastful

II. Girls
    a. Play in small groups or pairs
    b. Intimacy is the goal.
    c. Cooperative
    d. Avoid bragging

You will decide which summary technique works best for you based on the audience and purpose of your summary. For example, for an essay exam you may need to present more examples to convince your professor of your knowledge of the subject. Therefore, you might use a line-by-line summary. For a summary of a school organization's meeting, you may want to be brief to allow for adequate time for questions. In this case, you might choose the nutshell summary. For study notes, you may decide that the outline summary will best help you review the material for an exam.

Working Alone: Write a ten- to fifteen-line summary of this chapter to use for study notes. Then write another summary of this chapter for your instructor. Compare the results.

A Final Note

Summary writing is one of the more practical skills you will use in college. You will be asked to summarize throughout your college career. This chapter has focused on summarizing one piece of writing. In the chapters on evaluation, analysis, argument, and the research paper, you will use this valuable tool in combination with your own opinions and other resources.

Suggestions for Writing

1. Write an essay to incoming first-year students explaining why summaries are an essential part of learning in college. Your essay should contain advice

about how the students can use summary writing in their learning and how to write an effective summary.

2. Write a summary of one of the essays at the end of this chapter for your own use. Then write a summary of the same essay to be read by your instructor. Compare the two and explain the differences.

3. Write a brief autobiography using the techniques of summary writing.

4. Think of a movie or TV show that you have recently seen which is appropriate for both children and adults. Write two summaries of the show, the first for an audience of children, the second for an adult audience.

5. Write a summary of a novel which you have read, a concert which you have attended, or a tourist attraction which you have visited. Choose one of three audiences for your summary: a close friend, the readers of the college newspaper, or an elderly relative.

READINGS

WHAT'S IN A NAME?
SEUNG HEE SUH

1   "Okay then, I'm Erin," I said, "Yun, you're Katie, and Jong, your name is Allison." My two younger sisters and I decided on our new American names while we waited for the principal of our new school to come out and greet us. Unlike the other Korean kids we knew, our parents made us keep our Korean names when they enrolled us in our first American school. I grew tired of the puzzled faces when I told my name. Teachers got stuck when my name came up in the attendance call. People always asked me to repeat the name two or three times and no one ever got the pronunciation right. Attending a new school in a new town was my chance to take on a new identity. I could be more American with my new name. Adults won't bother me with questions about my name, then ask me to tell them stories of Korea. When they learn my new American name, I won't be singled out as the Asian kid. I could be another Jennifer, Kathy, or Mary.

2   However, the name wasn't enough to make me an American. My five sisters and I all took turns getting our hair permed. Mom sat down and carefully rolled our straight hairs and soaked them with chemicals. As a result, my hair-do was bigger than my body, but it was curly like the American girls'. No one will finger my hair and say, "It's so straight," as if straight hairs didn't belong in this country.

3   Rippled hair-do still didn't complete the look. In the classroom, the black-haired girl always stood out. In order to cure that problem, I brushed a syrup-like brown solution onto my hair. In minutes, the syrup gave me amber highlights, like the solution box said.

4   A girl named Erin with curly-brown hair still didn't look like the other kids. You could always find her face. That changed when I was old enough to wear make-up. Dark eyeliner outlined around the eyes and the brush of blue eye-shadow made my eyes bigger. Touch of peach blush on the cheeks narrowed my face. Before drawing my face, I pasted the skin with an ivory skin-tone cream. Now I was painted in colors and shapes like the other girls did in the bathroom before every class period.

5   In the morning, my sisters and I crowded around the bathroom mirror, curling our hair and layering on the make-up. Dad would look at us frowning and say, "Asian girls shouldn't wear blue paint and red lipstick, and why do you perm your hair?" I immediately dismissed his scolding. What does he know about modern girls anyway? He doesn't know about America. Mom understood why we clustered in front of the mirror. She bought us the make-up and permed our hair.

6   Later, Mom didn't have time to play with my hair, so I let the curls go straight. My hair was back in proportion to my body and it looked like the women on the cover of Mom's Korean magazines. But I was surprised; the girls at school commented, "You have such pretty hair; I wish my hair was straight." Strangers compared my hair with silk and wanted to caress it.

7   Also, the highlights dimmed after several washes. Someone asked me, "How do you get your hair color to be so black? I tried coloring but it didn't come out right." A smile came over me knowing than an American girl admired and wanted what I had as an Asian.

8   A man at my father's store told me, "You have very pretty eyes." The compliment surprised me because of the jokes and the ridicule I had heard about slanty-thin oriental eyes. I threw away the blush; the broken eyeshadow was never replaced, and I washed the white skin off my face.

9   On the college applications I wrote Seung Hee Suh and checked off the box for *Asian/Islander*. "What a pretty name. It sounds like 'song.'" People loved repeating my name. They wanted to hear it roll off their tongue. "Seung. What a great name. What does it mean?" they asked. "Endurance, never giving up," I replied and they would say, "I wish my name had a meaning."

10   My younger sister Yun said to me once, "I used to be ashamed and embarrassed to be an Asian, but I'm so glad now that I'm different. I like that people remember me and I can stick out in the crowd. I am glad my name is Yun." In few words, she had summed up what I had gone through and my attitude from the experience. It brought me comfort to know that my insecurities and pride were shared.

Topics for Thinking and Writing

1. What words, images, and phrases suggest to you the topic of Suh's essay?
2. You might think of Suh's main idea as being expressed in this two-part form: First, I felt _____, but then I felt _____. What details in the essay support the two parts of this statement of the main idea?
3. Using a T organizer as a prewriting strategy, write a nutshell summary of Suh's essay.

4. Write a short essay about a time when you wanted to change something about yourself. Why did you want to make the change? What did you discover about yourself during the process of trying to change?

5. Summarize, in nutshell form, your essay about changing something about yourself.

BEAUTY AND THE BEAST OF ADVERTISING
JEAN KILBOURNE

"You're a Halston woman from the very beginning," the advertisement proclaims. The model stares provocatively at the viewer, her long blonde hair waving around her face, her bare chest partially covered by two curved bottles that give the illusion of breasts and a cleavage.

The average American is accustomed to blue-eyed blondes seductively touting a variety of products. In this case, however, the blonde is about five years old.

Advertising is an over $130 billion a year industry and affects all of us throughout our lives. We are each exposed to over 1,500 ads a day, constituting perhaps the most powerful educational force in society. The average adult will spend one and one-half years of his/her life watching television commercials. But the ads sell a great deal more than products. They sell values, images and concepts of success and worth, love and sexuality, popularity and normalcy. They tell us who we are and who we should be. Sometimes they sell addictions.

4   Advertising is the foundation and economic lifeblood of the mass media. The primary purpose of the mass media is to deliver an audience to advertisers.

Adolescents are particularly vulnerable, however, because they are new and inexperienced consumers and are the prime targets of many advertisements. They are in the process of learning their values and roles and developing their self-concepts. Most teenagers are sensitive to peer pressure and find it difficult to resist or even question the dominant cultural messages perpetuated and reinforced by the media. Mass communication has made possible a kind of nationally distributed peer pressure that erodes private and individual values and standards.

But what does society, and especially teenagers, learn from the advertising messages that proliferate in the mass media? On the most obvious level they learn the stereotypes. Advertising creates a mythical, WASP-oriented world in which no one is ever ugly, overweight, poor, struggling or disabled either physically or mentally (unless you count the housewives who talk to little men in toilet bowls). And it is a world in which people talk only about products.

Housewives or Sex Objects

The aspect of advertising most in need of analysis and change is the portrayal of women. Scientific studies and the most casual viewing yield the same conclusion: Women are shown almost exclusively as housewives or sex objects.

8   The housewife, pathologically obsessed by cleanliness and lemon-fresh scents, debates cleaning products and worries about her husband's "ring around the collar."

The sex object is a mannequin, a shell. Conventional beauty is her only attribute. She has no lines or wrinkles (which would indicate she had the bad taste and poor judgment to grow older), no scars, or blemishes—indeed, she has no pores. She is thin, generally tall and long-legged, and, above all, she is young. All "beautiful" women in advertisements (including minority women), regardless of product or audience, conform to this norm. Women are constantly exhorted to emulate this ideal, to feel ashamed and guilty if they fail, and to feel that their desirability and lovability are contingent upon physical perfection.

Creating Artificiality

The image is artificial and can only be achieved artificially (even the "natural look" requires much preparation and expense). Beauty is something that comes from without: more than one million dollars is spent every hour on cosmetics. Desperate to conform to an ideal and impossible standard, many women go to great lengths to manipulate and change their faces and bodies. A woman is conditioned to view her face as a mask and her body as an object, as *things* separate from and more important than her real self, constantly in need of alteration, improvement, and disguise. She is made to feel dissatisfied with and ashamed of herself, whether she tries to achieve "the look" or not. Objectified constantly by others, she learns to objectify herself. (It is interesting to note that one in five college-age women have an eating disorder.)

"When *Glamour* magazine surveyed its readers in 1984, 75 percent felt too heavy and only 15 percent felt just right. Nearly half of those who were actually underweight reported feeling too fat and wanting to diet. Among a sample of college women, 40 percent felt overweight when only 12 percent actually were too heavy," according to Rita Freedman in her book *Beauty Bound*.

12   There is evidence that this preoccupation with weight begins at ever-earlier ages for women. According to a recent article in *New Age Journal*, "even grade-school girls are succumbing to stick-like standards of beauty enforced by a relentless parade of wasp-waisted fashion models, movie stars and pop idols." A study by a University of California professor showed that nearly 80 percent of fourth-grade girls in the Bay Area are watching their weight.

A recent *Wall Street Journal* survey of students in four Chicago-area schools found that more than half the fourth-grade girls were dieting and three-quarters felt they were overweight. One student said, "We don't expect boys to be that handsome. We take them as they are." Another added, "But boys expect girls to be perfect and beautiful. And skinny."

Dr. Steven Levenkron, author of *The Best Little Girl in the World*, the story of an anorexic, says his blood pressure soars every time he opens a magazine and finds an ad for women's fashions. "If I had my way," he said, "every one of them would have to carry a line saying, 'Caution: This model may be hazardous to your health.'"

Women are also dismembered in commercials, their bodies separated into parts in need of change or improvement. If a woman has "acceptable" breasts, then she must also be sure that her legs are worth watching, her hips slim, her feet sexy, and that her buttocks looks nude under her clothes ("like I'm not wearin' nothin'").

16   This image is difficult and costly to achieve and impossible to maintain—no one is flawless and everyone ages. Growing older is the great taboo. Woman are encouraged to remain little girls ("because innocence is sexier than you think"), to be passive and dependent, never to mature. The contradictory message—"sensual, but not too far from innocence"—places women in a double bind: somehow we are supposed to be both sexy and virginal, experienced and naïve, seductive and chaste. The disparagement of maturity is, of course, insulting and frustrating to adult women, and the implication that little girls are seductive is dangerous to real children.

Influencing Sexual Attitudes

Young people also learn a great deal about sexual attitudes from the media and from advertising in particular. Advertising's approach to sex is pornographic: it reduces people to objects and de-emphasizes human contact and individuality. This reduction of sexuality to a dirty joke and of people to objects is the real obscenity of the culture. Although the sexual sell, overt and subliminal, is at a fevered pitch in most commercials, there is at the same time a notable absence of sex as an important and profound human activity.

There have been some changes in the images of women. Indeed, a "new woman" has emerged in commercials in recent years. She is generally presented as superwoman, who manages to do all the work at home and on the job (with the help of a product, of course, not of her husband or children or friends), or as the liberated woman, who owes her independence and self-esteem to the products she uses. These new images do not represent any real progress but rather create a myth of progress, an illusion that reduces complex sociopolitical problems to mundane personal ones.

Advertising images do not cause these problems, but they contribute to them by creating a climate in which the marketing of women's bodies—the sexual sell and dismemberment, distorted body image ideal and children as sex objects—is seen as acceptable.

20   This is the real tragedy, that many women internalize these stereotypes and learn their "limitations," thus establishing a self-fulfilling prophecy. If one accepts these mythical and degrading images, to some extent one actualizes them. By remaining unaware of the profound seriousness of the ubiquitous influence, the redundant message and the subliminal impact of advertisements, we ignore one of the most powerful "educational" forces in the culture—one that greatly affects our self-images, our ability to relate to each other, and effectively destroys awareness and action that might help to change that climate.

Topics for Thinking and Writing

1. Using your own words, state the thesis of Kilbourne's essay.
2. In paragraphs 11 through 14, Kilbourne refers to statistics from published sources. Which of these statistics would you include in a summary? Explain your choice.

3. Identify some nonobjective, emotional words and phrases that Kilbourne uses.

4. This essay is divided into four main sections. What is the purpose of each section? Write a one-sentence summary of each of the four sections.

5. Write an objective nutshell summary of the essay.

"OUT, OUT—"
ROBERT FROST

The buzz saw snarled and rattled in the yard
And made dust and dropped stove-length sticks of wood,
Sweet-scented stuff when the breeze drew across it.
And from there those that lifted eyes could count
5   Five mountain ranges one behind the other
Under the sunset far into Vermont.
And the saw snarled and rattled, snarled and rattled,
As it ran light, or had to bear a load.
And nothing happened: day was all but done.
10   Call it a day, I wish they might have said
To please the boy by giving him the half hour
That a boy counts so much when saved from work.
His sister stood beside them in her apron
To tell them "Supper." At the word, the saw,
15   As if to prove saws knew what supper meant,
Leaped out at the boy's hand, or seemed to leap—
He must have given the hand. However it was,
Neither refused the meeting. But the hand!
The boy's first outcry was a rueful laugh,
20   As he swung toward them holding up the hand,
Half in appeal, but half as if to keep
The life from spilling. Then the boy saw all—
Since he was old enough to know, big boy
Doing a man's work, though a child at heart—
25   He saw all spoiled: "Don't let him cut my hand off—
The doctor, when he comes, Don't let him, sister!"
So. But the hand was gone already.
The doctor put him in the dark of ether.
He lay and puffed his lips out with his breath.
30   And then—the watcher at his pulse took fright.
No one believed. They listened at his heart.
Little—less—nothing!—and that ended it.
No more to build on there. And they, since they
Were not the one dead, turned to their affairs.

Topics for Thinking and Writing

1. What is the topic of the poem?
2. What are the possible theses of the poem?
3. The speaker of the poem is summarizing the event for his audience. What details does he present? What do you think the speaker wants us to know by presenting us the story with these details? Why?
4. How does the arrangement of the details affect the reader's response to the poem?
5. Is the speaker's summary of the event objective?
6. Write a one-paragraph nutshell summary of the poem.
7. Write a summary of an event which evoked strong emotion in you. Your summary should include the main idea and the essential details. Remember to write with objectivity.

THE TELEPHONE CALL
FLEUR ADCOCK

They asked me 'Are you sitting down?
Right? This is Universal Lotteries',
they said. 'You've won the top prize,
the Ultra-super Global Special.
5   What would you do with a million pounds?
Or, actually, with more than a million—
not that it makes a lot of difference
once you're a millionaire.' And they laughed.

'Are you OK?' they asked—'Still there?
10   Come on, now, tell us, how does it feel?'
I said 'I just … I can't believe it!'
They said 'That's what they all say.
What else? Go on, tell us about it.'
I said 'I feel the top of my head
15   has floated off, out through the window,
revolving like a flying saucer.'

'That's unusual' they said. 'Go on.'
I said 'I'm finding it hard to talk.
My throat's gone dry, my nose is tingling.
20   I think I'm going to sneeze—or cry.'
'That's right' they said, 'don't be ashamed
of giving way to your emotions.
It isn't every day you hear
you're going to get a million pounds.

25 Relax, now, have a little cry;
    we'll give you a moment …' 'Hang on!' I said.
    'I haven't bought a lottery ticket
    for years and years. And what did you say
    the company's called?' They laughed again.
30 'Not to worry about a ticket.
    We're Universal. We operate
    a Retrospective Chances Module.

    Nearly everyone's bought a ticket
    in some lottery or another,
35 once at least. We buy up the files,
    feed the names into our computer,
    and see who the lucky person is.'
    'Well, that's incredible' I said.
    'It's marvellous. I still can't quite …
40 I'll believe it when I see the cheque.'

    'Oh,' they said, 'there's no cheque.'
    'But the money?' 'We don't deal in money.
    Experiences are what we deal in.
    You've had a great experience, right?
45 Exciting? Something you'll remember?
    That's your prize. So congratulations
    from all of us at Universal.
    Have a nice day!' And the line went dead.

Topics for Thinking and Writing

1. Summarize the story told in the poem.
2. Think about an unexpected event that occurred in your own life. Write a brief summary of your initial reaction to that event and a brief summary of how you felt later when reflecting on it.
3. In a group, develop a list of the good and bad aspects of receiving a telephone call like the one that the poem's speaker receives.
4. How do you think you would feel if the events in the poem happened to you? How would you describe those feelings to someone else?
5. Write an account of a time when you did something to cheer someone else up. How did the person respond to you?

THE STORY OF AN HOUR
KATE CHOPIN

1 Knowing that Mrs. Mallard was afflicted with a heart trouble, great care was taken to break to her as gently as possible the news of her husband's death.

2   It was her sister Josephine who told her, in broken sentences, veiled hints that revealed in half concealing. Her husband's friend Richards was there, too, near her. It was he who had been in the newspaper office when intelligence of the railroad disaster was received, with Brently Mallard's name leading the list of "killed." He had only taken the time to assure himself of its truth by a second telegram, and had hastened to forestall any less careful, less tender friend in bearing the sad message.

3   She did not hear the story as many women have heard the same, with a paralyzed inability to accept its significance. She wept at once, with sudden, wild abandonment, in her sister's arms. When the storm of grief had spent itself she went away to her room alone. She would have no one follow her.

4   There stood, facing the open window, a comfortable, roomy armchair. Into this she sank, pressed down by a physical exhaustion that haunted her body and seemed to reach into her soul.

5   She could see in the open square before her house the tops of trees that were all aquiver with the new spring life. The delicious breath of rain was in the air. In the street below a peddler was crying his wares. The notes of a distant song which some one was singing reached her faintly, and countless sparrows were twittering in the eaves.

6   There were patches of blue sky showing here and there through the clouds that had met and piled above the other in the west facing her window.

7   She sat with her head thrown back upon the cushion of the chair quite motionless, except when a sob came up into her throat and shook her, as a child who has cried itself to sleep continues to sob in its dreams.

8   She was young, with a fair, calm face, whose lines bespoke repression and even a certain strength. But now there was a dull stare in her eyes, whose gaze was fixed away off yonder on one of those patches of blue sky. It was not a glance of reflection, but rather indicated a suspension of intelligent thought.

9   There was something coming to her and she was waiting for it, fearfully. What was it? She did not know; it was too subtle and elusive to name. But she felt it, creeping out of the sky, reaching toward her through the sounds, the scents, the color that filled the air.

10   Now her bosom rose and fell tumultuously. She was beginning to recognize this thing that was approaching to possess her, and she was striving to beat it back with her will—as powerless as her two white slender hands would have been.

11   When she abandoned herself a little whispered word escaped her slightly parted lips. She said it over and over under her breath: "Free, free, free!" The vacant stare and the look of terror that had followed it went from her eyes. They stayed keen and bright. Her pulses beat fast, and the coursing blood warmed and relaxed every inch of her body.

12   She did not stop to ask if it were not a monstrous joy that held her. A clear and exalted perception enabled her to dismiss the suggestion as trivial.

13   She knew that she would weep again when she saw the kind, tender hands folded in death; the face that had never looked save with love upon her, fixed and gray and dead. But she saw beyond that bitter moment a long procession of years to come that would belong to her absolutely. And she opened and spread her arms out to them in welcome.

14   There would be no one to live for her during those coming years; she would live for herself. There would be no powerful will bending her in that blind persistence with which men and women believe they have a right to impose a private will upon a fellow creature. A kind intention or a cruel intention made the act seem no less a crime as she looked upon it in that brief moment of illumination.

15   And yet she had loved him—sometimes. Often she had not. What did it matter! What could love, the unsolved mystery, count for in face of this possession of self-assertion which she suddenly recognized as the strongest impulse of her being.

16   "Free! Body and soul free!" she kept whispering.

17   Josephine was kneeling before the closed door with her lips to the keyhole, imploring for admission. "Louise, open the door! I beg; open the door—you will make yourself ill. What are you doing, Louise? For heaven's sake open the door."

18   "Go away. I am not making myself ill." No; she was drinking in a very elixir of life through that open window.

19   Her fancy was running riot along those days ahead of her. Spring days, and summer days, and all sorts of days that would be her own. She breathed a quick prayer that life might be long. It was only yesterday she had thought with a shudder that life might be long.

20   She arose at length and opened the door to her sister's importunities. There was a feverish triumph in her eyes, and she carried herself unwittingly like a goddess of Victory. She clasped her sister's waist, and together they descended the stairs. Richards stood waiting for them at the bottom.

21   Some one was opening the front door with a latchkey. It was Brently Mallard who entered, a little travel-stained, composedly carrying his gripsack and umbrella. He had been far from the scene of accident, and did not even know there had been one. He stood amazed at Josephine's piercing cry; at Richards' quick motion to screen him from the view of his wife.

22   But Richards was too late.

23   When the doctors came they said she had died of heart disease—of joy that kills.

Topics for Thinking and Writing

1. Write a one-sentence thesis statement which characterizes the marriage of Mrs. Mallard and her husband. Which lines from the story support your thesis? Now, write a one-paragraph summary of the marriage, incorporating two quotations from the story.
2. Before Mrs. Mallard cries, "Free, free, free," she looks out her window. What does she see? What do these images represent? How do the images lead to her cries about freedom?
3. Throughout the story a number of things happen which are the opposite of what we would expect in the situation. These "opposites" are called *ironies*. Identify the ironies in the story and write a paragraph summarizing your ideas.
4. Write a nutshell summary of the story for an audience of suspense lovers.
5. Write an outline summary of the story that you could use as a study guide for an upcoming exam.
6. Write a one-paragraph summary of how you would go about identifying the theme of this story.

Self-Assessment

Reread your self-assessment from the beginning of the chapter and answer the following questions.

What would I now change?

What do I now know about writing summaries?

Evaluating Writing/ Writing to Evaluate

8

A MEAL AT A FAST-FOOD STAND
YOUR MOM'S HOME COOKING
DINNER AT A GOURMET RESTAURANT

You can easily identify some of the distinctions among these eating experiences and the ways in which you evaluate and respond to each. You might enjoy fast food because of its convenience, particularly when you are in a hurry. You know you can count on the food's being the same at any stand of its kind. You aren't looking for a gourmand's delight but rather for quick service and a basic meal.

Although you might also respond to your mom's cooking in this way because of its familiarity, the quality of sameness is different from that of the offerings at the fast-food stand. With mom's cooking, there are emotional connections to earlier times when that meal was served. It's the freshness of the ingredients that you know she uses because you've been shopping with her. It's the particular care she takes in creating flavors that she knows will appeal to her family. And it's the sense of the tradition associated with her meals that makes them emotionally appealing to you. You are responding to the meal with emotion rather than with reason.

On the other hand, you are more likely to respond to a dinner at a gourmet restaurant with reason rather than emotion. Because of the prices and the complex combination of ingredients, you anticipate that the meal will be technically superb. You expect the food to offer fresh, original tastes presented with flair and excellence. You expect the service to be thoughtful and attentive.

In each of the previous examples, you have used your **evaluative** abilities. You have established standards by which you have judged the success of each dining experience. The standards, or criteria, for evaluation have differed with each situation and have been based on what makes sense for the situation. Just as you would not expect the meal at a fast-food restaurant to resemble a meal at your mother's or at a four-star restaurant, you likewise wouldn't judge them in the same way.

Just as you respond to what you eat, you also respond to what you read. You may respond emotionally, rationally, or in both ways. The reading may excite you. It may bore you. It may tell you something you did not know. It may show you something in a way that you have never before experienced. Unlike eating, however—when merely responding is enough—when you read, your job is not only to read but also to evaluate the reading.

Does the piece accomplish what the writer intended it to do? Is the writing appropriate for its intended audience? What is the main idea or thesis of the piece? Is that idea well supported by convincing examples? These are some of the questions that you, as a reader, should ask to establish the standards which you will use to evaluate the reading.

In similar fashion, as a writer, you often have to provide written answers to these questions. Also, as a writer, you will have to be able to evaluate your own writing. Learning how to evaluate writing—your own and others'—is important because in college you will be asked to write evaluations of readings and ideas. These evaluations may become a critical part of your writing and research. This chapter discusses these two important skills: reading to evaluate and writing evaluations.

Self-Assessment

Reading is an effort to bridge the gap between the mind of the reader and the mind of the writer. Reading is a lot harder than it appears to the casual observer. There are many approaches to reading, and everyone reads differently. Mortimer Adler, an editor of the Great Books series, believed that one should never read without a pen in hand to jot reactions in the margins. Yet other readers never mark a book.

What do *you* do when you read? If you are a careful reader, you should ask yourself these questions:

What do I already know about this?

What do I think of this?

Why is the writer telling me this?

The first two questions address what the reader already knows and is thinking. The third addresses what the reader imagines that the writer is thinking. This question is difficult to answer because it requires that the reader analyze the writer's thinking. It is not possible to be wrong about what you yourself are thinking, but it's not always easy to be right about somebody else's intentions. However, if your reading has been careful, there is a helpful "half-way" question that you can ask to bridge the gap between reader and writer: How has the writer influenced me so that I feel the way that I do?

As you answer the following, think about a type of reading you would find interesting.

1. When I'm reading, I identify the author's biases by looking for

2. When I'm reading, I decide that a thesis statement is strong if

3. When I'm reading, I identify the writer's purpose and audience by looking for

4. When I'm reading, I decide that the writer's examples are effective if they

What I know about reading to evaluate:	What I need to know about reading to evaluate:
What I know about writing evaluations:	What I need to know about writing evaluations:

Working Alone: Describe a science fiction film, romantic comedy, or action movie that you have recently seen. How would you evaluate this film as compared with others like it?

Working Together: Exchange papers with a classmate. Does your classmate have a carefully developed thesis and strong supporting examples? Write a quick evaluation of your peer's paper.

Responding to a Text: The Emotional and the Rational

People respond in two ways to what they read: emotionally and rationally. An emotional response is completely personal. It is based on your feelings about what you have read. A rational response may also be personal, but it is always evaluative because it's based on your thinking about the ideas that the writer hopes to convey and your weighing them to determine their validity and impact.

Since an emotional response to a text is purely personal, there is no "right" or "wrong" way to respond. However, an emotional response does not evaluate a piece of writing based upon its merits; it simply records how you felt about the piece.

Hundreds of thousands of people root for the Chicago Cubs or the Boston Red Sox every year because they have an emotional connection to the team. However, very few of them would make a rational claim that they support the most successful team in baseball. Similarly, it is possible for you to have an emotional connection to a piece of writing that—rationally—almost everyone else thinks is terrible—a poem from a loved one, for example. You may still enjoy the piece of writing because you have a pleasant emotional reaction to it, but that alone does not make the piece good writing.

Working Alone: Select a piece of writing or music or a painting which you like that conveys a powerful emotion for you. Describe your feelings about the work.

A rational response considers the writer's effectiveness by identifying the thesis and by evaluating the evidence and any arguments used to support the thesis. Making a rational evaluation means that you cannot criticize the author's position simply because you disagree with it. You must evaluate it based upon the logic and examples used to develop the thesis. Does the piece achieve what it set out to do?

In order to make a rational response to a piece of writing, you must evaluate it through both reading and writing.

Working Alone: Using the piece of writing or music or the painting that you chose for the previous exercise, write a short evaluation of it, concentrating on the technical merits of the piece instead of on the reasons why you like it.

Working Alone: Read the following two excerpts from music reviews of the same CD recording. How do they differ? Identify language used in each that makes the piece either emotional or rational.

> Anyone who comes away from The New Riders of the Apocalypse's newest release in a happy frame of mind needs to have that mind examined! The music is a terrible embarrassment: The melodies are childish, the lyrics lame, the vocals childish, and the musicianship just plain sloppy. I found myself imagining that I was caught in a time-warp, trapped in a garish 70s discotheque without my white polyester suit.

> The band's latest release suffers from a lack of strong material and the fresh musical ideas expected from a band of this caliber. The lyrics are too reminiscent of selections on the band's previous CDs. Even when the songs try to capture the live feel of a dance club, the musicianship is inconsistent, leaving this reviewer with the conviction that the group should have waited longer and rehearsed more to be sure that the material was up to the standard they set with last year's chart-topping *Valley of the Shadow.*

Writing an Evaluation

Writing an evaluation helps you clarify your ideas as you think about an experience or material that you have read. Often you write to **critique** what you read, as you might do for a literature course if you are asked to write a paper on a short story you've read. To critique, in this sense, doesn't mean to "criticize" or to find fault—though you certainly may negatively assess something. Instead, it refers to evaluating a text's strengths and weaknesses. This is similar to evaluating experiences you have had in other areas of your life. You might critique a film or a piece of music, for example, or evaluate a meal you have eaten in the college dining hall or in a fine restaurant.

Whenever you critique or evaluate something—whether it's a CD, a sporting event, a class, or a meal—you evaluate by using standards—or **criteria**—that apply to the situation. For example, if you were evaluating an Arnold Schwarzenegger movie, you'd probably use criteria related to action films. If you were evaluating the latest Julia Roberts film, you'd likely use criteria related to romantic comedies. Similarly, you establish criteria for evaluating a piece of writing.

When you are *reading* to evaluate, you are assessing the author's thesis, biases, examples, purpose, and audience. When you *write* an evaluation based on your reading of these elements—the **author's thesis, biases, examples, purpose,** and **audience**—they form the foundation stones of your evaluation. However, before you can begin to evaluate a piece of writing—your own or someone else's—you will need to find the foundation stones.

Foundation Stones of Evaluation

1. **Look for the main idea or thesis.**
2. **Find the biases.**
3. **Weigh the examples.**
4. **Identify the audience.**
5. **Assess the purpose.**

Chapter 7 discusses summary and introduces you to two of the foundation stones of evaluation. Writing summaries is a good way to capture main ideas and to distinguish between essential and nonessential supporting examples and details. Once you have produced a summary, you can begin to assess the strengths and weaknesses of the reading which you have summarized. The summary is also useful in helping you identify the remaining foundation stones of evaluation.

You will assess the same foundation stones when you evaluate your own writing. A key idea emphasized in this book and in this class is that writing is a process. Part of that process involves conducting an ongoing dialogue with yourself, asking questions and thereby evaluating your own writing. As a writer, you need to remember that your writing will be read by other people. Your assumptions about your audience and your purpose affect decisions about style and content. Likewise, knowing the biases you bring to your writing can help you present your ideas fairly.

Look for the Thesis: What Is the Author Saying?

Often the answer to the question "What is the author saying?" will be found in the thesis statement. For example, here is an excerpt from William Raspberry's essay "The Handicap of Definition":

I know all about bad schools, mean politicians, economics, deprivation, and racism. Still, it occurs to me that one of the heaviest burdens black Americans—and black children in particular—have to bear is the handicap of definition: the question of what it means to be black.

Raspberry's main idea, or his thesis, is found both in the title and in the second sentence of the opening paragraph. You may disagree with his assertion that the heaviest burden is one of definition, but to rationally and critically evaluate the essay, you must put your disagreement aside and focus on how well Raspberry presents his case for this thesis. To be convincing, he will need to cite specific examples of how definition is a handicap and how it particularly burdens children.

Once you know what the thesis of a passage is, you will be able to evaluate the idea on its own terms, not on whether or not you agree with it. As with summary, when evaluating a piece of writing, you are not agreeing or disagreeing with the thesis statement; you are simply identifying it. Later, you will determine whether the author has adequately supported the thesis.

Working Alone: Select a brief magazine article on a subject with which you are familiar. Then identify the thesis of the piece. Do the same for an article about a subject with which you are unfamiliar. Next, read both articles and write brief summaries of them.

Find the Bias: What Is the Writer's Personal View?

In addition to locating the main idea, finding out what the writer thinks about the main idea will help you to identify any bias in the writing. Bias is not necessarily bad; everybody has biases. Bias is the preexisting opinion of the author. For example, someone might be biased toward living in a small town rather than in a big city. This bias could be the result of positive experiences the person had while living in a small town. As John Mellencamp sings in "Small Town," he prefers small towns because he does not know enough about cities to judge them. This is his bias. It's not "against" anything and does not claim to be better or more important than anyone else's bias. It is simply the angle from which Mellencamp tells his story.

However, bias can affect the way in which an author writes. Both the writer's own biases and her assumptions about the audience's biases can influence her word choice, selection of examples, and purpose in writing. You might ask questions about the author's background, her interests, or her expertise on the particular topic. Although you may need to do some research to answer these questions, the answers may help you become more aware of the author's bias.

It's important to identify bias in order to begin thinking about the examples that support the thesis. Are the examples appropriate? Do they cover all of the points, or are parts of the argument not illustrated? How are the examples used? For instance, if an author is writing about the death penalty and supports it, he might use the example of the state of Texas, where the reintroduction of the death penalty has coincided with a decrease in the number of murders committed. The implication is that the reintroduction of the death penalty has caused the decline in the murder rate.

However, an author opposed to the death penalty might instead use Massachusetts as an example and point out that although the state does not have a death penalty, the number of murders committed there has decreased over the past few years. This example would seem to suggest that the death penalty does not affect the murder rate.

If you have identified the authors' biases—one in favor of the death penalty, the other opposed—you are now able to see why they used the examples that they did, and you can question whether either is giving you all of the facts.

To continue with this example, you would probably be more impressed by a writer with a bias who is careful to present the other side's key statistics and then explain why those figures don't necessarily prove what they seem to assert. The writer favoring the death penalty might deal with the case of Massachusetts by pointing out that the state has traditionally had a low murder rate, so any decline in the rate is statistically not as important as, say, the decline in the Texas murder rate. Similarly, the opponent of the death penalty might discuss economic factors in Texas, such as the rise in employment rates, to suggest that the decline in the murder rate may be linked only coincidentally to the reintroduction of the death penalty.

It is still up to you, the reader, to evaluate whether or not an argument is effective, but, by recognizing an author's bias, you are alert to the question of whether the idea being discussed is incomplete or detailed and thoughtfully developed.

Checklist for Finding the Biases

In order to effectively check for bias in writing, ask yourself the following questions as you read:

1. **What assumptions is the author making about the thesis/main idea?**
2. **What assumptions is the author making about the audience?**
3. **Does the author use words that are strongly emotional or value-laden?**
4. **What details does the author present to support the assumptions?**

Working Together: In a small group, read aloud a newspaper or magazine editorial. What are the biases that shape the writing? As a reader aware of bias, what would you wish to see the writer do differently to better make the case? Why?

Working Alone: Find a newspaper editorial or opinion piece with which you disagree. Evaluate the piece and then use your evaluation to demonstrate the strengths of the writing.

Weigh the Examples: Do They Provide Support?

After you have identified the main idea and found the biases, the next question to ask is whether the writer uses strong, reliable examples to support the main idea. For example, in the debate over the effects of second-hand smoke, there are two camps. One believes that second-hand smoke is dangerous and can lead to illnesses that can kill even nonsmokers. The other side argues that there is no scientific proof that second-hand smoke is harmful and that the opposition to smoking in public is depriving smokers of their rights. Neither of these positions is anything more than a statement of bias. You can only determine which has validity and which does not by examining the examples that each writer would use to support his or her case.

Evaluating writing does not necessarily involve deciding whether a writer is "right" or "wrong." More often, it involves deciding whether the writer has made a strong case. Consequently, in addition to the ideas and biases that the writer uses when developing a piece of writing, the examples that support her point of view are also crucial.

In the case of the second-hand smoke debate, those examples might include details such as scientific studies, actuarial tables, and testimony from individuals and experts. Remember, however, the writer's choice of examples may reflect bias. Examples from experts such as the American Medical Association will be more reliable than the statement of a friend. Also, consider how current the data presented are. Statistics from long ago may not be relevant in the present situation. As a reader, one thing you should look for is the amount of attention the writer gives to explaining the methods by which the data were obtained. You should also examine the care with which the writer demonstrates why the examples support the case.

Generally, the better the writer explains the connection between the examples and the main idea, the stronger the idea. The more powerful the evidence, the more carefully the writer will demonstrate its pertinence.

Checklist for Weighing the Examples

To effectively check for valid examples in writing, ask yourself the following questions as you read:

1. Is the relationship between a point and an example explained? (If not, why is the example included?)
2. If a comparison is being made, is the comparison valid? (Remember, comparing apples to oranges may be useless.)
3. Is the example from a reliable source?
4. Is the example current?

Evaluating Web Sites

Evaluating sources you have found on the Internet requires asking yourself additional questions besides those listed in the Examples Checklist. Consider the following:

1. Who created the web site? Is the web site owner named? If so, does he or she have a contact address listed?
2. Is the web site associated with an educational, government, or public institution?
3. Is the web site associated with a private or commercial organization?
4. Is the organization with which the web site is associated reputable?
5. Is the web site an advertisement?
6. How recently was the information on the web site updated?

Working Alone:

1. Find a web page on a topic that interests you. In writing, evaluate the web page's thesis statement, bias, and examples. Then answer the additional web site questions previously listed.
2. In light of the evaluation, what changes would you make if you were in charge of the web page? Why would you make these changes?

Identify the Audience: For Whom Is the Piece Written?

Lastly, you should consider the audience of the piece of writing which you are evaluating as well as the audience for your written evaluation. You can determine the audience for the *writing* by examining the title, word choice, sentence structure, and examples that the writer uses. What does the writer assume about the audience's background knowledge of the topic? Are those assumptions appropriate?

When you are writing an *evaluation* of a work, it is likewise important to identify *your* audience. For instance, if your audience knows a lot about the subject of the piece of writing which you are evaluating, you might want to be specific in your references to the strengths and weaknesses of the piece. However, if your audience is unfamiliar with the general topic, you might want to explain why you are making your particular assessment.

Imagine, for example, that you are evaluating an article about new space station technology for a professor of astronomy or physics. Since your audience is likely to be well informed about the topic, part of your evaluation could be a passage like this one:

> Alison Sneider's effective article relies in particular upon the excellent earlier work of Morgan and Webster. She painstakingly develops the argument of both of these pioneer researchers to explain how the basic frame of a living section need not be reinforced to compensate for the necessary centrifugal forces. Her thorough summary of their work should prove helpful to those with some prior knowledge in the field. Her understanding of Morgan's views is especially strong, and she uses Webster's ideas about the relatively benign nature of the space environment imaginatively, if not fully convincingly.

The previous evaluation assumes that the reader knows what "centrifugal forces" are and why they are necessary. The writer also assumes that the reader is familiar with Morgan's and Webster's "pioneer" research. The use of words like *compensate* and *benign* suggests an educated reader.

If the reader of your evaluation is unfamiliar with the subject you are writing about—or has a different level of education—you will need to explain the basis of your evaluation more carefully:

> Alison Sneider deals with one of the major worries facing the designers of the space station: in order to create a place that will allow astronauts to live and work comfortably, just how strong does the frame of the living section need to be to withstand the pressures created as it spins in space? She highlights the most essential aspects of an essay by Morgan which discusses the stresses that could build up around the

joints of the living section. Sneider also uses his demonstration of the stress to convincingly show that, with a few modifications to basic designs, much lighter material can be used. She also insightfully uses Webster's work on the cumulative effects of the pinpricks created by the hundreds of miniature meteors that will hit the space station to try to show that lighter material will not be a danger to astronauts because of these collisions. Although the language of both Morgan and Webster is technical and hard to understand, Sneider's writing is clear and easy to understand.

The previous evaluation explains centrifugal force and the work of both Morgan and Webster in order to help the reader grasp ideas which may not be familiar.

Working Alone: Select an article on a topic with which you are familiar. Write two evaluations, one for an audience which is unfamiliar with the topic and one for an audience which knows it well.

Working Together: With a peer, discuss the differences between the two evaluations you have each written. What are the specific differences? How do the differences demonstrate an awareness of audience?

Assess the Purpose: Is It Achieved?

As readers, we all sometimes make the mistake of assuming that writing that is about topics we find interesting is good writing and writing about other topics is not so good. In truth, writing is good if it accomplishes its writer's purpose.

Once you have identified the thesis of the piece of writing which you are evaluating, the writer's bias, and the examples which support the thesis, you must now consider the purpose of the piece. What did the writer intend to do by writing this piece? Was it meant to inform? To persuade? To entertain? Was the purpose achieved?

Chapter 3 suggests that all writing is done with a purpose in mind. One of the ways in which you judge the effectiveness of writing—your own and others'—is to determine whether the purpose has been achieved.

If the writer's purpose was to inform, you can ask yourself if you have learned anything new from the piece. If the intent was to persuade, have you been convinced by the author? If the purpose was to entertain, were you amused by the piece? Can you cite particular word choices and examples that helped you discover the purpose of the writing?

Read the following passage to determine its purpose. Then explain what aspects of the piece helped you make your decision.

Women writers were the best-selling authors of the mid-nineteenth century in America. In fact, Nathaniel Hawthorne accused these "damn'd scribbling women" of thwarting the opportunity for male authors to make a decent living. These prolific women thought of themselves as professionals, not as artists. Their personal goals were to help support their families through their writings. They were interested in encouraging the women who read them to find their inner strengths, to overcome obstacles, and to live harmonious, helpful lives. Their fiction often told the story of the young girl forced to make her own way in a world that was hostile to her. Through this journey, she learned to rely on moral courage, her intelligence, and the friendship of other women. Female readers of the day were inspired by these "scribbling" women to examine their lives and to make what subtle changes they could. The most well-loved of the day were Fanny Fern, Susan Warner, and, of course, Harriet Beecher Stowe, the renowned author of *Uncle Tom's Cabin*.

The previous piece is about American women writers of the nineteenth century. Its basic purpose is to inform the audience of the goals and success of these women writers. As you evaluate the piece, ask yourself: Has the writing accomplished what it says it will do? Have I learned something new from it? Since its purpose is to inform, you shouldn't fault it for failing to amuse or persuade you. Rather, you should expect it to clearly and straightforwardly present its information.

Working Alone: Read a front-page article in a newspaper and then answer these questions: What was the purpose of the article? How effective was the writer in achieving the purpose? What strategies did the writer use to achieve the purpose? Use the Purpose Checklist first introduced in Chapter 3 and presented again here with a few changes:

Purpose Checklist

When checking for purpose in writing, ask yourself the following questions as you read:

What is the author's purpose for writing this piece?

What should the audience know, feel, or think after reading the piece?

What choices has the writer made to cause the readers' reactions to the piece?

Working Together: Working in a group, create a short list of popular television shows. Then identify the main purpose of each—to get laughs, to inform, to stimulate ideas, and so on—and name ways in which each show achieves (or fails to achieve) this purpose.

Return to the three dining experiences described at the beginning of this chapter. For you to evaluate them fairly, it's important to remember that you are, in effect, doing a "blind taste test"—that is, you are considering them based upon criteria that you have established: flavor, quality of ingredients, service, and so on. Certainly you may have an emotional reaction to any one of the experiences—who is going to knock Mom's cooking?—but you must leave that out if you're going to be objective in your evaluation.

Likewise, when you are reading to evaluate, it's important to remember that you are considering the work rationally, *not* emotionally. It doesn't matter whether you personally agree with the argument or not. What you are doing is determining whether the writer has made the argument well, based upon the previously mentioned criteria—the main idea, the bias, the examples, the purpose, and the audience.

You have probably already noticed that the questions you've asked when preparing your evaluation also offer you a plan for the structure of your written evaluation. An evaluation can usually be developed in this pattern:

Author, title, year

Author's main idea/thesis

Author's bias

Examples

Audience

Purpose

Very often, *you* will be the reader of your own evaluation, as when you are preparing notes for a research paper. Your evaluation will tell you how well you have understood the original piece and therefore will be a helpful tool for learning. However, you still have to think about what you know about the subject and write your evaluation accordingly. Don't forget that you will probably use your evaluation when you are busy writing the longer project of which it might become a part. You may be too busy to remember the full details of the work that you are evaluating, so your evaluation must make sense to you on its own.

Working Together:

1. In a group, discuss how a written evaluation of a piece of writing differs from a summary of the same writing.
2. Discuss with a peer how well the foundation stones for evaluating writing apply to other media. For example, would you evaluate a movie or a web page in the same way? Why or why not? Make a list of similarities and/or differences.

Working Alone: Take a summary which you wrote for the previous chapter and turn it into an evaluation. What changes did you make? Why?

The hardest writing to evaluate is your own. It's difficult to see the gaps, the mistakes, and the assumptions you have made because you are so familiar with the work. But you have honed your critical skills by evaluating others' writing and by writing those evaluations. You can now apply the same foundations of evaluation to your own work. Therefore, you should evaluate your own writing, just as you would evaluate other people's. Ask yourself:

Have I clearly stated my thesis?

What are my biases?

Do I provide strong and valid details and examples?

Do I have a clear sense of my audience?

Do I achieve my stated purpose?

After you have let a piece of your own writing sit for a few days so that you have had time to achieve some distance from it, reread it as if it were someone else's work. Identify the main idea or thesis. Is this what you intended to say? Recognize the bias that you brought to the work. For example, if you are writing about field hockey, you might have assumed that it's a sport for women. However, after reading more about it, you may have discovered that in some countries, it's a major men's sport with professional leagues and highly successful national teams. How has your bias affected your writing? Don't forget to consider the biases of your readers. In this country, your readers would be surprised to read a paper about men's field hockey. Did you take that fact into account?

What examples do you use? Are they the best that you could find—or just the ones you happened to remember? Do you explain how the examples support your thesis? What could be done to make the examples even more useful? And finally, does your piece succeed in fulfilling its purpose? How? Or if it doesn't, why not?

A Final Note

Remembering the foundation stones of evaluation and bringing them to each piece of writing that you do strengthens both your writing skills and your self-assessment skills. Of course, evaluating your own work is often harder than evaluating someone else's, but if you have been careful to ask yourself what you were doing during each stage of your work—and why you were doing it—you have already done much of the evaluation that goes into making a piece of writing successful.

Other readers will be evaluating your work, whether formally or not. You owe it to yourself to evaluate your own work first. The better you evaluate your own work, the better others will judge your writing to be.

Suggestions for Writing

1. Select two advertisements for the same product that appear in or on different media (for example, in a daily newspaper and on the radio, or on the Internet and on TV). Why are the two advertisements different? How effective are they? Why?

2. Imagine that you have been assigned to design a questionnaire that asks fellow students their opinions about their educational experiences at your college. What questions would you ask? Why?

3. Write a book, music, or film review for your school newspaper. What criteria would you use to produce a rational evaluation? Can you identify words that you have used that show an emotional response?

4. Write an evaluation of your own writing process. Include the criteria on which you are basing your evaluation.

5. Write an evaluation of a car you own or have owned.

READINGS

A VETERAN REMEMBERS
HOWARD ZINN

Let's go back to the beginning of Veterans Day. It used to be Armistice Day, because at the 11th hour of the 11th day of the 11th month of 1918, World War I came to an end.

We must not forget that conflict. It revealed the essence of war, of all wars, because however "just" or "humanitarian" may be the claims, at the irreducible core of all war is the slaughter of the innocent, organized by national leaders, accompanied by lies. World War I was its epitome, as generals and politicians sent young men forward from their trenches, bayonets fixed, to gain a few miles, even a few yards, at frightful cost.

In July 1916 the British General Douglas Haig ordered 11 divisions of English soldiers to climb out of their trenches and move toward the German lines. The six German divisions opened up with their machine guns. Of the 110,000 who attacked, more than half were killed or wounded—all those bodies strewn on no man's land, the ghostly territory between the contending trenches. That scenario went on for years. In the first battle of the Marne there were a million casualties, 500,000 on each side.

The soldiers began to rebel, which is always the most heroic thing soldiers can do, for which they should be given medals. In the French Army, out of 112 divisions, 68 would have mutinies. Fifty men would be shot by firing squads.

Three of those executions became the basis for the late filmmaker Stanley Kubrick's antiwar masterpiece, "Paths of Glory." In that film a pompous general castigates his soldiers for retreating and talks of "patriotism." Kirk Douglas, the lieutenant colonel who defends his men, enrages the general by quoting the famous lines of Samuel Johnson: "Patriotism is the last refuge of a scoundrel."

The supposed moral justification of that war (the evil Kaiser, the Belgian babies) disintegrated quickly after it ended with sudden recognition of the 10 million dead in the mud of France and the gassed, shellshocked, and limbless veterans confronting the world.

The ugliness of that war was uncomplicated by the moral righteousness that made later wars, from World War II on, unsullied in our memory, or at least acceptable. Vietnam was the stark exception. But even there our national leaders have worked hard to smother what they call "the Vietnam syndrome." They want us to forget what we learned at the Vietnam War's end: that our leaders cannot be trusted, that modern war is inevitably a war against civilians and particularly children, that only a determined citizenry can stop the government when it embarks on mass murder.

Our decent impulse, to recognize the ordeal of our veterans, has been used to obscure the fact that they died, they were crippled, for no good cause other than the power and profit of a few. Veterans Day, instead of an occasion for denouncing war, has become an occasion for bringing out the flags, the uniforms, the martial music, the patriotic speeches reeking with hypocrisy. Those who name holidays, playing on our genuine feeling for veterans, have turned a day that celebrated the end of a horror into a day to honor militarism.

As a combat veteran myself, of a "good war," against fascism, I do not want the recognition of my service to be used as a glorification of war. At the end of that war, in which 50 million died, the people of the world should have shouted "Enough!" We should have decided that from that moment on, we would renounce war—and there would be no Korean War, Vietnam War, Panama War, Grenada War, Gulf War, Balkan War.

The reason for such a decision is that war in our time—whatever "humanitarian" motives are claimed by our political leaders—is always a war against children: the child amputees created by our bombing of Yugoslavia, the hundreds of thousands of Iraqi children dead as a result of our postwar sanctions. Veterans Day should be an occasion for a national vow: No more war victims on the other side; no more war veterans on our side.

Topics for Thinking and Writing

1. This piece was written as a newspaper editorial for Veterans Day. What points is the author attempting to make? Does he state his thesis?
2. What evidence does the author present to support his ideas? Evaluate his argument in light of this evidence.
3. This piece stirred reader reaction when it first appeared. Why do you think it did?
4. What does the fact that Zinn is a veteran of World War II add to his case?
5. In a few paragraphs, contrast this editorial with views that you would be more likely to find in most newspapers on Veterans Day.
6. Write a piece that opposes Zinn's claim that soldiers who rebel should be given medals.

POOR MAN AS GOURMAND*
RUSSELL BAKER

As chance would have it, the very evening Craig Claiborne ate his historic $4,000 dinner for two with 31 dishes and nine wines in Paris, a Lucullan repast for one was prepared and consumed in New York by this correspondent, no slouch himself when it comes to titillating the palate.

Mr. Claiborne won his meal in a television fund-raising auction and had it professionally prepared. Mine was created from spur-of-the-moment inspiration, ne-

*Editors' Title

cessitated when I discovered a note on the stove saying, "Am eating out with Dora and Imogene—make dinner for yourself." It was from the person who regularly does the cooking at my house and though disconcerted at first, I quickly rose to the challenge.

The meal opened with a 1975 Diet Pepsi, served in a disposable bottle. Although the bouquet was negligible, its distinct metallic aftertaste evoked memories of tin cans one had licked experimentally in the first flush of childhood curiosity.

To create the balance of tastes so cherished by the epicurean palate, I followed with a paté de fruites de nuts of Georgia, prepared according to my own recipe. A half-inch layer of creamy-style peanut butter is troweled onto a graham cracker, then half a banana is crudely diced and pressed firmly into the peanut butter and cemented in place as it were by a second graham cracker.

The accompanying drink was cold milk served in a wide-brimmed jelly glass. This is essential to proper consumption of the paté, since the entire confection must be dipped into the milk to soften it for eating. In making the presentation to the mouth, one must beware lest the milk-soaked portion of the sandwich fall onto the necktie. Thus seasoned gourmandisers follow the old maxim of the Breton chefs and "bring the mouth to the jelly glass."

At this point in the meal, the stomach was ready for serious eating, and I prepared beans with bacon grease, a dish I perfected in 1937 while developing my cuisine du dépression.

The dish is started by placing a pan over a very high flame until it becomes dangerously hot. A can of Heinz's pork and beans is then emptied into the pan and allowed to char until it reaches the consistency of hardening concrete. Three strips of bacon are fried to crisps, and when the beans have formed huge dense clots firmly welded to the pan, the bacon grease is poured in and stirred vigorously with a large screw driver.

This not only adds flavor, but also loosens some of the beans from the side of the pan. Leaving the flame high, I stirred in a three-day-old spaghetti sauce found in the refrigerator, added a sprinkle of chili powder, a large dollop of Major Grey's chutney and a tablespoon of bicarbonate of soda to make the whole dish rise.

Beans and bacon grease is always eaten from the pan with a tablespoon while standing over the kitchen sink. The pan must be thrown away immediately. The correct drink with this dish is a straight shot of room-temperature gin. I had a Gilbey's 1975, which was superb.

For the meat course, I had fried bologna á la Nutley, Nouveau Jersey. Six slices of A&P bologna were placed in an ungreased frying pan over maximum heat and held down by a long fork until the entire house filled with smoke. The bologna was turned, fried the same length of time on the other side, then served on air-filled white bread with thick lashings of mayonnaise.

The correct drink for fried bologna á la Nutley, Nouveau Jersey, is a 1927 Nehi Cola, but since my cellar, alas, had none, I had to make do with a second shot of Gilbey's 1975.

The cheese course was deliciously simple—a single slice of Kraft's individually wrapped yellow sandwich cheese, which was flavored by vigorous rubbing over the bottom of the frying pan to soak up the rich bologna juices. Wine being absolutely de rigueur with cheese, I chose a 1974 Muscatel, flavored with a maraschino cherry, and afterwards cleared my palate with three pickled martini onions.

It was time for the fruit. I chose a Del Monte tinned pear, which, regrettably, slipped from the spoon and fell on the floor, necessitating its being blotted with a paper towel to remove cat hairs. To compensate for the resulting loss of pear syrup, I dipped it lightly in hot-dog relish which created a unique flavor.

With the pear I drank two shots of Gilbey's 1975 and one shot of Wolfschmidt vodka (non-vintage), the Gilbey's having been exhausted.

At last it was time for the dish the entire meal had been building toward—dessert. With a paring knife, I ripped into a fresh package of Oreos, produced a bowl of My-T-Fine chocolate pudding which had been coagulating in the refrigerator for days and, using a potato masher, crushed a dozen Oreos into the pudding. It was immense.

Between mouthfuls, I sipped a tall, bubbling tumbler of cool Bromo-Seltzer, and finished with six ounces of Maalox. It couldn't have been better.

Topics for Thinking and Writing

1. What are some instances in which Baker adapts his language to the language of food writing?
2. Clearly Baker is enjoying himself as he writes. Cite some lines that show his delight.
3. In this piece, written in 1975, Baker adopts a playful tone and spoofs (makes fun of) the idea of writing seriously about food. Write a one-paragraph spoof in which you imitate a particular kind of writing (for example, a piece about cars, music, or sports).
4. Select a restaurant review from a newspaper or magazine and evaluate it for language, audience, and purpose.
5. Write a review of a meal you've recently enjoyed (or hated) in the college dining hall or at a restaurant. Consider such factors as presentation of food, ingredients, taste, size of portions, and price.

THE PITCHER
ROBERT FRANCIS

His art is eccentricity, his aim
How not to hit the mark he seems to aim at,

His passion how to avoid the obvious,
His technique how to vary the avoidance.

5   The others throw to be comprehended. He
Throws to be a moment misunderstood.

Yet not too much. Not errant, arrant, wild,
But every seeming aberration willed.

Not to, yet still, still to communicate
10 Making the batter understand too late.

Topics for Thinking and Writing

1. According to the poet, what are the criteria by which pitching is judged?
2. Which specific lines express those criteria and how the pitcher meets them?
3. What is Francis's thesis about the skill or "art" of pitching?
4. Write a paragraph which expresses the poet's thesis.
5. Write a short essay about a skill that you possess and the criteria used to evaluate that skill.

MOVING CAMP TOO FAR
NILA NORTHSUN

i can't speak of
    many moons
    moving camp on travois[1]
I can't tell of
5   the last great battle
    counting coup[2] or
    taking scalp
i don't know what it
    was to hunt buffalo
10   or do the ghost dance
but
i can see an eagle
    almost extinct
15   on slurpee plastic cups
i can travel to powwows
    in campers & winnebagos
i can eat buffalo meat
    at the tourist burger stand
I can dance to indian music
20   rock-n-roll hey-a-hey-o
i can
    & unfortunately
    i do

---

[1]*travois* a frame slung between poles and pulled by a dog or horse, used by Plains Indians to carry goods and belongings.
[2]*counting coup* telling stories of one's adventures in battle

Topics for Thinking and Writing

1. Identify Northsun's audience and purpose in this poem. Evaluate how her audience and purpose might have influenced the way in which the poem is written.
2. Describe Northsun's bias. Quote one passage that reflects her bias. Evaluate how her biases might have influenced her writing of the poem.
3. Rewrite this poem in paragraph form. Use words, sentences, and ideas that reflect the same biases and purpose.
4. Describe a stereotype of a social, religious, or ethnic group of which you are a member. Write an essay evaluating the biases of the media in representing— or misrepresenting—members of this group. Use specific examples of news reports, commercials, and television shows to support your evaluation.

CATHEDRAL
RAYMOND CARVER

This blind man, an old friend of my wife's, he was on his way to spend the night. His wife had died. So he was visiting the dead wife's relatives in Connecticut. He called my wife from his in-laws'. Arrangements were made. He would come by train, a five-hour trip, and my wife would meet him at the station. She hadn't seen him since she worked for him one summer in Seattle ten years ago. But she and the blind man had kept in touch. They made tapes and mailed them back and forth. I wasn't enthusiastic about his visit. He was no one I knew. And his being blind bothered me. My idea of blindness came from the movies. In the movies, the blind moved slowly and never laughed. Sometimes they were led by seeing-eye dogs. A blind man in my house was not something I looked forward to.

That summer in Seattle she had needed a job. She didn't have any money. The man she was going to marry at the end of the summer was in officers' training school. He didn't have any money, either. But she was in love with the guy, and he was in love with her, etc. She'd seen something in the paper: HELP WANTED—*Reading to Blind Man,* and a telephone number. She phoned and went over, was hired on the spot. She'd worked with this blind man all summer. She read stuff to him, case studies, reports, that sort of thing. She helped him organize his little office in the county social-service department. They'd become good friends, my wife and the blind man. How do I know these things? She told me. And she told me something else. On her last day in the office, the blind man asked if he could touch her face. She agreed to this. She told me he touched his fingers to every part of her face, her nose—even her neck! She never forgot it. She even tried to write a poem about it. She was always trying to write a poem. She wrote a poem or two every year, usually after something really important had happened to her.

When we first started going out together, she showed me the poem. In the poem, she recalled his fingers and the way they had moved around over her face. In the poem, she talked about what she had felt at the time, about what went through her mind when the blind man touched her nose and lips. I can remember I didn't think much of the poem. Of course, I didn't tell her that. Maybe I just don't understand poetry. I admit it's not the first thing I reach for when I pick up something to read.

Anyway, this man who'd first enjoyed her favors, the officer-to-be, he'd been her childhood sweetheart. So okay. I'm saying that at the end of the summer she let the blind man run his hands over her face, said goodbye to him, married her childhood etc., who was now a commissioned officer, and she moved away from Seattle. But they'd kept in touch, she and the blind man. She made the first contact after a year or so. She called him up one night from an Air Force base in Alabama. She wanted to talk. They talked. He asked her to send a tape and tell him about her life. She did this. She sent the tape. On the tape, she told the blind man about her husband and about their life together in the military. She told the blind man she loved her husband but she didn't like it where they lived and she didn't like it that he was part of the military-industrial thing. She told the blind man she'd written a poem and he was in it. She told him that she was writing a poem about what it was like to be an Air Force officer's wife. The poem wasn't finished yet. She was still writing it. The blind man made a tape. He sent her the tape. She made a tape. This went on for years. My wife's officer was posted to one base and then another. She sent tapes from Moody AFB, McGuire, McConnell, and finally Travis, near Sacramento, where one night she got to feeling lonely and cut off from people she kept losing in that moving-around life. She got to feeling she couldn't go it another step. She went in and swallowed all the pills and capsules in the medicine chest and washed them down with a bottle of gin. Then she got into a hot bath and passed out.

5   But instead of dying, she got sick. She threw up. Her officer—why should he have a name? he was the childhood sweetheart, and what more does he want?—came home from somewhere, found her, and called the ambulance. In time, she put it all on a tape and sent the tape to the blind man. Over the years, she put all kinds of stuff on tapes and sent the tapes off lickety-split. Next to writing a poem every year, I think it was her chief means of recreation. On one tape, she told the blind man she'd decided to live away from her officer for a time. On another tape, she told him about her divorce. She and I began going out, and of course she told her blind man about it. She told him everything, or so it seemed to me. Once she asked me if I'd like to hear the latest tape from the blind man. This was a year ago. I was on the tape, she said. So I said okay, I'd listen to it. I got us drinks and we settled down in the living room. We made ready to listen. First she inserted the tape into the player and adjusted a couple of dials. Then she pushed a lever. The tape squeaked and someone began to talk in this loud voice. She lowered the volume. After a few minutes of harmless chitchat, I heard my own name in the mouth of this stranger, this blind man I didn't even know! And then this: "From all you've said about him, I can only conclude—" But we were interrupted, a knock at the door, something, and we didn't ever get back to the tape. Maybe it was just as well. I'd heard all I wanted to.

Now this same blind man was coming to sleep in my house.

"Maybe I could take him bowling," I said to my wife. She was at the draining board doing scalloped potatoes. She put down the knife she was using and turned around.

"If you love me," she said, "you can do this for me. If you don't love me, okay. But if you had a friend, any friend, and the friend came to visit, I'd make him feel comfortable." She wiped her hands with the dish towel.

"I don't have any blind friends," I said.

10   "You don't have *any* friends," she said. "Period. Besides," she said, "goddamn it, his wife's just died! Don't you understand that? The man's lost his wife!"

I didn't answer. She'd told me a little about the blind man's wife. Her name was Beulah. Beulah! That's a name for a colored woman.

"Was his wife a Negro?" I asked.

"Are you crazy?" my wife said. "Have you just flipped or something?" She picked up a potato. I saw it hit the floor, then roll under the stove. "What's wrong with you?" she said. "Are you drunk?"

"I'm just asking," I said.

15   Right then my wife filled me in with more detail than I cared to know. I made a drink and sat at the kitchen table to listen. Pieces of the story began to fall into place.

Beulah had gone to work for the blind man the summer after my wife had stopped working for him. Pretty soon Beulah and the blind man had themselves a church wedding. It was a little wedding—who'd want to go to such a wedding in the first place?—just the two of them, plus the minister and the minister's wife. But it was a church wedding just the same. It was what Beulah had wanted, he'd said. But even then Beulah must have been carrying the cancer in her glands. After they had been inseparable for eight years—my wife's word, *inseparable*—Beulah's health went into a rapid decline. She died in a Seattle hospital room, the blind man sitting beside the bed and holding on to her hand. They'd married, lived and worked together, slept together—had sex, sure—and then the blind man had to bury her. All this without his having ever seen what the goddamned woman looked like. It was beyond my understanding. Hearing this, I felt sorry for the blind man for a little bit. And then I found myself thinking what a pitiful life this woman must have led. Imagine a woman who could never see herself as she was seen in the eyes of her loved one. A woman who could go on day after day and never receive the smallest compliment from her beloved. A woman whose husband could never read the expression on her face, be it misery or something better. Someone who could wear makeup or not—what difference to him? She could, if she wanted, wear green eye-shadow around one eye, a straight pin in her nostril, yellow slacks, and purple shoes, no matter. And then to slip off into death, the blind man's hand on her hand, his blind eyes streaming tears—I'm imagining now—her last thought maybe this: that he never even knew what she looked like, and she on an express to the grave. Robert was left with a small insurance policy and a half of a twenty-peso Mexican coin. The other half of the coin went into the box with her. Pathetic.

So when the time rolled around, my wife went to the depot to pick him up. With nothing to do but wait—sure, I blamed him for that—I was having a drink and watching the TV when I heard the car pull into the drive. I got up from the sofa with my drink and went to the window to have a look.

I saw my wife laughing as she parked the car. I saw her get out of the car and shut the door. She was still wearing a smile. Just amazing. She went around to the other side of the car to where the blind man was already starting to get out. This blind man, feature this, he was wearing a full beard! A beard on a blind man! Too much, I say. The blind man reached into the back seat and dragged out a suitcase. My wife took his arm, shut the car door, and, talking all the way, moved him down the drive and then up the steps to the front porch. I turned off the TV. I finished my drink, rinsed the glass, dried my hands. Then I went to the door.

My wife said, "I want you to meet Robert. Robert, this is my husband. I've told you all about him." She was beaming. She had this blind man by his coat sleeve.

20   The blind man let go of his suitcase and up came his hand. I took it. He squeezed hard, held my hand, and then he let it go.

"I feel like we've already met," he boomed.

"Likewise," I said. I didn't know what else to say. Then I said, "Welcome. I've heard a lot about you." We began to move then, a little group, from the porch into the living room, my wife guiding him by the arm. The blind man was carrying his suitcase in his other hand. My wife said things like, "To your left here, Robert. That's right. Now watch it, there's a chair. That's it. Sit down right here. This is the sofa. We just bought this sofa two weeks ago."

I started to say something about the old sofa. I'd liked that old sofa. But I didn't say anything. Then I wanted to say something else, small-talk, about the scenic ride along the Hudson. How going *to* New York, you should sit on the right-hand side of the train, and coming *from* New York, the left-hand side.

"Did you have a good train ride?" I said. "Which side of the train did you sit on, by the way?"

25   "What a question, which side!" my wife said. "What's it matter which side?" she said.

"I just asked," I said.

"Right side," the blind man said. "I hadn't been on a train in nearly forty years. Not since I was a kid. With my folks. That's been a long time. I'd nearly forgotten the sensation. I have winter in my beard now," he said. "So I've been told, anyway. Do I look distinguished, my dear?" the blind man said to my wife.

"You look distinguished, Robert," she said. "Robert," she said. "Robert, it's just so good to see you."

My wife finally took her eyes off the blind man and looked at me. I had the feeling she didn't like what she saw. I shrugged.

30   I've never met, or personally known, anyone who was blind. This blind man was late forties, a heavy-set, balding man with stooped shoulders, as if he carried a great weight there. He wore brown slacks, brown shoes, a light-brown shirt, a tie, a sports coat. Spiffy. He also had this full beard. But he didn't use a cane and he didn't wear dark glasses. I'd always thought dark glasses were a must for the blind. Fact was, I wished he had a pair. At first glance, his eyes looked like anyone else's eyes. But if you looked close, there was something different about them. Too much white in the iris, for one thing, and the pupils seemed to move around in the sockets without his knowing it or being able to stop it. Creepy. As I stared at his face, I saw the left pupil turn in toward his nose while the other made an effort to keep in one place. But it was only an effort, for that eye was on the roam without his knowing it or wanting it to be.

I said, "Let me get you a drink. What's your pleasure? We have a little of everything. It's one of our pastimes."

"Bub, I'm a Scotch man myself," he said fast enough in this big voice.

"Right," I said. Bub! "Sure you are. I knew it."

He let his fingers touch his suitcase, which was sitting alongside the sofa. He was taking his bearings. I didn't blame him for that.

35 "I'll move that up to your room," my wife said.

"No, that's fine," the blind man said loudly. "It can go up when I go up."

"A little water with the Scotch?" I said.

"Very little," he said.

"I knew it," I said.

40 He said, "Just a tad. The Irish actor, Barry Fitzgerald? I'm like that fellow. When I drink water, Fitzgerald said, I drink water. When I drink whiskey, I drink whiskey." My wife laughed. The blind man brought his hand up under his beard. He lifted his beard slowly and let it drop.

I did the drinks, three big glasses of Scotch with a splash of water in each. Then we made ourselves comfortable and talked about Robert's travels. First the long flight from the West Coast to Connecticut, we covered that. Then from Connecticut up here by train. We had another drink concerning that leg of the trip.

I remembered having read somewhere that the blind didn't smoke because, as speculation had it, they couldn't see the smoke they exhaled. I thought I knew that much and that much only about blind people. But this blind man smoked his cigarette down to the nubbin and then lit another one. This blind man filled his ashtray and my wife emptied it.

When we sat down at the table for dinner, we had another drink. My wife heaped Robert's plate with cube steak, scalloped potatoes, green beans. I buttered him up two slices of bread. I said, "Here's bread and butter for you." I swallowed some of my drink. "Now let us pray," I said, and the blind man lowered his head. My wife looked at me, her mouth agape. "Pray the phone won't ring and the food doesn't get cold," I said.

We dug in. We ate everything there was to eat on the table. We ate like there was no tomorrow. We didn't talk. We ate. We scarfed. We grazed that table. We were into serious eating. The blind man had right away located his foods, he knew just where everything was on his plate. I watched with admiration as he used his knife and fork on the meat. He'd cut two pieces of meat, fork the meat into his mouth, and then go all out for the scalloped potatoes, the beans next, and then he'd tear off a hunk of buttered bread and eat that. He'd follow this up with a big drink of milk. It didn't seem to bother him to use his fingers once in a while, either.

45 We finished everything, including half a strawberry pie. For a few moments, we sat as if stunned. Sweat beaded on our faces. Finally, we got up from the table and left the dirty places. We didn't look back. We took ourselves into the living room and sank into our places again. Robert and my wife sat on the sofa. I took the big chair. We had us two or three more drinks while they talked about the the major things that had come to pass for them in the past ten years. For the most part, I just listened. Now and then I joined in. I didn't want him to think I'd left the room, and I didn't want her to think I was feeling left out. They talked of things that had happened to them—to them!—these past ten years. I waited in vain to hear my name on my wife's sweet lips: "And then my dear husband came into my life"—something like that. But I heard nothing of the sort. More talk of Robert. Robert had done a little of everything, it seemed, a regular blind jack-of-all-trades. But most recently he and his wife had had an Amway distributorship, from which, I gathered, they'd earned their living, such as it was. The blind man was also a ham radio operator. He talked in his loud voice about conversations he'd had with fellow operators in Guam, in the Philippines, in Alaska, and even in Tahiti. He said he'd have a lot of

friends there if he ever wanted to go visit those places. From time to time, he'd turn his blind face toward me, put his hand under his beard, ask me something. How long had I been in my present position? (Three years.) Did I like my work? (I didn't.) Was I going to stay with it? (What were the options?) Finally, when I thought he was beginning to run down, I got up and turned on the TV.

My wife looked at me with irritation. She was heading toward a boil. Then she looked at the blind man and said, "Robert, do you have a TV?"

The blind man said, "My dear, I have two TVs. I have a color set and a black-and-white thing, an old relic. It's funny, but if I turn the TV on and I'm always turning it on, I turn on the color set. It's funny, don't you think?"

I didn't know what to say to that. I had absolutely nothing to say to that. No opinion. So I watched the news program and tried to listen to what the announcer was saying.

"This is a color TV," the blind man said. "Don't ask me how, but I can tell."

50 "We traded up a while ago," I said.

The blind man had another taste of his drink. He lifted his beard, sniffed it, and let it fall. He leaned forward on the sofa. He positioned his ashtray on the coffee table, then put the lighter to his cigarette. He leaned back on the sofa and crossed his legs at the ankles.

My wife covered her mouth, and then she yawned. She stretched. She said, "I think I'll go upstairs and put on my robe. I think I'll change into something else. Robert, you make yourself comfortable," she said.

"I'm comfortable," the blind man said.

"I want you to feel comfortable in this house," she said.

55 "I am comfortable," the blind man said.

After she'd left the room, he and I listened to the weather report and then to the sports roundup. By that time, she'd been gone so long I didn't know if she was going to come back. I thought she might have gone to bed. I wished she'd come back downstairs. I didn't want to be left alone with a blind man. I asked him if he wanted another drink, and he said sure. Then I asked if he wanted to smoke some dope with me. I said I'd just rolled a number. I hadn't, but I planned to do so in about two shakes.

"I'll try some with you," he said.

"Damn right," I said. "That's the stuff."

I got our drinks and sat down on the sofa with him. Then I rolled us two fat numbers. I lit one and passed it. I brought it to his fingers. He took it and inhaled.

60 "Hold it as long as you can," I said. I could tell he didn't know the first thing.

My wife came back downstairs wearing her pink robe and her pink slippers.

"What do I smell?" she said.

"We thought we'd have us some cannabis," I said.

My wife gave me a savage look. Then she looked at the blind man and said, "Robert, I didn't know you smoked."

65 He said, "I do now, my dear. There's a first time for everything. But I don't feel anything yet."

"This stuff is pretty mellow," I said. "This stuff is mild. It's dope you can reason with," I said. "It doesn't mess you up."

"Not much it doesn't, bub," he said, and laughed.

My wife sat on the sofa between the blind man and me. I passed her the number. She took it and toked and then passed it back to me. "Which way is this going?" she said. Then she said, "I shouldn't be smoking this. I can hardly keep my eyes open as it is. That dinner did me in. I shouldn't have eaten so much."

"It was the strawberry pie," the blind man said. "That's what did it," he said, and he laughed his big laugh. Then he shook his head.

70 "There's more strawberry pie," I said.

"Do you want some more, Robert?" my wife said.

"Maybe in a little while," he said.

We gave our attention to the TV. My wife yawned again. She said, "Your bed is made up when you feel like going to bed, Robert. I know you must have had a long day. When you're ready to go to bed, say so." She pulled his arm. "Robert?"

He came to and said, "I've had a real nice time. This beats tapes, doesn't it?"

75 I said, "Coming at you," and I put the number between his fingers. He inhaled, held the smoke, and then let it go. It was like he'd been doing it since he was nine years old.

"Thanks, bub," he said. "But I think this is all for me. I think I'm beginning to feel it," he said. He held the burning roach out for my wife.

"Same here," she said. "Ditto. Me, too." She took the roach and passed it to me. "I may just sit here for a while between you two guys with my eyes closed. But don't let me bother you, okay? Either one of you. If it bothers you, say so. Otherwise, I may just sit here with my eyes closed until you're ready to go to bed," she said. "The bed's made up, Robert, when you're ready. It's right next to our room at the top of the stairs. We'll show you up when you're ready. You wake me up now, you guys, if I fall asleep." She said that and then she closed her eyes and went to sleep.

The news program ended. I got up and changed the channel. I sat back down on the sofa. I wished my wife hadn't pooped out. Her head lay across the back of the sofa, her mouth open. She'd turned so that her robe slipped away from her legs, exposing a juicy thigh. I reached to draw her robe back over her, and it was then that I glanced at the blind man. What the hell! I flipped the robe open again.

"You say when you want some strawberry pie," I said.

80 "I will," he said.

I said, "Are you tired? Do you want me to take you up to your bed? Are you ready to hit the hay?"

"Not yet," He said. "No, I'll stay up with you, bub. If that's all right. I'll stay up until you're ready to turn in. We haven't had a chance to talk. Know what I mean? I feel like me and her monopolized the evening." He lifted his beard and he let it fall. He picked up his cigarettes and his lighter.

"That's all right," I said. Then I said, "I'm glad for the company."

And I guess I was. Every night I smoked dope and stayed up as long as I could before I fell asleep. My wife and I hardly ever went to bed at the same time. When I did go to sleep, I had these dreams. Sometimes I'd wake up from one of them, my heart going crazy.

85 Something about the church and the Middle Ages was on the TV. Not your run-of-the-mill TV fare. I wanted to watch something else. I turned to the other

channels. But there was nothing on them, either. So I turned back to the first channel and apologized.

"Bub, it's all right," the blind man said. "It's fine with me. Whatever you want to watch is okay. I'm always learning something. Learning never ends. It won't hurt me to learn something tonight. I got ears," he said.

We didn't say anything for a time. He was leaning forward with his head turned at me, his right ear aimed in the direction of the set. Very disconcerting. Now and then his eyelids drooped and then they snapped open again. Now and then he put his fingers into his beard and tugged, like he was thinking about something he was hearing on the television.

On the screen, a group of men wearing cowls was being set upon and tormented by men dressed in skeleton costumes and men dressed as devils. The men dressed as devils wore devil masks, horns, and long tails. This pageant was part of a procession. The Englishman who was narrating the thing said it took place in Spain once a year. I tried to explain to the blind man what was happening.

"Skeletons," he said. "I know about skeletons," he said, and he nodded.

90   The TV showed this one cathedral. Then there was a long, slow look at another one. Finally, the picture switched to the famous one in Paris, with its flying buttresses and its spires reaching up to the clouds. The camera pulled away to show the whole of the cathedral rising above the skyline.

There were times when the Englishman who was telling the thing would shut up, would simply let the camera move around the cathedrals. Or else the camera would tour the countryside, men in fields walking behind oxen. I waited as long as I could. Then I felt I had to say something. I said, "They're showing the outside of this cathedral now. Gargoyles. Little statues carved to look like monsters. Now I guess they're in Italy. Yeah, they're in Italy. There's paintings on the walls of this one church."

"Are those fresco paintings, bub?" he asked, and he sipped from his drink.

I reached for my glass. But it was empty. I tried to remember what I could remember. "You're asking me are those frescoes?" I said. "That's a good question. I don't know."

The camera moved to a cathedral outside Lisbon. The differences in the Portuguese cathedral compared with the French and Italian were not that great. But they were there. Mostly the interior stuff. Then something occurred to me, and I said, "Something has occurred to me. Do you have any idea what a cathedral is? What they look like, that is? Do you follow me? If somebody says cathedral to you, do you have any notion what they're talking about? Do you know the difference between that and a Baptist church, say?"

95   He let the smoke dribble from his mouth. "I know they took hundreds of workers fifty or a hundred years to build," he said. "I just heard the man say that, of course. I know generations of the same families worked on a cathedral. I heard him say that, too. The men who began their life's work on them, they never lived to see the completion of their work. In that wise, bub, they're no different from the rest of us, right?" He laughed. Then his eyelids drooped again. His head nodded. He seemed to be snoozing. Maybe he was imagining himself in Portugal. The TV was showing another cathedral now. This one was in Germany. The Englishman's voice droned on. "Cathedrals," the blind man said. He sat up and rolled his head

back and forth. "If you want the truth, bub, that's about all I know. What I just said. What I heard him say. But maybe you could describe one to me? I wish you'd do it. I'd like that. If you want to know, I really don't have a good idea."

I stared hard at the shot of the cathedral on the TV. How could I even begin to describe it? But say my life depended on it. Say my life was being threatened by an insane guy who said I had to do it or else.

I stared some more at the cathedral before the picture flipped off into the countryside. There was no use. I turned to the blind man and said, "To begin with, they're very tall." I was looking around the room for clues. "They reach way up. Up and up. Toward the sky. They're so big, some of them, they have to have these supports. To help hold them up, so to speak. These supports are called buttresses. They remind me of viaducts, for some reason. But maybe you don't know viaducts, either? Sometimes the cathedrals have devils and such carved into the front. Sometimes lords and ladies. Don't ask me why this is," I said.

He was nodding. The whole upper part of his body seemed to be moving back and forth.

"I'm no doing so good, am I?" I said.

100   He stopped nodding and leaned forward on the edge of the sofa. As he listened to me, he was running his fingers through his beard. I wasn't getting through to him, I could see that. But he waited for me to go on just the same. He nodded, like he was trying to encourage me. I tried to think what else to say. "They're really big," I said. "They're massive. They're built of stone. Marble, too, sometimes. In those olden days, when they built cathedrals, men wanted to be close to God. In those olden days, God was an important part of everyone's life. You could tell this from their cathedral-building. I'm sorry," I said, "but it looks like that's the best I can do for you. I'm just no good at it."

"That's all right, bub," the blind man said. "Hey, listen. I hope you don't mind my asking you. Can I ask you something? Let me ask you a simple question, yes or no. I'm just curious and there's no offense. You're my host. But let me ask if you are in any way religious? You don't mind my asking?"

I shook my head. He couldn't see that, though. A wink is the same as a nod to a blind man. "I guess I don't believe in it. In anything. Sometimes it's hard. You know what I'm saying?"

"Sure, I do," he said.

"Right," I said.

105   The Englishman was still holding forth. My wife sighed in her sleep. She drew a long breath and went on with her sleeping.

"You'll have to forgive me," I said. "But I can't tell you what a cathedral looks like. It just isn't in me to do it. I can't do any more than I've done."

The blind man sat very still, his head down, as he listened to me.

I said, "The truth is, cathedrals don't mean anything special to me. Nothing. Cathedrals. They're something to look at on late-night TV. That's all they are."

It was then that the blind man cleared his throat. He brought something up. He took a handkerchief from his back pocket. Then he said, "I get it, bub. It's okay. It happens. Don't worry about it," he said. "Hey, listen to me. Will you do me a favor? I got an idea. Why don't you find us some heavy paper? And a pen. We'll do something. We'll draw one together. Get us a pen and some heavy paper. Go on, bub, get the stuff," he said.

110   So I went upstairs. My legs felt like they didn't have any strength in them. They felt like they did after I'd done some running. In my wife's room, I looked around. I found some ballpoints in a little basket on her table. And then I tried to think where to look for the kind of paper he was talking about.

Downstairs, in the kitchen, I found a shopping bag with onion skins in the bottom of the bag. I emptied the bag and shook it. I brought it into the living room and sat down with it near his legs. I moved some things, smoothed the wrinkles from the bag, spread it out on the coffee table.

The blind man got down from the sofa and sat next to me on the carpet.

He ran his fingers over the paper. He went up and down the sides of the paper. The edges, even the edges. He fingered the corners.

"All right," he said. "All right, let's do her."

115   He found my hand, the hand with the pen. He closed his hand over my hand. "Go ahead, bub, draw," he said. "Draw. You'll see. I'll follow along with you. It'll be okay. Just begin now like I'm telling you. You'll see. Draw," the blind man said.

So I began. First I drew a box that looked like a house. It could have been the house I lived in. Then I put a roof on it. At either end of the roof, I drew spires. Crazy.

"Swell," he said. "Terrific. You're doing fine," he said. "Never thought anything like this could happen in your lifetime, did you, bub? Well, it's a strange life, we all know that. Go on now. Keep it up."

I put in windows with arches. I drew flying buttresses. I hung great doors. I couldn't stop. The TV station went off the air. I put down the pen and closed and opened my fingers. The blind man felt around over the paper. He moved the tips of his fingers over the paper, all over what I had drawn, and he nodded.

"Doing fine," the blind man said.

120   I took up the pen again, and he found my hand. I kept at it. I'm no artist. But I kept drawing just the same.

My wife opened up her eyes and gazed at us. She sat up on the sofa, her robe hanging open. She said, "What are you doing? Tell me, I want to know."

I didn't answer her.

The blind man said, "We're drawing a cathedral. Me and him are working on it. Press hard," he said to me. "That's right. That's good," he said. "Sure. You got it, bub, I can tell. You didn't think you could. But you can, can't you? You're cooking with gas now. You know what I'm saying? We're going to really have us something here in a minute. How's the old arm?" he said. "Put some people in there now. What's a cathedral without people?"

My wife said, "What's going on? Robert, what are you doing? What's going on?"

125   "It's all right," he said to her. "Close your eyes now," the blind man said to me. I did it. I closed them just like he said.

"Are they closed?" he said. "Don't fudge."

"They're closed," I said.

"Keep them that way," he said. He said, "Don't stop now. Draw."

130   So we kept on with it. His fingers rode my fingers as my hand went over the paper. It was like nothing else in my life up to now.

Then he said, "I think that's it. I think you got it," he said. "Take a look. What do you think?"

But I had my eyes closed. I thought I'd keep them that way for a little longer. I thought it was something I ought to do.

"Well?" he said. "Are you looking?"

My eyes were still closed. I was in my house. I knew that. But I didn't feel like I was inside anything.

135   "It's really something," I said.

Topics for Thinking and Writing

1. What are some biases against blind people expressed by the narrator of the story?
2. With what examples does the narrator support his views? Is his support effective? Why or why not?
3. Does the narrator respond emotionally or rationally to the blind man's visit? What evidence supports your decision?
4. What point do you think Carver is making about contemporary people? What examples does Carver use to support his point?
5. Write a short essay discussing a time when you responded emotionally to a person you had just met.
6. Write a short essay evaluating the narrator's marriage. On what criteria are you basing your evaluation?

Self-Assessment

Reread the self-assessment that opens this chapter. Then answer the following questions.

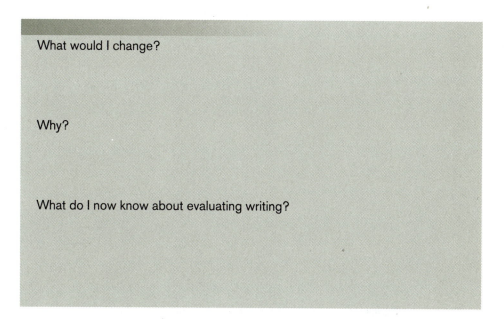

What would I change?

Why?

What do I now know about evaluating writing?

Analysis: Looking at the Parts/ Examining the Whole

GILLS
SCALES
BONES

Many years ago, a popular Harvard professor would present each of the students in his comparative anatomy course with a preserved fish on the first day of class. He would instruct them to look at the fish and jot down in their notebooks any observations they might make. Some students finished in a few minutes; others took longer, but by the end of the lab period, all had filled a page or two with notes. They were surprised, therefore, when at the next class, the professor presented them with the *same fish* and invited their observations once more. He did the same for the next several classes. Then he provided the students with tools to further examine the fish: magnifying lenses, scalpels, tweezers, glass slides, and so on.

The students, who thought they had seen all there was to see during the first session, ended up spending most of the entire semester examining the fish. As a result, they learned some of the most essential lessons that a scientist—*and a writer*—can learn. They learned the habits of patience and close observation, of really looking. More than simply seeing the outer form of a fish, they were able to make connections and to view the various parts in connection to the whole fish. They came to understand how design aided function and how gills, scales, fins, and the inner organs were all part of a complex whole. They saw that they could begin to **define** the parts, to **compare** certain parts to other parts, to **outline the process**—step-by-step—of how each part worked, to see how the functioning of one part **caused an effect** to occur in another part, and to understand how the fish fit into a **classification** system of species.

As writers and as students, you will often be asked to engage in similar activities. You will be asked to look closely at or listen to assigned readings, current events, art objects, lectures, or political speeches. You will be asked to reflect on your observations and to interpret, through writing, what you have read or heard. One way of writing about your reflections is through **analysis.** To analyze means to break something into its parts, to become aware of how those parts connect to each other, and to understand the function of the parts in relationship to the whole. This chapter presents methods of analysis which include **definition, process, comparison-contrast, classification,** and **cause and effect**.

Working Together: With a partner, spend some time examining something closely. For example, you might look at an object or a machine in your room, an animal, or a plant. Then write a paragraph explaining the parts you discovered. Next, compare your paragraphs. In what ways are they similar? In what ways are they different?

Self-Assessment

Whenever you have a decision to make and you weigh the pros and cons of various options, you are engaging in analysis. You may have recently conducted an analysis when choosing a college to attend. As part of the decision-making process, you probably engaged in several methods of analysis. You may have looked at the various parts of each college in relationship to the whole college's culture. You likely looked at tuition, class size, the number of course offerings, facilities, the library, and student services as you tried to define the culture of each college you were considering. You may have compared one college with another, based on a specific comparison of their facilities and programs. Or you may have classified the colleges in categories based on tuition, admissions criteria, and so on.

Looking at such factors when selecting a college is only one of many types of analysis you have already done. You use your skills of analysis every day. You've probably previously written directions telling a friend how to do something, compared one movie with another, defined a term for a child, and thought about the causes of situations in which you've found yourself. Each time you engaged in one of these activities, whether in writing or in speaking, you were using a type of analysis.

1. I have written the following types of papers (check each type that applies and write the topic of the paper alongside it):
   - Definition of what something is
   - Directions telling how to do something
   - Comparison and contrast of different items
   - Classification of items by categories
   - Explanation of cause and effect

2. Of the types I have checked, the most difficult to write was _____.

3. What made this paper difficult to write was _____.

4. If I were going to rewrite this paper, I would _____.

5. I have previously used some type of analysis (comparison, definition, and so on) to make the following decision:

6. I am likely to use some type of analysis (comparison and contrast, classification, and so on)

    A. in these courses: _____.

    B. in these life situations: _____.

What I know about writing analyses:	What I want to know about writing analyses:

Working Alone: Write a paragraph about why it is important to develop the skill of analysis.

What Is Analysis?

Chapter 8 asks you to look at the parts of writing—your own and others'—and to evaluate those parts for bias, thesis, evidence, and so on. Any topic can be divided into its components. This process is **analysis,** a term which comes from a Greek word meaning "to break into parts." When you hear a rattle in your car, you ask yourself which part is broken. When you decide to begin a diet, you consider the calories of certain foods to determine which to eliminate. Often, your teachers will break their lectures into parts. For example, in psychology the instructor may present material on human development in stages ranging from fetal, to infant, to toddler, and so on. In biology, animals may be classified by species. Your U.S. history textbook may be organized by decades, which are then divided to focus on economic, political, and cultural aspects. In physics, you will look at the components of the atom—the neutrons, protons, and electrons.

Working Together: With a partner, break the following down into analyzable parts:

• a sport of your choice
• a poem of your choice
• a library of your choice
• a restaurant of your choice

Then write an outline of your analysis.

Writing An Analysis: Parts to Whole

Throughout the course of your education, on tests and in papers, you have been—and will be—asked to interpret or analyze some content or topic and to present that analysis in writing. You may be asked to examine the causes of the Civil War in a history class, to analyze the personality of the protagonist in a short story, or to compare the duties of a state senator with those of a state representative. As in all writing, you will need to develop a thesis which states the main idea of your interpretation, and you will need to develop that idea with evidence and examples. When writing analyses, you can first begin to examine a topic by looking at the various parts of the whole and the relationships among them.

To better understand these relationships, you might ask yourself:

- Into what basic parts can this subject/object be broken?
- What part do I want to explore in more depth?
- What do I know about this part?
- What's interesting to me about this part?
- What will I need to find out about this part?
- How can I find this information?
- What function does this part perform?
- How does this part contribute to the whole?
- What would happen to the whole without this part?
- How can I best present this part's relationship to the whole?

Using a graphic organizer can help you to answer these questions and to begin to see the relationship of the parts to the whole. For example, imagine that you have been asked to write an analysis of the following poem by Ralph Waldo Emerson.

CONCORD HYMN
RALPH WALDO EMERSON

By the rude bridge that arched the flood
Their flag to April's breeze unfurled,
Here once the embattled farmers stood
And fired the shot heard round the world.

The foe long since in silence slept;
Alike the conqueror silent sleeps;
And Time the ruined bridge has swept
Down the dark stream which seaward creeps.

On this green bank, by this soft stream,
We set today a votive stone;
That memory may their deed redeem,
When, like our sires, our sons are gone.

Spirit, that made those heroes dare
To die, and leave their children free,
Bid time and Nature gently spare
The shaft we raise to them and thee.

You might begin by using a graphic organizer to help you visualize the various parts of the poem. Your completed graphic could look like this:

Notice that this organizer lists four aspects of the poem which could be analyzed: word choice, rhyme, setting, and theme. Each of these parts can be broken down further. For example, you might break setting down into time and place. You could decide that setting is the aspect of the poem that you want to analyze. As you read through the poem, you may notice Emerson seems to be talking about two settings—one at the occasion of the poem's delivery, the other in the past. You begin to realize that the present event, the dedication of the statue, is a result of the war that was fought long before. You also realize that the "freedom" of the poem's listeners stems from the war that the soldiers fought in the past. You recognize that your parts-to-whole analysis is taking on a specific shape. You see that the setting causes readers to think of those who have sacrificed their lives for them. Consequently, your thesis will express the method of analysis your essay will use:

> Emerson reminds us on this Patriot's Day of the effects of the sacrifice those in the past have made for us.

After you've stated your thesis, you will closely examine and explain how nouns and verbs in the poem support your thesis. These explanations in the body of your paper will become the evidence. In your conclusion, you will make the connection between the causes (word choices) and the reader's overall awareness (the effect). The structure of your essay will be as follows:

Thesis

Cause one (part one—the war)

Cause two (part two—the sacrifice)

Cause three (part three—the present setting)

Effect

Working Alone:
Choose a song that you like. Then break the song into its parts. Pick one of those parts and write a paragraph analyzing the part in relationship to the whole song.

Working Together:
1. Look at one of your textbooks. How is the subject organized (broken into parts)?
2. Look at the statistics listed for a specific team player in the sports section of a newspaper. What can you assume about the player's performance from the statistics? What might you suppose about the team's performance after looking at four or more individual players' statistics?

Methods of Analysis

The effect of the word choices in Emerson's poem led you to develop a **cause-and-effect** thesis which analyzed the relationship between the parts and the whole. However, cause-and-effect is only one of a number of methods of analysis you can choose to use. Your choice of method will depend on your topic and the relationship you wish to examine between that topic's parts and its whole. The following are some common methods of analysis:

Definition	What is it? What are its features?
Process Analysis	How did you do that? How did that happen?
Comparison-Contrast	How are they the same? How are they different?
Classification	What are its features? To what group does it belong?
Cause and Effect	Why did it happen? How did it happen? What will happen?

The method which you choose will be determined by the thesis you decide to develop, the purpose of the piece of writing, and the audience for whom you are writing. For example, imagine that your task is to write a plan to improve the playing of your school's soccer team. If you were writing for the players, you might choose to organize your essay by using a **process analysis** which teaches them, step-by-step, how to execute a penalty kick. If you were writing for the alumni, you might show how alumni support could bolster team morale and school spirit—thus, you would demonstrate **cause and effect**. For the athletic office, you might use **definition** to establish the team's ideals and style of play, and then use **classification** to group the types of teams and players in the league. For the coaching staff, you might **compare and contrast** the team's style of play with that of an opponent.

Working Together: With a classmate, read the following thesis statements and decide which method of analysis each would warrant.

1. The showmanship of the band Phish is similar to that of the Grateful Dead.
2. The anti-Vietnam war movement in this country grew out of a number of historical events.
3. Major depression falls under the category of affective disorders.
4. Happiness means having good friends.
5. The keys to a perfect summer are good weather and good times.

Each method of analysis has its own guidelines that will help you structure your writing. Each is covered in detail in the next section.

Definition

What is it?

What are its features?

Definition, a common tool in writing, explains what you mean by a specific term or idea. You use definition every day. There are two broad categories of definition:

standard, or "simple," definition, and "extended" definition. A simple definition tends to be short, usually consisting of two or three sentences. An extended definition is more elaborate and may consist of several paragraphs or even several pages.

No matter what type of definition you are writing, the pattern of organization is basically the same. Definitions can be structured by using three basic components:

1. The item to be defined
2. The general category of the item
3. The distinguishing (special) features of the item

For example, a **simple definition** of the term *schizophrenia* would look something like this:

Schizophrenia is a type of psychosis characterized by disturbances in thought and language including delusions, hallucinations, and neologisms.

In this one-sentence definition, notice the three parts indicated: 1) the term—*schizophrenia*, 2) the category—psychosis, and 3) the distinguishing features—disturbances in thought and language. This is one way to define the term; obviously, there are others. The way in which you choose to explain a term depends on your audience and purpose. The previous definition would be appropriate if your purpose was to give a simple definition to a general audience.

If, however, you were writing a definition essay for your psychology class, you would probably write a more complicated, detailed definition than the previous one. This longer definition is known as an **extended definition.** Since this definition can be lengthy, it is organized as you would organize an essay. However, the essential structure of an extended definition is still the same as that of a simple definition. You identify the term that you are defining and place the item in a general category. This becomes the thesis and helps to focus the essay. Your explanation of the distinguishing features will form the body of the essay. In the body, you might use one paragraph or more to explain in detail each feature of the item which you are defining. In an extended definition you will probably also use examples and analogies to illustrate your ideas.

For example, an extended definition of *schizophrenia* might identify the history of diagnosing the disorder, the possible causes, the treatments currently in use, the effects of the disease on the families of schizophrenics, the different clinical subtypes, and the current prognoses for the disorder. The beginning of such an essay might look like this:

Schizophrenia is generally considered the most severe of the mental illnesses. It falls into the category of psychosis. The schizophrenic may experience disturbances in any one or more of the following areas: thought, perception, language, motor behavior, or mood.

The disordered thought of the schizophrenic may manifest itself in a variety of delusions ranging from notions of grandiosity to thoughts of persecution. The schizophrenic may believe himself to be a famous person and adopt the characteristics of that person. The persecution delusions are often quite frightening to the schizophrenic for they convince him that he is not safe from others. He may think that an innocent look from another person is really a stare of animosity and hatred or that the harmless overtures of kindness from others are, in fact, threats of bodily harm.

Oftentimes the disturbances of thought are compounded by perceptual difficulties. The most common are auditory hallucinations, or the "hearing of voices." These voices quite often reinforce the terror of the persecution delusions and may tell the patient to harm himself in some way. Over 50 percent of schizophrenics report experiencing auditory hallucinations. Less frequently reported are visual, olfactory, and tactile hallucinations.

As you see from this extended definition, after the term *schizophrenia* is simply defined in the introduction, the following paragraphs provide more details about it. The term's distinguishing features are presented in general form in the thesis and elaborated upon in the body of the paper. If the essay were to continue, subsequent paragraphs would cover speech, motor, and mood disturbances.

You might graphically represent the structure of the essay like this:

Introduction (thesis/simple definition)
Distinguishing feature 1 and supporting details
Distinguishing feature 2 and supporting details
Distinguishing feature 3 and supporting details
Distinguishing feature 4 and supporting details
Conclusion

Working Alone:

1. Write a simple definition for a term with which you are familiar. Decide who the audience is for your definition.
2. Next, write a simple definition of the same term for a different audience.
3. Write an outline for an extended definition of the same term for one of the audiences you have chosen.

Working Together:

1. With a partner, read some simple definitions that you find in a textbook. What are the parts of the definitions?
2. What do you notice about the structure of the definitions?

Process Analysis

How did you do that?
How did it happen?

Process analysis explains a procedure. Whenever you write directions telling how to complete a task or explaining how something happens, you are analyzing a procedure. There are two types of process analysis, **directional** and **informational.** When writing a directional process analysis, your purpose is to give directions telling how to complete a task. For example, you might write out the directions to the site of a party, instructions on how to assemble a computer, or a recipe for your favorite dish. When writing an informational process analysis, your purpose is to explain how something happens. This analysis is written with the goal of providing information rather than directions or instructions. For example, your explanation of how you write a paper will differ from your instructions to others on how to write a paper.

Working Together: With a partner, identify the following processes as either directional or informational. Then explain your choices.
1. How to appeal a grade
2. How you study for an exam
3. How to change a flat tire
4. How you silence a crying baby

Writing a Directional Process Analysis

As anyone who has gotten lost trying to follow directions to a party or who has bought a product requiring assembly knows, writing a directional process can be deceptively tricky. One wrong step can make the process unclear and can lead the reader astray. Part of the difficulty in writing this type of analysis occurs when the writer fails to see the procedure from the reader's point of view and assumes that details obvious to him will also be obvious to the reader. You can overcome this difficulty by keeping the following guidelines in mind as you create your directions and develop your process analysis:

1. Identify the process in the opening paragraph.
2. List any tools, parts, or equipment that will be needed to complete the process.
3. State the point at which the process begins.
4. Explain the steps in proper sequence.
5. Use strong transition words such as *first, next,* and *finally.*
6. Signal when the process is completed.

Read the following example of a directional process analysis.

HOW TO PASTE A DOCUMENT INTO AN EMAIL FROM A WORD PROGRAM

In order to paste a document from a Word program into an email, you should **first** go to your email writing center and address your email to the person to whom you wish to send it. **Next,** you can write a quick opening to the addressee in the message box, letting her know what you will be pasting in. **Then** open your word processing program and pull up the document you wish to send in the email. **Now,** select the document by clicking on "Select all" on your edit menu; **then** click on the icon for "Copy." Close the document. You are **now** back at your email screen. **Next,** place your cursor into your message box and click on the right-hand side of the mouse. **When** the menu appears, click on "Paste." Your document should **now** appear in the message box. Complete whatever message you wish to forward to the addressee and send off the email. You have **now** successfully pasted a document into an email!

Notice that the writer uses the second-person pronoun *you* throughout the paragraph. Directional processes are addressed to the second-person audience. In the opening of the essay, the writer states the process that is to be explained. The word *first* signals the beginning of the process. The writer also uses transition words such as *next, then,* and *now* in the paragraph to signal the sequence of the steps. The last sentence indicates that the process is complete.

Working Alone: Write a directional process on one of the following topics.

How to appeal a grade

How to use the reference section of the library

How to run a successful student government campaign

How to change your major

How to do something (for example, explain the steps involved in planting tomatoes or making a quilt)

Working Together: Exchange papers with a fellow student who has written on the same topic that you have. Which details are similar and which are different in your directions? How do you account for those differences?

Comparison and Contrast

How are they the same?
How are they different?

As the term suggests, *comparison and contrast* analyzes the similarities and differences of items. You use comparison and contrast frequently in your daily life. When deciding which computer to buy or whether Mark McGwire is a better hitter than Babe Ruth, you are likely to use comparison and contrast. Similarly, in school you would use comparison and contrast when your instructor asks you to discuss the similarities and differences between John Donne's love poems and his religious poems or to explain the differences between the American and French revolutions.

When formulating and writing a comparison and contrast, the first step is to identify a **basis for comparison.** For example, when determining whether the 1960s movie *Cape Fear* is better than the 1990s remake, you might base your comparison on camera techniques, development of suspense, acting, and pacing.

Once you have decided on one or more points of comparison, these will become part of your essay's thesis. The body of the essay can then be organized in two different ways:

The block method
The alternating (or point-by point) method

The *block method* organizes the body of the essay in two blocks. That is, the first part of the essay discusses all the points of comparison for Item A; the second part discusses all the points for Item B. For example, if you were to compare the two versions of *Cape Fear,* you might first talk about the original film's pacing, camera work and editing, and acting. In the second part of the essay, you would discuss the same aspects of the remake.

The block essay can be represented in this way:

I. Introduction
   A. Thesis
   B. Basis for comparison
II. Block 1: Original version of *Cape Fear*
   A. Pacing
   B. Camera work and editing
   C. Acting
III. Block 2: Remake of *Cape Fear*
   A. Pacing
   B. Camera work and editing
   C. Acting
IV. Conclusion

Here is how the written essay might look:

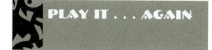
PLAY IT . . . AGAIN

During the last decade, Hollywood has become enraptured with the idea of remaking films from its own past. Given the arsenal of new technologies available to the modern filmmaker and the greater freedom in what can be shown on screen, it's tempting to assume that the remakes are better films than the originals. The fact is, some clearly are better; others clearly are not (as critics asked after the remake of Hitchcock's classic, *Psycho,* "Why bother?"). But rather than get locked in that debate, it's interesting to look at what the remake trend reveals about the changing styles of Hollywood and the tastes of the movie-going public.

A good place to look is at the two film versions of *Cape Fear.* Originally made in 1962 and remade in 1991, and based upon John D. McDonald's 1957 novel, *The Executioners, Cape Fear* is a story of an ex-convict's hunger to take revenge on the lawyer who bungled his case. By means of his sociopathic cunning and loopholes in the legal system, he terrorizes the man and his family and turns their stable, everyday world upside down. Both versions tell the same story, but the differences are most notable in the pacing, in the camera work and editing, and in the acting.

In the original film, director J. Lee Thompson allows the story to find its own pace, gradually letting tension build as the viewer meets the characters and discovers, as they do, their predicament. From this point on, it's a matter of tightening the screws of conflict until the full terror is felt. As is typical of the period, the camera work, editing, and use of black and white cinematography are unremarkable. The camera moves unobtrusively, telling the story with a variety of long, medium, and close-up shots. The editing is in the seamless, "invisible" style that Hollywood was then known for. Thompson is careful not to call attention to the camera, instead allowing the script and actors to reveal the story.

Gregory Peck, Robert Mitchum, and Polly Bergen head the cast, with Peck as Sam Bowden, the attorney and family man being pursued by the vengeful Max Cady. As always, Peck is restrained, almost stiff, a gray flannel man in a civilized world. Cady, a convicted rapist recently released from prison and nursing his hatred for Bowden, is portrayed by Mitchum, who uses his swagger and sneering smile to imply rather than state the twisted depths of Cady's psyche. And Bergen is a stylish 1950s-style housewife.

Martin Scorsese's remake of *Cape Fear*, although telling the same story, is a strikingly different film. He opts for full speed, plunging the viewer headlong into the story from the opening scene and maintaining a relentless pace until the very end. His camera work and editing are anything but invisible. Instead, Scorsese adopts a "slash-and-burn" approach, using the camera to turn plot flips, to spy on people's secret lives, and to render the violence of the action. In one scene the camera actually goes topsy-turvy to create for the viewer the feeling of being caught in a raging river. On another occasion, the director employs infrared effects to put the viewer off guard.

Nick Nolte plays Sam Bowden with some of the restraint Peck used, giving the viewer reason to believe that Sam is a good citizen with a just cause, but at times he seems to be as off guard as the viewer feels, caught in a world he suddenly can't recognize. The biggest departure in acting, however, is Robert De Niro's Max Cady. As the sociopathic ex-con bent on destruction, De Niro is completely over the top. Appearing for the role like an escapee from Gold's Gym with his pumped-up pecs and biceps and his apocalyptic ravings, he chews the scenery. He even takes a page from another Mitchum role (in *Night of the Hunter*) by having the words *love* and *hate* tattooed on his fists. Jessica Lange portrays Sam's wife with a suggestion that she has steamy depths of her own. As a nice bit of homage to the original, both Peck and Mitchum have cameo roles in the remake.

Whereas the original *Cape Fear* offers itself to us as a slice of life from a slower, 1950s world, the remake, with its dazzling Technicolor and camera pyrotechnics, and influenced by the pacing of TV shows, fairly screams, "Look at me! I'm a 1990s movie!" Both films are well made and enjoyable, though they were clearly designed by different Hollywoods with different audiences in mind.

The *alternating—or point-by-point—method* switches back and forth between Item A and Item B in each section of the essay. In this case, still using the *Cape Fear* example, you would discuss the original film's pacing, then the remake's pacing; the original's camera work and editing, then the remake's camera work and editing, and so on. The alternating essay can be outlined this way:

I. Introduction
   A. Thesis
   B. Basis for comparison
II. Point 1: Pacing
   A. Original film
   B. Remake

III. Point 2: Camera work and editing
  A. Original film
  B. Remake
IV. Point 3: Acting
  A. Original film
  B. Remake
 V. Conclusion

Here is how the essay might be written:

PLAY IT . . . AGAIN

During the last decade, Hollywood has become enraptured with the idea of re-making films from its own past. Given the arsenal of new technologies available to the modern filmmaker and the greater freedom in what can be shown on screen, it's tempting to assume that the remakes are better than the originals. The fact is, some clearly are better; others clearly are not (as critics asked after the re-make of Hitchcock's classic, *Psycho,* "Why bother?") But rather than get locked in that debate, it's interesting to look at what the remake trend reveals about the changing styles of Hollywood and the tastes of the movie-going public.

A good place to look is at the two film versions of *Cape Fear.* Originally made in 1962 and remade in 1991, and based upon John D. MacDonald's 1957 novel, *The Executioners, Cape Fear* is a story of an ex-convict's hunger for revenge on the lawyer who bungled his case. By means of his sociopathic cunning and loopholes in the legal system, he terrorizes the man and his family and turns their stable, everyday world upside down. Both versions tell the same story, but the differences are most notable in the pacing, in the camera work and editing, and in the acting.

In the original film, director J. Lee Thompson allows the story to find its own pace, gradually letting tension build as the viewer meets the characters and dis-covers, as they do, their predicament. From this point on, it's a matter of tighten-ing the screws of conflict until the full terror is felt. The remake of *Cape Fear,* on the other hand, opts for full speed, plunging the viewer headlong into the story from the opening scene and maintaining a relentless pace to the very end. In both ver-sions—the slower 1962 film and the modern, TV-influenced film—the results are satisfying, yet each film reflects its own time.

The camera work and editing likewise reveal differences. As is typical of the earlier period, the 1962 film is shot in black and white. The camera moves unob-trusively, telling the story through a variety of long, medium, and close-up shots. The editing is in the seamless, "invisible" style that Hollywood was then known for. Thompson is careful not to call attention to the camera, instead allowing the actors and the script to reveal the story. With director Martin Scorsese, on the other hand, the shooting and editing are anything but invisible. His camera bobs and weaves to turn plot flips, to spy on people's secret lives, and to render the vi-olence of the action. In one scene the camera actually goes topsy-turvy to create for the viewer the feeling of being caught in a raging river. On another occasion, Scorsese employs infrared effects to put the viewer off guard.

Both films have star power. Gregory Peck, Robert Mitchum, and Polly Bergen head the cast of the 1962 version; Nick Nolte, Robert De Niro, and Jessica Lange do the same in the remake. In the acting styles, however, the differences are marked. Peck is Sam Bowden, the attorney and family man being pursued by the vengeful Max Cady. As always, Peck is restrained, almost stiff, a gray flannel man in a civilized world. Cady, a convicted rapist recently released from prison and nursing his hatred for Bowden, is portrayed by Mitchum, who uses his swagger and sneering smile to imply rather than state the twisted depths of Cady's psyche. In the remake, Nolte plays Sam Bowden with some of the restraint Peck used, giving the viewer reason to believe that Sam is a good citizen with a just cause, but there's a hint of hidden secrets in him, too. The biggest departure in acting, however, is De Niro's Max Cady. As the sociopathic ex-con bent on destruction, De Niro is completely over the top. Appearing for the role like an escapee from Gold's Gym with his pumped-up pecs and biceps and his apocalyptic ravings, he chews the scenery. He also takes a page from another Mitchum role (in *Night of the Hunter*) by having the words *love* and *hate* tattooed on his fists. The women in each film, too, are very different. Bergen portrays a stylish 1950s-style housewife while Lange's character has steamy depths of her own. As a nice bit of homage to the original, both Peck and Mitchum have cameo roles in the remake.

Whereas the original *Cape Fear* offers itself to us as a black-and-white slice of life, the remake, with its dazzling Technicolor and camera pyrotechnics, fairly screams, "Look at me! I'm a 1990s movie!" Both films are well made and enjoyable, though they were clearly designed by different Hollywoods with different audiences in mind.

Regardless of the method of organization that you use, follow these guidelines for writing your comparison-and-contrast essay:

Choose two items that can be logically compared and contrasted.

Decide on the basis (bases) of comparison.

Write a thesis that includes the bases.

Select a form, either block or alternating.

Working Together: With a classmate, discuss possible points of comparison for the following pairs:

two current teenage singing heartthrobs
two local restaurants
a comedy show from the past and a current comedy show

Working Alone: Write a paragraph comparing two items with which you are familiar.

Classification

What are its significant features?
To what group does it belong?

What section of the newspaper do you read first? Sports? Business? Entertainment? If you were looking for a job, you would probably turn to Help Wanted, and depending on the kind of job you were seeking, you would then turn to a particular part of the Help Wanted section such as Medical, Professional, or Technical Help. Imagine how difficult it would be to find a job listing if they were not arranged in categories or *classified* according to similarity.

Classification is a method of analysis used to organize items into groups based on a common characteristic. This is an important skill that can help you organize and understand the world around you. When you study biology, you learn the basic classifications of plants and animals, and under the category *animals,* you find another set of classifications—mammals, amphibians, reptiles, and so on. When you study literature, you learn that literature is frequently classified as poetry, drama, or fiction. On a restaurant menu, foods might be separated into salads, entrees, and desserts. In each of these categories, items are grouped together according to shared features. Such groupings help you make sense of your world.

Classification is also an important tool to help you organize your ideas in writing. When using classification to develop an idea in an essay, keep the following points in mind:

1. Identify significant distinguishing features to organize the items into groups or classes.
2. A significant distinguishing feature is determined by your purpose in organizing the classification for your particular audience.

Suppose you have been asked to write an analysis of the learning styles of the student body at your school or a paper analyzing the top fashion models of the past decade. One obvious way to approach either task is to group the students or fashion models according to some shared significant features. For example, in writing about the student body, you might establish categories based on age, test performance, or cultural background. However, it would be useless to classify students based on their height and hair color because such classifications would yield little meaningful information for gaining an understanding of student learning styles. Height and hair color, however, might be significant features to use in an essay examining changing trends in fashion modeling and could lead to a greater understanding of this subject. You might also use classifications such as age and weight. Remember that when you choose a significant feature to organize a category of classification, each item which you place in the category must have a connection to that feature.

Organizing a Classification

Thesis: Identifies the topic, the major categories, and the distinguishing features

First Category: Specific examples and details that explain their connection to the distinguishing feature

Second Category: Specific examples and details that explain their connection to the distinguishing feature

Third Category: Specific examples and details that share a distinguishing feature

Conclusion: Restates or refers back to the thesis

The following is an excerpt from an essay classifying the fictional detective story into categories. There are more categories than the three discussed in this excerpt, but you can see how classification works by reading this sample.

Within the broad definition of the *mystery novel,* there are various categories into which such books are usually placed. The simplest division is into the categories of "amateurs" and "pros." That is, the person(s) solving the mystery are either working professionals (cops and private investigators) or amateur sleuths who do it as a hobby. Within these two broad categories, there are further ways to classify mystery novels.

One very popular form of mystery novel has long been the "cozy," a name which derives from the fact that they almost always have a "homey" feel, with little graphic violence. The crime-solving is done by amateur, or "armchair," sleuths. Rex Stout's books featuring Nero Wolfe, who never leaves the penthouse where he tends his orchids but always manages to solve crimes, are a good example of this form. The prototype of the cozy, however, is Agatha Christie's Miss Marple.

The most popular mysteries in Britain have for many years been "locked room" stories. In these tales, as the name implies, the murder occurs in a specific place, the "locked room," with a limited number of suspects. The detective—either a pro or an amateur—has to determine who the murderer is and how he or she managed to commit the crime without any of the other possible suspects noticing. In the most intricate "locked room" mysteries, the body is alone in the room, and the challenge is figuring out who managed to kill a person and leave the scene while making it look as if no one but the victim was present. Again, a master practitioner of this type of tale was Agatha Christie, with her hero Hercule Poirot.

The "police procedural" is a mystery form in which the emphasis is on the painstaking and often authentically detailed investigative work that is carried out by police detectives and forensic technicians. Most notable in this category is Ed McBain's 87th Precinct series. The idea behind the police procedural is also perhaps familiar to TV viewers through shows such as "Law and Order" and "Homicide."

One final category worth noting is the "hard-boiled" mystery novel. This type of book generally features a PI (private investigator) who takes on cases for hire. Frequently, he is a loner who has trouble with police, women, and alcohol, in no particular order. The most famous of the early detectives in this mold were Dashiell Hammett's Sam Spade, featured in *The Maltese Falcon,* and Raymond Chandler's Philip Marlowe in novels such as *The Big Sleep.* Both of these characters, by the way, were portrayed in the movies by Humphrey Bogart. More recently, the hard-boiled novel has been opened up by women writers such as Sara Paretsky and Sue Grafton, who depict the crime solving of female PIs.

Working Alone: Write a classification of the students in your English class. Then list the primary categories you have used to organize the classification.

Working Together: Working with a classmate, identify at least two significant features that you would use to organize a classification of the following subjects. List at least two specific examples for each category.

1. Players in a particular sport
2. Types of teachers you encountered in high school
3. Fashion statements for people in your age group
4. The types of music played on a local radio station

The significant features which you use to organize a classification will depend on your purpose for writing for a particular audience. For instance, imagine that your mother is thinking of applying to the school that you are currently attending, and she's asked you to describe the student body. Since your purpose is to provide information to help her decide whether the school is the right choice for her, you might use age groups, educational goals, and the personal interests of the students as a way of organizing the classification. With your mother as your audience, your purpose is to help her decide whether she will have any classmates her age or who would share her interests.

If, on the other hand, your psychology professor has asked you to write an analysis of the benefits of particular classroom activities in helping students understand course material, you might use the students' learning styles as the significant feature for organizing the analysis. In structuring this classification, your purpose is to let your psychology professor know that you understand the different ways in which students learn new information.

Working Alone: Select one of the topics you identified in the last Working Together activity. Then write two analyses that classify this topic for different purposes and different audiences.

Cause and Effect

Why did it happen?
What will happen?

"Why did I fail the math test?" "What will happen if I cram all night for the next exam?" You engage in this type of thinking every day. Often you try to understand why things happened: "Why did I fail the test?" Every time you face a decision, you weigh the effects of the choices: "What will happen if I cram all night?"

Considering the reasons why something happens and anticipating the consequences that will follow are common ways of analyzing and understanding events and actions. Your history teacher might ask you what events caused World War I. Your writing teacher might ask you what will be the effect of beginning your essay with a blunt, surprising fact. In both situations you would be considering the consequences of events, and you would be engaging in a type of thinking commonly referred to as **causal analysis.**

Analyzing cause and effect and writing the causal analysis seem relatively easy. However, there are two difficulties of which you should be aware:

1. Distinguishing between coincidence and true causes
2. Organizing the causes and effects in a logical sequence

Sometimes events happen so close together or appear to have such a close relationship that it seems logical to assume that one event caused the other. In cause-and-effect analysis, it is important to determine whether or not there is a causal relationship between events and to be sure that it's not just a coincidence that one event followed another. For example, suppose a total eclipse of the sun was followed by an earthquake. In ancient times it would not have been unusual for people to connect the two events and to assume that the eclipse caused the earthquake. However, scientific evidence indicates that the true cause of an earthquake is the buildup in seismic pressure along a fault line and that there is no connection between an earthquake and an eclipse. In this example, these two events are linked by coincidence, not by cause.

Superstitions are another common example of mistaking a coincidence for a cause or an effect: "Because I wore my lucky T-shirt, I did well on the exam (therefore, if I wear the shirt again, I won't need to study for tomorrow's test!)." Because mistaking a coincidence for a true cause or effect is dangerous in this type of analysis, it's important that you make sure that there is really a relationship between the events. One simple way to check is to ask whether the same cause or effect would result if particular events were left out of the sequence. ("If I'd worn a different T-shirt, would I have passed the exam?") If the same cause or effect would have resulted, perhaps the link is insignificant or merely coincidental.

A cause-and-effect analysis might read like this:

Language experts bemoan the fact that today's young adults have limited vocabularies which lead to diminished speech. These critics point to excessive TV viewing, the popularity of video games, and the breakdown of family communication as the causes of this increasing inarticulation.

The average twenty-year-old has watched more than six hours of TV a day for at least sixteen years. During the viewing hours of the 1980s and 1990s, the young adult heard 50 percent fewer and less difficult words than viewers had in previous decades. The speech patterns of TV became the speech patterns of the viewer. The results? Lots of "okays," "likes," and "yeahs" connected with pauses and little else.

Video games and the solitary nature of play associated with them are also culprits contributing to the young adult's lack of language skills. Although the games may be played alongside a friend, they require little, if any, verbal communication. A few grunts, booms, and "got 'em" are the extent of the conversation.

Dinner around the table was once often a time for the family to talk about the day's events, both local and global. However, those times are few and far between for the modern family. First, dual working parents may not be home at the same time. Also, kids are often involved in many organized activities which frequently run through the dinner hour. Conversation, if held at all, tends to be around who needs to be picked up at what practice field and who's doing the driving the next day.

With the inarticulate speech of TV role models, solitary game playing, and rushed dinner hours, is it any wonder that today's young people have fewer and fewer words at their disposal?

What are the effects that the writer establishes in this essay? What does she list as the causes?

Working Together:
1. With a fellow student, identify the causes of one of the following:
   A. The reason why a particular team won a world championship
   B. Why one make of automobile costs significantly more than another
2. Then identify some of the effects of the following:
   A. Higher gasoline prices
   B. Prolonged drought in the Midwest

The other difficulty in writing a cause-and-effect essay is organizing the events in a logical sequence. There are two basic methods of organization for the cause-and-effect essay:

1. Identifying several causes that result in one particular effect
2. Identifying one cause that results in several effects

In the first method of organization, the thesis is built on the effect that will be proven by the causes explained in the body of the essay. The following is a typical thesis built in this way:

The baby boom, a dramatic increase in the birth rate between 1945 and 1960, was caused by several events which occurred at the same time.

In the second method of organization, the thesis is built on the cause that will be proven by the effects explained in the body of the essay. The following is a typical thesis built in this way:

As the baby boom generation has aged, it has had a dramatic effect on American culture and government.

These methods of constructing a cause-and-effect essay might be graphically represented in these ways:

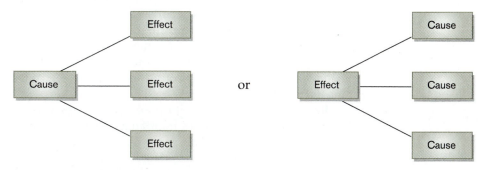

A Final Note On Writing An Analysis

This chapter has explained analysis by focusing on five separate methods which you might use to organize an analytical essay. However, often as you write an essay, you might use more than one method of analysis to explain your ideas. For example, if you were writing an essay on your favorite ethnic food, you might use **definition** to explain what it is, **process analysis** to explain how to make it, comparison and contrast to liken it to a more familiar food, **classification** to place it into a particular category, and **cause and effect** to discuss its nutritional benefits. You probably wouldn't use all of these methods in the same essay, but as you are becoming aware by now, writing is rarely such a neat process that you will always use only one of the methods of analysis as you develop your ideas.

In writing analyses, remember these key points:

1. Keep your analysis focused on one or two aspects of your topic.
2. Make sure that you define all of the terms and ideas for your audience. You can use your skill of summary writing to help you establish the background for your analysis.
3. Be sure that you support your analysis with concrete evidence.
4. Write with an objective tone. You are choosing the topic and the thesis, but the analysis should not be a personal, emotional response to the topic.

Throughout this text, you have been breaking down writing into its various parts. You have looked at the role of audience and purpose. You have seen process divided into prewriting, writing, revising, and editing; you have also looked at the components of an essay—the introduction, thesis, body, and conclusion. You have read an in-depth discussion of each of these aspects of writing. You have become aware of the ways in which each aspect contributes to the final product— the written text. Most important, you have assessed the writing of others as well as your own writing to determine how well the components fit together. In other words, you have analyzed writing.

Suggestions for Writing

1. Using any poem from the readings in this book, examine the lines for some interesting words. Then write a parts-to-whole analysis in which you show how the words you've selected relate to the larger meanings of the poem.
2. Select a term or expression from one of your hobbies and write an extended definition of it. (For example, if you were writing about surfing, you might define the term *goofy foot.* If you were writing about music, you might examine the word *feedback.*)
3. Write an informational or directional process analysis about something you do regularly but write about it for an audience who know nothing about the process. (For example, changing a flat tire, tying a necktie, or applying eye makeup.)
4. Referring to the Working Together activity on page 200, (compare and/or contrast two singing heartthrobs, TV shows, and so on), develop a compare/contrast essay. Remember to use either a block or an alternating method of organization.
5. Examine a desk drawer (or bureau drawer, wastebasket, glove compartment, and so on) and then write an essay analyzing its contents using classification.
6. Reflect on a change in your thinking or behavior that you've made since starting college. Then write a causal analysis in which you explore the causes or the effects of the change.

READINGƒ

THE DIƒCOVERY OF WHAT IT MEANƒ TO BE AN AMERICAN
JAMES BALDWIN

"It is a complex fate to be an American," Henry James observed, and the principal discovery an American writer makes in Europe is just how complex this fate is. America's history, her aspirations, her peculiar triumphs, her even more peculiar defeats, and her position in the world—yesterday and today—are all so profoundly and stubbornly unique that the very word "America" remains a new, almost completely undefined and extremely controversial proper noun. No one in the world seems to know exactly what it describes, not even we motley millions who call ourselves Americans.

I left America because I doubted my ability to survive the fury of the color problem here. (Sometimes I still do.) I wanted to prevent myself from becoming *merely* a Negro; or, even, merely a Negro writer. I wanted to find out in what way the *specialness* of my experience could be made to connect me with other people instead of dividing me from them. (I was as isolated from Negroes as I was from whites, which is what happens when a Negro begins, at bottom, to believe what white people say about him.)

In my necessity to find the terms on which my experience could be related to that of others, Negroes and whites, writers and non-writers, I proved, to my astonishment, to be as American as any Texas GI. And I found my experience was shared by every American writer I knew in Paris. Like me, they had been divorced from their origins, and it turned out to make very little difference that the origins of white Americans were European and mine were African—they were no more at home in Europe than I was.

The fact that I was the son of a slave and they were the sons of free men meant less, by the time we confronted each other on European soil, than the fact that we were both searching for our separate identities. When we had found these, we seemed to be saying, why, then, we would no longer need to cling to the shame and bitterness which had divided us so long.

It became terribly clear in Europe, as it never had been here, that we knew more about each other than any European ever could. And it also became clear that, no matter where our fathers had been born, or what they had endured, the fact of Europe had formed us both, was part of our identity and part of our inheritance.

I had been in Paris a couple of years before any of this became clear to me. When it did, I, like many a writer before me upon the discovery that his props have all been knocked out from under him, suffered a species of breakdown and was carried off to the mountains of Switzerland. There, in that absolutely alabaster landscape, armed with two Bessie Smith records and a typewriter, I began to try to recreate the life that I had first known as a child and from which I had spent so many years in flight.

It was Bessie Smith, through her tone and her cadence, who helped me to dig back to the way I myself must have spoken when I was a pickaninny, and to remember the things I had heard and seen and felt. I had buried them very deep. I had never listened to Bessie Smith in America (in the same way that, for years, I would not touch watermelon), but in Europe she helped to reconcile me to being a "nigger."

I do not think that I could have made this reconciliation here. Once I was able to accept my role—as distinguished, I must say, from my "place"—in the extraordinary drama which is America, I was released from the illusion that I hated America.

The story of what can happen to an American Negro writer in Europe simply illustrates, in some relief, what can happen to any American writer there. It is not meant, of course, to imply that it happens to them all, for Europe can be very crippling, too; and, anyway, a writer, when he has made his first breakthrough, has simply won a crucial skirmish in a dangerous, unending, and unpredictable battle. Still, the breakthrough is important, and the point is that an American writer, in order to achieve it, very often has to leave this country.

The American writer, in Europe, is released, first of all, from the necessity of apologizing for himself. It is not until he *is* released from the habit of flexing his muscles and proving that he is just a "regular guy" that he realizes how crippling this habit has been. It is not necessary for him, there, to pretend to be something he is not, for the artist does not encounter in Europe the same suspicion he encounters here. Whatever the Europeans may actually think of artists, they have killed enough of them off by now to know that they are as real—and as persistent—as rain, snow, taxes, or businessmen.

Of course, the reason for Europe's comparative clarity concerning the different functions of men in society is that European society has always been divided into classes in a way that American society never has been. A European writer considers himself to be part of an old and honorable tradition—of intellectual activity, of letters—and his choice of a vocation does not cause him any uneasy wonder as to whether or not it will cost him all his friends. But this tradition does not exist in America.

On the contrary, we have a very deep-seated distrust of real intellectual effort (probably because we suspect that it will destroy, as I hope it does, that myth of America to which we cling so desperately). An American writer fights his way to one of the lowest rungs on the American social ladder by means of pure bullheadedness and an indescribable series of odd jobs. He probably *has* been a "regular fellow" for much of his adult life, and it is not easy for him to step out of that lukewarm bath.

We must, however, consider a rather serious paradox: though American society is more mobile than Europe's, it is easier to cut across social and occupational lines there than it is here. This has something to do, I think, with the problem of status in American life. Where everyone has status, it is also perfectly possible, after all, that no one has. It seems inevitable, in any case, that a man may become uneasy as to just what his status is.

But Europeans have lived with the idea of status for a long time. A man can be as proud of being a good waiter as of being a good actor, and, in neither case, feel threatened. And this means that the actor and the waiter can have a freer and more genuinely friendly relationship in Europe than they are likely to have here. The waiter does not feel, with obscure resentment, that the actor has "made it," and the actor is not tormented by the fear that he may find himself, tomorrow, once again a waiter.

This lack of what may roughly be called social paranoia causes the American writer in Europe to feel—almost certainly for the first time in his life—that he can reach out to everyone, that he is accessible to everyone and open to everything. This is an extraordinary feeling. He feels, so to speak, his own weight, his own value.

It is as though he suddenly came out of a dark tunnel and found himself beneath the open sky. And, in fact, in Paris, I began to see the sky for what seemed to be the first time. It was borne in on me—and it did not make me feel melancholy—that this sky had been there before I was born and would be there when I was dead. And it was up to me, therefore, to make of my brief opportunity the most that could be made.

I was born in New York, but have lived only in pockets of it. In Paris, I lived in all parts of the city—on the Right Bank and the Left, among the bourgeoisie and among *les misérables,* and knew all kinds of people, from pimps and prostitutes in Pigalle to Egyptian bankers in Neuilly. This may sound extremely unprincipled or even obscurely immoral: I found it healthy. I love to talk to people, all kinds of people, and almost everyone, as I hope we still know, loves a man who loves to listen.

This perpetual dealing with people very different from myself caused a shattering in me of preconceptions I scarcely knew I held. The writer is meeting in Europe people who are not American, whose sense of reality is entirely different from his own. They may love or hate or admire or fear or envy this country—they see it, in any case, from another point of view, and this forces the writer to reconsider many things he had always taken for granted. This reassessment, which can be very painful, is also very valuable.

This freedom, like all freedom, has its dangers and its responsibilities. One day it begins to be borne in on the writer, and with great force, that he is living in Europe as an American. If he were living there as a European, he would be living on a different and far less attractive continent.

This crucial day may be the day on which an Algerian taxi-driver tells him how it feels to be an Algerian in Paris. It may be the day on which he passes a café terrace and catches a glimpse of the tense, intelligent, and troubled face of Albert Camus. Or it may be the day on which someone asks him to explain Little Rock and he begins to feel that it would be simpler—and, corny as the words may sound, more honorable—to *go* to Little Rock than sit in Europe, on an American passport, trying to explain it.

This is a personal day, a terrible day, the day to which his entire sojourn has been tending. It is the day he realizes that there are no untroubled countries in this fearfully troubled world; that if he has been preparing himself for anything in Europe, he has been preparing himself—for America. In short, the freedom that the

American writer finds in Europe brings him, full circle, back to himself, with the responsibility for his development where it always was: in his own hands.

Even the most incorrigible maverick has to be born somewhere. He may leave the group that produced him—he may be forced to—but nothing will efface his origins, the marks of which he carries with him everywhere. I think it is important to know this and even find it a matter for rejoicing, as the strongest people do, regardless of their station. On this acceptance, literally, the life of a writer depends.

The charge has often been made against American writers that they do not describe society, and have no interest in it. They only describe individuals in opposition to it, or isolated from it. Of course, what the American writer is describing is his own situation. But what is *Anna Karenina* describing if not the tragic fate of the isolated individual, at odds with her time and place?

The real difference is that Tolstoy was describing an old and dense society in which everything seemed—to the people in it, though not to Tolstoy—to be fixed forever. And the book is a masterpiece because Tolstoy was able to fathom, and make us see, the hidden laws which really governed this society and made Anna's doom inevitable.

American writers do not have a fixed society to describe. The only society they know is one in which nothing is fixed and in which the individual must fight for his identity. This is a rich confusion, indeed, and it creates for the American writer unprecedented opportunities.

That the tensions of American life, as well as the possibilities, are tremendous is certainly not even a question. But these are dealt with in contemporary literature mainly compulsively; that is, the book is more likely to be a symptom of our tension than an examination of it. The time has come, God knows, for us to examine ourselves, but we can do this only if we are willing to free ourselves of the myth of America and try to find out what is really happening here.

Every society is really governed by hidden laws, by unspoken but profound assumptions on the part of the people, and ours is no exception. It is up to the American writer to find out what these laws and assumptions are. In a society much given to smashing taboos without thereby managing to be liberated from them, it will be no easy matter.

It is no wonder, in the meantime, that the American writer keeps running off to Europe. He needs sustenance for his journey and the best models he can find. Europe has what we do not have yet, a sense of the mysterious and inexorable limits of life, a sense, in a word, of tragedy. And we have what they sorely need: a new sense of life's possibilities.

In this endeavor to wed the vision of the Old World with that of the New, it is the writer, not the statesman, who is our strongest arm. Though we do not wholly believe it yet, the interior life is a real life, and the intangible dreams of people have a tangible effect on the world.

Topics for Thinking and Writing

1. James Baldwin's "discovery" of his Americanness became possible when he moved to Paris. Why was it necessary for him to move abroad before this could happen?

2. In a small group, identify various badges by which you might be identified, e.g., *student*, *friend*, and so on. Discuss how you would define these terms. What experiences have helped to shape these definitions?

3. At the end of the essay, Baldwin writes that Europe has something to offer America, and America something to offer Europe. When you're defining an idea or an experience, how important is it to have something with which to contrast it? Why?

4. How does Baldwin define *being an American* in this essay? Write a brief piece discussing how this definition differs from or is similar to the way that you would define the term.

5. This essay was originally published in 1959. Write a brief piece discussing which of Baldwin's assumptions are still valid today and which are not.

CONVERSATIONAL BALLGAMES
NANCY MASTERSON SAKAMOTO

1   After I was married and had lived in Japan for a while, my Japanese gradually improved to the point where I could take part in simple conversations with my husband and his friends and family. And I began to notice that often, when I joined in, the others would look startled, and the conversational topic would come to a halt. After this happened several times, it became clear to me that I was doing something wrong. But for a long time, I didn't know what it was.

2   Finally, after listening carefully to many Japanese conversations, I discovered what my problem was. Even though I was speaking Japanese, I was handling the conversation in a western way.

3   Japanese-style conversations develop quite differently from western-style conversations. And the difference isn't only in the languages. I realized that just as I kept trying to hold western-style conversations even when I was speaking Japanese, so my English students kept trying to hold Japanese-style conversations even when they were speaking English. We were unconsciously playing entirely different conversational ballgames.

4   A western-style conversation between two people is like a game of tennis. If I introduce a topic, a conversational ball, I expect you to hit it back. If you agree with me, I don't expect you simply to agree and do nothing more. I expect you to add something—a reason for agreeing, another example, or an elaboration to carry the idea further. But I don't expect you always to agree. I am just as happy if you question me, or challenge me, or completely disagree with me. Whether you agree or disagree, your response will return the ball to me.

5   And then it is my turn again. I don't serve a new ball from my original starting line. I hit your ball back again from where it has bounced. I carry your idea further, or answer your questions or objections, or challenge or question you. And so the ball goes back and forth, with each of us doing our best to give it a new twist, an original spin, or a powerful smash.

6   And the more vigorous the action, the more interesting and exciting the game. Of course, if one of us gets angry, it spoils the conversation, just as it spoils a tennis game. But getting excited is not at all the same as getting angry. After all, we are

not trying to hit each other. We are trying to hit the ball. So long as we attack only each other's opinions, and do not attack each other personally, we don't expect anyone to get hurt. A good conversation is supposed to be interesting and exciting.

7   If there are more than two people in the conversation, then it is like doubles in tennis, or like volleyball. There's no waiting in line. Whoever is nearest and quickest hits the ball, and if you step back, someone else will hit it. No one stops the game to give you a turn. You're responsible for taking your own turn.

8   But whether it's two players or a group, everyone does his best to keep the ball going, and no one person has the ball for very long.

9   A Japanese-style conversation, however, is not at all like tennis or volleyball. It's like bowling. You wait for your turn. And you always know your place in line. It depends on such things as whether you are older or younger, a close friend or a relative stranger to the previous speaker, in a senior or junior position, and so on.

10   When your turn comes, you step up to the starting line with your bowling ball, and carefully bowl it. Everyone else stands back and watches politely, murmuring encouragement. Everyone waits until the ball has reached the end of the alley, and watches to see if it knocks down all the pins, or only some of them, or none of them. There is a pause, while everyone registers your score.

11   Then, after everyone is sure that you have completely finished your turn, the next person in line steps up to the same starting line, with a different ball. He doesn't return your ball, and he does not begin from where your ball stopped. There is no back and forth at all. All the balls run parallel. And there is always a suitable pause between turns. There is no rush, no excitement, no scramble for the ball.

12   No wonder everyone looked startled when I took part in Japanese conversations. I paid no attention to whose turn it was, and kept snatching the ball halfway down the alley and throwing it back at the bowler. Of course the conversation died. I was playing the wrong game.

13   This explains why it is almost impossible to get a western-style conversation or discussion going with English students in Japan. I used to think that the problem was their lack of English language ability. But I finally came to realize that the biggest problem is that they, too, are playing the wrong game.

14   Whenever I serve a volleyball, everyone just stands back and watches it fall, with occasional murmurs of encouragement. No one hits it back. Everyone waits until I call on someone to take a turn. And when that person speaks, he doesn't hit my ball back. He serves a new ball. Again, everyone just watches it fall.

15   So I call on someone else. This person does not refer to what the previous speaker has said. He also serves a new ball. Nobody seems to have paid any attention to what anyone else has said. Everyone begins again from the same starting line, and all the balls run parallel. There is never any back and forth. Everyone is trying to bowl with a volleyball.

16   And if I try a simpler conversation, with only two of us, then the other person tries to bowl with my tennis ball. No wonder foreign English teachers in Japan get discouraged.

17   Now that you know about the difference in the conversational ballgames, you may think that all your troubles are over. But if you have been trained all your life to play one game, it is no simple matter to switch to another, even if you know the rules. Knowing the rules is not at all the same thing as playing the game.

18   Even now, during a conversation in Japanese I will notice a startled reaction, and belatedly realize that once again I have rudely interrupted by instinctively trying to hit back the other person's bowling ball. It is no easier for me to "just listen" during a conversation, than it is for my Japanese students to "just relax" when speaking with foreigners. Now I can truly sympathize with how hard they must find it to try to carry on a western-style conversation.

19   If I have not yet learned to do conversational bowling in Japanese, at least I have figured out one thing that puzzled me for a long time. After his first trip to America, my husband complained that Americans asked him so many questions and made him talk so much at the dinner table that he never had a chance to eat. When I asked him why he couldn't talk and eat at the same time, he said that Japanese do not customarily think that dinner, especially on fairly formal occasions, is a suitable time for extended conversation.

20   Since westerners think that conversation is an indispensable part of dining, and indeed would consider it impolite not to converse with one's dinner partner, I found this Japanese custom rather strange. Still, I could accept it as a cultural difference even though I didn't really understand it. But when my husband added, in explanation, that Japanese consider it extremely rude to talk with one's mouth full, I got confused. Talking with one's mouth full is certainly not an American custom. We think it very rude, too. Yet we still manage to to talk a lot and eat at the same time. How do we do it?

Topics for Thinking and Writing

1. This essay compares and contrasts Japanese and American cultures. What is the basis of the comparison? Which method of organization, block or alternating, is used to organize the comparison?
2. What secondary topic does Sakamoto discuss in paragraphs 19 and 20? Why do you think she felt it necessary to include a brief discussion of this topic?
3. Sakamoto compares conversational styles to a type of ball game. Point to specific examples of ball games she uses to develop the comparison. In what ways is the idea of comparing a conversation to a ball game effective? In what ways might it be ineffective or inaccurate?
4. Using Sakamoto's essay as a model, write a comparison of the conversational styles of two cultural, ethnic, or age groups.
5. Write a comparison of the different conversational styles you would use with an audience of your peers and with an audience of authority, such as your boss or your instructor.

THE HANDSHAKE
RUSSELL BAKER

1   One of the worst handshakes I have ever been involved in occurred a few weeks ago in the Middle West. This hand placed itself in my hand, as hands commonly do when their proprietors are being introduced, and immediately made itself at home.

2   Usually hands are satisfied to drop in for a second or two and then go on about their business, but I could tell from the feel of this hand that it was of a mind to settle in for a long stay. Being a social coward, I didn't want to eject it forcibly, so I attempted a subtle withdrawal by moving my torso out of the area occupied by its proprietor.

3   The hand was not to be evicted that easily. It nestled in snugly between my palm and finger tips and dragged its proprietor right along behind it as I crossed the floor. The proprietor didn't seem to notice. Maybe he didn't like that particular hand anymore and hoped it would run off with somebody else so he could find happiness with another hand he was keeping in an apartment downtown.

4   In any case, it was obvious that if it stayed much longer I'd never be able to get rid of it without becoming vulnerable to prosecution for abandonment and non-support. At that point, one of those hearty men who prowl crowded rooms in search of hands to maul spotted mine, tossed out the long-term tenant and moved his own hand in for a display of pure brute strength.

5   I was so grateful for relief that I barely screamed as his ferocious hand ravaged my knuckles and reduced my fingertips to pulp. This is a kind of handshake I used to dread before discovering that the faster you surrender, the quicker the agony stops. Hands like this are out to embarrass the man they belong to, and usually succeed. You can always recognize him. His smile is wide, but his teeth are gritted as the hand moves in on the host hand.

6   His smile is wide because he wanted to be thought a good fellow, and his teeth are gritted because he knows what his despicable hand is about to do. It is about to plunge into your hand with the fury of a berserk Viking and engage in trials of muscularity aimed at forcing the loser to burn his hut, slaughter the cattle and surrender the women.

7   Give that hand the satisfaction of combat in your palm and the pain will be prolonged. But go limp from wrist to finger tip the instant it arrives and it will be content with a quick devastation. When hands like this call, their purpose is to make your hand look contemptible before the world. Give them satisfaction right away and they'll save the worst for the next victim.

8   My own hand is not very comfortable in the intimate society of other hands and cannot understand the necessity for these constant visitations by strange fists, fingers, knuckles, palms, nails, lifelines, love lines, cuticle, small bones, short bristles. I understand, of course. It is peculiarly American, as forming queues is peculiarly English and 10 o'clock dining is peculiarly Spanish.

9   I have tried to persuade my hand that it is a small duty it must pay for our national character, and the hand has agreed to do its best, but sometimes it is still astonished by the hands that come to call. It has never decided, for example, how to entertain the hand that leaves everything but four fingers outside the door.

10   In these cases the hand reaches out to welcome the caller into the parlor and finds itself clutching only a handful of finger tips, which feel like a few spears of overcooked asparagus. Hands like this seem to feel adequately entertained after a light squeeze, but it is very hard to tell whether they might not be secretly yearning to have their fingernails pulled.

11   Not long ago, a man extended his arm in my direction and my hand felt itself entertaining a cold, limp, gelatinous object weighing less than half a pound by the

feel of it. A hand's natural instinct at such a visitation is to place the material under refrigeration until autopsy, and mine would certainly have done so had I not happened to glance down and note that the object was another hand.

12   It obviously did not want to be shaken, squeezed, kneaded, pummeled or massaged. It just wanted to lie there and be left alone. I was surprised that this man would let a hand in that condition go out, much less let it try to hobnob with other hands, for all the spirit had long since been drained out of it.

13   My own hand, which is merciful, would doubtless have tried to lend it a cup of warmth, but I intervened. It can be dangerous interfering in relationships between a man and his hand, and after all, there is no law saying a man can't treat his hand any way he wants to.

14   So I gave the order and my hand handed the hand back to the man, and then another hand came along and ruined my knuckles while smiling around gritted teeth.

Topics for Thinking and Writing

1. What type of introduction strategy does Baker use to draw in the reader? How effective is this strategy?

2. Although Baker doesn't formally tell us that he is categorizing handshakes, he does set up a classification system in the essay. What categories does he use? What aspects of handshakes does he explore in each category? How does he achieve a balance among the categories in the essay?

3. Part of the appeal of Baker's essay is his expectation that his audience will be familiar with the subject and will have experienced similar circumstances. What words, phrases, and images does he use to let his readers know that he expects that familiarity?

4. Write a short essay in which you describe a social custom using categories. Possible topics include telephone greetings, answering machine messages, and e-mail openers.

TOP OF THE FOOD CHAIN
T. CORAGHESSAN BOYLE

The thing was, we had a little problem with the insect vector there, and believe me, your tamer stuff, your Malathion and pyrethrum and the rest of the so-called environmentally safe products didn't begin to make a dent in it, not a dent, I mean it was utterly useless—we might as well have been spraying with Chanel Number 5 for all the good it did. And you've got to realize these people were literally covered with insects day and night—and the fact that they hardly wore any clothes just compounded the problem. Picture if you can, gentlemen, a naked little two-year-old boy so black with flies and mosquitoes it looks like he's wearing long johns, or the young mother so racked with the malarial shakes she can't even lift a diet Coke to her lips—it was pathetic, just pathetic, like something out of the Dark Ages. . . . Well, anyway, the decision was made to go with DDT. In the short term. Just to get the situation under control, you understand.

Yes, that's right, Senator, *DDT*: Dichlorodiphenyltrichloroethane.

Yes, I'm well aware of that fact, sir. But just because *we* banned it domestically, under pressure from the birdwatching contingent and the hopheads down at the EPA, it doesn't necessarily follow that the rest of the world—especially the developing world—is about to jump on the bandwagon. And that's the key word here, Senator: *developing*. You've got to realize this is Borneo we're talking about here, not Port Townsend or Enumclaw. These people don't know from square one about sanitation, disease control, pest eradication—or even personal hygiene, if you want to come right down to it. It rains a hundred and twenty inches a year, minimum. They dig up roots in the jungle. They've still got headhunters along the Rajang River, for god's sake.

And please don't forget they *asked* us to come in there, practically begged us—and not only the World Health Organization, but the Sultan of Brunei and the government in Sarawak too. We did what we could to accommodate them and reach our objective in the shortest period of time and by the most direct and effective means. We went to the air. Obviously. And no one could have foreseen the consequences, no one, not even if we'd gone out and generated a hundred environmental-impact statements—it was just one of those things, a freak occurrence, and there's no defense against that. Not that I know of, anyway. . . .

Caterpillars? Yes, Senator, that's correct. That was the first sign: caterpillars.

But let me backtrack a minute here. You see, out in the bush they have these roofs made of thatched palm leaves—you'll see them in the towns too, even in Bintulu or Brunei—and they're really pretty effective, you'd be surprised. A hundred and twenty inches of rain, they've got to figure a way to keep it out of the hut, and for centuries, this was it. Palm leaves. Well, it was about a month after we sprayed for the final time and I'm sitting at my desk in the trailer thinking about the drainage project at Kuching, enjoying the fact that for the first time in maybe a year I'm not smearing mosquitoes all over the back of my neck, when there's a knock at the door. It's this elderly gentleman, tattooed from head to toe, dressed only in a pair of running shorts—they love those shorts, by the way, the shiny material and the tight machine-stitching, the whole country, men and women and children, they can't get enough of them. . . . Anyway, he's the headman of the local village and he's very excited, something about the roofs—*atap*, they call them. That's all he can say, *atap, atap,* over and over again.

It's raining, of course. It's always raining. So I shrug into my rain slicker, start up the 4X4 and go have a look. Sure enough, all the *atap* roofs are collapsing, not only in his village, but throughout the target area. The people are all huddled there in their running shorts, looking pretty miserable, and one after another the roofs keep falling in, it's bewildering, and gradually I realize the headman's diatribe has begun to feature a new term I was unfamiliar with at the time—the word for caterpillar, as it turns out, in the Iban dialect. But who was to make the connection between three passes with the crop duster and all these staved-in roofs?

Our people finally sorted it out a couple weeks later. The chemical, which, by the way, cut down the number of mosquitoes exponentially, had the unfortunate side effect of killing off this little wasp—I've got the scientific name for it somewhere in my report here, if you're interested—that preyed on a type of caterpillar that in turn ate palm leaves. Well, with the wasps gone, the caterpillars hatched out with nothing to keep them in check and chewed the roofs to pieces, and that was unfortunate, we admit it, and we had a real cost overrun on replacing those roofs with tin . . . but the people were happier, I think, in the long run, because let's face it, no matter how tightly you weave those palm leaves, they're just not going to keep the water out like tin. Of course, nothing's perfect, and we had a lot of complaints about the rain drumming on the panels, people unable to sleep and what-have-you. . . .

Yes, sir, that's correct—the flies were next.

Well, you've got to understand the magnitude of the fly problem in Borneo, there's nothing like it here to compare it with, except maybe a garbage strike in New York. Every minute of every day you've got flies everywhere, up your nose, in your mouth, your ears, your eyes, flies in your rice, your Coke, your Singapore sling and your gin rickey. It's enough to drive you to distraction, not to mention the diseases these things carry, from dysentery to typhoid to cholera and back round the loop again. And once the mosquito population was down, the flies seemed to breed up to fill in the gap—Borneo wouldn't be Borneo without some damned insect blackening the air.

Of course, this was before our people had tracked down the problem with the caterpillars and the wasps and all of that, and so we figured we'd had a big success with the mosquitoes, why not a series of ground sweeps, mount a fogger in the back of a Suzuki Brat and sanitize the huts, not to mention the open sewers, which as you know are nothing but a breeding ground for flies, chiggers and biting insects of every sort. At least it was an error of commission rather than omission. At least we were trying.

I watched the flies go down myself. One day they were so thick in the trailer I couldn't even *find* my paperwork, let alone attempt to get through it, and the next they were collecting on the windows, bumbling around like they were drunk. A day later they were gone. Just like that. From a million flies in the trailer to none. . . .

Well, no one could have foreseen that, Senator.

The geckos ate the flies, yes. You're all familiar with geckos, I assume, gentlemen? These are the lizards you've seen during your trips to Hawaii, very colorful, patrolling the house for roaches and flies, almost like pets, but of course they're wild animals, never lose sight of that, and just about as unsanitary as anything I can think of, except maybe flies.

Yes, well don't forget, sir, we're viewing this with twenty-twenty hindsight, but at the time no one gave a thought to geckos or what they ate—they were just another fact of life in the tropics. Mosquitoes, lizards, scorpions, leeches—you name it, they've got it. When the flies began piling up on the windowsills like drift, naturally the geckos feasted on them, stuffing themselves till they looked like sausages crawling up the walls. Where before they moved so fast you could never be sure you'd seen them, now they waddled across the floor, laid around in the corners, clung to the air vents like magnets—and even then no one paid much attention to them till they started turning belly-up in the streets. Believe me, we confirmed a lot of things there about the buildup of these products as you move up the food chain and the efficacy—or lack thereof—of certain methods, no doubt about that. . . .

The cats? That's where it got sticky, really sticky. You see, nobody really lost any sleep over a pile of dead lizards—though we did the tests routinely and the tests confirmed what we'd expected, that is, the product had been concentrated in the geckos because of the sheer number of contaminated flies they consumed. But lizards are one thing and cats are another. These people really have an affection for their cats—no house, no hut, no matter how primitive, is without at least a couple of them. Mangy-looking things, long-legged and scrawny, maybe, not at all the sort of animal you'd see here, but there it was: they loved their cats. Because the cats were functional, you understand—without them, the place would have been swimming in rodents inside of a week.

You're right there, Senator, yes—that's exactly what happened.

You see, the cats had a field day with these feeble geckos—you can imagine, if any of you have ever owned a cat, the kind of joy these animals must have experienced to see their nemesis, this ultra-quick lizard, and it's just barely creeping across the floor like a bug. Well, to make a long story short, the cats ate up every dead and dying gecko in the country, from snout to tail, and then the cats began to die . . . which to my mind would have been no great loss if it wasn't for the rats. Suddenly there were rats everywhere—you couldn't drive down the street without running over half-a-dozen of them at a time. They fouled the grain supplies, fell in the wells and died, bit infants as they slept in their cradles. But that wasn't the worst, not by a long shot. No, things really went down the tube after that. Within the month we were getting scattered reports of bubonic plague, and of course we tracked them all down and made sure the people got a round of treatment with antibiotics, but still we lost a few and the rats kept coming. . . .

It was my plan, yes. I was brainstorming one night, rats scuttling all over the trailer like something out of a cheap horror film, the villagers in a panic over the threat of the plague and the stream of nonstop hysterical reports from the interior—people were turning black, swelling up and bursting, that sort of thing—well, as I say, I came up with a plan, a stopgap, not perfect, not cheap; but at this juncture, I'm sure you'll agree, something had to be implemented.

We wound up going as far as Australia for some of the cats, cleaning out the SPCA facilities and what-have-you, though we rounded most of them up in Indonesia and Singapore—approximately fourteen thousand in all. And yes, it cost us—cost us upfront purchase money and aircraft fuel and pilots' overtime and all the rest of it—but we really felt there was no alternative. It was like all nature had turned against us.

And yet still, all things considered, we made a lot of friends for the U.S.A. the day we dropped those cats, and you should have seen them, gentlemen, the little parachutes and harnesses we'd tricked up, fourteen thousand of them, cats in every color of the rainbow, cats with one ear, no ears, half a tail, three-legged cats, cats that could have taken pride of show in Springfield, Massachusetts, and all of them twirling down out of the sky like great big oversized snowflakes. . . .

It was something. It was really something.

Of course, you've all seen the reports. There were other factors we hadn't counted on, adverse conditions in the paddies and manioc fields—we don't to this day know what predatory species were inadvertently killed off by the initial sprayings, it's just a mystery—but the weevils and whatnot took a pretty heavy toll on the crops that year, and by the time we dropped the cats, well, the people were pretty hungry, and I suppose it was inevitable that we lost a good proportion of them right then and there. But we've got a CARE program going there now, and something hit the rat population—we still don't know what, a virus, we think—and the geckos, they tell me, are making a comeback.

So what I'm saying is, it could be worse, and to every cloud a silver lining, wouldn't you agree, gentlemen?

Topics for Thinking and Writing

1. The story demonstrates the theory known as the "law of unintended consequences." In a small group, identify other examples of this law that are in effect, either from your own lives or from events about which you have read or heard.
2. "Top of the Food Chain" first appeared in *Harper's* magazine. Using your library's resources, find that issue and the ones immediately following it which contain letters about the story. Write a discussion of how the letters you read about the story may have changed your original thoughts about the story.
3. In a small group discuss whether you think the author is making a point about the politics of insect control. What examples did you consider in order to come to your conclusion?
4. Imagine that you are a member of the Senate committee that is hearing this report. Write a response to the testimony highlighting the areas you think are most important and state why you consider them important.

GENESIS 6

12   And God looked upon the earth, and, behold, it was corrupt; for all flesh had corrupted his way upon the earth.

13   And God said unto Noah, The end of all flesh is come before me; for the earth is filled with violence through them; and, behold, I will destroy them with the earth.

14   Make thee an ark of gopher wood; rooms shalt thou make in the ark, and shalt pitch it within and without with pitch.

15   And this *is the fashion* which thou shalt make it *of:* The length of the ark *shall be* three hundred cubits, and the height of it thirty cubits.

16   A window shalt thou make to the ark, and in a cubit shalt thou finish it above; and the door of the ark shalt thou set in the side thereof; *with* lower, second, and third *stories* shalt thou make it.

17   And, behold, I, even I, do bring a flood of waters upon the earth, to destroy all flesh, wherein *is* the breath of life, from under heaven; *and* every thing that *is* in the earth shall die.

18   But with thee I will establish my covenant, and thou shalt come into the ark, thou, and thy sons, and thy wife, and thy sons' wives with thee.

19   And of every living thing of all flesh, two of every *sort* shalt thou bring into the ark, to keep *them* alive with thee; they shall be male and female.

20   Of fowls after their kind, and of cattle after their kind, of every creeping thing of the earth after his kind, two of every *sort* shall come unto thee, to keep *them* alive.

21   And take thou unto thee of all food that is eaten, and thou shalt gather *it* to thee; and it shall be for food for thee, and for them.

22   Thus did Noah; according to all that God commanded him, so did he.

Topics for Thinking and Writing

1. Is the passage from Genesis 6 an example of a directional or an informational process? Why?
2. Discuss the steps that God commands Noah to take in building the Ark. How do they follow the guidelines of a process analysis?
3. Imagine that you receive an ark-building kit which contains the instruction found in the passage. Are there steps where you might want more explicit instructions? If so, write out the additional directions you would like to see included in the kit.
4. Take a set of instructions you have for something you have put together around the house or use a process essay you have previously written. Rewrite the instructions or essay, imitating Biblical form.
5. Write an informational process analysis describing the steps you took to develop your imitative passage.

Self-Assessment

Reread the self-assessment that opens this chapter. Then answer the following questions.

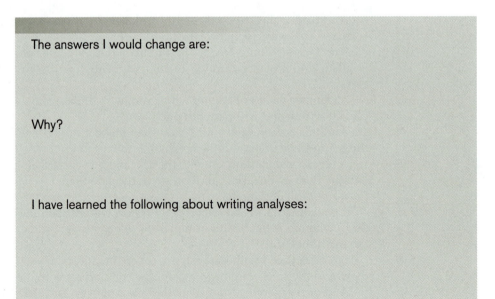

The answers I would change are:

Why?

I have learned the following about writing analyses:

Persuasion: Making Your Case in Writing

"THAT'S RIDICULOUS!"
"I DISAGREE."
"LET ME EXPLAIN."

If you are answering someone else's ideas in writing, it is not enough simply to write that you disagree. Just as when you are discussing which is the better of two movies, you won't win the argument merely by saying, "That's ridiculous!" if your friend names *The Battleship Potemkin* when you think *Titanic* is the better film. You might feel better by saying—or even shouting,—"Baloney!" in response to your friend's opinion, but you haven't convinced anybody about the validity of *your* opinion, least of all your friend.

Similarly, saying, "I disagree" when you friend suggests that you try the latest trend in body piercing might stop her from pushing you into the tattoo parlor, but, again, it does not explain why you don't think the experience is for you.

To make sure that other people see your point of view, the best thing to do is to say, "Let me explain," and then to state clearly your position as eloquently as possible. This reply is even more necessary when you are responding in writing to someone else's idea.

Making an argument when you write is not the same as arguing with someone, at least not as most people use the word *arguing* in everyday speech. When you write a persuasive essay, you are trying to get your readers to agree with you. As you have noticed throughout this book, the way in which you make your case—your "argument"—will depend upon your purpose and your audience.

There are various techniques for writing an argument, but all of them involve winning your readers over by using one of two basic approaches: relying on facts and examples to convince them or appealing to their emotions. When you explain your position politely, carefully, and with respect for others, you are making an argument (though to help avoid confusing this process with the everyday meaning of the word *argument*, it might be easier to think of what you are doing as *seeking to persuade*.) Whichever words you use, what you are doing is writing to convince somebody else that your idea is best, or at least worth considering.

Self-Assessment

When you seek to persuade someone that your idea has merit, what do you do? First of all, it is usually helpful to clearly understand the idea yourself. Sometimes, you might *think* that you know what you mean, but when you try to tell other people, the idea comes out in a confusing order or with certain parts missing. Second, you should consider what the other person probably thinks about the idea. If someone whom you are trying to convince to buy organic fruit already wears only natural wool or cotton clothing, you can assume he is likely to be sympathetic to your ideas about the importance of avoiding chemical pesticides. However, if you know that he also wraps everything in plastic and loves fast food, you can guess that he probably won't be impressed by your appeals to purchase natural foods and will need to be persuaded in some other way. Third, you should consider evidence that will support your case. What proof do you have that your opinion is valid?

As you can see, writing an argument builds upon skills you have already practiced in writing summaries, evaluations, and analyses. It also—like all writing—requires that you think about purpose and audience.

1. The most difficult time that I have had convincing someone else of the validity of my argument was when _____.

2. What made the previous idea so hard to convince others to believe was _____
_____.

3. In order to convince people of the validity of that idea, I _____
_____.

4. During the past year, the most significant change of mind I have had was _____
_____.

5. What changed my mind about this subject was _____
_____.

6. I think that the important elements of persuasion are _____
_____.

What I know about my process of writing an argument:	What will I need to know to make my process more effective?

Working Together: In a small group, select one movie, book, or CD released during the past year which you all enjoyed. If you wanted to convince someone who knows nothing about it that your choice is worth seeing, reading, or hearing, on which aspects would you concentrate? Why?

Working Alone: Write a brief piece recounting a time when you last disagreed with a friend or colleague with whom you have since reached a peaceful agreement. Describe your audience and purpose and explain the way in which you prepared your argument.

The Argument

There are two basic ways to make an argument. You can appeal to your readers' feelings or to their thoughts. To put it another way, your appeal can be either **emotional** or **rational.** Each of these appeals has its place, but one is the better choice for your writing. Which do you think it is? Why?

Whenever a salesperson, a politician, a cheerleader, or an evangelist urges us—from a public platform—to adopt a particular view, chances are good that the appeal being made is to our emotions. Also, in private our friends and loved ones may often use emotional appeals to get us to do something. Hollywood movies, popular music, and literature often appeal to us on an emotional level, getting us to identify with a mood, a character, or a cause. As playwright Tennessee Williams said of his appealing to emotions in such plays as *The Glass Menagerie* and *A Streetcar Named Desire,* you "raise the temperature of the audience, you key them up, then you can tell them anything."

While an appeal to emotion can be effective, it's worth noting that, as Irish writer Jonathan Swift said three hundred years ago, such an appeal will rarely move "our spirits deep enough to last till the next morning, or rather to the next meal." There are, then, limits to using emotional appeals. Thoughtful readers will often dismiss an argument that seeks to win their agreement with emotions. Even if they don't reject it out of hand, many people, as Swift suggests, will forget an emotional appeal before their next meal. You will discover, therefore, that a written argument usually works best when it is based on logic and appeals to reason.

In the Academy Award-winning film *Philadelphia,* an attorney played by Denzel Washington defends another attorney portrayed by Tom Hanks in a wrongful firing suit. Amid the emotionally charged storm of issues surrounding the case, Washington's character maintains a steady course of reason. He doesn't have to agree with the feelings involved—in fact, he has some personal resistance to them—but he makes his case rationally. Slowly, he undermines the powerful opposing arguments by showing how they are based upon emotions such as hatred and fear (some of which he personally shares). It's a tough fight, but he sticks to logic and reason and ultimately persuades the jury and the viewers to accept his argument.

Although both emotion and reason have their place, it's best to begin your preparation for persuasive writing by considering how to write a rational argument.

Shaping the Argument

Chapter 9 shows the way in which analysis takes one part of a whole and uses it to explain how the whole works. Persuasive papers are like analytical papers in that they also use several smaller facts and examples to create a whole or complete argument.

When you write a persuasive paper, in many important ways the task is just like writing any other essay. To begin, you need a thesis (the main point with which you are trying to persuade your readers to agree). From there you build a body of evidence to support your case, seeking to persuade your readers by showing how a series of parts adds up to a whole. And finally, you must conclude.

A persuasive essay might be set up in the following way:

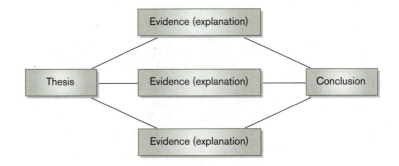

Here is one way this plan might look in brief written form:

Many young fans would argue that rock 'n' roll has undergone dramatic changes during its nearly fifty years of history. "Just look at the current bands!" they'll say. In one important way, however, rock hasn't changed at all. The lineup of instruments has remained the same.

From its roots in rhythm and blues and hillbilly music of the late 1940s and early 1950s, the sound of rock 'n' roll has been built upon the use of drums and electric guitars to provide rhythm and melody. Generally, this has meant a set of drums and at least one guitar, though more typically it includes a lead, a rhythm, and a bass guitar. Although there have been various additions at times—such as horns, keyboards, synthesizers—the basic instruments of rock have steadily remained the same. This fact helps give rock music a common thread.

This thread can be seen in any examination of key artists and groups ranging from Chuck Berry in the 1950s to the Beatles in the 1960s, Aerosmith in the 1970s, and Madonna in the 1980s to contemporary performers such as Sheryl Crow and Stone Temple Pilots. As different as these artists are in terms of the style and content of their music, their dominant instrumental sounds are all created with electric guitars and drums.

Although the profusion of rock music will continue for generations to come, the basic sounds will still be formed by the same instruments: the guitar and drums. As Bob Seeger says, [Rock 'n' roll remembers its roots.]

If you were developing an essay along these lines, you would probably want to expand on the key points and provide further evidence to support your point of view. However, even in this short example, you can see that the basic essay structure discussed in Chapter 5 is used. There's an introduction which includes a thesis statement (that is, a clear expression of your purpose), a body, and a conclusion.

The writer's thesis is supported by various examples of evidence (a list of instruments and performers) which she then explains to demonstrate how each one supports the thesis. She mentions another point of view—that there are sometimes other instruments involved—but then addresses it by stating that even with the addition of these instruments, drums and guitars remain at the heart of the rock 'n' roll sound. Finally, there is a conclusion which reminds the reader of the thesis and by doing so underscores that the argument based on the evidence convincingly supports the thesis—though, again, some added details would help make the case even more strongly.

A rational argument will usually persuade an audience. While they are reading it—or listening to it—the clarity and strength of the examples will often be so convincing that the audience will agree with the point of view of the writer or speaker. For example, in the essay about rock 'n' roll, the author uses Chuck Berry, the Beatles, and other performers to make her point. Afterwards, analysis or evaluation might help reveal weaknesses in the argument, but even then, analysis will show that the argument is based upon logic and evidence.

The more evidence you present, the better, as long as you are not repeating yourself and you can show that your evidence supports your thesis. Therefore, more often than not, writing an argument essay will require that you do some research to find facts and examples that can support your point.

Evidence and Explanation

To make your argument persuasive, you will need to provide evidence and examples and to explain how they support your case. Some of the most useful forms of evidence are commonly known facts, statistics, anecdotes, analogies, and appeals to authority.

Commonly Known Facts: Sometimes a **commonly known fact** can be used to help make your case. For example, in an essay arguing that America needs to develop better volcano warning systems, you could point out that most volcanoes are active around the so-called Ring of Fire and that part of this ring runs right along the U.S. Pacific coast.

There are four basic types of commonly known facts that you can use without providing documentation.

- *Historical facts*, e.g., Delaware was the first state to ratify the Constitution of the United States
- *Scientific facts*, e.g., water freezes at 0° Celsius
- *Geographical facts*, e.g., the Nile is the longest river in Africa
- *Biographical facts*, e.g., Carrie Fisher is Debbie Reynolds's daughter

Note: For any other type of information, you should always identify its source.

If you were developing the previously discussed essay on rock 'n' roll, you might incorporate some commonly known facts:

> Even the Beatles's crowning achievement, *Sergeant Pepper's Lonely Hearts Club Band*, considered by many fans and critics alike to be the greatest rock album ever recorded, although heavy in its use of innovative studio techniques and other instruments (including a full symphony orchestra), still relies primarily on electric guitars and Ringo's drums to create its sound.

In the previous passage, you would not need to cite any sources because this is considered commonly known historical information. Later, however, if you wished to add authority to your essay, you might decide to quote a rock critic or musician or to use an anecdote about the Beatles.

Statistics: Using **statistics**—numerical descriptions of specific events or numerical approximations that apply to a large population—is another powerful way to strengthen an argument. The first kinds of statistics are the result of specific measurements of specific actions. For example, each basketball season statisticians keep track of the points scored, number of rebounds, and so on. However, the statistics for each player are unique. You wouldn't use the details of, for example, Rebecca Lobo's rebounding to draw any conclusions about how good a rebounder Lisa Leslie is.

The other types of statistics are more general—the population of a country, say, or the average family income. Each month the U.S. government announces the percentage increase—or, occasionally, the decrease—in the consumer price index (CPI). This statistic measures the average price paid for a "basket" of goods that each household typically buys each month. This measure of inflation does not tell how much the cost of a particular item (toothpaste, for example) increased or decreased; it only indicates what the change in cost of a range of products was. In other words, although you can use the consumer price index to determine how much more, on average, it costs to live now than it did a year ago, you cannot use the CPI to say anything specific about the price of a particular item. The cost of long-distance phone calls, for example, has decreased during the past few years even though the CPI has risen.

When using statistical examples, you must ensure that the statistic you use is appropriate, and you must explain why the statistic is applicable to your argument. For example, you might have statistics showing that the fuel efficiency of Ford cars has improved by 12 percent during the past five years. This information does not allow you to say anything about the fuel efficiency of Ford trucks or General Motors cars. On the other hand, statistics that demonstrate that the fuel efficiency of U.S. manufacturers' cars has improved by 6 percent during the same period allow you to generalize about the products of Ford, GM, and DaimlerChrysler.

Once again, if you were developing the previous essay on rock 'n' roll, you might decide to include statistics to support your thesis.

> According to *Rocker* magazine, 99 percent of rock bands feature at least one guitar, and 84 percent use two or more whereas only 21 percent employ keyboards, and a mere 6 percent use horns.

Working Together: With a few classmates, go through the most recent edition of your local daily paper. Look for statistics that have been used in stories. Then decide whether these statistics are descriptive or approximate. Which are used appropriately, and which are not?

Working Alone: Use the statistics that you have found to support an argument.

Anecdotes: These are brief stories of people's experiences—your own or others'. Sometimes they can be used to help support an argument. As with statistics, however, when using anecdotes, it is important to explain how they apply to your thesis. You will need to prove their validity as part of the evidence supporting your argument. For example, you might have gone on a fishing trip to a stream famous for its trout. You may decide to use the story of the trip in your essay. If you failed to catch any fish, that fact might not indicate that trout numbers are declining in that stream; it could simply mean that you weren't lucky that day. However, if you have won the state trout fishing championship for the past four years, this anecdote could be used to discuss the probable decline in trout numbers. As always, when you use an example, you need to explain to the reader why the anecdote helps to support your thesis.

When developing the essay on rock 'n' roll, anecdotes could be used to support your case:

> When they were just schoolboys growing up in England after the Second World War, Eric Clapton, George Harrison, Keith Richards, and Jimmy Page all had one thing in common: They would lie awake at night to listen to radio stations in hopes of hearing some of the American rock 'n' roll songs that occasionally got played.

From this point, it might be useful to develop the idea that those early years of hearing American rock and rhythm and blues music had a profound influence on these young English kids, all of whom went on to become legendary guitar players.

Working Together: With some classmates, look through a recent magazine article. What anecdotes are used to support the writer's thesis? Are they helpful? Why? Why not?

Working Alone: Go to a web page or Internet story about a topic that you find interesting. After reading the material that you found there, write an anecdote that you might post on the site. Accompany that with a brief explanation of what the anecdote says about your topic and why it would be a good addition to the other material you have found.

Analogies: An **analogy** is a kind of comparison which typically compares different kinds of things but finds their points of similarity. Sometimes it can serve your purpose to compare two events or situations to suggest probable similarities. This is what medical researchers do when they expose rats to particular chemicals to see if they will develop cancer tumors. If the rats do, scientists argue by analogy that the same chemicals may also be carcinogens for people. Or you might compare the cultural life of your college to a desert oasis, thus emphasizing the idea that there's a richness of cultural offerings in an otherwise barren place. Of course, analogies cannot themselves prove an argument. Rats are not people; however, when analogies are used in conjunction with other types of examples, they can strengthen an argument.

By using an analogy comparing the role of the guitar in a rock band with the use of the violin in a symphony orchestra, you might help your reader understand the thesis of your rock 'n' roll essay:

> Although an orchestra is a group of musicians playing various instruments, if a single instrument could be said to unify an orchestra's sound, it would be the violin. In a similar fashion, the electric guitar is the unifying instrument for a rock 'n' roll band.

Working Together: In a small group, imagine that you are writing a letter to the president of your college asking for one course that is not currently offered to be added to the catalog. What would the course be? Develop your argument by using an analogy in order to be as convincing as possible.

Appeals to Authority: An **appeal to authority** uses the words or ideas of an expert on a topic. Sometimes it can be useful to show that a person who knows far more about the subject than you (or your readers) does agree with you. For example, if you are writing about housing conditions in East St. Louis, you could consider any comments that local Habitat for Humanity leaders may have made on the subject. There are cases, too, where experts in another field have comments pertinent to your topic. If Albert Einstein had said something about space travel, and you are writing about that topic, his opinions might be well worth including. Remember, though, that just because someone is famous does not mean that he is an expert on everything. George Lucas might have a lot to say about filmmaking, but you'd probably want to be wary of using his ideas to design spacecraft for NASA. Likewise, although Denzel Washington can convincingly portray an attorney on screen, would you want him to represent you in court? As with using an analogy, you need to ensure that the authority to whom you are appealing is appropriate for the topic.

In developing the persuasive essay on the instruments of rock, quoting guitar legend Jimi Hendrix might strengthen your point:

Hendrix said, "Just because a guitar's been used certain ways a long time don't mean it's a tired old instrument and there ain't other ways nobody's thought of yet. I want to be the one to find out some of them new ways."

Working Alone: Pick two or three topics about which you might write a persuasive paper—such as dieting, the benefits of exercise, or government support for health care. Then use the Internet to find various people's comments on these subjects. Which of these people would be suitable authorities for you to use to support your idea, and which would not? How did you decide?

A Warning: As with all the writing you do, writing a persuasive paper requires you to consider your audience and your purpose. When you write an argument, you want to remember that your reader will have time to go back over your essay and reread it if she wishes. Rereading an essay that relies upon the types of examples which form the basis of a persuasive essay allows the reader an opportunity to look for errors in logic. These are called **fallacies.** One of the easiest to make is the **hasty generalization,** the mistake of "jumping to the conclusion" that because one thing is true, related points must be also true. An example would be to say that because one model of small car is dangerous, all small cars are dangerous.

Working Together: With a peer, read through a long article of your choice in a popular magazine and look for any arguments that appear to be fallacies—that is, look for arguments that do not prove what the author says they do. How are those arguments fallacies?

Working Alone: Write a brief piece based on the previous activity that refutes what you consider the most important of the fallacies. (If you did not do the previous activity, read a long article in a popular magazine, identify the fallacies, and then write about them.)

These are the principal ways in which you can build a persuasive argument. The broader the variety of types of argument you can use, the better. An essay that uses statistics, commonly known facts, and an anecdote or two, for example, will often be stronger than an essay that simply relies on analogy. But not every argument lends itself to every type of example. As with all essays, purpose and audience will determine the content. An argument aimed at research scientists might concentrate on statistics and analogy. One for sports fans might use anecdotes about the feats of players.

Whatever you do, though, perhaps the most important component of writing a persuasive essay is to make sure that your examples are appropriate for your argument. As a writer, you are also responsible for making sure that you have made it very clear to your reader how your examples work to support your argument. You must, in other words, explain yourself.

Organizing Your Essay

In simple terms, writing persuasively involves stating your argument (your thesis, or what it is you want to prove), presenting your evidence—in each case explaining what that evidence does to support your argument—and drawing your case together in a conclusion. You shouldn't be surprised to discover that this is exactly the same basic structure you'd use for writing almost any essay. The following are some additional guidelines to keep in mind when you begin to write an argument.

State your thesis clearly. Both you and your reader need to understand clearly what you're trying to prove.

Briefly acknowledge any opposing views. Doing this will deflect any claims that you're stacking the cards.

Build toward your strongest evidence. In presenting your evidence, it's usually best to start with what you consider your weaker evidence and move toward your strongest evidence to clinch the argument.

Provide smooth transitions. When moving from one piece of evidence to the next, be sure that you do so smoothly, following the principles of logical transition. Remember, good writing *flows.*

Restate your thesis. When drawing your conclusion, it's usually a good idea to remind your reader (and yourself) what you've attempted to prove. By doing so, you can check your essay to be sure that the trail of evidence leads to your conclusion.

Suggestions for Writing

1. Find an editorial in a newspaper or magazine that takes a stand on an issue. Then write your own editorial on the same subject, taking a different stance and seeking to persuade the same audience that the first editorial addressed.
2. Find the budget (or part of the budget) of your college's student government program. Then write a letter to the president of your school arguing that more money should be allocated for the program.
3. Imagine that your favorite television show is about to be canceled. Write a persuasive letter to the network's head of programming asking to have the program renewed.
4. Write an editorial for your local paper seeking to persuade its readers that the TV show described in suggestion 3 should be renewed.
5. You have just heard that a neighborhood park used by young children will have its toddler play area replaced by a full-sized basketball court. Write an essay that you would present to your local government opposing this change.
6. There are not enough full-sized basketball courts in your community to accommodate all who wish to participate in the town league. Write an essay to your local government arguing that a children's playground should be converted to a full-size basketball court.
7. Write an essay to persuade your readers that a particular CD, book, or movie was the most overrated of the past twenty years.
8. Write an essay to persuade your readers that a particular CD, book, or movie released during the past twenty years deserves more recognition than it has received thus far.

9. Closely watch your favorite TV show. Then write a persuasive essay to convince your fellow students to watch the show's next episode.

READINGS

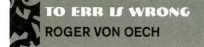

TO ERR IS WRONG
ROGER VON OECH

1   In the summer of 1979, Boston Red Sox first baseman Carl Yastrzemski became the fifteenth player in baseball history to reach the three thousand hit plateau. This event drew a lot of media attention, and for about a week prior to the attainment of this goal, hundreds of reports covered Yaz's every move. Finally, one reporter asked, "Hey Yaz, aren't you afraid all of this attention will go to your head?" Yastrzemski replied, "I look at it this way: in my career I've been up to bat over ten thousand times. That means I've been unsuccessful at the plate over seven thousand times. That fact alone keeps me from getting a swollen head."

2   Most people consider success and failure as opposites, but they are actually both products of the same process. As Yaz suggests, an activity which produces a hit may also produce a miss. It is the same with creative thinking; the same energy which generates good creative ideas also produces errors.

Many people, however, are not comfortable with errors. Our educational system, based on "the right answer" belief, cultivates our thinking in another, more conservative way. From an early age, we are taught that right answers are good and incorrect answers are bad. This value is deeply embedded in the incentive system used in most schools:

Right over 90% of the time = "A"

Right over 80% of the time = "B"

Right over 70% of the time = "C"

Right over 60% of the time = "D"

Less than 60% correct, you fail.

3   From this we learn to be right as often as possible and to keep our mistakes to a minimum. We learn, in other words, that "to err is wrong."

Playing It Safe

4   With this kind of attitude, you aren't going to be taking too many chances. If you learn that failing even a little penalizes you (e.g., being wrong only 15% of the time garners you only a "B" performance), you learn not to make mistakes. And

more important, you learn not to put yourself in situations where you might fail. This leads to conservative thought patterns designed to avoid the stigma our society puts on "failure."

5   I have a friend who recently graduated from college with a Master's degree in Journalism. For the last six months, she has been trying to find a job, but to no avail. I talked with her about her situation, and realized that her problem is that she doesn't know how to fail. She went through eighteen years of schooling without ever failing an examination, a paper, a midterm, a pop-quiz, or a final. Now, she is reluctant to try any approaches where she might fail. She has been conditioned to believe that failure is bad in and of itself, rather than a potential stepping stone to new ideas.

6   Look around. How many middle managers, housewives, administrators, teachers, and other people do you see who are afraid to try anything new because of this fear of failure? Most of us have learned not to make mistakes in public. As a result, we remove ourselves from many learning experiences except for those occurring in the most private circumstances.

A Different Logic

7   From a practical point of view, "to err is wrong" makes sense. Our survival in the everyday world requires us to perform thousands of small tasks without failure. Think about it: you wouldn't last very long if you were to step out in front of traffic or stick your hand into a pot of boiling water. In addition, engineers whose bridges collapse, stock brokers who lose money for their clients and copywriters whose ad campaigns decrease sales won't keep their jobs very long.

8   Nevertheless, too great an adherence to the belief "to err is wrong" can greatly undermine your attempts to generate new ideas. If you're more concerned with producing right answers than generating original ideas, you'll probably make uncritical use of the rules, formulae, and procedures used to obtain these right answers. By doing this, you'll by-pass the germinal phase of the creative process, and thus spend little time testing assumptions, challenging the rules, asking what-if questions, or just playing around with the problem. All of these techniques will produce some correct answers, but in the germinal phase errors are viewed as a necessary by-product of creative thinking. As Yaz would put it, "If you want the hits, be prepared for the misses." That's the way the game of life goes.

Errors as Stepping Stones

9   Whenever an error pops up, the usual response is, "Jeez, another screwup, what went wrong this time?" The creative thinker, on the other hand, will realize the potential value of errors, and perhaps say something like, "Would you look at that! Where can it lead our thinking?" And then he or she will go on to use the error as a steeping stone to a new idea. As a matter of fact, the whole history of discovery is filled with people who used erroneous assumptions and failed ideas as stepping stones to new ideas. Columbus thought he was finding a shorter route

to India. Johannes Kepler stumbled on to the idea of interplanetary gravity because of assumptions which were right for the wrong reasons. And, Thomas Edison knew 1800 ways *not* to build a light bulb.

10   The following story about the automotive genius Charles Kettering exemplifies the spirit of working through erroneous assumption to good ideas. In 1912, when the automobile industry was just beginning to grow, Kettering was interested in improving gasoline-engine efficiency. The problem he faced was "knock," the phenomenon in which gasoline takes too long to burn in the cylinder—thereby reducing efficiency.

11   Kettering began searching for ways to eliminate the "knock." He thought to himself, "How can I get the gasoline to combust in the cylinder at an earlier time?" The key concept here is "early." Searching for analogous situations, he looked around for models of "things that happen early." He thought of historical models, physical models, and biological models. Finally, he remembered a particular plant, the trailing arbutus, which "happens early," i.e., it blooms in the snow ("earlier" than other plants). One of this plant's chief characteristics is its red leaves which help the plant retain light at certain wavelengths. Kettering figured that it must be the color red which made the trailing arbutus bloom earlier.

12   Now came the critical step in Kettering's chain of thought. He asked himself, "How can I make the gasoline red? Perhaps I'll put red dye in the gasoline—maybe that'll make it combust earlier." He looked around his workshop, and found that he didn't have any red dye. But he did have some iodine—perhaps that would do. He added the iodine to the gasoline and, lo and behold, the engine didn't "knock."

13   Several days later, Kettering wanted to make sure that it was the redness of the iodine which had in fact solved his problem. He got some red dye and added it to the gasoline. Nothing happened! Kettering then realized that it wasn't the "redness" which had solved the "knock" problem, but certain other properties of iodine. In this case, an error had proven to be a stepping stone to a better idea. Had he known that "redness" alone was not the solution, he may not have found his way to the additives in iodine.

Negative Feedback

14   Errors serve another useful purpose: they tell us when to change direction. When things are going smoothly, we generally don't think about them. To a great extent, this is because we function according to the principle of negative feedback. Often it is only when things or people fail to do their job that they get our attention. For example, you are probably not thinking about your kneecaps right now; that's because everything is fine with them. The same goes for your elbows: they are also performing their function—no problem at all. But if you were to break a leg, you would immediately notice all of the things you could no longer do, but which you used to take for granted.

15   Negative feedback means that the current approach is not working, and it is up to you to figure out a new one. We learn by trial and error, not by trial and rightness. If we did things correctly every time, we would never have to change

direction—we'd just continue the current course and end up with more of the same.

16   For example, after the supertanker *Amoco Cadiz* broke up off the coast of Brittany in the spring of 1978, thereby polluting the coast with hundreds of thousands of tons of oil, the oil industry rethought many of its safety standards regarding petroleum transport. The same thing happened after the accident at [the] Three Mile Island nuclear reactor in 1979—many procedures and safety standards were changed.

17   Neil Goldschmidt, former Secretary of Transportation, had this to say about the Bay Area Rapid Transit (BART):

> It's gotten too fashionable around the country to beat up on BART and not give credit to the vision that put this system in place. We have learned from BART around the country. The lessons were put to use in Washington, in Atlanta, in Buffalo, and other cities where we are building mass transit systems. One of the lessons is not to build a system like BART.

We learn by our failures. A person's errors are the whacks that lead him to think something different.

Trying New Things

18   Your error rate in any activity is a function of your familiarity with that activity. If you are doing things that are routine and have a high likelihood of correctness, then you will probably make very few errors. But if you are doing things that have no precedence in your experience or are trying different approaches, then you will be making your share of mistakes. Innovators may not bat a thousand—far from it—but they do get new ideas.

19   The creative director of an advertising agency told me that he isn't happy unless he is failing at least half of the time. As he puts it, "If you are going to be original, you are going to be wrong a lot."

20   One of my clients, the president of a fast-growing computer company, tells his people: "We're innovators. We're doing things nobody has ever done before. Therefore, we are going to be making mistakes. My advice to you: make your mistakes, but make them in a hurry."

21   Another client, a division manager of a high-technology company, asked his vice president of engineering what percentage of their new products should be successful in the marketplace. The answer he received was "about 50%." The division manager replied, "That's too high. 30% is a better target; otherwise we'll be too conservative in our planning."

22   Along similar lines, in the banking industry, it is said that if the credit manager never has to default any of his loans, it's a sure sign he's not being aggressive enough in the marketplace.

23   Thomas J. Watson, the founder of IBM, has similar words: "The way to succeed is to double your failure rate."

24   Thus, errors, at the very least, are a sign that we are diverging from the main road and trying different approaches.

Nature's Errors

25   Nature serves as a good example of how trial and error can be used to make changes. Every now and then genetic mutations occur—errors in gene reproduction. Most of the time, these mutations have a deleterious effect on the species, and they drop out of the gene pool. But occasionally, a mutation provides the species with something beneficial, and that change will be passed on to future generations. The rich variety of all species is due to this trial and error process. If there had never been any mutations from the first amoeba, where would we be now?

Summary

26   There are places where errors are inappropriate, but the germinal phase of the creative process isn't one of them. Errors are a sign that you are diverging from the well-traveled path. If you're not failing every now and then, it's a sign that you're not being very innovative.

> *Tip #1:*
> If you make an error, use it as a stepping stone to a new idea you might not have otherwise discovered.

> *Tip #2:*
> Differentiate between errors of "commission" and those of "omission." The latter can be more costly than the former. If you're not making any errors, you might ask yourself, "How many opportunities am I missing by not being more aggressive?"

> *Tip #3:*
> Strengthen your "risk muscle." Everyone has one, but you have to exercise it or else it will atrophy. Make it a point to take at least one risk every twenty-four hours.

> *Tip #4:*
> Remember these two benefits of failure. First, if you do fail, you learn what doesn't work; and second, the failure gives you an opportunity to try a new approach.

Topics for Thinking and Writing

1. What is the thesis of Von Oech's argument?
2. What specific types of evidence does the author use to prove his thesis?
3. Which type of evidence presented strikes you as being the strongest? Why?
4. Von Oech presents his view of the American educational system's attitude toward student errors. Write a paragraph agreeing or disagreeing with his position.
5. Write an essay about a time when your making an error led to greater understanding.
6. Write an essay about a classroom environment which would encourage making errors as part of growth and learning. What would be the role of the teacher? The role of the students? What would the classroom look like?

I SEEN WHERE A WOODCHUCK HAD CAME AND WENT
BY TIM TRASK

My grandmother is lying back against the elevated head of the hospital bed watching my daughter put the camcorder on the tripod. Audrey just turned twelve. Grammie is almost ninety. Audrey's brown hair keeps falling in front of her eyes as she works to thread the mounting screw into the camera body. Grammie shows some amusement by a liveliness in her eyes, but otherwise, she lies calm, almost lifeless, her sparse, wavy, white hair spread out around her like an aura, merging at its ends with the whiteness of the pillow slipcase. Audrey doesn't notice these things. She's finally got the screw started and her whole young body is alive around the tripod, tightening.

She wanted to make the trip to visit Grammie, but she didn't want to bring the camcorder. And she didn't want to conduct a formal interview either, but I talked her into it.

"Look, Audrey," I said. "You were the one who wanted us to get this camcorder so we could start keeping a family history."

Of course that hadn't been her real reason. That had just been her argument with me. And it worked, too. So now we are actually using the expensive gadget for something useful. We've made a list of "starter" questions and I've tried to show her how to listen and ask follow-up questions to get the real material.

"Your great-grandmother has lived through two world wars and the great depression," I had reminded her as the elevator brought us up to Grammie's floor. "She's seen kings and czars replaced by committees. She's lived through more presidents than you have years. She's nearly as old as the century itself and remembers most of it."

"I know that," Audrey had replied as though I always insulted her intelligence.

I have helped Audrey get ready by clipping a small microphone to Grammie's bedclothes, and now I hand her the wire so she can plug it in.

"She wants to be a great film maker—an artist," I say to Grammie.

Audrey sticks her tongue out at me as she plugs in the microphone connector.

"You should encourage her, David dear," Grammie says.

"But an artist?" I say. "She comes from a family of teachers." Both my parents were teachers, as I am, and as Grammie was. I feel I'm honoring her when I suggest the profession to Audrey. A teacher—or maybe a doctor or lawyer. Those are practical jobs that—well, a professional can always be an artist, but to be an artist without something to fall back on . . .

"OK, I'm ready," Audrey says.

"Goodness," Grammie says, her voice just a faint version of what I remember from years ago. "I feel like a celebrity."

She glances merrily over at me, and I can't help but recall the doctor's gently chiding voice just a few moments ago in the hall as she cast a skeptical glance at the video equipment and said, "She could go any time, you know. Don't grill her too severely."

But I know that telling her stories has always brought Grammie most to life, and Audrey is her favorite great-grandchild. Besides, I'm watching.

After about five minutes, I see it's not working. Audrey has let the machine get between her and Grammie. She's just reading the questions off the sheet we prepared earlier and not listening to the answers. She's had Grammie list all the siblings she's outlived and tell how her grandparents lived and where, and she's gotten dates of birth and death, but she's just looking to the next item on the list—not responding with any human questions. She's too distracted by the electronic image in the viewfinder. She has her other eye shut, and both ears are covered by the walkman headphones plugged into the back of the camcorder.

I walk over and gently remove the headphones, putting them on my own head. Grammie's voice, amplified through them, sounds younger, more forceful. It startles me for a moment, and it reminds me.

I lean closer to Audrey's ear and whisper, "Ask her about teaching in Hamlin." Hamlin is a backwoods town in northern Maine where Grammie taught for a few years after World War I. She's always told amusing anecdotes about the local people of the area, particularly those who lived on the ridge, on the fringes of civilized life. Audrey hasn't heard these stories, I know.

Audrey nods and waits politely for a pause in Grammie's family history. I unplug the headphones and take them with me to my seat on the silver radiator by the window to resume my watch, feeling smug. This will be a treat for Audrey.

"Daddy wants you to tell me about teaching in Hamlin."

"He always liked those stories," Grammie says, "but there's one he never heard."

That can't be possible, I think. I've heard all her school-teaching stories at least five times—some at least ten or more.

"Well, then, tell us, by all means," I say.

"I never told this story because it was never the right time," Grammie says softly. "I guess this is the right time.

"It was my first year of teaching and I had five pupils in a one-room schoolhouse up on the ridge."

Grammie is one of the few people I've ever heard talk about students as pupils. "Pupils are all eyes" is one of her favorite sayings, and she says it with a kind of gravity I've never quite understood.

"It was at the end of a long winter," she continues, "and we'd been cooped up huddled around the woodstove for months, and I'd been trying to pour knowledge into their poor brains the whole time. It was my first year teaching, remember.

"One boy, Sam Clark, was old enough to be in the fourth grade, but he was only in the second. We all considered him to be very slow—all the people in Hamlin, I mean. They said his mother was his sister. Things like that happened on the ridge, and I thought that was the reason. We never talked about it, but everyone thought they knew."

I look over at Audrey. She's paying attention now. The camera is recording, but she's looking with both eyes at Grammie.

"His mother was his sister? What do you mean, Grammie?"

"You know what I mean, child. I mean his mother and he had the same father."

I've heard her talk about intermarriage on the ridge before, but never with a name or a particular relationship. It never seemed real before. I'm listening, too.

"I couldn't get Sam to write anything at all, and I'd been plaguing him all winter to write something on his own. Oh, he'd copy things from a book or answer questions, but he wouldn't write anything like the other children would—didn't seem able to use his mind.

"Finally, I gave up. I blamed it on the incest—in my own mind, you know—and told him if he couldn't, he couldn't. He should just do the best he could."

Her skin is pale. So pale I begin to be frightened for her. "Maybe we'd better stop now," I say.

"Oh no," she says. "It's taken me nearly fifty years to tell this story and I'm not going to stop now."

She says it with such strength that I'm even more concerned. She even tries to sit up, thrusting her thin elbows into the mattress. I don't even try to correct her mistake. It's been more like seventy years or more since she taught on the ridge. Fifty years only took it back to just around World War II.

"OK, Grammie. Just go on." I get up and reach over to pat her shoulder. "I just thought it might be too hard for you."

"It *is* hard," she says, and her eyes flash in a way I haven't seen in nearly thirty years, since she reprimanded me for pulling my sister's hair.

"The next day Sam Clark came to school earlier than the other pupils and walked into the classroom with his eyes cast down. I said, 'Why Sam, you're early.'

"He said, 'I gotta work today. Here's my story.'

"He thrust a crumpled up piece of paper at me and ran from the school building before I could recover from my surprise.

"I smoothed out the sheet of paper which was all stained and had some numbers on the other side and looked at where he had scrawled his name, 'Sam Clark,' and then this sentence: 'I seen where a woodchuck had came and went.' That was the whole story."

Audrey laughs.

"I seen where a woodchuck had came and went," Grammie repeats. "That was it. And you would have laughed even more if you'd *seen* his 'story.' Nearly every word was misspelled." She raises her hand and lets it drop back to the bed as she says "every word."

I find myself smiling, too. Grammie has always been a stickler for spelling and grammar. She still is. In fact, she corrected me on something about a month ago, the last time I visited her.

"I sat down and wept," she continues. "I thought, this poor boy can't help it. I knew he must have slaved over that sentence, and he was so self-conscious he couldn't bear to be around when I read it, like he was revealing a secret. And he hadn't been able to write anything at all until I'd given up on him. It was a desperate sentence.

"And it made him seem even more hopeless to me. Here was a boy who'd had four years of schooling and had finally broken his long silence to write something which had some significance for him, but couldn't possibly be considered to be a *story* or a composition of any sort. And he'd inherited a butchered sense of verb tenses from his incestuous parents. To me, grammar and morality seemed intimately intertwined, and here was proof I could not teach this child anything because of the way his life and mind were."

"But Grammie," I interrupt, more for Audrey's benefit than anything else. "At least he wrote something, and it was about something he'd observed himself."

She silences me by raising her hand. "I'm telling the story. You listen and you might learn something."

This isn't going exactly the way I want. I've learned a good deal from this woman. I've learned that every person deserves the best efforts of a teacher. I've learned never to give up on a human being who wants to learn. I've learned that the child who seems the most stupid may have as much potential as the child who is the best "pupil." And I've learned not to judge children by their parents or siblings. Those are some of the reasons I wanted her to tell stories about teaching in Hamlin.

"The next day," Grammie continues, "Sam Clark didn't come to school. I read his story again after the other children left—not that I had to. It's the kind of thing you never forget after hearing it once. I decided then and there that he needed special treatment and that I was going to lie to get him back to school.

"So I went to his house that afternoon to speak with his father. His father told me school was too hard for Sam. He had enough education anyway. He could read and write and he could do his numbers and that was all he needed. He was going to work from now on. After all, he was ten years old.

"I asked to see Sam. He came in from the fields, all sweaty. I told him his story was wonderful. I told him I hadn't really understood him until I read that story. I told him I wanted him back in school the next day and I wanted him to write more.

"He came back. For the next two years he worked and worked. I saw him get to the point where he could spell most of the words he used, but he just couldn't get the grammar right, especially verbs. I tried to teach him how to love God and his country and to be honest and loyal. He was a good boy deep down where it counts.

"Then I married your great-grandfather and moved away. I never saw those children again. I left thinking Sam Clark would end up just like his father and all those other godforsaken people on the ridge. What chance did they have?"

"But you say he'd made progress," I say hopefully.

"Oh, not really. I went back to teaching when your mother entered school, you know, in a town where people were better off—went to church, had fine homes. And by the standards of the children in that town, Sam hadn't made much progress. He was twelve years old when I left. Look at Audrey here. If you can think of the most ignorant child you know her age, Sam Clark would make that child seem quite clever."

"But Audrey's had advantages," I say. "Besides, you always told me that you never know the potential a child has. You know, 'pupils are all eyes'—that stuff."

"I'm telling you *why*," she says with a good deal of heat.

Audrey breaks in. "I kind of like that story," she says. "The woodchuck, I mean. It's kind of eerie. He didn't see the woodchuck. He just saw its tracks. And the way he said it—He said he 'seen' where it 'had came and went.' I like that. I don't know why, exactly. I just like it."

"So do I," I add hastily, inspired by Audrey's insight. "Audrey's right. 'I saw a woodchuck's tracks' just doesn't have the same power."

Grammie smiles. "And I thought I was going to teach you two something.

"But that's not the end of the story," she continues. "Years later I read an article in *National Geographic* about a young graduate student from the University of Paris—an paleontologist—who discovered the oldest human tracks ever found in the United States. This man found some fossilized tracks that were more than 10,000 years old in sandstone in the Colorado River. He'd been digging in the Grand Canyon and discovered the footprints of an animal, I think it was an elk, being stalked by a man. He'd written an article recreating the entire scene and the way of life for this stalker's people just from analyzing the tracks he'd seen there. He'd found the one place on the entire continent which by accidents of geology and weather had recorded this one day's events, waited 10,000 years, and then revealed them just like that.

"Reading this article made me think of Sam. He was the only person I'd ever known to make so much of a bunch of footprints. It made me think. You think of that—it'd been over twenty years since that boy had written that sentence, and it was still on my mind.

I laugh. "Grammie," I say, "I can't believe you've never told this story before."

Audrey is quiet, but it's clear she's about to ask something. Finally, she says, "Grammie, do you think Sam Clark could have grown up to do that kind of work? Be a paleontologist?"

"Do I think it!" Grammie exclaims. "Young lady, I *know* it.That young man's name—the one in the *National Geographic*, I mean—was Samuel Clark."

"You mean?" Audrey asks.

Grammie waves her question off. "There was a picture of him squatting beside the footprints of the man and the elk, pointing. He'd grown some, and he wore glasses, but I thought I could see a resemblance to the same Sam Clark I'd dismissed in grammar school as hopeless."

"But . . . ," I sputter.

"What I didn't realize until I read that article," Grammie continues, ignoring my attempt to speak, "was that this young boy had put his entire soul into that one sentence. Where I saw misspelled words and improper verb tenses was a *sentence*. And what a sentence! A sentence he'd labored over until he got it perfect. The sentence of a soul. And I missed it! I *dis*missed it! And here he'd followed that sentence and developed it and made something great out of it. And I, his so-called teacher . . ."

"But you . . . ," I begin to protest.

"I *lied*," she cries. "I never *really* thought he had any promise.

"I drove up to the ridge to see if I could find his father. I wanted to write to Sam and apologize—tell him how proud I was he'd done so well.

I parked my car on the road in front of his house. The yard was full of old cars and parts, like a junkyard. Three or four filthy, beautiful little children were playing around them, having a great time. The house had aged to a slate gray—weathered wood with no paint. An old man came out, and it took me a while to realize he was Sam's father.

"He didn't remember me. Sam had a bunch of teachers, he said, and he couldn't remember them all. Sam had 'learnt more'n he should of,' he said. 'Always wanted to be someone else.' I showed him the *National Geographic* magazine and he couldn't make any sense of the pictures. Finally I asked him straight out if the young man in the pictures was Sam.

"He looked sharply at me as if I'd taken leave of my senses. 'Sam went over across,' he said as if I should have known. 'He was too old to go, and I told him so. Never came back.'"

"What'd he mean, Grammie?" Audrey asks.

"He was killed in the war, Audrey honey. It was an awful time."

"So he wasn't …" Audrey begins to ask.

"No," Grammie sighs. "The Samuel Clark in the magazine wasn't my Sam Clark." She's looking at Audrey the whole time—as if I'm no longer present.

The doctor is suddenly there, and I don't know how long she's been in the room. "I think that's enough for today," she says in a hushed tone, walking over and picking up Grammie's arm to check her pulse.

"I was hoping it was the same Sam Clark," Audrey says to Grammie.

"So was I," I say.

"He should have been," Audrey says, still looking at Grammie.

"I know," I say.

"Why wasn't he?" she asks, somewhat indignantly.

Grammie's head sinks slightly into the pillow and a smile of satisfaction lights her face. I walk over to remove the microphone and kiss her goodbye.

"She asks the right questions, David," she says as I lean over her.

"I know," I say, even though I don't quite understand why she says it that particular way.

* * *

Audrey and I are alone in the elevator going down. She's cradling the camera in her arms. I'm carrying the tripod in my hand. She looks lonely with her thoughts, and I put my free arm around her.

"I wish we lived closer so you could spend more time with her," I say.

"I *am* going to make movies," Audrey says in a determined manner, pulling away from me. "You'll see."

I'm about to repeat my argument about a job to fall back on, but something makes me hesitate for the briefest instant just as it dawns on me that Grammie has just taught me one more lesson.

Topics for Thinking and Writing

1. While not a typical "argument," this piece nevertheless involves persuasion. What are some of the persuasive devices the author uses? What does Grammie persuade Audrey of? What does she persuade her grandson of?

2. Although she is a teacher, Grammie learns some lessons herself as a result of her experience with Sam Clark. What are they, and why has she waited all this time to tell the story?

3. Grammie's teaching techniques change from her first year of teaching to later. Contrast the differences. Which technique is more effective? Why?

4. Based upon what you know about writing, what could Sam do to make his one-sentence essay stronger?

5. Given Sam's limitations as a learner, write a paragraph arguing that Sam should or should not be allowed to continue as a student.

6. Sam's father tells Grammie that Sam has enough education. Write a short essay to persuade Sam's father that his son deserves more education.

I HAVE A DREAM
MARTIN LUTHER KING, JR.

I am happy to join with you today in what will go down in history as the greatest demonstration for freedom in the history of our nation.

Five score years ago a great American in whose symbolic shadow we stand today signed the Emancipation Proclamation. This momentous decree came as a great beacon light of hope to millions of Negro slaves who had been seared in the flames of withering injustice. It came as a joyous daybreak to end the long night of their captivity. But one hundred years later the Negro still is not free. One hundred years later the life of the Negro is still sadly crippled by the manacles of segregation and the chains of discrimination. One hundred years later the Negro lives on a lonely island of poverty in the midst of a vast ocean of material prosperity. One hundred years later the Negro is still languished in the corners of American society and finds himself in exile in his own land. So we've come here today to dramatize a shameful condition.

In a sense we've come to our nation's capital to cash a check. When the architects of our Republic wrote the magnificent words of the Constitution and the Declaration of Independence, they were signing a promissory note to which every American was to fall heir. This note was a promise that all men—yes, black men as well as white men—would be guaranteed the unalienable rights of life, liberty and the pursuit of happiness. It is obvious today that America has defaulted on this promissory note insofar as her citizens of color are concerned. Instead of honoring this sacred obligation, America has given the Negro people a bad check, a check which has come back marked "insufficient funds."

But we refuse to believe that the bank of justice is bankrupt. We refuse to believe that there are insufficient funds in the great vaults of opportunity of this nation. So we've come to cash this check, a check that will give us upon demand the riches of freedom and the security of justice.

We have also come to this hallowed spot to remind America of the fierce urgency of now. This is no time to engage in the luxury of cooling off or to take the tranquilizing drug of gradualism. Now is the time to make real the promises of democracy. Now is the time to rise from the dark and desolate valley of segregation to the sunlit path of racial justice. Now is the time to lift our nation from the quicksands of racial injustice to the solid rock of brotherhood.

Now is the time to make justice a reality for all of God's children. It would be fatal for the nation to overlook the urgency of the moment. This sweltering summer of the Negro's legitimate discontent will not pass until there is an invigorating autumn of freedom and equality—nineteen sixty-three is not an end but a beginning. Those who hope that the Negro needed to blow off steam and will now be content will have a rude awakening if the nation returns to business as usual.

There will be neither rest nor tranquility in America until the Negro is granted his citizenship rights. The whirlwinds of revolt will continue to shake the foundations of our nation until the bright day of justice emerges.

But there is something that I must say to my people who stand on the worn threshold which leads into the palace of justice. In the process of gaining our rightful place we must not be guilty of wrongful deeds. Let us not seek to satisfy our thirst for freedom by drinking from the cup of bitterness and hatred.

We must forever conduct our struggle on the high plane of dignity and discipline. We must not allow our creative protests to degenerate into physical violence. Again and again we must rise to the majestic heights of meeting physical force with soul force. The marvelous new militancy which has engulfed the Negro community must not lead us to a distrust of all white people, for many of our white brothers, as evidenced by their presence here today, have come to realize that their destiny is tied up with our destiny. They have come to realize that their freedom is inextricably bound to our freedom. We cannot walk alone. And as we walk we must make the pledge that we shall always march ahead. We cannot turn back.

There are those who are asking the devotees of civil rights, "When will you be satisfied?"

We can never be satisfied as long as the Negro is the victim of the unspeakable horrors of police brutality.

We can never be satisfied as long as our bodies, heavy with the fatigue of travel, cannot gain lodging in the motels of the highways and the hotels of the cities.

We cannot be satisfied as long as the Negro's basic mobility is from a smaller ghetto to a larger one. We can never be satisfied as long as our children are stripped of their selfhood and robbed of their dignity by signs stating "For Whites Only."

We cannot be satisfied as long as the Negro in Mississippi cannot vote and the Negro in New York believes he has nothing for which to vote.

No, no, we are not satisfied, and we will not be satisfied until justice rolls down like waters and righteousness like a mighty stream.

I am not unmindful that some of you have come here out of great trials and tribulations. Some of you have come fresh from narrow jail cells. Some of you have come from areas where your quest for freedom left you battered by the storms of persecution and staggered by the winds of police brutality. You have been the veterans of creative suffering.

Continue to work with the faith that unearned suffering is redemptive. Go back to Mississippi, go back to Alabama, go back to South Carolina, go back to Georgia, go back to Louisiana, go back to the slums and ghettos of our Northern cities, knowing that somehow this situation can and will be changed. Let us not wallow in the valley of despair.

I say to you today, my friends, so even though we face the difficulties of today and tomorrow, I still have a dream. It is a dream deeply rooted in the American dream. I have a dream that one day this nation will rise up, live out the true meaning of its creed: "We hold these truths to be self-evident, that all men are created equal."

I have a dream that one day on the red hills of Georgia sons of former slaves and the sons of former slave-owners will be able to sit down together at the table of brotherhood. I have a dream that one day even the state of Mississippi, a state sweltering with the heat of injustice, sweltering with the heat of oppression, will be transformed into an oasis of freedom and justice.

I have a dream that my four little children will one day live in a nation where they will not be judged by the color of their skin but by the content of their character. I have a dream today. I have a dream that one day down in Alabama, with its vicious racists, with its governor having his lips dripping with the words of interposition and nullification, one day right there in Alabama little black boys and black girls will be able to join hands with little white boys and white girls as sisters and brothers.

I have a dream today. I have a dream that one day every valley shall be exalted, every hill and mountain shall be made low. The rough places will be made plain, and the crooked places will be made straight. And the glory of the Lord shall be revealed, and all flesh shall see it together. This is our hope. This is the faith that I go back to the South with. With this faith we will be able to hew out of the mountain of despair a stone of hope. With this faith we will be able to transform the jangling discords of our nation into a beautiful symphony of brotherhood. With this faith we will be able to work together, to pray together, to struggle together, to go to jail together, to stand up for freedom together, knowing that we will be free one day.

This will be the day, this will be the day when all of God's children will be able to sing with new meaning, "My country, 'tis of thee, sweet land of liberty, of thee I sing. Land where my fathers died, land of the pilgrim's pride, from every mountainside, let freedom ring." And if America is to be a great nation, this must become true. So let freedom ring from the prodigious hilltops of New Hampshire. Let freedom ring from the mighty mountains of New York. Let freedom ring from the heightening Alleghenies of Pennsylvania. Let freedom ring from the snowcapped Rockies of Colorado. Let freedom ring from the curvaceous slopes of California.

But not only that. Let freedom ring from Stone Mountain of Georgia. Let freedom ring from Lookout Mountain of Tennessee. Let freedom ring from every hill and molehill of Mississippi, from every mountainside. Let freedom ring.

And when this happens, when we allow freedom [to] ring—when we let it ring from every village and every hamlet, from every state and every city, we will be able to speed up that day when all of God's children, black men and white men, Jews and Gentiles, Protestants and Catholics, will be able to join hands and sing in the words of the old Negro spiritual, "Free at last, Free at last, Thank God a-mighty, We are free at last."

Topics for Thinking and Writing

1. Although this was originally delivered as a speech, it is also a piece of prose writing. Is its primary appeal emotional or rational? Explain your answer.
2. Point to word and sentence patterns that King uses (for example, repetition). What purposes do these serve? Do they work as well in writing as they might in speech?
3. What is the purpose of this speech? Who is the intended audience?
4. Find an audiotape version of King's speech. Listen to it and do a freewrite or write a journal entry, recording your responses as you listen.

5. Write an essay in which you make a rational case for your own views on a subject such as tolerance or discrimination.

TO THE LADY
MITSUYE YAMADA

The one in San Francisco who asked:
Why did the Japanese Americans let
the government put them in
those camps without protest?

5 Come to think of it I
        should've run off to Canada
        should've hijacked a plane to Algeria
        should've pulled myself up from my
        bra straps
10   and kicked'm in the groin
        should've bombed a bank
        should've holed myself up in a
        woodframe house
        and let you watch me
15   burn up on the six o'clock news
        should've run howling down the street
        naked and assaulted you at breakfast
        by AP wirephoto
        should've screamed bloody murder
20   like Kitty Genovese

        Then
YOU would've
        come to my aid in shining armor
        laid yourself across the railroad track
25   marched on Washington
        tattooed a Star of David on your arm
        written six million enraged
        letters to Congress

        But we didn't draw the line
30   anywhere
        law and order Executive Order 9066
        social order moral order internal order

        YOU let'm
        I let'm
35   All are punished.

Topics for Thinking and Writing

1. Who is the poet's audience for this poem? What do you know about this audience?
2. Working with a classmate, identify as many of the historical references as you can. (You may want to use the library or the Internet for your research.)
3. Why does the poet include references to twentieth-century events?
4. How do you interpret the poem's final stanza?
5. Write about an incident during which the U.S. government did something that seems to violate certain principles held in high esteem by Americans.

THE UNICORN IN THE GARDEN
JAMES THURBER

Once upon a sunny morning a man who sat in a breakfast nook looked up from his scrambled eggs to see a white unicorn with a gold horn quietly cropping the roses in the garden. The man went up to the bedroom where his wife was still asleep and woke her. "There's a unicorn in the garden," he said. "Eating roses." She opened one unfriendly eye and looked at him. "The unicorn is a mythical beast," she said, and turned her back on him. The man walked slowly downstairs and out into the garden. The unicorn was still there; he was now browsing among the tulips. "Here, unicorn," said the man, and he pulled up a lily and gave it to him. The unicorn ate it gravely. With a high heart, because there was a unicorn in his garden, the man went upstairs and roused his wife again. "The unicorn," he said, "ate a lily." His wife sat up in bed and looked at him, coldly. "You are a booby," she said, "and I am going to have you put in the booby-hatch." The man, who had never liked the words "booby" and "booby-hatch," and who liked them even less on a shining morning when there was a unicorn in the garden, thought for a moment. "We'll see about that," he said. He walked over to the door. "He has a golden horn in the middle of his forehead," he told her. Then he went back to the garden to watch the unicorn; but the unicorn had gone away. The man sat down among the roses and went to sleep.

As soon as the husband had gone out of the house, the wife got up and dressed as fast as she could. She was very excited and there was a gloat in her eye. She telephoned the police and she telephoned a psychiatrist; she told them to hurry to her house and bring a strait-jacket. When the police and the psychiatrist arrived they sat down in chairs and looked at her, with great interest. "My husband," she said, "saw a unicorn this morning." The police looked at the psychiatrist and the psychiatrist looked at the police. "He told me it ate a lily," she said. The psychiatrist looked at the police and the police looked at the psychiatrist. "He told me it had a golden horn in the middle of its forehead," she said. At a solemn signal from the psychiatrist, the police leaped from their chairs and seized the wife. They had a hard time subduing her, for she put up a terrific struggle, but they finally subdued her. Just as they got her into the strait-jacket, the husband came back into the house.

"Did you tell your wife you saw a unicorn?" asked the police. "Of course not," said the husband. "The unicorn is a mythical beast." "That's all I wanted to know," said the psychiatrist. "Take her away. I'm sorry, sir, but your wife is as crazy as a jay bird." So they took her away, cursing and screaming, and shut her up in an institution. The husband lived happily ever after.

Moral: Don't count your boobies until they are hatched.

Topics for Thinking and Writing

1. Why did the police and the psychiatrist believe the husband and not the wife at the end of this story?
2. "The Unicorn in the Garden" was written to illustrate a moral, or point, of a story. In a group, think of your own moral. In what ways might you write a story to illustrate this moral?
3. Select one of the stories which you read and thought about in this book. Then rewrite that story on your own.
4. How would you persuade someone to believe you if you had seen a unicorn?
5. Write a brief account of what happened in "The Unicorn in the Garden" from the wife's point of view.

Self-Assessment

Reread the self-assessment that opens this chapter. Then answer the following questions.

The answers that I would now change are:

Why?

I have learned the following things about writing persuasively:

Writing the Research Paper

LIBRARY
LABORATORY
LIFE

When you think of doing research, you may imagine yourself spending hours in the library. It's true that when it comes to researching, a library is a valuable source, but it isn't the only one. Research can be done through trial and error, as in a laboratory experiment, or through observation to see how things work. At other times, research might involve drawing on your own experiences. Regardless of the form it takes, researching is an essential skill.

As you have probably discovered by now, much of the writing you've done (and will do) in college involves obtaining information from sources. When writing a comparison-and-contrast paper about a fast-food restaurant and a gourmet restaurant, you may have needed to find facts about prices, ingredients, and nutritional value. When making a persuasive argument about the need for election reform, you may have gathered voting data from library sources. To write a lab report, you likely went outside on a field trip or spent time experimenting and recording your results. For an opinion piece for the school newspaper, you may have surveyed classmates. In other words, there have already been times when you have had to gather information by making observations or by using sources, ideas, and words other than your own. This finding of information and using it effectively in your work is called *doing research*.

In your career, you may find yourself conducting original research of various kinds; for now, however, your most likely use for research will be to write research papers. It is essential, therefore, to know how to locate information, how to evaluate it for usefulness and accuracy, how to incorporate it into your own writing, and how to document (or give credit to) the sources you use.

Self-Assessment

A research paper begins with your curiosity. As the name suggests, a research paper is a piece of writing based upon the use of other sources to answer a question or support a position. However, a research paper is not merely a stringing together of material from those other sources. Sometimes, a research paper will be informative; more often, it will also be persuasive. Generally speaking, in a research writing assignment, you set out to answer a question which you have raised. Very often this is an implied question—that is, one which you have in mind but won't necessarily mention in your research paper. The following are some examples: What happens when we deprive a plant of sunlight? Does the nuclear arsenal of the former Soviet Union represent a threat to world stability? How have public attitudes toward drunk driving changed during the past decade? There are an infinite number of other questions you could ask. The research paper is written to support the answer you've found to one question and to argue for your answer.

1. I would define a *research paper* as _____

   _____

2. I have written research papers in the following subjects: _____

   _____

3. I have used the following sources to write research papers. (Place a check mark beside the sources which you have used.)
   The library
   The Internet
   Personal experience
   Books
   Magazines
   Newspapers
   Electronic databases
   TV and films
   Interviews
   Other

4. Of the previous items which I have checked, I found the following to be most

   helpful because _____

   _____

5. My understanding of plagiarism is _____

   _____

6. The way I avoid plagiarism is _____

_____

7. I have difficulty with the following aspects of writing a research paper:
   Coming up with a topic
   Creating a research question or stating a thesis for my paper
   Finding sources to support my ideas
   Evaluating sources for accuracy
   Knowing how to quote someone else's words
   Taking notes
   Organizing my notes
   Outlining the paper
   Writing the paper

What I know about writing a research paper:

What I want to learn about writing a research paper:

Steps for Writing the Research Paper

Unlike some writing in which you can rely entirely on your own knowledge or experience to develop a topic, writing a research paper requires that you go outside your own knowledge to other sources. Because you have to go outside of yourself, and because writing a research paper takes a considerable amount of time, it is important that you plan your strategy. Here are a series of steps that will help you manage the length and flow of information in your research paper:

• Choose and evaluate a topic
• Develop the research question
• Research the question
• Evaluate sources
• Take notes
• Create a working thesis and an outline
• Organize your ideas
• Write the paper
• Credit the sources that you have used

Choosing and Evaluating a Topic

Topics for research papers may be assigned by your instructor. However, as you progress in your college career, you will probably be required to develop your own topics for research. Since finding an appropriate topic is a critical step in the research process, it is important that you spend some time selecting a topic that will lead to a successful final paper.

Think of the early stages of this assignment as you would those of any other writing assignment. Use the prewriting strategies that you would normally use to help you discover topics that you might want to explore further. Your goal at this stage of the process is simply to discover general topics that interest you. Remember that you are going to be stuck with whatever topic you choose for a long time, so the first rule of finding a topic is to select one that you would like to know more about and that genuinely interests you. The last thing you want to do is end up in the library researching and writing about a topic that bores you.

The basic rule of finding a topic that interests you applies in all subject areas you will study in college. So when you are assigned an open topic in a specialized course such as business management, art history, or biology, remember to begin your search by exploring topics in the discipline about which you would like to learn more. You might, for example, want to understand the differences in business management styles between the United States and Japan, know why Andy Warhol is considered a pioneer in twentieth-century American painting, or learn the ecological importance of wetlands.

Because not all topics that interest you will be appropriate for a research paper assignment, your next step in finding a topic is to evaluate your list of potential topics. Here are some general guidelines for evaluating a topic:

- Choose a topic that interests you.
- Choose a topic that is appropriate for research.
- Choose a topic that fulfills the requirements of the research assignment.
- Limit your topic to a manageable scope.
- Don't choose a topic that is too broad.
- Don't choose a topic that is completely personal.

Working Alone: Use your personal interest as a basis for brainstorming possible topics for research in two courses which you are currently taking. Try to develop as many topics as you can. Continue working even after you first run out of ideas. Remember, good, original ideas often come late in a brainstorm.

Consider the following topics:

The causes of World War II

Friendships

Why I like country music.

The first two topics are much too broad. The topics would be impossible to cover in a research paper. The third topic is not appropriate for research because it will simply lead to an expression of personal preference. Each of these three topics could be made appropriate for research by limiting or rewording the topic:

The major events that caused the United States to enter World War II

The differences between male and female friendships

Country music reflects the concerns of American culture.

Working Together: Reword the following topics so that they are limited and appropriate for a research paper.

1. Rock 'n' roll
2. Human development
3. The Internet
4. Studying in college
5. Losing weight
6. Exercise
7. Illegal drugs
8. Meeting people
9. Family
10. The importance of computers

Working Alone: Review the list of topics you brainstormed for the Working Alone section on the previous page.

1. Place an asterisk beside each topic that you think would be appropriate for research.
2. Restate the topics so that they are limited and manageable for research.

Developing the Research Question

Once you have found an appropriate topic, your next step is to develop a *research question*. This question will help you identify the specific aspect of the topic you wish to research. It will also help to focus and direct the early stages of your research. To formulate your research question, rephrase your limited topic in question form. Here are some examples of how the previously mentioned limited topics might be restated as appropriate research questions:

What were the major events that caused the United States to enter World War II?

What are the differences between male and female same-sex friendships?

Does country music reflect the social issues of modern America?

At this stage of the research process, you may have some answers to your questions. For example, you might know some of the general events that led America into the war, you might have observed that men and women talk to their friends in different ways, and you might think that country music reflects America's concern with romance. These general ideas and possible answers to your questions may also help to focus your research.

Working Alone: Develop a research question for two of the items on your limited topic list.

Researching the Question

Once you have decided on a research question, you can begin to search for sources to help you answer the question. But before your search begins, you can take two steps which will not only make your search more efficient and successful but also might lead to a working thesis for the development of your paper:

1. **Break your topic or question into parts.**
2. **Ask yourself what you already know about the research question and the topic.**

Breaking the topic or question into parts will help you find information when you search. One strategy for discovery is to brainstorm words and subtopics for exploration. For example, if your question is "What are the differences between male and female same-sex friendships?" obvious parts are "male friendships" and "female friendships." However, if you brainstorm some possible subtopics or avenues, you might develop a list which includes "friendships in early childhood," "adolescence and friendships," "teams and friendships," "adult friendships," "workplace friendships," "male-female communication patterns," "friendships and college," "famous friendships in history and literature," and "'buddy' films."

Working Together: Exchange research questions with a classmate. Brainstorm a list of parts into which the questions can be broken.

Asking yourself what you already know about your topic and coming up with possible answers to your research question is a second strategy. In fact, your own knowledge about your topic is your first source. For example, for the paper on gender and friendship, you may realize that you have observed differences between your friendships and those of your siblings of the opposite sex. You may also realize that your definition of *friendship* has changed as you have grown older. In addition, you may have read about some great friendships in history and what characterized them as successful.

Working Alone: Use the following box to list what information you already know about your research question and topic, how you know that information, and what you will still need to find out through research.

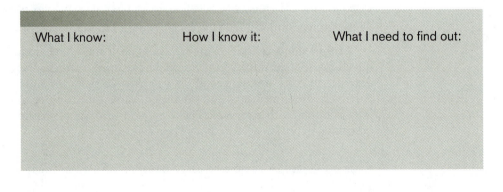

What I know:	How I know it:	What I need to find out:

Listing what you know and what you need to find out is a good starting point for your research. The more specific the words are on your brainstorm list of what you already know, the easier it will be to find sources.

Types of Sources

Sources are divided into two general categories: **primary sources** and **secondary sources.** Examples of primary sources include firsthand accounts of some occurrences, diary entries, poems, short stories, songs, interviews, letters, and government documents. Secondary sources include commentaries, analyses, and interpretations of someone else's work or of an event.

Sources can also be divided into **popular** sources and **academic** sources. Although the lines between these two types of sources are not always clear, there is some general agreement in the academic world about how sources can be classified. Magazines and newspapers are usually considered popular sources; journals of specific academic or professional disciplines and government documents are academic sources. You should check with your instructor to learn the type of sources he or she prefers that you use.

Working Together: Working with a classmate, place the following sources into these four categories: primary, secondary, popular, academic (there may be some overlapping).

Time magazine
An interview with a state official
A copy of a letter written by Eleanor Roosevelt
The *Wall Street Journal*
Journal of American Literature
A book review of *The Scarlet Letter*
A chapter of *The Scarlet Letter*
A copy of local building codes

For the research paper on gender and friendships, you may decide that you want to use a combination of primary and secondary sources. For primary sources, you might conduct interviews with your male and female peers. You could also observe the interactions of children at the local playground or at a preschool. For secondary sources, you might read academic articles in the *Journal of Child Psychology* as well as articles from a popular source such as *Parenting* magazine.

Using the Library

Your next step is to visit the library and to gather information which will help you answer your research question. Your college library staff is prepared to help you learn about the various sources available and how to access them.

Most libraries have three standard areas:

1. **The Reference Section**—noncirculating materials (encyclopedias, dictionaries, atlases, annals, bibliographies, and so on)
2. **The Paper Collection**—books, journals, newspapers, magazines, government documents
3. **The Computer Collection** (databases, online collections, the Internet)

Efficiently using all of the sources in the library can save you time. Don't limit yourself to just the Internet or electronic sources. The paper collection is easy to use and accessible.

The Reference Section: The reference section is a good place to begin your search because it is easy to use and will contain general information on your topic. Most reference sections are organized by subject; for example, all literature sources are located in one area and all history information in another.

This section also contains general and specialized encyclopedias, general and specialized dictionaries, atlases, almanacs, bibliographies, and indexes of published works. Sources in the reference section can provide you with an overview of your topic. For example, the specialized *Encyclopedia of Psychology* may give you some general background information about gender roles in society and children's play. The *Reader's Guide to Periodical Literature* may contain a listing of articles written about your topic. Although you will probably not cite encyclopedias in your research paper, the background information will help you to find more specific sources by giving you additional key words to use in your search. (Note: You can photocopy materials from the reference section, but the original materials may not be taken out of the library.)

Working Alone: Take a tour of the reference section of the library. Make a list of the sources which might prove helpful in answering a research question of your choice. Write down the name of each source and its location in the reference section.

The Paper Collection: The **paper collection** is the library's collection of sources printed on paper: magazines, newspapers, periodicals, journals, and books. Today, most libraries have electronic catalogs of their paper holdings. You can usually search the library's catalog for its paper collection in four ways:

1. Author search
2. Title search
3. Subject search
4. Key word search

Most sources are entered into the library's catalog by *call number*. For example, you could search for Deborah Tannen's book *You Just Don't Understand: Men and Women in Conversation* in four ways—by author, by title, by subject, or by key word.

Author: Deborah Tannen

Title: *You Just Don't Understand: Men and Women in Conversation*

Subject: Friendships and gender

Key word: friendships, gender differences in speech, male and female relationships

Each search will produce the source under the same call number, regardless of the search method used.

Working Alone: Refer to your brainstorm list about your topic to find as many ways to search as possible. Then access the electronic catalog of your library and conduct subject and key word searches of your topic. Write down or print out the names of the sources.

You can find your library's holdings that are related to your topic by conducting a catalog search, but you can find additional sources by walking through the aisles where the books are shelved. Use the call number of one source which you have found in the catalog. After locating that book, look at the titles of the books that are shelved around it. You may discover another source by using this method. Sometimes the old-fashioned method of searching by walking down aisles, reading titles, pulling books off shelves, and looking through tables of contents and indexes will yield unexpected treasures.

The Electronic Collection: Today's libraries often keep a portion of their **periodical collection** in computerized databases. Periodicals are publications issued at regular intervals such as daily, weekly, or monthly. Examples include the *New York Times*, *Sports Illustrated*, *Composition Chronicle*, and *Psychology Today*.

Many libraries today contain electronic databases that store full and partial texts of periodical articles. Often these articles contain *abstracts*—summaries of the articles' main ideas. You can search these databases for sources for your topic by author, title, subject, and key word. You should check with your librarian to find out what databases and periodicals are electronically available to you.

Working Alone: Using the database/periodical options available at your library, conduct a search on your topic. Print out a list of any sources that you think might be useful in answering your research question.

The Internet: One of the most popular ways to search for information today is via the Internet. There are numerous search engines which "crawl" through the Web locating information related to topics. However, despite its popularity and appearance of speed, the Web is often the least efficient means of finding substantive information for your research. Remember that usually when researching a college paper, you will be looking for scholarly discussions and evidence which support your paper's thesis. The Web can provide you with statistics and demographics but is less likely to provide you with in-depth discussions. Another problem with the Web is that search engines explore by using broad concepts, not specific terms. For example, a search on "friendship" brings up sites on "friendship rings" and "friendship cakes."

Working Alone: Conduct a web search on your topic.

1. How many sites located on the first two pages of the results screen were specifically related to your topic? How many were unrelated?
2. Click onto one of the sites. Does it contain the kind of information that you expected to find?

Evaluating Sources

Good evaluation at the beginning of your search will make the search process easier for you. You can think of evaluation in two ways:

1. An evaluation of the reliability and validity of the source
2. An evaluation of the source's usefulness in answering your research question

Since there is so much information available to you today, how will you know which is accurate, valid, and reliable? First, it's important to consider the source from which you are taking the information. You can begin to check for validity by learning about the author. A biographical dictionary housed in the reference section of the library may be able to give you information about the author and his known expertise in the field. Also, if the author is quoted or mentioned in other sources which you are using, these references can be a strong indication that the author is well known in the field.

Besides checking information about the author and the reliability of the general source, it's also important to consider the publication date of the specific information that you are using. Some topics, such as those related to science and health, may require that you use current information. Other topics may need a more historical view and will require sources from different historical periods.

Here is a quick list of questions to ask yourself about the reliability and validity of sources:

1. Is the source from which you are taking the article considered reliable?
2. Is the author well known in the field and considered an expert?
3. Is the information current or outdated?

Web Site Evaluation

Web site evaluations require that you be particularly careful because anyone can post information on the Web. If the site is sponsored by an educational institution (.edu), a government office (.gov), or a well-known public organization (.org), it is more likely to be acceptable to your instructors as a source than a commercial site (.com) or an individual's home page (.com or .edu) would be.

You should also evaluate the source further. Use the following questions as guidelines:

1. Who created the web site? Is the web site owner named? If so, does he or she have a contact address?
2. Is the web site associated with an educational, government, or public institution?
3. Is the web site associated with a private or commercial organization?
4. Is the organization with which the site is associated reputable?
5. Is the web site an advertisement?
6. How recently was the information on the web site updated?
7. Is the information on the web site supported by other sources which you have obtained?

Working Alone: Using an Internet search engine, conduct a search on your topic. Then conduct Web site evaluations of some of the sources you have found.

Working Alone: Using a biographical dictionary, check the author of a source that you are using. What kinds of information does the entry in the dictionary give you? If you are unable to locate the author's name in the dictionary, ask the librarian about other means of checking. You might also ask your professor for suggestions.

After you have evaluated your sources and found them to be appropriate, you should determine whether the sources will help you answer your research question. If you are using a periodical article that contains an abstract, first read the abstract to find out what the article is about. If there is no abstract, quickly skim the article, reading the introduction, conclusion, and topic sentences of the body paragraphs. These two methods should help you determine whether the piece is worth examining more closely.

Taking Notes

Once you have decided that the sources you have found are reliable, valid, and potentially useful, you can efficiently organize your sources by using a note-card system. Using 4 × 6-inch index cards, list all of the essential bibliographical information for a source on one side of a card. Generally, this information will include the author, title, publisher, place of publication, and publication date of each source. The requirements for citing commonly used sources can be found in the Quick MLA Guide at the end of this chapter. (For complete information on citing sources, you may wish to consult the *MLA Handbook for Writers of Research Papers* available in your library.) Use one card for each source. Your stack of cards will become your **working bibliography** of your sources. Then, when you are ready to type your list of references, all you have to do is alphabetize your stack of cards.

Back of Note Card

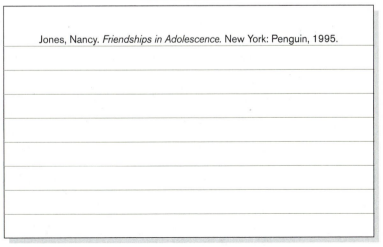

Jones, Nancy. *Friendships in Adolescence.* New York: Penguin, 1995.

On the other side of each note card, you will write the information from the source that you want to use to support the thesis of your paper. Use the following format:

1. Label the upper-left-hand corner of the note card with either the author's last name or a key word from the source's title.
2. Leave the upper-right-hand corner of the note card blank for now.

Front of Note Card

Jones
(Information)
(Page numbers on which the information was found)

Once you have set up your card, you are ready to write out the information you wish to store on it. There are three standard forms which you can use to record the information:

• Summary
• Paraphrase
• Quotation

For example, let's say that you have decided to use the following information on friendships from the book *Friendships in Adolescence*:

Not only do friendships with peers become significantly more important in adolescence than in middle childhood, but both the nature of the relationships and the influence the peers have on the individual also significantly change. In middle childhood, friendships for both boys and girls are based on mutually shared activities, time, and space. For example, children in the same classroom, on the same sports teams, and in the same neighborhood become quick friends. In middle childhood, when access to the friend becomes difficult, the friendships end. The influence of peers on likes and dislikes is almost nonexistent for this developmental period. On the other hand, in adolescence, friendships are based on mutual trust, respect, and shared values, as well as on shared interests. Because of increasing mobility and independence, teens are less dependent on physical proximity for friendships to continue. The approval of friends for choices in music, dress, and activities becomes paramount in the teenage years.

A Summary Card: The summary technique most suitable for note-card preparation is the nutshell summary, in which you condense the source's material by capturing the main ideas and essential details (see Chapter 7). On the note card, you will write, in your own words, the information that you think you might use in your paper. Remember to keep in mind the question that you are answering and the ways in which the information from the source will help you to answer that question. Your summary should state the gist of the author's point. Be sure to list the pages on which the information is located.

A summary card on the previous excerpt might look like this:

Summary Card

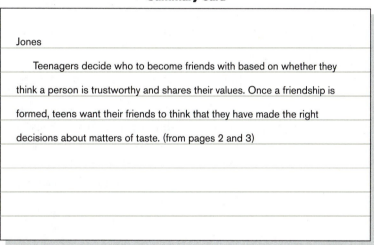

Jones

    Teenagers decide who to become friends with based on whether they

think a person is trustworthy and shares their values. Once a friendship is

formed, teens want their friends to think that they have made the right

decisions about matters of taste. (from pages 2 and 3)

Remember that you are only summarizing the part of the source which helps you answer your research question.

Working Alone: Using a source for your research paper, write a summary card by using the sample summary card as an example.

A Paraphrase Card: In a paraphrase, you follow the original author's form more closely. You still use your own words and sentence structure, but you capture more of the original because you feel that it's important to present the author's full points to support your thesis. Often, a paraphrase is almost as long as the original passage, whereas a summary is a significantly condensed version of the original. Write your paraphrase on the note card (if you need to use two note cards, label the second "continuation" and be sure to write the author's name in the upper-left-hand corner). List the page numbers. On the back of the card, write all of the necessary bibliographical information.

Here is an example of a paraphrase card of the friendship excerpt:

Paraphrase Card

Jones

Friendships of teenagers differ a lot from the friendships of younger kids.

Younger children tend to pick their friends because they live near them, go to

school with them, or play with them. These kids don't really care whether their

friends like what they wear or the games they want to play. However, teenagers

care very much about what their friends think about their tastes in music and

clothes. They also pick friends because they realize that friendship should be

based on trust. Another factor for teens in picking friends is figuring out who

feels the same way about the world that they do. (from pages 2 and 3)

Working Alone: Using the same source that you used for your summary card, write a paraphrase card by using the sample paraphrase card as an example.

Direct Quotation: Sometimes you will want to use the author's exact words in your paper. Most often, direct quotations are used when they add "spice" to your writing or more creatively state the point you are trying to make. It's important to be exact when you are copying down the author's words.

Direct Quotation

Jones

"The approval of friends for choices in music, dress, and activities

becomes paramount in the teenage years."

(from page 2)

You should have at least one note card for each source that you use. You may not end up using the information on all of the cards, but it's better to start out with more rather than not enough information. In the next section of this chapter, you will learn how to write an outline for your paper. After completing your outline, you will go back to your note cards and, in the upper-right-hand corner, you will **code** the card to a section of your outline.

Note: **Plagiarism** is using the words or ideas of another writer without giving credit to the person. You can avoid plagiarizing by citing the sources of all borrowed words and ideas and by remembering to do the following:

1. Write your summary and paraphrases in your own words.
2. Put quotation marks around direct quotations.
3. Include the bibliographical information for source material.

Doing these three things will help you to avoid plagiarizing. In this chapter you will learn what types of information need to be cited. But it is always better to err on the side of caution; that is, when you aren't sure whether you should cite a source, you should include the citation.

Plagiarism is the inevitable result of using sources without crediting them. **It is always academically unacceptable.**

Creating a Working Thesis and an Outline

The information that you have compiled in response to your research question should help you formulate a **working thesis.** The working thesis is your answer to the research question. In other words, the working thesis should be developed from your responses to the facts, ideas, and opinions that you encountered as you were conducting research and compiling notes.

Here are some examples of working theses:

- Although the bombing of Pearl Harbor was the specific event that caused America to enter World War II, there were also significant economic factors that prompted America's entry.
- Men's and women's friendships differ in their levels of openness and intimacy.
- Country music reflects America's preoccupation with the problems of romantic love.

Creating the working thesis is the first step in the process of writing the paper. As with any other paper you would write, the working thesis will guide your writing as you organize and manage the information you expect to include in the paper.

You will use your working thesis to create an **outline** of your paper. The outline should identify the paper's major sections—the main points that you expect to use to support or explain your thesis. As you complete your paper, you will develop these sections with explanatory details and examples.

Because there are many aspects to manage while completing the research paper, creating an outline of the paper will help you to visualize how the parts will fit together. This outline will become your road map as you complete each section of the paper.

The outline is also important because it breaks a large writing task into several smaller and more manageable parts. Using an outline enables you to think of a ten-page paper as a compilation of short papers on specific parts of your thesis.

For example, a basic outline might look something like this:

I. Introduction and Thesis: Country music reflects America's preoccupation with the problems of romantic love.

II. Body
  A. Songs about lost love
  B. Songs about abuse in love relationships
  C. Songs about loneliness (being without love)
  D. Songs about being in the wrong relationships

III. Conclusion

Working Alone: Take a moment to flip through the pages of this chapter. Notice that the chapter is divided into sections and that each section is identified by a heading. You could think of these headings as forming a basic outline of the chapter. Use the headings to outline the chapter's major sections. How does this outline help you to visualize the writing process for the research paper?

Organizing Your Notes

By writing an outline, you have identified the sequence of the major sections of your paper. The outline becomes your guide as you map out ways to organize your notes to fit into the flow of the paper. This is a critical step in completing the paper, so organizing your notes carefully will make writing the paper much easier.

To begin organizing your notes, first review your note cards and group them by category. That is, notes about the same topic should be grouped together. The categories which you use should match the sections that you have identified in the outline. As you group the cards, place a description of the topic in the upper-right-hand corner. The description could be a key word from the section of the outline. This will serve as a quick reference when you begin to connect the cards to the specific sections of the paper.

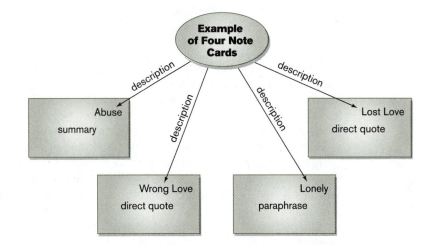

Each of these cards should correspond to a section of the outline. Cards that do not seem to fit into a section of the outline should be placed aside. The information on those cards might be useful later in the writing process.

Writing the Research Paper

After you have completed your outline and grouped your cards, you are ready to write your research paper. Employ the writing strategies you have developed throughout this writing course. Use any of the prewriting strategies you have found effective: brainstorming, freewriting, webbing, and so on. You will follow the same process of drafting, revising, and editing for the research paper that you have followed for all of the papers you have previously written.

The difference between writing this research paper and writing your previous papers is that the examples you will now use to support your thesis will be derived from the sources you have gathered, evaluated, and organized. A strong research paper balances the way *your ideas* are used with summaries, paraphrases, and direct quotations of *other people's ideas and words.* Remember that you must cite the sources that you use. It is also important to remember that *you* control the use of the sources and the writing; the sources never control your writing.

Following these steps will help you maintain control of the paper.

1. Write one section of the paper in your own words without using your sources.
2. Read the section that you have written and decide which of your ideas need to be specifically supported with material from outside sources.
3. Look through your set of note cards which is coded to this section.
4. Decide which of the note cards contain material that will most effectively support your ideas.
5. Smoothly incorporate that material into your writing.

You can blend others' ideas into your own writing by carefully using words of **attribution.** A word of attribution is a signal to the reader that borrowed material is about to be introduced.

Example: **According to** Bonetti, the "days of football's glory years are gone."
Bonetti **argues** that "the days of football's glory years are gone."

In the following box you will find some of the more common attribution words. Choose the word that best illustrates the point of view presented in the material that you are quoting or paraphrasing.

Attribution Words				
says	insists	agrees	disagrees	states
points out	relates	comments	suggests	discovered
describes	defends	argues	notes	thinks
analyzes	reports	observes	finds	asks
records	warns	predicts	asserts	explains
writes	according to	demonstrates	concludes	shows

You can incorporate quotations into your sentences in two ways:

1. By using the full quotation in your sentence
2. By using part of the quotation in your sentence

The following are some examples of ways to incorporate full or partial quotations into a paper.

Example of Quotation from Source: "The majority of Little League fathers studied said that during their sons' season, they experienced numerous dreams of their own Little League games. These dreams often left them with feelings of anxiety, failure, and sadness."

Full Quotation in Paper: Jones reports that "the majority of Little League fathers studied said that during their sons' season, they experienced numerous dreams of their own Little League games. These dreams often left them with feelings of anxiety, failure, and sadness."

Partial Quotation in Paper: When their kids are playing ball, Jones reports dads say that they have "numerous dreams of their own Little League games" and that when they awaken from these dreams, they have "feelings of anxiety, failure, and sadness."

When the quotation is more than four lines of your text, it is presented after a colon and is indented five spaces.

Example of Quotation from Source: "I thought at first that I was enjoying my son's games, but with each game, I grew more and more anxious. Sometimes, I found myself getting angry at my son, much too angry. At other times, I felt indescribably sad, kind of longing for something. One night I particularly remember looking at my kid at bat and thinking how I could do it better than him. Now, that's ridiculous, isn't it? I mean, I'm thirty-five years old. Why would I feel this need to be competitive with my son—dumb, dumb!"

Indented Quotation in Paper: Bill, one father of an eleven-year-old player, poignantly says:

> I thought at first that I was enjoying my son's games, but with each game, I grew more and more anxious. Sometimes, I found myself getting angry at my son, much too angry. At other times, I felt indescribably sad, kind of longing for something. One night I particularly remember looking at my kid at bat and thinking how I could do it better than him. Now, that's ridiculous, isn't it? I mean, I'm thirty-five years old. Why would I feel this need to be competitive with my son—dumb, dumb!

Note: Remember that you must always incorporate quotations into your sentences. Quotations can never stand alone in the body of your paper.

Using direct quotations in your paper often requires special use of punctuation. In the following box, you will find some general guidelines for punctuating the research paper.

Punctuation and the Research Paper

Quotation Marks

1. Use double quotation marks to indicate quoted material.
2. Use single quotation marks to indicate a quotation within a quotation.

Examples:

1. The bond trader said, "The stock market is going haywire today."
2. He said, "The business reporter on the evening news announced, 'The stock market is going haywire today.'"

Introducing a Quotation

1. Use a comma or a colon to introduce a quotation when it creates a break with the flow of your own writing. In general, the greater the break with your own sentence, the more likely the colon is appropriate. (See previous examples in this box.)
2. Always use a colon to introduce longer quotations that are extracted from a text. (See example on page 286.)

Punctuation of Quotations

1. The punctuation of a quotation should appear exactly as it does in the original material.
2. Commas and periods are always placed inside the quotation marks.

Example: The research report stated, "A majority of the people favored a repeal of the newest tax law."

If the quotation is introduced by "that" you can use a lower case letter to begin the quoted material.

Example: The research report stated that "a majority of ..." etc.

3. Question marks and exclamation points may be placed inside or outside the quoted material. If they are a part of the original material, they should be placed inside the quotation marks. If, on the other hand, they are a part of *your* sentence, they should be placed outside the quotation marks.

Example: Smith asks a pertinent question, "What is the likelihood, then, that the law will be overturned?"

Example: What is the role that the "voter should play in the repeal of the law"?

Adding Material to the Original Quotation

Use *brackets* [ ] to indicate an addition to the original quotation. Since quotations are direct copies of original material, any addition you make to the original must be indicated within the quotation by placing the addition within a pair of brackets. (*continued*)

(continued)

Example:

Original: "The women were not expected to write about issues outside of their sphere of experience."

Addition: "The women [of the late 1800s] were not expected to write about issues outside of their sphere of experience."

Omitting Material from the Original Quotation
Use *ellipsis points* (three spaced periods ...) to indicate the omission of words, phrases, or sentences from the original quotation. It might be necessary to condense an original quotation to make it fit more smoothly into your own writing. Ellipsis points are a signal to the reader that some material has been deleted from the original. Remember, however, that you cannot change the author's original meaning through deletion.

Example:

Original: "The women were not expected to write about issues outside of their sphere of experience. No women were expected to know about the difficulties faced by a nation's people during war. Nor were women expected to understand the intricacies of business negotiations and labor practices. And as far as politics were concerned, women were not to have intimate knowledge of the machinations associated with building power and influence in government. Because women rarely operated in spheres outside of the home, they could not write about these spheres with any degree of reality; thus, they should not attempt to do so."

Omission: "The women were not expected ... to know about ... war, ... business negotiations and labor practices, [or] ... building power and influence in government.... [T]hey could not write about these spheres with any degree of reality; ..."

Paraphrases and summaries are blended into your writing in the same way that direct quotations are—through attribution.

Note: Paraphrases and summaries of another person's ideas must also be cited to avoid plagiarism.

Original Passage:

Today's political speeches have less content than the speeches of years ago. In part, this is because candidates are appealing to the broad audience made available to them through TV and radio. Fifty years ago, politicians delivered speeches to local audiences. Each speech dealt with the issues relevant to that audience. Each speech was filled with concrete details. The candidate was not afraid to use strong, powerful language and words with some meat to them. Today, politicians know that their speeches will be heard and reported on from one end of the country to the other. They don't want to offend anyone, so what we get is blandspeak, nothing to sink one's teeth into.

John Stevens

Example of Summary Integration:

> Stevens suggests that the absence of specifics in today's political speeches is caused by the politician's fear of offending any audience. Today's candidate knows that his speech is not local, but global—everyone around the country, through media, will have access to it. Therefore, he delivers the least concrete, and the blandest, speech that he can.

Crediting the Sources That You Use

As the previous examples illustrate, you will be incorporating the ideas or words of other people to support your thesis. Whenever you do this, you *must* stop and consider whether or not you need to give credit for these ideas.

As a rule of thumb, you could think about giving credit in this way: If you looked something up, and you have used it in your writing, you must give credit for it. However, there are very specific circumstances in which you don't need to document your sources.

The following are four basic types of commonly known facts that you can use without providing documentation. You should always cite the source of any other type of information that you use.

Historical facts, e. g., Delaware was the first state to ratify the Constitution of the United States.

Scientific facts, e. g., water freezes at 0° Celsius.

Geographical facts, e. g., the Nile is the longest river in Africa.

Biographical facts, e. g., Carrie Fisher is Debbie Reynolds's daughter.

If you are in doubt, give credit to avoid the risk of plagiarizing the source.

Working Alone: Which of the following statements would require documentation and which would not?

- Grover Cleveland was President of the United States from 1885 to 1889 and from 1893 to 1897.
- His first inaugural address mentioned the loss of the vast herds of buffalo that used to roam the Great Plains.
- "Catfish" Hunter was given his nickname by the owner of the Dodgers.
- Boise is the capital of Idaho.
- The average SAT score of entering students at East State University is 1270.
- Fewer than one in one hundred live births of cattle in northern Finland shows evidence of genetic damage as a consequence of the Chernobyl nuclear accident.

How to Give Credit

When you are writing your paper, you should always acknowledge the sources of your information. MLA style requires that you cite sources within the text of your paper. You normally do this by placing the information about the source in parentheses immediately after the borrowed material. Include three pieces of information the first time that you mention a source: the author, the title, and the page number or numbers. After your first mention of a source, you only need to give the author's last name and the page number or numbers in additional citations.

There are two other points to remember. Sometimes the information you use may not have a title or may not credit an author; in such cases, just provide as much information as you can so that the reader can identify the source. For example, you might need to cite a magazine title if the author and article title are not given. Also, do not refer to material you have obtained from electronic sources by page number because the page numbers will differ from computer to computer. In this case, you should provide a paragraph number rather than a page number.

You may mention only the author's last name and the page (or paragraph) number after you have given all of the information in your first citation of the source. There are two ways to present this information in your first citation.

Mention the author of the quotation and the title of the work in your sentence and then put the page number in parentheses after the quotation.

One of the most important observations Nancy Jones makes about relationships in *Friendships in Adolescence* is that "friendships with peers become significantly more important in adolescence than in middle childhood" (2).

Put the author of the quotation, title, and page number in parentheses after the quotation.

It is important to remember that "friendships with peers become significantly more important in adolescence than in middle childhood" (Nancy Jones, *Friendships in Adolescence* 2).

Note: Usually, your writing will be smoother if you can mention the author and title in the portion written in your own words, but you should judge for yourself which option sounds better. In either case, the page number always goes in parentheses.

If you've already mentioned the work once before, you can document your source for a quotation in the following way.

Hancock has suggested that "if we all got an extra hour of sleep every night, the number of road accidents would decrease by a factor of two" (67).

There are also formats you should follow when citing the source of a paraphrase.

Name the author within your paraphrase and then put the title and page number in parentheses.

One of the most interesting ideas that Renee Marcotte presents is the suggestion that changes in the frequency of air travel have led to an increase in the number of airborne diseases infecting Americans ("Infectious Disease Transmission in Air Transport" 23).

Documenting your source for a paraphrase after you have already mentioned the work once before.

The frequency of earthquakes with a magnitude greater than 6.0 on the Richter scale in the San Francisco area before the big earthquake of 1906, Rowe reminds us, is starting to bear an uncanny resemblance to current seismic events in the Bay Area (par. 4).

Remember, you put other source information, such as web addresses, in the Works Cited section. Keep the essay itself as free of clutter as possible.

Working Alone: The following are five short passages. For each one, write a paragraph by using some or all of the passage.

- For one passage, include the author's name and title of the work within your own wording.
- For another, identify the author within your own wording but place the work's title in parentheses.
- For the third passage, create a paraphrase and assume that you have already identified the author and the work's title in an earlier citation.
- For the fourth passage, paraphrase the quotation and incorporate the author's name into your wording. Assume that you have not mentioned the work previously in your paper.
- For the final sample, quote from some or all of the passage and place all of the necessary information in parentheses. Assume that you have not mentioned the work earlier in your paper.

Passage One:

A defender and advocate of Catholic rights in Britain and Ireland, Edmund Burke's defense of the British political system was practical rather than theoretical. Although his body of work can cumulatively be read as a systemic defense of the ideals of parliamentary democracy and a broad franchise, Burke's individual works are often specific responses to specific situations, and his political philosophy is not systematic in any modern sense of the word.

Source: Tim Westfall, *The Life and Writings of Edmund Burke,* Dublin: Street Corner Press, 1997. 17.

Passage Two:

A more plausible guess as to his [Vitaly Shevoroshkin's] occupation would be leader of a philosophical school whose upshot is unmitigated despair, as if he has long lived under the burden of some insight into the human condition which you would just soon he didn't share with you.
Source: Robert Wright, "Quest for the Mother Tongue." *Atlantic Monthly.* Apr. 1991: 39.

Passage Three:

If medical practitioners wanted to save lives … instead of making money out of people they would unite to prevent diseases, not work separately to cure them. The cause of most illness has been known since the sixth century before Christ, when the Greeks made a goddess of Hygiene.
Source: Alasdair Gray, *Poor Things*. New York: Harcourt Brace Jovanovich, 1992. 23–24.

Passage Four:

Golf is not a game of chance … and failure lies entirely with the individual. When I miss a crucial putt … I know the reason is not that I misread the green or put too much pace on the ball, but because I am, at core, a weak and silly man.
Source: Joel Achenbach, "Looking Out For the Bogeyman on Texas' Tour 18," *Smithsonian,* August 1993, 50.

Passage Five

Maria Edgeworth's own life was increasingly centered around her family's estate and in practicing what she had preached. Her neighbors and tenants recorded her tireless efforts on behalf of the poor and destitute during the Great Famine. The success of her work in those difficult times is testified to in the relatively few names of émigrés from her parish appearing in the rolls of the famine ships or in the records at their final ports of call abroad. The death rate, too, although higher than in preceding years, was noticeably lower in her parish than in many of the surrounding communities (Djrianna Betts, *A Quick Guide to the Life of Maria Edgeworth,* <http://www.irelandbio.org./c18/author/edgeworth>par. 5).

Working Together: Using the MLA guide at the end of this chapter, create a Works Cited page for these five passages. Assume that you have used all five in your essay.

A Final Note

As you finish reading this chapter, you will probably be completing a draft of an assigned research paper. No doubt you have discovered that writing a research paper is one of the more difficult writing tasks which you have encountered in college. But going through the process of writing one will help you develop writing skills that you will use throughout your life. In your other college courses, on the job, and in your personal life, locating information, evaluating its usefulness to you, and organizing that information so that it best helps you meet your needs are writing skills that you will use again and again. Like the other skills you have learned as you have progressed through this course, these are skills that you can now add to your life as a writer.

Sample Research Paper

Once you have prepared to write your research paper, the big moment comes. The following is a research paper written by a student using the techniques and approaches discussed in this chapter. Notes have been added to highlight various aspects of both her writing style and the mechanics of citing sources that she has used.

Remember, what you are looking at is a final draft, the last stage of a process in which the student drafted, wrote, and revised versions of her paper. She received help both from her instructor and from classmates as the various drafts took shape.

Sample Research Paper

So You Want to Be a Parent?

by
Elizabeth D. Kanavos

Professor Donald Cocci
15 November 2000

When World War II ended, America had become a country that believed in technology, in advances in society, and in science. It followed that to be a good parent, you had to know the latest ideas about raising children. "It was 1946 when I became a mother," Anne Raeburn remembers, "and I absolutely believed there had to be a better way to raise children than in the past" (*Forty Years of Parenting* 38). In 1946, that better way was most famously described in Dr. Benjamin Spock's *The Common Sense Book of Baby and Child Care.*

Spock's basic idea was that babies were not helpless blobs. Babies, he said, were alert, conscious, loving creatures who responded better to nurturing than to the old ideas that children should be seen but not heard. "I always knew that having a baby in the house was not just a matter of going about business as before," Celia Amhara, a nurse at Mercy Hospital in St. Louis, Missouri, told researchers Donna Raposo and Corey Campbell when explaining why she was so taken with Dr. Spock's ideas (qtd. in *Fifty Years of Caring for Baby* 57). When she became pregnant with her first child, Ms. Amhara left her job, prepared her home, and became Dr. Spock's ideal mother: there for her child, always caring for him, and always challenging and encouraging him.

Today, however, many of us know that America now is not like America was then. In Dr. Spock's world, mothers stayed home with their children, and fathers went to work. Children were raised in two-parent homes. One income was enough for a family of four or five. What do we have today? For most of us, one income is not enough to support ourselves, never mind any children we might have. Many of us who are raising children are working one or two jobs, trying to go to school, and struggling to pay the bills for health care, a car, and food. And then there's the cost of childcare.

Who has time anymore for Dr. Spock's advice? This paper looks at how times have changed since Dr. Spock's book was published and attempts to show that much of the advice we get today has nothing to do with the reality millions of mothers face every day.

Of course America has changed. And with the changes have come new ideas about raising children, but those ideas often miss one important point. For example, Richard Harris calls for a return to an understanding that "Boundaries Work." According to Harris,

---

Quotation marks show where a quotation begins and ends.
The author's full name is given the first time you use it.
The title of the book from which you quote.
The page number of the quote.
Book titles are in italics.

On second mention, give only last name of author.
Paraphrase of author's idea. No page number is given if paraphrase is of more than one or two pages.

Here you are quoting what one person told the author. Use "qtd. in."

Here is the research question—and here is the thesis.

Magazine and journal article titles appear in quotation marks.

If the quotation is more than 4 lines of your type, indent it 5 spaces on the right.

Indented quotations are double-spaced and do not use quotation marks.

Word in brackets was added by author of paper to help reader understand the quotation.

Pages 17 and 18 are quoted here.

A child, especially a baby or toddler, does not know what is safe and what is not. She does not know what is acceptable behavior and what is not. He does not know whether he is allowed to do something or not. Most of all, a child likes to ask why, likes to explore the limits of his world [but] this is not a world in which the idea that "anything goes" is either wise or practical. Children need limits and they need to learn them quickly and for good. [17–18]

For Harris and people like him, child raising is a job requiring hard work and perseverance. He may be right, but Harris seems to assume that parents have all the time in the world to spend with their children.

This just isn't true. And it's a good thing some people recognize this. One great resource is the web page maintained by the Council for Children. It makes it clear that "well over half the children under five in America spend some part of at least three days a week with all aspects of care provided for them by someone other than the primary care giver" (par. 3). Furthermore, the Council notes that "39 per cent of [the] children in America under the age of ten in 1997 spent at least one working year of their first five years in day care" (par. 9). And, finally, the Council reports that "62 per cent of all grandparents in America report having provided at least some full-time day care to a grandchild at some stage of the child's first five years" (par. 12).

Most web pages don't have an author's name. If your source doesn't, use the name of the page's creating agency.

Give web page quotations by paragraph number.

Today, the question of caring for America's children is so serious that the National Research Council (NRC) thought it necessary to prepare a major report—*Who Cares for America's Children*—examining the relationships among parents, children, and other care providers. One other point is that "although women's labor force participation in the United States has increased in almost every decade since 1890, the dramatic increase … during the past decade represents a fundamental change in the day-to-day life of many American women" (NRC 21). To say nothing of their children!

Identify an agency first and then record its abbreviation.

Using three ellipses points shows you have left out some words that were in the original.

You can put an author in parentheses or in text.

This is certainly something that bothers women with children who have to work outside of the house and perhaps have to go to college to take classes as well. It is obvious to these mothers that they are relying on someone else to help establish their children's character and attitudes.

"I have to work two jobs just to pay rent and buy the food for little Zach and me," says one student interviewed at Central Community College, Alana Tserios. "I don't want to do this," she goes on,
explaining:

> but both my jobs are part-time, so they don't pay for health care, and they
> don't help with childcare. To work one job, I really have to work another just
> to pay for what it takes to do that first job. And I don't intend to be working
> part-time my whole life, so I have to go to school to get a degree, so Zach's
> got to learn a lot from someone other than me.

Luckily for this student, her local church group helps with childcare
much of the time, "and [she likes to] … know where Zach is and
who is teaching him," but twice a week she has to send him to a
local daycare group. "I mean, I talked to them, and I explained my
situation and what I wanted and all," she says, "but in the end, there
are only so many I can afford," so the daycare her son gets is not really all that much under her control.

But daycare is not always a bad idea. In fact, it may often be a
good idea. Research conducted for the Association of State and
Local Child Service Providers shows that children who attend daycare full-time for some or most of their pre-first-grade years are no
more likely to do poorly in school than children who spend more
time at home (*The Effects of Daycare on the Success of Children in
Grades One Through Three*). An article in the *Daily News and Chronicle*,
"Children Flourish in a Happy Setting," provides further discussion
of the association's research. One additional point is worth noting:
By third grade it was impossible even to guess with any accuracy
which children had ever attended daycare and which had not (Janis
Marone A3), further suggesting that it is the quality of care which
matters at least as much as who the provider is.

In some cases, children who have been in daycare will do better
in school than those who have not. "This study demonstrates what
we have sensed all along," Gerri Portan told WWTV, showing that
"what goes on where children spend their time is as important as
where they spend it."

That is a sentiment that Perri Ambrose agrees with. "I stayed
home with my daughter Rose Marie for the first year and a half after

---

This information comes from a personal interview. State where the interview took place.

As this quotation is from an interview, you cannot give a page or paragraph number.

Newspaper titles are in italics. The title of the article in a newspaper is in quotation marks.

Author's name and page number. Newspapers are often in sections so you must give the section letter, too.

WWTV is a TV station. Other details regarding the source go in Works Cited.

These quotations are from a speech. In text, name the venue of the speech; other info can go in the Works Cited.

she was born," she told an audience at Central Community College. "Two things happened to me: I was tired all the time, and I got shut off from many of my friends whom I just didn't have the energy to see anymore." As for her daughter, Ambrose says that "Rose Marie got bored. She spent a lot of time in our small apartment. I didn't want her watching TV all day, but I found that by the time I'd gotten everything done, there just wasn't time left to go to the park or whatever."

When she took a job last July, Ambrose was able to put Rose Marie in her company's on-site daycare program. "The change in my daughter was remarkable," she said. "Almost from the first day she became much friendlier and more active. She started talking a lot more, moving around more. It was just like she was a different, better person."

The title of an article in an academic journal.
Three authors for one title

In "Transgenerational Trends in Parental Care Choice Concerns," a study by Jon Worley, Jill Jones, and Michael Pugh, the authors show that childcare is becoming more and more important to parents as well as to children, not only because of financial constraints but because new parents are looking for ways to "socialize their children into an environment that is controlled, relatively predictable, and which at least partially resembles the playground experiences that

they remember from their own childhood" (179). Worley and his co-authors suggest that although the adults of America remain too busy to recapture the leisure days of their youth, they would like their children to experience "the structured and yet generally playful world" that they remember from their own childhoods (189).

The conclusion restates the thesis

Someone is raising our children, and it is very often not who the "experts" think it is. Perhaps it's time that we put away all the books and tried to figure out a way to ensure children are well cared for wherever they are.

[1]
Works Cited

[2] [3] [4] [5]
Ambrose, Perri. Address. Conf. on Student Life in the '90s. Gentry Hall, Central

[6] [7] [8]
Community College, Athol, MA. 6 Nov. 1999.

[9] [10]
Association of State and Local Child Service Providers. *The Effects of Day Care on*

the Success of Children in Grades One Through Three. New Orleans: ASLCSP, [11] [12]

[13]
1998.

[14] [15] [16] [17]
Council for Children. "Who Looks After the Children?" 6 June 1999. 11 Nov. 1999.

[18]
<http://www.childcouncil.org/childstudy/surveys/childcare/htm>.

[19] [20] [21]
Harris, Richard. "Boundaries Work." *Good Parenting: The Magazine of the Healthy*

[22] [23]
Family. Aug. 1998: 15–21.

[24] [25]
Hayes, Cheryl D., John L. Palmer, and Martha J. Zaslow, eds. *Who Cares for Amer-*

ica's Children? Washington, D.C.: National Academy, 1990.
[26] [27] [28]

1 Always on a new page. Centered. Capitalize the "W" and "C."	14 Corporate author
	15 Title of home page
2 Last name	16 Date page updated
3 First name	17 Date page retrieved
4 Details of conference where speech was given	18 Address is given between < and >
	19 Author
5 Building where speech given	20 Magazine article title
6 Name of host institution	21 Title of magazine
7 Town	22 Month, year of publication
8 Date of speech	23 Pages of article
9 Corporate author	24 Three editors
10 Title of study	25 Title of article
11 Place of publication	26 Place of publication
12 Publisher	27 Publisher
13 Date of publication	28 Year of publication

²⁹   ³⁰   ³¹
Marone, Janis. "Children Flourish in a Happy Setting." *Daily News and Chronicle*. 7

   ³²   ³³ ³⁴   ³⁵   ³⁶   ³⁷
June 1998, city. ed.: A3. *Infotrac: Magazine Index Plus*. Online. 12 Nov. 1999.

   ³⁸   ³⁹   ⁴⁰   ⁴¹   ⁴²
Portan, Gerri. Interview with Petra Moralis. *Six O'Clock News*. WWTV, Newbury-

   ⁴³
port, MA. 8 June 1998.

⁴⁴   ⁴⁵   ⁴⁶ ⁴⁷ ⁴⁸
Raeburn, Anne. *Forty Years of Parenting*. Boston: Fleet, 1998.

            ⁴⁹   ⁵⁰   ⁵¹
Raposo, Donna, and Corey Campbell. *Fifty Years of Caring for Baby*. San Luis

         ⁵² ⁵³
Obispo, CA: Traders', 1996.

⁵⁴   ⁵⁵   ⁵⁶   ⁵⁷
Spock, Benjamin. *The Common Sense Book of Baby and Child Care*. New York: Duell,

            ⁵⁸
Sloan, & Pearce, 1946.

⁵⁹   ⁶⁰   ⁶¹
Tserios, Alana. Personal Interview. 17 Nov. 1999.

29	Author	46	Place of publication
30	Title of newspaper article	47	Publisher
31	Title of newspaper	48	Year of publication
32	Date of article	49	The authors
33	Edition	50	Title of book
34	Page number	51	Place of publication
35	Database article retrieved from	52	Publisher
36	How database accessed	53	Year of publication
37	Date of retrieval	54	Author
38	Person interviewed	55	Book title
39	Interviewer	56	Place of publication
40	Show	57	Publisher
41	TV station	58	Year of publication
42	Location of station	59	Person interviewed
43	Date of broadcast	60	Interview by author
44	Author	61	Date of interview
45	Book title		

62
63
Worley, Jon, Jill Jones, and Michael Pugh. "Transgenerational Trends in Parental

64   65   66   67
Care Choice Concerns." *Journal of Parenting* 25 (1998): 176–194.

62 Three authors
63 Title of article
64 Title of journal

65 Volume number
66 Year
67 Page numbers of whole article

Style Notes:

All entries end with a period.

All entries which run for more than one line are indented on the second and following lines.

For the names of book publishers, you do not use words such as *press* or *inc.*

This list is in alphabetical order.

A Quick MLA Guide

Below is a list of the bibliographical forms for some of the more common sources you are likely to use for a research paper. A more complete listing can be found in your college library or online. These sources will be listed in alphabetical order on a Works Cited page. This page is usually the last page of your research paper.

Books

1. Book with one author

     1   2   3

Deering, Jyl. *Teenage Idols*. Boston: Heart Press, 1999.

2. Book with two or more authors.

      4

Campbell, Corey, and Masuka Clary. *Solitaire Lives On*. New York: Games,

  5 1988.

3. Book with four or more authors

       6

Vaughn, Melody P., et al. *Reading for Life*. Portland: U of Maine P, 1997.

4. Book with editor or editors

     7

Mandino, Tom. ed. *Billiards, Snooker, and Kitchen Pool*. Cambridge: Harvard, 1996.

5. Work in an anthology

    8   9   10   11

Hancock, Mandy. "Love in Film." *Romance at the Cinema*. Ed. Robert Jones.

    12   13   14

Chicago: Delta, 1987. 25–32.

1 last name, first name	8 author's last name, first name
2 title, capitalized and underlined	9 title of included work
3 place of publication: publisher, date	10 title of anthology
4 reverse only the first name	11 editor's first name, editor's last name
5 indent 1/2 inch	12 place of publication, publisher
6 Use all names or first name and "et al." (Latin for "and others")	13 date
7 include the abbreviation "ed." or "eds."	14 pages covered by the work

6. Reference book

15   16   17   18

"Naturalism and Realism." Encyclopedia of Literary Forms. 4th ed. 1981.

7. Book with unnamed author

19

A Book of Widgits. 10th ed. Trenton: Dynamo, 1996.

Articles

8. Article in a daily/weekly magazine or newspaper

20   21   22   23

Brown, Casey. "Sports for the Middle-Schooler." *Teen Sports* 6 June 1995: 23–26.

9. Article in a monthly or bi-monthly magazine.

24

Santello, Sarah. "Pumpkin Art." *Design* Oct. 1983: 17.

10. Article in a scholarly journal, continuously paged throughout volume

25   26   27   28

Mandino, Michelle. "Eleanor Roosevelt." *Journal of the Great Depression* 35 (1988):

101–122.

11. Article in a scholarly journal, paged by issue

29

Daniel, Alex. "Princesses as Icons." *Journal of Myth and Culture* 78.3 (1997): 23–45.

15 title of article
16 title of reference book
17 edition number
18 date of publication
19 title first (Do not use "a," "an," or "the" when you alphabetize your list.)
20 last name, first name
21 article title
22 magazine name underlined

23 day, month year: page numbers
24 month, year
25 last name, first name
26 article title
27 journal underlined
28 volume number date in parentheses: page numbers
29 issue number after the volume number, separated by a period

Online Sources

In general, give enough information so that your reader can take the same path as you to find the information. Record as much information as possible, since sites often change addresses. Include, when possible, an author, title, title of online source, date when the source was posted or updated, the sponsor of the source, and the date that you accessed the source. Place the web address last. For the rest of the general bibliographical information, follow the form for print sources.

Example:

Godden, [30] Missy. "Houses [31] on Parade." Decorating [32] 5 Nov. [33] 1998. 8 July [34] 1999.

<http://www.dec.com/houses.html>. [35]

Miscellaneous

12. Letter, personal communication, or interview

Keyes, Penney. Personal interview. 11 Nov. 1973.

Nienaber, Jackie. Letter to the author. 25 September 1951.

13. A television or radio program

"Malls and Magic." [36] The Teen Show. [37] Exec. prod. Brittany Lynn. [38] WBZ, [39] Boston. [40] 13

June [41] 1976.

14. Lecture, live performance

D'Anjou, Sara. [42] "Study Skills Strategies." [43] Newbury College Faculty Convention. [44]

Brookline. [45] 10 Sept. [46] 1995.

30 author	39 station
31 title of article	40 city
32 online magazine	41 date
33 date of article	42 lecturer
34 date retrieved	43 title of lecture
35 web address	44 to whom lecture presented
36 title of episode	45 place
37 title of show	46 date
38 producer	

15. Film or videotape

47   48   49   50   51   52

Skiing at Mount Kilmore. Videocassette. Mindy Hall. JUMP Media, 1998. VHS. 60

min.

16. Sound recording

53   54   55   56

Keyes, Francis Scott. The Star-Spangled Banner. Mary Leeonce. Audiocassette.

57
Columbia, 1997.

17. Government publication

58   59   60

Massachusetts. Department of Higher Education. *Paying for Your Child's Education.*

61   62
Boston, 1997.

47 title of video	55 performer
48 type of medium	56 type
49 producer	57 production company, date
50 distributor	58 govt. place
51 date	59 govt. agency
52 length	60 title of work (use author if named)
53 composer	61 city
54 title	62 date

Self-Assessment

Reread your self-assessment which opens this chapter. Then answer the following questions.

What would I change?

Why?

What do I now know about writing a research paper?

Your Portfolio: Assessing Your Writing

**PRACTICE
REHEARSAL
PERFORMANCE**

Very few of us are lucky enough to be naturally gifted at what we do. Just as the concert violinist we watch perform does not walk onto the stage without first having practiced, so also can we not write for other readers without first practicing.

Long before the violinist performed Beethoven's *Violin Concerto*, she began to practice the piece, a few bars at a time, building slowly to an entire movement. Whenever necessary, she would stop, think her process through, repeat the passage that gave her difficulty, and play it over and over again until she got it right.

Once the violinist believes that she is playing the piece as she wants to, she will begin rehearsals. She might now play the piece from beginning to end for a small invited audience. As she listens to her performance and to the acoustics in the hall and keeps track of the time, she might ask herself, "Am I playing the piece too loudly, too quickly, too haphazardly?" Even now, she is not yet ready to play in public. It will take her more than one rehearsal before she is comfortable with the way in which she is performing the piece.

Finally, she will walk out onto the stage in front of several thousand people and have just one chance to get Beethoven's *Violin Concerto* right. If the practice and the rehearsal have gone well, so will the performance.

Your writing is just like her performance. The more you practice and the more you rehearse, the better your finished work will be. As you have read and done the assignments in this book, you have been practicing. This section is your opportunity to "rehearse" your writing. Once you have finished rehearsing, you will finally be ready to walk confidently onto the stage and perform.

Introduction

This portfolio is built upon two pillars: your writing and your analysis of that writing. You are encouraged to reread the writing you have already done for the course and to select particular samples of your work to support your analyses of that work. This final practice session of self-assessment will help you to understand how you write, and which ways of writing work most effectively for you so that you can continue to improve your writing throughout your college education and for the rest of your life. The portfolio assignment asks you to take a step beyond simply meeting the requirements of a writing course and to start understanding how you can apply what you have learned about writing to other situations that you are likely to encounter.

Throughout this semester you have been practicing using self-assessment to improve the overall quality of your writing. At a certain stage, it is always necessary to test what you have learned from practice. This section explains how to go about preparing a portfolio to do just that: to test yourself to see how successful all of your practicing has been. It includes specific directions for writing four pieces so that you can see exactly what you are expected to do. Because writing is an important lifelong skill, you owe it to yourself to commit fully to the process, to spend sufficient time in the library, and to use enough out-of-class time to create the best portfolio you can.

The Philosophy Behind the Portfolio

Your writing portfolio is not designed to reevaluate the work you have done in this course. Although your portfolio will include two or three samples of your work from this semester, those samples will be included as evidence to support your self-assessment. *The writing portfolio is designed to ensure that you understand that writing is a process and that producing effective writing requires time, commitment, and revision.* A writing course is not completed in the weeks that you spend in the classroom. Instead, during those weeks the course introduces you to ways of thinking about writing that will equip you to write successfully throughout your personal and professional life. As part of that process, compiling and analyzing your portfolio should demonstrate your own approaches to writing, illustrate the ways in which you use those strategies, and examine their effectiveness.

In short, creating the portfolio will encourage self-reflection about your work during the semester. It asks you to think about what you have learned about your own writing techniques and about the effectiveness of those techniques. In asking you to reflect upon your own work, the portfolio assignment will show you that you have the tools to produce powerful, effective writing on any subject.

The Portfolio's Content

In keeping with the philosophy behind the portfolio assignment, you will write four pieces dealing with four specific aspects of writing:

1. How you write
2. How you decide when your writing is good enough to be read by others
3. How writing for your professional field differs from writing for an English course
4. How you assess a piece of your own writing by using the skills you have acquired during this course.

Each assignment asks you to take a specific approach to the topic about which you are writing. The guide sheets are designed to help you understand and identify the important parts of each piece. These sheets will also help you find specific prompts to help you understand the questions the reader expects you to answer. Each guide sheet has certain words printed in boldface type asking you, for example, to "quote" or "demonstrate" some aspect of your work. You should pay particular attention to these words as you write.

Each self-assessment that you write should be accompanied by the piece of writing which you are evaluating.

Deciding What to Say in Each Piece

Because the portfolio is an instrument of self-reflection and self-assessment, there are no absolutely wrong or right answers.

Personal Practice Defines Content

Often in writing there is no "right" answer. The samples used in each portfolio will vary from person to person; the quality of the samples is what you will assess. The more care and attention you give to your unique answers, the better you will do.

For each piece that you write, you will be asked to examine a particular aspect of your writing. You will have to demonstrate how you use the various techniques you discuss to create a good paper. Each assignment asks you to reflect upon your work to convince your reader that your approach to the specific aspects inquired about on the corresponding guide sheet are techniques which work for you. Because there is no "right" answer, your reader will be looking for a clear, convincing statement of what your strategy is whenever you write a paper and why your strategy works for you.

Specific Instructions for Each Piece

Each piece you will write should meet certain expectations which will be outlined on the corresponding guide sheet. Pay particular attention to these guidelines. If the directions for one assignment consist of one sentence and another assignment's directions are five or six sentences long, it is unlikely your reader will expect each aspect of the two assignments to be addressed at the same length. Also, if you are asked to "quote" from your work, it is a good idea to do so. Don't simply *say* that you did something; *show* in your response *how* you did it. For example, when you are asked to discuss "significant" changes that you made to an essay, try to write about more than your spelling corrections.

The first assignment, for example, asks what you do when you write a paper. You might have been taught in class about brainstorming, freewriting, prewriting, branching, or some other method of getting started. In this assignment, you are not being asked to complete a paper; you are being asked to write about what *you* personally do when beginning to work on a paper. The assignment then asks you to walk your reader through each step of your process. Thus, the "correct" answer is to explain clearly to your reader what you do and not to worry about how anyone else might write an essay.

While producing this clear and convincing statement, you will come to understand the approach you take to writing and to see the strengths and weaknesses of that approach. In this way, you will be able, next semester and beyond, to plan sufficient time in your schedule to ensure that all that you learned this semester about your writing skills can be used in the future to create the most effective writing you are capable of producing.

Presentation of Your Portfolio

Your portfolio is a professional document designed to demonstrate your own writing skills and your understanding of those skills. If your instructor has particular presentation guidelines, you should follow those. If not, you should still present your portfolio in as professional a manner as possible.

Piece One—Assess Your Recursive Process

Attach an example of your writing that best demonstrates the entire process you use to write a paper most effectively. The supporting material should include **all** the work you have done to **complete one essay.** This may include brainstorming, prewriting, drafting, notes for each revision, peer review responses, conference prompts, and the final graded paper.

Your self-assessment should demonstrate your understanding that writing is a recursive process which requires drafting, rewriting, editing, and revision. Write about each of the following categories.

- Clearly **explain** each step you take when writing an essay—from generating the idea and supporting details, through each stage of your drafting, up to completion of the final paper.
- Which **one** part of this process did you find most valuable? Why?
- **Quoting** from each of your drafts and any notes you may have made, **show** where you made **significant** changes as your essay developed. **Explain** why you made those changes and **show** how they improved the essay as a whole. Be sure to point out significant changes, not just superficial changes in spelling and grammar.

Piece One—Mechanics and Organization

Writing is evaluated on its mechanical and organizational merits as well as on its content. For this portfolio piece, you should take particular care to ensure that your writing meets the criteria of good mechanics and organization to the very best of your ability. As you write this self-assessment for your portfolio, keep in mind everything that you have learned thus far about the structure of writing as well as what you have learned about content.

- Your **spelling** should be accurate. Your sentences should be **grammatically correct** and should demonstrate your ability to **vary your sentence structure** to avoid repetitive writing. Your **word usage** should demonstrate your command of vocabulary and your ability to use language accurately and effectively.
- Your essay should include a strong, effective **introduction** and **conclusion.**
- Your **thesis** should be clearly stated and well supported throughout your essay.
- Your **paragraphs** should each contain a clear topic sentence, should keep to that topic, and should progress in a logical order.

Note: Key words and phrases in student responses that follow have been bold-faced for emphasis.

SAMPLE ONE

Each of us uses a different process for writing. For some, writing a paper is easy; for others, it's like going to the dentist. The whole idea of writing can be difficult, but it does get easier with practice. It also gets easier once you are able to figure out what works for you and what doesn't. At least, that's what I've discovered during this semester.

I think that I've figured out my process by writing my assignments for this course. I now know that it's important for me to do some kind of **prewriting.** What seems to work best for me is **brainstorming and freewriting.** As much as I hated to admit this at the beginning of the semester, I also know that I have to **draft and redraft** if I want to improve my paper and make it as good as I can. I've learned that I can't just redraft right away. Most of the time, I can't look at my essay for a few days after writing it. Then, when I pick it up, I see the changes I need to make. I also like to have my teacher look at my draft; sometimes I also have my classmates look at it. Even after drafting a second time, I know that I still have to do that final **edit** to check for grammar and spelling errors. Only after I've followed this process do I feel somewhat confident about my paper.

I used this process when I wrote my essay "Growing Up with Troop 2259." First, I **brainstormed** some experiences that I had in high school which showed that I was growing up. I came up with a list that included the volunteer work I had done, the part-time jobs I had held, my changes in study habits, and my understanding of some of my family's problems.

I next took each of the items on the list and **freewrote** about them. I realized that writing about volunteering to help run a Brownie troop was the easiest and most enjoyable topic for me to write about. I also realized how much I had learned about myself and responsibility by participating in this activity.

The next step in writing this paper was to develop a **thesis statement:** "I grew up when I helped to run a third-grade Brownie troop." After I wrote the thesis, I came up with supporting ideas and then wrote the first draft. When I had a conference with my teacher and read my draft out loud, I noticed that there were some good examples in it, but what I had was really just a list of what I had done. I wasn't really connecting the activities to my thesis about growing up. For example, I told about taking the kids on a nature walk and how much fun we had, but I didn't tell how that demonstrated my sense of responsibility. **In the second draft, I expanded the thesis** to include some ways in which I think I matured. The new thesis said, "Helping to run troop 2259 made me more responsible, more creative, more understanding, and less selfish." Once I had changed my thesis, I made sure that all my examples were specifically related to it. For example, I added to the nature walk example descriptions of how I showed the girls some safety precautions and how I planned the activity with the children's fun in mind, not mine. I explained that I "read up on science activities for third graders" and "taught the kids what poison ivy looked like."

I also realized that I needed to show more clearly what I had expected helping with a troop to be like and what it really required of me. I had left this part out of the first draft, but when I **redrafted, I included this information because it showed how much I had learned.** Doing this added a whole new section to my second draft.

I also made a **significant change in my second draft when I reorganized my examples.** Instead of just listing them, I thought about what each showed about my growing maturity and which of them was most important. I now arranged my paragraphs in order from least significant to most significant. I decided to move paragraph 5 (about being responsible for troop finances) to the paragraph 3 position. I then moved paragraph 3 (about teaching the kids to help others in the community) to the paragraph 5 position. By rearranging these paragraphs, I think I gave the reader a better idea of what I considered to be most important about my experience.

A final significant change that I made was in the introduction. First, I had an ordinary paragraph which said basically that I learned a lot about myself and others when I helped the troop. I had a lot of general words like *trust, responsibility,* and *helpfulness* in it. It seemed kind of boring to me and to my peer reviewers. I decided to change it. In the second draft, I told a short anecdote of a particularly good memory of the troop that illustrated my relationship with them and how they helped me to grow up. I told about the time that the girls pointed out to me the mistakes I had made when I tried to teach them to cook. The fact that I could take criticism from the girls, learn from the criticism, and laugh with the girls about the experience showed how they helped me to grow. My classmates said that they liked the story.

The most helpful part of the writing process for me is revising. I never realized the importance of rewriting my papers. Now that I see how much stronger my writing can be, I realize that I need to spend more time redoing my papers.

I am proud of the final draft of the essay. I know that it could probably still be improved, but I also know that because I carefully went through these steps when writing, this paper is much better than those which I used to write.

Piece Two—Assess Your Best Piece of Writing

Attach the piece of writing you have done this semester which you consider to be your best work to date. Write **persuasively** to demonstrate why this sample of your writing is the best piece you have written this semester. **Identify** the criteria by which you judge writing **in general** and then **show** how your example meets, or exceeds, your standards of good writing.

Write about both of the following categories.

- **Identify** as many components of good writing as possible (other than grammar and spelling). **Explain** why any piece of writing must have these components to ensure that the reader remains interested and understands the ideas which the writer wishes to communicate.
- **Quoting** examples from your work, demonstrate how they meet certain criteria which you previously identified. **Explain** how your examples achieve what you say they do.

Piece Two—Mechanics and Organization

Writing is evaluated on its mechanical and organizational merits as well as on its content. For this portfolio piece, you should take particular care to ensure that your writing meets the criteria of using good mechanics and having good organization to the very best of your ability. As you write this self-assessment for your portfolio, keep in mind everything that you have learned thus far about the structure of writing as well as what you have learned about content.

- Your **spelling** should be accurate. Your sentences should be **grammatically correct** and should demonstrate your ability to **vary your sentence structure** to avoid repetitive writing. Your **word usage** should demonstrate your command of vocabulary and your ability to use language accurately and effectively.
- Your essay should include a strong, effective **introduction** and **conclusion.**
- Your **thesis** should be clearly stated and well supported throughout your essay.
- Your **paragraphs** should each contain a clear topic sentence, should keep to that topic, and should progress in a logical order.

SAMPLE TWO

I think that my essay "How to Successfully Live with Strangers" is my best essay of the semester. I believe that it meets the **criteria of good writing** in which not only I believe but in which most people believe: **awareness of audience, a strong thesis, specific examples, logical flow, and variety in sentence structure and wording.**

First, it has a **strong sense of audience.** I decided to write the essay for high school seniors who are planning to live on a college campus. I imagined what they would want to know about. I also imagined that I could send the essay back to my high school for publication in the school's paper. I picked the words that I thought students could relate to and gave examples that I thought would be practical but also funny. I was careful not to be too negative because I didn't want to scare them. I decided to use both *I* and *you* in the essay so that my audience could feel as if I were talking directly to them from experience. I start off saying, "A year ago I was in your shoes—thinking about college, all the studying, all the new people to meet, and mostly about sharing a room with a complete stranger. Well, I'm here to tell you that there's stuff you can do ahead of time and the minute you arrive at school which will help you live in peace!"

A good essay needs **a strong thesis** which lets the audience know where the essay is headed. This opening that I just quoted is also my thesis statement. I think that this statement is clear. The readers should expect my paper to contain lots of practical advice on what they can do to have peace with a roommate.

Next, a good essay has **lots of specific examples and details** which support the thesis. I include in my essay details about writing letters to your new roommate over the summer to decide who's bringing what to the room and to find out about the roommate's study habits, sleeping habits, tastes in music, and interests. I say, "The more you can know about each other ahead of time, the easier it will be to come up with guidelines you both can live with." I support the thesis even more with some funny and not-so-funny examples of what can happen when roommates don't take the time to communicate. I tell about how my roommates and I all arrived on campus with room-size rugs and microwaves. I also talk about how miscommunication about sleeping arrangements almost led to a big fight.

Another criterion for good writing is that it has a logical flow that is smooth. A good flow helps the reader to follow the ideas and to see the connections among the ideas. I make sure that I connect the different pieces of advice with strong transitions. I don't just use *and* or *then*. I try to use transitions which show the relationships among the ideas. I use words like *because, since,* and *although*. For example, I write, "Although each of you comes from a different background, you have something that you all share—a room on this campus!" I also ordered my information in a time sequence (from the day when roommates are first assigned to the day when students finally arrive on campus).

Finally, I try to **vary my sentences and use strong wording** throughout the essay. I use a combination of short and long sentences and make sure that my words are colorful and will appeal to a high school audience. For example, instead of saying, "You should have open and direct communication with each other," I write, "You need to just talk—get it out!"

While this essay is not perfect, I think it meets some of the criteria of good writing. It's a logically developed "how-to" essay that I hope will be helpful to the audience for which it was designed.

Piece Three—Assess a Piece of Writing from a Professional Journal

This piece of writing differs from the others which you are asked to write for your portfolio. In this case, you are to use a piece of writing from a professional journal or magazine to **explain** how **audience** and **purpose** influence **language** and **style**. Attach a suitable piece of work from an appropriate professional journal. You should look for a piece of writing with language and structure that are specific to a particular field of study. You should, therefore, probably look in a specialized source. *Time* magazine, for example, is unlikely to be an appropriate source.

Write about each of the following categories.

- **Describe** the type of person who would read this article and explain **why** the piece was written. Your description should focus on the audience's area of expertise.
- Provide **quotations** from the piece and **explain how** those quotations use language and abbreviations that could only be understood by someone familiar with the subject.
- Discuss the **organization** of the piece and **explain** why it is organized in this way.
- Provide **appropriate documentation** as necessary. (A Works Cited page is part of the documentation.)

Piece Three—Mechanics and Organization

Writing is evaluated on its mechanical and organizational merits as well as on its content. For this portfolio piece, you should take particular care to ensure that your writing meets the criteria of good mechanics and organization to the very best of your ability. As you write this self-assessment for your portfolio, keep in mind everything that you have learned thus far about the structure of writing as well as what you have learned about content.

- Your **spelling** should be accurate. Your sentences should be **grammatically correct** and should demonstrate your ability to **vary your sentence structure** to avoid repetitive writing. Your **word usage** should demonstrate your command of vocabulary and your ability to use language accurately and effectively.
- Your essay should include a strong, effective **introduction** and **conclusion.**
- Your **thesis** should be clearly stated and well supported throughout your essay.
- Your **paragraphs** should each contain a clear topic sentence, should keep to that topic, and should progress in a logical order.

SAMPLE THREE

My major is psychology. In this essay I am analyzing a piece of writing from the *Journal of Adolescent Behavior.* The specific article by Rachel Ayres is entitled "Hiding Practices of Anorexics." I will look at the **audience, the purpose, the use of language, and the organization of the piece to show that the article was written for a specific audience.**

This professional article presents a study which looked at some ways in which "adolescent anorexic girls try to hide their weight loss, try to deceive others about their eating habits, while using denial as a defense" (Ayres 456). **The article was** written for professionals in the field of psychology such as therapists and school counselors. Psychology students might also like the article, but some of it may be a little difficult for introductory students. **The article's purpose is to inform** this audience of some of the study's findings and to encourage professionals to be on the lookout for some of these behaviors.

The writer of this article assumes that the readers have a lot of background knowledge, not only about anorexia but also about psychological methods of conducting studies. The reader needs to **know language** such as "control groups and experimental groups." The author also uses words from statistics such as *validity*, *reliability*, and *norm groups*. The reader also has to know what anorexia is and what treatments are used for teens today. The treatments are named but not defined. For example, the author talks about "rational-emotive," "cognitive-based" and "behavior modification" without saying what they are. An audience of trained psychologists would know that these terms are types of therapies. The vocabulary that the author uses clearly shows that she is writing for an audience familiar with the language of the field.

The article follows the traditional form for an article in a professional psychology journal. It starts out with an abstract that summarizes the main idea of the study and follows with a review of the current literature on the topic of the study. The abstract lets the readers know whether or not the article will interest them. The literature review tells the readers what others have said about the subject. Next, the writer presents the parts of the study: the subjects observed, the methods used to get the information, and the results. The article then contains a discussion of the results and what those results mean for treatment and other studies. Finally, there is a References page so that the reader knows the sources of the in-text citations. This reference list is helpful to professionals in the field if they want to read more about the topic. Professionals in the field would expect an article in one of their journals to follow this format.

After reading this article from this journal, I realize how writing changes when a writer has a particular audience in mind. I would not write in this way for a general audience, but maybe someday I will when I enter my profession.

Work Cited

Ayres, Rachel. "Hiding Practices of Anorexics." *Journal of Adolescent Psychology* 46 (1998): 456–82.

Piece Four—Assess Your Earliest Work

Attach the earliest complete piece of writing you did this semester and **analyze** its **strengths** and **weaknesses.** As well as doing this, you are encouraged to provide a **plan** for revising the work. You do not need to rewrite the piece; just explain what you would do if you were given the opportunity to revise it.

Write about each of the following categories.

• By **quoting** specific passages, explain what is good about this sample of your work and what is weak. You should pay particular attention to the criteria of a good essay which you identified in portfolio piece 2. How does this sample **meet** those criteria? How does it **fall short**?

- Using specific examples, **explain** how you would revise and strengthen the next draft of this essay if you were given the opportunity to do so.
- **How** do the changes which you have outlined demonstrate how you have changed as a writer since you originally wrote the piece? Be **specific.**

Piece Four—Mechanics and Organization

Writing is evaluated on its mechanical and organizational merits as well as on its content. For this portfolio piece, you should take particular care to ensure that your writing meets the criteria of good mechanics and organization to the very best of your ability. As you write this self-assessment for your portfolio, keep in mind everything that you have learned thus far about the structure of writing as well as what you have learned about content.

- Your **spelling** should be accurate. Your sentences should be **grammatically correct** and should demonstrate your ability to **vary your sentence structure** to avoid repetitive writing. Your **word usage** should demonstrate your command of vocabulary and your ability to use language accurately and effectively.
- Your essay should include a strong, effective **introduction** and **conclusion.**
- Your **thesis** should be clearly stated and well supported throughout your essay.
- Your **paragraphs** should each contain a clear topic sentence, should keep to that topic, and should progress in a logical order.

SAMPLE FOUR

When I came to college, I thought I was a pretty strong writer. However, after reading the essay which I wrote at the beginning of the semester, I see that I had a long way to go and that I needed this writing course! I'm not saying that the essay doesn't have some good points, but it could definitely be improved.

I had to write the essay for my English class. I was told to write about a good friend and to tell why that person was important to me. I had two days to write the essay, which was supposed to be about three pages long. I have to admit that I wrote it the night before the day that it was due. I did not use any prewriting strategies. I basically sat at the computer and wrote. Now I realize that what I have is pretty much a freewrite. It doesn't have a clear thesis followed by paragraphs which develop the thesis. I wouldn't even call it a first draft.

First, I will talk about its strengths, or maybe I should say its *potential* strengths. I think that the reader can see from the essay that I have been close to my friend Penney for many years. **I do give some background about our friendship** and talk about how we first met in the sixth grade. **I am specific here** when I talk about our meeting on the soccer field and how we spent about an hour talking after practice. I place this background in the introduction, which seems like a **logical place for it.** I end the first paragraph by saying, "Penney is my best friend, then and now." This is a sort of thesis statement and lets the reader know what the paper will be about.

However, now that I have reread the essay, **the thesis seems too short and too general.** If I had the chance to rewrite the essay, **I would expand the thesis** to include the reasons why she is my best friend. I might write, "Penny was and still is my best friend, then and now, because she's always there for me, because she's kind and generous, and because she lets me be who I am." I think that this expanded thesis would help me to organize the paragraphs which follow it.

Besides having a thesis which is not strong, the paragraphs that follow don't have enough concrete details. **I use too many abstract terms and general statements.** For example, I say that Penney is "trustworthy," "kind," "nonjudgmental," and "loyal." But I don't illustrate any of those qualities with specific details. I don't give examples which show that she's any of those things. If I were to rewrite this essay, **I would develop each of the ideas in the thesis statements with stories** which would demonstrate that she's all of those things. I would tell of the times when she has unselfishly helped me. I would show her many acts of kindness. For example, I would write about the volunteer work she does with the Big Sisters and how she's gotten me involved.

Last, I realize that I just ran out of steam at the end of the essay. I have a one-line conclusion: "I hope Penny and I will remain friends for a long time." If I had the chance to revise, **I would definitely work on expanding the conclusion.** I might end with a short but effective story that really captures our friendship.

As I review this essay, I realize how far I have come in my writing. I am better able to see what I need to do to make my work stronger. I know that I need to develop a thesis. I know that I have to plan how to support that thesis by using some prewriting activities. I also realize how important it is to reread my work, and I plan to revise at least twice. I have some definite ideas about what makes writing effective, and I have some strategies which can help me use those ideas. I think I'm off to a good start!

Addendum

Using the rules of writing is not like using magic. It takes patience and practice. You can memorize the rules, but if you do only that, you'll probably soon forget them. You are more likely to remember how to use the rules when you use your critical reading skills to evaluate and assess your own writing. Think about how you use the rules of writing and ask yourself if there's a better way to use them to make your writing more effective.

However, looking at your own writing is often not enough. You also need to apply your reading skills to all of the texts that you read. **Becoming a careful reader of other people's writing is one of the best ways to improve your own writing.** As you read, observe the ways in which other writers use punctuation. Notice how other writers use the comma, the semicolon, and the colon. Ask yourself why a writer used a particular punctuation mark. Ask yourself why a phrase was placed in a certain position. Ask yourself if the writer has made it clear about whom he is talking in a particular sentence. Ask yourself how you might rewrite the sentence so that it would make more sense to you. Ask yourself about the writer's word choices and her sentence construction. How do these choices add to the overall style of the piece? What other choices might the writer have made? What different choices might you have made?

Memorizing is important and helpful, but if you bring the skills of careful reading and self-assessment to your review of your essays, with time and patience you will gradually learn to use the rules of writing to express your ideas with clarity and confidence.

Ten Punctuation Tips for Writing

1. A semicolon separates complete ideas.
2. A colon introduces or points to an idea.
3. A comma and a coordinating conjunction separate complete ideas.
4. A comma alone cannot separate complete ideas.
5. A single comma should not come between a verb and its subject or complement.
6. An exclamation point is used to show extraordinary emphasis.
7. Quotation marks are used in pairs to indicate direct speech and quoted material.
8. An apostrophe is used to show ownership.
9. An apostrophe indicates that letters have been omitted from a word.
10. Italics or quotation marks are used to indicate titles of works.

1. A semicolon separates complete ideas. A semicolon functions like a period. Think of it as a red light that tells you to stop.

Incorrect: *I like the challenge of trout fishing; especially in the early spring.*

The semicolon is incorrect because the phrase *especially in the spring* cannot stand alone as a complete sentence.

Correct: *Mary went to the early show; Jim went home to study.*

If you use the semicolon correctly, there should be a group of words on either side of it that functions as a complete idea (that is, an "independent clause" or a group of words containing a subject and verb that can stand alone).

Exercises: Correct the semicolon errors in the following sentences. Place a *C* in the blanks beside those sentences that are correct.

_____ 1a. Josh ran a personal best in the last marathon, Andrea withdrew from the race because of an injury.

_____ 1b. Many students like to stay up late; they also get up late and miss early classes.

_____ 1c. Maria left early to go to the library; because she has a lot of reading to do for her paper.

_____ 1d. Antonio Carlos Jobim is a great Brazilian songwriter, Carlo Ponte comes from Italy.

_____ 1e. Listening to classical music helps me to study; I usually listen to it every night.

---

2. A colon introduces or points to an idea. It should not be used to separate complete ideas. Think of it as a green light that tells you to read on.

Incorrect: _The theater committee considered three new promotions an open house for the entire weekend, a big party on opening night, and a week-long telemarketing campaign._

There should be a colon after the word _promotions_ because what follows is an explanation of what the three promotions were.

Correct: _If you really want to understand Shakespeare's tragedies, you should read the following plays: Hamlet, Macbeth, King Lear, and Romeo and Juliet._
In Act V of Hamlet, Hamlet picks up a skull in a graveyard and says to Horatio: "Alas, poor Yorick, I knew him, Horatio."

Notice that in the first correct example, the colon after the word _plays_ introduces the plays which you should read to understand Shakespeare. In the second example, the colon is used to introduce the quotation which follows after the word _Horatio_. In both instances, the colon points to or introduces what follows.

Note that colons are also used after the salutation in a formal business letter.

Correct: _Dear Mr. Alvares:_
Dear Fellow Students:

Exercises: Correct the colon errors in the following sentences. Place a _C_ in the blanks beside those sentences that are correct.

_____ 2a. Mandy lived for one thing only; rock 'n' roll.

_____ 2b. If you want to improve your writing, you should do three things: practice, practice, practice.

_____ 2c. John F. Kennedy said. "Ask not what your country can do for you. Ask what you can do for your country."

_____ 2d. The students need to vote on the following issues. The budget, new officers, and events for the upcoming semester.

_____ 2e. When I walked into the chemistry lab, I saw something very surprising: The students were actually laughing and having fun.

3. Use a comma and a coordinating conjunction (*and, but, yet, or, nor, for, so*) instead of a period to separate complete ideas.

Incorrect: *I spent all night on the Internet, and the morning in the library.*
I like to go to live concerts, but not to dance clubs.

Like the period and the semicolon, a comma with a coordinating conjunction must have a complete idea on either side. In the two previous examples, the idea after the coordinating conjunction is incomplete, so the comma should not be used.

Correct: *The computers are on the first floor, and the books are on the third floor.*
Maria got an A on the final exam, but Danielle barely got a passing grade.

In the two correct examples, the comma and the coordinating conjunction separate ideas (independent clauses) that could stand alone as complete sentences. Substituting a period in these examples would create two grammatically correct sentences.

Exercises: Correct the comma and coordinating conjunction errors in the following sentences. Place a *C* in the blanks beside those sentences which are correct.

_____ 3a. The delivery truck came early this morning but the driver did not have a package for you.

_____ 3b. Dancing is a great way to get exercise and it also is a good way to release your frustrations and to be creative.

_____ 3c. You could either listen to the radio, or watch television but you can't do both at the same time.

_____ 3d. Neither Jamie nor Andres had attended the lecture but they acted as if they were experts on the subject.

_____ 3e. Imelda must make up the last test and the last paper or she will fail this course and have to retake it next semester.

4. A comma alone cannot separate complete ideas.

Incorrect: *Maria likes New York salsa, she could dance to salsa all night.*
The fans left before the game had ended, the players walked off the field in disgust.

The student body voted for a bigger budget, the college president approved their decision.

Notice that the comma here is **spliced between** the two ideas. It is not strong enough to separate the ideas on either side. The error can be easily corrected by using a period, a semicolon, or a comma with a coordinating conjunction (*and, but, so, for, or, nor, yet*).

Correct: *Maria likes New York salsa; she could dance to salsa all night.*

The fans left before the game had ended and the players walked off the field in disgust.

The student body voted for a bigger budget; the college president approved their decision.

Exercises: Correct the comma errors in the following sentences. Place a C in the blanks next to those sentences which are correct.

_____ 4a. The Clash were probably the best rock band of the early eighties, they were another successful English export.

_____ 4b. The English literature lecture was really interesting, but the handouts were a bit confusing.

_____ 4c. I love the smell of bacon on Saturday morning, it reminds me of those lazy days of childhood.

_____ 4d. Maureen planted her tomato plants too early, and they were killed by a late frost.

_____ 4e. The food in the dining hall is usually not that interesting, the salad bar looks like the weeds from a lost garden.

5. A single comma should not come between a verb and its subject or complement.

Incorrect: *Mambo, a type of dance that originated in Cuba is very passionate and energetic.*

Carmella sings with great tenderness and feeling, the traditional love songs of old Mexico.

In the first example, the comma comes between the verb *is* and its subject, *Mambo*. In the second example the comma comes between the verb *sings* and its direct object, *songs*.

One possible way of correcting the first example is to use two commas and to treat the idea as an addition to the basic sentence.

Correct: *Mambo, a type of dance that originated in Cuba, is very energetic and passionate.*

The second example could be corrected by rewriting or reordering the ideas in the sentence.

Correct: *Carmella sings the traditional love songs of old Mexico with great tenderness and feeling.*

Exercises: Correct the comma errors in the following sentences. Place a C in the blanks beside those sentences which are correct.

_____ 5a. Although he is most famous for his plays, Shakespeare the dramatist, wrote many beautiful love poems.

_____ 5b. The football team was determined to win the game, and to get to the playoffs.

_____ 5c. Daniella, the woman in our art history class, grew up near Florence, Italy.

_____ 5d. *The Mona Lisa,* Leonardo Da Vinci's most famous painting is in the Louvre museum in Paris.

_____ 5e. The campus crime patrol found many lapses in security, and unsafe conditions.

6. An exclamation point is used to show extraordinary emphasis. However, if you use it too often, it loses its emphatic power.

Incorrect: *Wow! The concert was fantastic! When the band's rhythm section got going, the place really rocked!*

The overuse of the exclamation point causes it to be read as just another punctuation mark and not as the emphatic mark that the writer intended.

Correct: *The concert was fantastic! When the band's rhythm section got going, the place really rocked.*

Exercises: Correct the exclamation point errors in the following sentences by adding exclamation points where they may be appropriate and deleting them when they are overused. Place a C in the blanks next to those sentences that are correct.

_____ 6a. Yea. We're leaving on vacation a day earlier than we had planned.

_____ 6b. I can't believe that it's snowing! I'm so happy! That means a day off from school!

_____ 6c. What a relief! The professor gave us a two-week extension on the project.

_____ 6d. The two candidates for school council president are debating tonight!

_____ 6e. You're kidding! The tickets for the concert are already sold out?

> **7. Quotation marks are used in pairs to indicate direct speech and quoted material.** Quotation marks are not used to indicate indirect speech (paraphrases).

Incorrect: *The teacher asked us if "We were going to study the text to prepare for the next exam."*

According to Andy Warhol, in the future everyone will be famous for fifteen minutes.

In the first example, the speaker is reporting what the teacher said. We are not hearing the teacher's words directly, but we are hearing them indirectly through the voice of another speaker. In the second example, what Andy Warhol said should be contained within quotation marks because it is a direct quotation.

Correct: *The teacher asked us, "Are you going to study the text to prepare for the exam?"*

According to Andy Warhol, "In the future, everyone will be famous for fifteen minutes."

Exercises: Correct the quotation mark errors in the following sentences. Place a C in the blanks next to those sentences that are correct.

_____ 7a. The guest lecturer asked the audience if "they had ever experienced any psychic phenomena."

_____ 7b. She said that "she was going to be out of school for a week."

_____ 7c. According to Shakespeare, "The course of true love never did run smooth."

_____ 7d. The professor announced I have scheduled a test for next Tuesday.

_____ 7e. The professor announced that she was canceling the scheduled test.

> **8. Use an apostrophe to show ownership.** An apostrophe is not used to form a plural.

Incorrect: *Because there will not be enough opening positions', Johns car will not compete in the upcoming races'.*

In this example, *positions* and *races* are simple plurals. There should not be an apostrophe after the *s* in those words. However, there should be an apostrophe before the *s* in *John's* to indicate that he owns or possesses the car ("the car *of* John").

Correct: *Because there will not be enough opening positions, John's car will not compete in the next race.*

The drivers' knowledge of the track is very important in the men's qualifying round.

All nouns form the singular possessive by adding an *'s* to the word. Form the plural possessive of regular plurals (words that form the plural by adding *s* or *es*) by first forming the plural of the word and by then placing an apostrophe after the *s*. Words with irregular plurals—such as man (men), child (children), or deer (deer)—form the plural possessive by first forming the plural of the word and then by adding *'s* (men's, children's, deer's).

Exercises: Correct the apostrophe errors in the following sentences. Place a *C* in the blanks beside those sentences that are correct.

_____ 8a. Suzannes books' were found on the table near the door of the cafeteria.

_____ 8b. We won the game because our goalie's skill proved too much for the other team's attempted shots on goal.

_____ 8c. The womens' swim team was victorious over its long-time rivals'.

_____ 8d. Toni Morrisons' novels present the reader with poetic language and vibrant imagery.

_____ 8e. The children's literature course requires the students to read to children in the community.

> **9. Use an apostrophe to indicate that letters have been omitted from a word.**

Incorrect: *Many people dont appreciate the early music that forms the roots of rock 'n' roll.*

In the previous sentence *don't* could be rewritten as *do not,* but the words have been contracted, or made shorter, by omitting the letter *o.* The same is true of *rock 'n' roll,* which has been contracted by leaving out the *a* and *d* in *and.*

Correct: *Many people don't appreciate the early music that forms the roots of rock 'n' roll.*

Notice that in the correct sentence an apostrophe is used in each position in which a letter has been omitted.

Exercises: Correct the apostrophe errors in the following sentences. Place a *C* in the blanks beside those sentences that are correct.

_____ 9a. We wont be able to attend the Sargent exhibit at the museum because of a previous commitment.

_____ 9b. He didnt' vote in the last senate election because he disliked all of the candidates.

_____ 9c. It's difficult to say what caused the fight to break out at the concert.

_____ 9d. The library cant order the materials on such short notice.

_____ 9e. Because of a budget crunch, the shuttle service won't be running on Sundays.

---

10. Italics or quotation marks are used to indicate titles of works.

Incorrect: E. B. White's classic essay *Once More to the Lake* is in *The Collected Essays of E. B. White.*

In this example, the two titles need to have special treatment so that the reader is aware that the writer is citing titles of works.

Correct: E. B. White's classic essay "Once More to the Lake" is in *The Collected Essays of E. B. White.*

The first title is in quotation marks because it is the title of a smaller work. The second title is italicized because it is a longer, or whole, work. Simply states, titles of short works go inside quotation marks. Titles of longer whole works are italicized. Place **quotation marks** around the titles of essays, poems, articles, chapters, short stories, and other titles within a whole work. **Italicize** the titles of magazines, newspapers, novels, encyclopedias, and journals. Underlining such titles is also acceptable if you are unable to italicize.

Only titles which you are citing get special treatment. You would not italicize or place quotation marks around the title of your own work. For example, the title of your essay should not be placed inside quotation marks or italicized.

Exercises: Correct the errors in italics or quotation mark used in the following sentences. Place a *C* in the blanks beside those sentences that are correct.

_____ 10a. The short story A Good Man Is Hard to Find is typical of Flannery O' Connor's use of gothic imagery.

———— 10b. Next week, in Social Issues II, we will begin to read the "New York Times" on a daily basis.

———— 10c. The chapter *The Sweetheart of Song Tra Bong* is one of the most powerful in Tim O'Brien's novel "The Things They Carried."

———— 10d. Mary used research from the article "Three Causes of Schizophrenia" that she found in the *Journal of Abnormal Psychology.*

———— 10e. Poe's The Raven is one of the most frightening and eerie poems ever written.

Ten Usage Tips for Good Writing

1. A sentence needs to contain a main verb and its subject and to express a complete idea. Note: a verb ending in *-ing* needs a helping verb to be a main verb.
2. Avoid run-on sentences by placing a semicolon (;) or a comma and a coordinating conjunction between complete ideas. The coordinating conjunctions are *and, but, or, nor, yet, for,* and *so.*
3. A verb must always agree with its subject in number (singular or plural).
4. When a verb is separated from its subject by a phrase, make sure that the verb agrees with its subject in number.
5. A pronoun takes the place of a noun; therefore, you must clearly indicate which noun the pronoun is replacing. (The noun being replaced is called the *antecedent*).
6. Not only does a pronoun require an antecedent, it also has to agree with that antecedent in number (singular or plural).
7. First and third person pronouns change form to indicate whether they are the subject or the object of the action of the verb or the object of a preposition.
8. Make sure that the parts of a sentence which explain an action or idea (*modifiers*) are positioned as closely as possible to that action or idea.
9. Avoid placing dangling modifiers at the beginning of sentences.
10. A series of similar words or phrases in a sentence should be constructed in the same way. This construction is called *parallelism.*

1. A sentence needs to contain a main verb and its subject and to express a complete idea. Note: A verb ending in *-ing* needs a helping verb to be a main verb.

Incorrect: *Sitting in the park, Mary saw the ducks.*

Although the second of these word groups (*Mary saw the ducks*) is a sentence—that is, it has both a subject and a verb and expresses a complete idea—the first group of words (*Sitting in the park*) is not a sentence. *Sitting* is the gerund (a verbal which functions as a noun) of the verb *to sit*, so it cannot serve as a verb in the first part of the sentence.

Correct: *While she was sitting in the park, Mary saw the ducks.*

Exercises: Correct the incomplete sentences in the following sentences. Place a *C* in the blanks beside the sentences which are correct.

_____ 1a. I like ice cream. Particularly on a hot summer's day.

_____ 1b. Dancing at the concert. I bumped into all types of people.

_____ 1c. Hawthorne wrote a number of chilling stories. While living in Salem, Massachusetts.

_____ 1d. Since I moved to California, I've grown to love the taste of avocados.

_____ 1e. After swimming for a few minutes. I felt a cramp in my leg.

---

2. Avoid run-on sentences by placing a semi-colon (;) or a comma and a coordinating conjunction between complete ideas. The coordinating conjunctions are *and, or, but, nor, yet, for,* and *so.*

Incorrect: *Many people listen to the radio in the morning but few people listen to the radio after dinner.*

Mary ate pizza and hamburger almost every night she couldn't fit into any of her clothes by the end of the semester.

In the first example, the coordinating conjunction alone is not strong enough to separate the two complete ideas (independent clauses) on either side of it.

Correct: *Many people listen to the radio in the morning, but few people listen to the radio after dinner.*

Many people listen to the radio in the morning; few people listen to the radio after dinner.

In the second example, the two complete ideas have no punctuation between them. Here are some ways to add stronger punctuation:

Correct: *Mary ate pizza and hamburgers almost every night, so she couldn't fit into any of her clothes by the end of the semester.*

Mary ate pizza and hamburgers almost every night; she couldn't fit into any of her clothes by the end of the semester.

Notice that you can test to see if you have a run-on sentence by placing a period where the two ideas are connected. If each idea can stand alone as a sentence, then you should use a semicolon or a comma and a coordinating conjunction to separate them.

Exercises: Correct the run-on sentence errors in the following sentences. Place a C in the blanks beside the sentences that are correct.

_____ 2a. Stephen King writes bestsellers, he's also considered to be a strong screenwriter.

_____ 2b. Writers revise and revise their work; they know that rewriting will strengthen it.

_____ 2c. The basketball game went into double overtime, it was one of the best games the fans had ever seen.

_____ 2d. King Lear is often thought of as foolish, he does not recognize the false flattery of his eldest daughters.

_____ 2e. T. S. Eliot wrote many famous poems and plays but some people think his biggest influence was in literary criticism.

> **3. A verb must always agree with its subject in number (singular and plural).**

Incorrect: *Helena (singular) go (plural) to Dublin every summer.*
Helena and Ryan (plural) goes (singular) to Dublin every summer.

In the first sentence the subject, *Helena,* is singular; the verb, *go,* is plural. They do not agree. In the second sentence, the subject, *Helena and Ryan,* is plural (a compound subject); the verb, *goes,* is singular. They, too, do not agree.

Correct: *Helena goes to Dublin every summer.*
Helena and Ryan go to Dublin every summer.

In the first corrected sentence, the subject, *Helena,* is singular. The verb, *goes,* is also singular. Therefore, they agree. In the second sentence, the subject is *Helena and Ryan.* This is a plural subject which agrees with the verb, *go.*

Exercises: Correct the errors in subject-verb agreement in the following sentences. Place a C in the blanks beside the sentences that are correct.

_____ 3a. Romeo and Juliet dances together at the costume ball.

_____ 3b. The fashion industry now sell clothing not only in stores but also over the Internet.

_____ 3c. Monica and John serve as representatives for the Admissions Department.

_____ 3d. Rhyme and rhythm add to the unique sound of Robert Frost's poetry.

_____ 3e. The interior designer carefully survey the space before she begins to sketch out a design.

4. When a verb is separated from its subject by a phrase, make sure that the verb agrees with the subject in number.

Incorrect: _The chef, as well as the bakers, think that the presentation of the food is as important as the taste._

The subject of the sentence is _chef,_ which is singular. The verb, _think,_ is plural in this case; therefore, it does not agree with the subject.

Correct: _The chef, as well as the bakers, thinks that the presentation of the food is as important as the taste._

In this example, the verb, _thinks,_ is singular and agrees with the singular subject, _chef._

Exercises: Correct the subject-verb agreement errors in the following sentences. Place a _C_ in the blanks beside the sentences which are correct.

_____ 4a. The dancers of the Russian ballet school leaps across the stage.

_____ 4b. Each of the girls, costumed in colorful tutus, dazzles the audience with her skill.

_____ 4c. The accompanying music, played by concert violinists, fill the hall with magic.

_____ 4d. The readers of Edgar Allan Poe meets once a week for dinner at the House of Poe.

_____ 4e. The island, known for its gorgeous beaches, offer snorkeling and scuba diving.

5. A pronoun takes the place of a noun; therefore, you must clearly indicate which noun the pronoun is replacing. (The noun being replaced is called the *antecedent*.) You should not write *she, it, this,* or *that* if the pronoun does not have an antecedent.

Incorrect: *The political speech and the handout from the campaign were both informative, but it was more specific.*

In this sentence there are two possible antecedents for the pronoun *it*. They are *political speech* and *handout*. The reader would not know to which antecedent *it* was referring.

Correct: *The political speech and the handout from the campaign were both informative, but the handout was more specific.*

The sentence has been corrected by changing the pronoun to a noun.

Exercises: Revise the following sentences to make the pronouns and their antecedents clearer. Place a *C* in the blanks beside the sentences which are correct. Treat the sentences as if they were all part of one essay.

_____ 5a. We watched a film version of *Hamlet* before we read the play in class. Most of us liked it better.

_____ 5b. Hamlet and Laertes both wish to avenge the deaths of their fathers, but he is the more decisive of the two.

_____ 5c. Shakespeare presents desirable female characters in the play— Gertrude and Ophelia. If I had to choose a character to play, I would pick her.

_____ 5d. The gravediggers add comic relief to Hamlet's brooding in the play. Their scene with him is a theatrical classic.

_____ 5e. Hamlet has powerful scenes with both Gertrude and Ophelia. She really loves him.

6. Not only does a pronoun require an antecedent, it also has to agree with its antecedent in number (singular or plural).

Incorrect: *Peter was unable to find a BMW that he wanted to buy. This situation made them sad.*

Peter is just one person, so the use of the pronoun *them* in this sentence is confusing.

Correct: *Peter was unable to find a BMW that he wanted to buy. This situation made him sad.*

Peter was unable to find a BMW that he wanted to buy. This situation made his family sad.

In the first corrected version, the singular pronoun *him* refers to the noun *Peter,* which is its antecedent. In the second corrected version, the pronoun *them* is replaced by the noun *family.* This option also avoids confusing the reader.

Exercises: Correct the following errors or confusions in pronoun-antecedent agreement. Place a C in the blanks besides the sentences which are correct. There is more than one possible way to correct the errors.

_____ 6a. Huck and Jim think that his days are better spent on the raft.

_____ 6b. Each girl decorated their dorm rooms with stuffed animals.

_____ 6c. The boys in the rock band styled their hair in crewcuts similar to the hairstyles of rock 'n' roll groups of the 1950s.

_____ 6d. Tom pocketed seven balls in a row in the billiards game. They were happy with his performance.

_____ 6e. John, along with Bill and Joe, registered for their classes during the lunch break.

7. First and third person pronouns change form to indicate whether they are the subject or the object of the action of the verb or the object of a preposition.

Incorrect: *Mary and me are going to audition for the musical.*

Let me know when it is convenient for you and I to meet.

The professor met Sally and I at the theater.

Pronouns that receive the action of verbs or that are objects of prepositions should be written in the objective form. Pronouns that are subjects of sentences should be written in the subjective form.

Correct: *Mary and I are going to audition for the musical.*

Let me know when it is convenient for you and me to meet.

The professor met Sally and me at the theater.

Use *I*, *we*, *he*, *she*, or *they* when the pronoun is the subject. Use *me*, *us*, *him*, *her*, or *them* when the pronoun is the object.

Exercises: Correct the errors in subjective-objective pronoun use in the following sentences. Place a *C* in the blanks beside the sentences that are correct.

_____ 7a. Just between you and I, I never liked studying grammar.

_____ 7b. We met her at the embassy, and she took a photograph of we as we shook hands with the ambassador.

_____ 7c. Jerry, Michaela, and me formed a counterculture rock group called Fried Fish.

_____ 7d. The instructor gave the final exam to his students, and they gave a copy of the exam to John and me.

_____ 7e. The other class causes a good deal of trouble, but us students are always cooperative and eager.

---

8. Make sure that the parts of a sentence which explain an action or idea (*modifiers*) are positioned as closely as possible to that action or idea.

Incorrect: *We took the entrance exam for the college in the small dining hall.*
The traffic officer placed a ticket on your car in the white hat.
Many students failed the course unexpectedly.

In each of these examples, the underlined group of words is misplaced, causing the reader to misinterpret the writer's meaning.

Correct: *We took the college entrance exam in the small dining hall.*
The traffic officer in the white hat placed a ticket on your car.
Many students unexpectedly failed the course.

Placing a modifier close to the word that it describes will also affect the meaning of the sentence.

Examples: *I **only** like early hip-hop music.*
***Only** I like early hip-hop music.*
*I like **only** early hip-hop music.*
*I like early hip-hop music **only**.*

Exercises: Correct the misplaced modifiers in the following sentences. Place a *C* in the blanks beside the sentences that are correct.

_____ 8a. The makeup classes were scheduled for the sick professor's course at the end of the semester.

_____ 8b. The woman danced the rumba in a Brazilian costume.

_____ 8c. I finished my paper for my business course ten minutes before it was due.

_____ 8d. I scanned the book on dieting on the Internet quickly.

_____ 8e. Tom Thumb was a member of P. T. Barnum's show the smallest man in the world.

9. Avoid placing dangling modifiers at the beginning of sentences.

dangling modifier
Incorrect: *Swimming to shore, the wave crashed over me.*

In this example, the wave is swimming.
There are two ways to fix a sentence which contains a dangling modifier:

1. Keep the modifier. Make the noun or pronoun being described the subject of the independent clause that follows the modifier.

Example: *Swimming to shore, I felt the wave crashing over me.*

2. Change the dangling modifier so that it has its own subject and verb.

Example: *While I was swimming to shore, the wave crashed over me.*

Exercises: Correct the dangling modifier errors in the following sentences. Place a C in the blanks beside the sentences that are correct.

_____ 9a. Dancing at the club, the money fell out of my pocket.

_____ 9b. Rushing up the sidelines, the ball was almost dribbled out of bounds.

_____ 9c. Ignoring the critics, Twain continued to promote his controversial book, *The Adventures of Huckleberry Finn.*

_____ 9d. Furiously drawing, the pen slipped from my hand.

_____ 9e. After campaigning day after day for two months, the election was a welcome relief.

10. A series of similar words or phrases in a sentence should be constructed in the same way. This construction is called *parallelism*.

Incorrect: *Maria was going to write a letter, read a novel, and was finding a present for her cousin.*

The three items in the list—"to write a letter," "read a novel," and "finding a present"—should be constructed in the same way.

Correct: *Maria was going to write a letter, to read a novel, and to find a present for her cousin.*

The three infinitive phrases in the list—"to write a letter," "to read a novel," and "to find a present"—are now constructed in parallel form.

Exercises: Correct the errors in parallelism in the following sentences. Place a C in the blanks beside the sentences which are correct.

_____ 10a. The dining hall at the college prides itself on good service, delicious food, and making sure that the portions are large.

_____ 10b. Swimming, lacrosse, and taking archery are the three physical education course options for the spring semester.

_____ 10c. Don was known for his sense of humor, how he helped others, and ability to find solutions to difficult problems.

_____ 10d. The poetry of Emily Dickinson is marked by complex imagery, unique use of punctuation, and concise word choice.

_____ 10e. Playing the piano, knitting mittens for the homeless, and good books are three hobbies of mine.

Ten Style Tips for Good Writing

Here are ten simple things you can do to improve your writing:

1. Write about what you know.
2. Make sure that the subject interests you.
3. Have a reader in mind.
4. Don't just "tell"—"show"!
5. Deliver on the promises that you make to your reader.
6. Use concrete and specific language.
7. Eliminate words that don't pull their own weight.
8. Resist using the passive voice.
9. Revise; revise; revise.
10. Do it!

1. **Write about what you know.** There's an amusing scene at the beginning of the Beatles's animated film *Yellow Submarine* in which Ringo, moping around Liverpool on a Saturday night, complains, "Nothing exciting ever 'appens to me." In the background, unseen by Ringo, is a strange yellow submarine watching him through its periscope. What he doesn't know—but what the viewers do!—is that his life is about to get very exciting.

   You may sometimes feel as if nothing exciting ever comes your way. You may imagine that other peoples' lives and experiences are more interesting than your own. For this reason, you may be tempted to write about exotic themes and to set your essays and stories in faraway or imaginary experiences. The problem with this strategy is that you often won't know enough about these places or experiences to make them seem real or believable—and nothing sends an audience away unsatisfied more quickly than writing that rings false. And remember, holding your audience is a goal of all writers.

   A better strategy is to write about places, events, processes, or people that you already know something about. Don't worry if you think that they're boring—as Ringo's life in Liverpool must have seemed to him—seeing them with a fresh eye can enliven your depiction of them. Plus, not everyone has had *your* experiences, so they may well be new for your reader. Remember, it isn't the experience itself but rather the way in which you write about it that will make the experience enjoyable for your reader.

2. **Make sure that the subject interests you.** This is simple. A goal for many writers is to make their work "unputdownable." But if what you're writing about doesn't hold *your* interest, you can forget about its ever interesting somebody else. Therefore, whenever possible, select writing topics about which you are passionate—or at least that truly interest you. Even when this isn't possible—and with some assignments, it won't be—try to approach your material in different ways that will stir your interest. Writing is one of the best ways for you to learn about new things or to learn new things about familiar topics. Suppose, for example, that you have a paper due for a biology class. You might choose to examine the squirrels that you always see hopping around campus, or a tree outside your window which you've looked at a hundred times but have never really *seen*. Also, as you write, keep your reader in mind.

3. **Have a reader in mind.** When asked for whom he writes, John Updike once revealed that he imagines a young woman who might walk into a public library in the Midwest, take his book off the shelf, read the first page, and then decide she has to read the rest. This is a very specifically imagined audience, but given that Updike is one of the most admired and widely published modern American authors, he certainly seems to be doing something that is reaching readers.

   You may write with your teacher or your mother in mind, or a dear friend, or a group of people with whom you share an interest in your topic. The key is, as you've seen in Chapter 2, to think about your audience. Remember the advice about "hopping the fence" and put yourself in the place of somebody who is reading your words. Imagine someone actually sitting down reading and reacting to what you've written. And maybe, if you do this well, your reader will feel like Holden Caulfield in *The Catcher in the Rye* and will want to call you up to talk.

4. **Don't just "tell"—"show"!** When you say that an essay or another piece of writing "comes alive," you probably mean that you're able to picture it in your mind. You see, hear, smell, taste, touch, and emotionally experience parts of the story. As a writer, to be able to do this, you must engage your reader's senses.

    The difference between merely *telling* and really *showing* is the difference between "the kitchen was messy" and "there were dishes and scorched pans heaped in the sink. Newspapers littered the table. In one corner, a spider had knit a web that glittered in the morning sun seeping palely through the dingy window."

    With telling, you make it easy for your readers to stay outside your writing. With showing, you put the readers inside, where you want them. Contrast "I was scared" with "My stomach was clenched as tight as a fist. My breath came in shallow heaves, and I felt I couldn't get enough air. A scream rose in my brain, and I wanted to run, but my knees had turned to taffy."

    As you write, "Show; don't tell!" should be a dictum that you recite to yourself as often as you must as a reminder that the best writing engages a reader—makes the act of reading worthwhile—which, after all, is the unspoken promise that you make to your reader.

5. **Deliver on the promises that you make to your reader.** This tip relates to your having a clear thesis—both in mind and on paper—when you set out to write. Your thesis statement tells your reader what to expect in the sentences, paragraphs, and pages that follow. The thesis statement leads to your readers' payoff. It becomes a kind of contract with your audience that says: If you read this, I promise to delight you, inform you, persuade you, make you laugh, cry, and tremble.... Pick the words that apply, but whatever they are, *deliver*. And continually check yourself to be sure that you are delivering on what you say you're going to do. Whether you're writing to inform, persuade, or entertain, if the piece is to be worth reading, you must deliver.

6. **Use concrete and specific language.** The most powerful language is that which enables your reader to experience what you are writing about. Some guaranteed ways to achieve this effect are with writing that appeals to the senses and with writing that conveys action and emotion. In other words, writing that *shows* rather than just *tells*.

    Look at the following passage: *Running across the campus, she felt really good. When she got to class, she was happy.* Now, contrast it with this passage: *Jogging across the campus, with the maple leaves crackling underfoot, she experienced a sense of well-being. Her skin felt aglow, and her breath made puffs of frost on the autumn air. When she got to class, she was glad to be alive.*

    The first passage is vague or "soft"; it's not specific and does little to bring the reader into the piece. The second passage is concrete and more specific, making an appeal to the senses and conveying movement and action—thus bringing the reader in.

7. **Eliminate words that don't pull their own weight.** Remember when you wrote your first book reports in school? You probably wrote passages like this one: *Animal Farm by George Orwell is a really good book. The author is English. English authors write good books. This book is good because it tells all about modern life in the twentieth century.* After thirty-five words, what do you really know? Very little. In weak writing there are usually words just hitching a ride, doing no work of their own. By eliminating such words, you get a lighter, more efficient passage like this one: *George Orwell's Animal Farm is a chilling fable about socialism.* Here you have ten words, each doing its job to help express an idea.

   Imagine that your writing is like the spring in one of those little wind-up toys. When it's wound, the compressed spring contains a lot of energy to make the toy "go." Similarly, writing that is concise, that's doing its job with the fewest necessary (and well-chosen) words, can have a lot of energy to make your essay go. This doesn't mean you should slash every word in sight, but you will do yourself a favor if you make sure that your words and examples are expressing your ideas.

8. **Resist using the passive voice.** The *passive* voice puts emphasis on the receiver of the action; the *active* voice emphasizes the performer of the action. Or, said another way, with the passive voice, an action is done to someone or something; with the active voice, the person or thing performs the action. Contrast the following sentences:

   The piano was played by her.
   She played the piano.
   The story was covered by *Time* magazine.
   Time magazine covered the story.

   In version 2 of each case, the active voice is more concise and direct. This doesn't mean that there is no place for passive voice, but as a general practice, you should avoid using it and should use the active voice instead. By reading your writing aloud, you can often rely on your ear to tell you which construction works best.

9. **Revise; revise; revise.** Why does a very good basketball player still practice shooting foul shots? Why does an accomplished musician still play scales? Because they want to remain good and become even better performers. Practicing is their version of revising. Professional writers often spend more of their time revising than composing the first draft.

   You no doubt have a classmate who boasts that she sits down the night before a writing assignment is due and knocks it out in one session, hands it in, and gets a good grade. Even if this is true—and it sounds dubious—the truth is that with revision, her work could be even better.

10. **Do it!** You've got a headache. Your favorite show is on TV. It's game six of the playoffs. Your pencil broke. There's always mañana. These are all fine excuses for putting off writing, but they are still excuses. The best thing to do when you've got work to write is to *do it*. Make some time; sit down and write.

    Sometimes the sheer size of a task—a research paper, say—can be overwhelming, but the thing to remember is that you don't have to do it all at once. Nor must you get it right the first time. If people had to, no one would ever write a book (or run a marathon, cook a Thanksgiving dinner, or raise kids). All writing has to start somewhere.

As you've been learning throughout your use of this book, the best writing often doesn't come until after you've already written at least one draft. Doing this frees you from worrying about the task and lets you go to work to produce something really good. So when you're uncertain, put some of those prewriting strategies to work and get something down on paper. Just do it.

If you've been practicing the techniques which this book presents, you are in the process of becoming an ever-improving writer. Congratulations. But no book or teacher can do the writing for you. That's your part of the deal. And the rewards … well, those are yours, too.

Acknowledgments

Chapter 1 Page 11, "The Quarry," by David Daniel. Reprinted by permission from David Daniel; page 13, "Polaroids," from *Bird by Bird* by Anne Lamott. Copyright © 1994 by Anne Lamott. Reprinted by permission of Pantheon Books, a division of Random House, Inc.; page 15, "Digging," from *Opened Ground: Selected Poems 1966-1998* by Seamus Heaney. Copyright © 1998 by Seamus Heaney. Reprinted by permission of Farrar, Straus and Giroux, LLC; page 16, "The Thought Fox," from *Selected Poems 1957-1967* by Ted Hughes. Copyright © 1957 by Ted Hughes. Originally appeared in *The New Yorker*. Reprinted by permission of HarperCollins Publishers, Inc.; page 17, "Spin," from *The Things They Carried* by Tim O'Brien. Copyright © 1990 by Tim O'Brien. Reprinted by permission of Houghton Mifflin Company/Seymour Lawrence. All rights reserved.

Chapter 2 Page 32, "Black Men and Public Space," by Brent Staples. Appeared in *Ms. Magazine,* September 1986. Reprinted by permission from Brent Staples; page 35, "How We Listen," from *What To Listen For in Music* by Aaron Copland. Reprinted by permission of the Aaron Copland Fund for Music, Inc., copyright owner; page 37, lyrics to "The Times They Are A-Changin," by Bob Dylan. Copyright © 1963, 1964 by Warner Bros. Music. Copyright renewed 1991 by Special Rider Music. All rights reserved. International copyright secured. Reprinted by permission; page 39, "Dream Deferred," from *Collected Poems* by Langston Hughes. Copyright © 1994 by the Estate of Langston Hughes. Reprinted by permission of Alfred A. Knopf, a division of Random House, Inc.; page 40, "Girl," from *At the Bottom of the River* by Jamaica Kincaid. Copyright © 1983 by Jamaica Kincaid. Reprinted by permission of Farrar, Straus and Giroux, LLC.

Chapter 3 Page 53, "The Great Person-Hold Cover Debate: A Modest Proposal for Anyone Who Thinks the Word 'He' is Just Plain Easier..." by Lindsy Van Gelder, originally appeared in *Ms. Magazine,* April 1980 issue. Reprinted by permission from Lindsy Van Gelder; page 55, "Last Rites for Indian Dead," by Suzan Shown Harjo. Copyright 1989 *Los Angeles Times.* Reprinted by permission from the *Los Angeles Times* and from Morning Star Foundation; page 57, "The Sacred," from *Between Angels* by Stephen Dunn. Copyright ©1989 by Stephen Dunn. Used by permission of W. W. Norton & Company, Inc; page 58, "Dulce Et Decorum Est," by Wilfred Owen, from *The Collected Poems of Wilfred Owen,* copyright ©1963 by Chatto & Windus, Ltd. Reprinted by permission of New Directions Publishing Corp.; page 59, "The Lesson," from *Gorilla, My Love* by Toni Cade Bambara. Copyright © 1972 by Toni Cade Bambara. Reprinted by permission of Random House, Inc.

Chapter 4 Page 79, "October Burial," from *The Tamarack Writers* by David Daniel. Reprinted by permission from David Daniel; page 80, "Original Detail," from *Writing Down the Bones* by Natalie Goldberg ©1986. Reprinted by arrangement with Shambhala Publications, Inc., Boston, *www.shambhala.com*; page 81, "The Writer," from *The Mind Reader* by Richard Wilbur ©1971. Reprinted by permission of Harcourt, Inc; page 82, "Constantly Risking Absurdity," from *A Coney Island of the Mind* by Lawrence Ferlinghetti, copyright © 1958. Reprinted by permission of New Directions Publishing Corp.; page 83, "No One's a Mystery," by Elizabeth Tallent from *Time with Children* ©1986 by Alfred A. Knopf.

Chapter 5 Page 98, "Football Season," from *The Music School: A Collection of Short Stories* by John Updike. Copyright ©1966 by John Updike. Reprinted by permission of Alfred A. Knopf, a division of Random House, Inc.; page 102, "Writing Drafts," from *The Writer's Companion* by Richard Marius. Copyright ©1991 by McGraw-Hill. Reprinted by permission from the McGraw-Hill Companies; page 104, "In My Craft or Sullen Art," from *The Poems of Dylan Thomas* by Dylan Thomas. Copyright ©1946 by New Directions Publishing Corp. Reprinted by permission of New Directions Publishing Corp.; page 105, "For the Young Who Want To," from *Circles on the Water* by Marge Piercy. Copyright ©1982 by Marge Piercy. Reprinted by permission of Alfred A. Knopf, a division of Random House, Inc.; page 106, "Pattern for Survival," from *The Shores of Space* by Richard Matheson. Reprinted by permission of Don Congdon Associates, Inc. Copyright ©1955 by Fantasy House, Inc., renewed 1983 by Richard Matheson.

Chapter 6 Page 124, "Two Past Midnight," from *Four Past Midnight* by Stephen King. Copyright ©1990 by Stephen King. Used by permission of Viking Penguin, a division of Penguin Putnam, Inc.; page 125, "Revising," from *Writing Well,* 6th ed. by Donald Hall. Copyright 1988 by Donald Hall. Reprinted by permission of Addison-Wesley Educational Publishers, Inc.; page 129, "The Author to Her Book," by Anne Bradstreet; page 130, "Theme for English B," from *Collected Poems* by Langston Hughes. Copyright ©1994 by the Estate of Langston Hughes. Reprinted by permission of Alfred A. Knopf, a division of Random House, Inc.;

page 131, "The Stolen Party," by Liliana Heker, ©1982, which appeared in *Other Fires: Short Fiction by Latin American Women,* edited and translated by Alberto Manguel, ©1985. Reprinted by permission of Westwood Creative Artists, Ltd.

Chapter 7   Page 157, "Different Worlds of Words," from *You Just Don't Understand* by Deborah Tannen. Copyright ©1990 by Deborah Tannen. Reprinted by permission of HarperCollins Publishers, Inc., William Morrow; page 166, "What's in a Name?" from *The Essay Collection* by Lynn Z. Bloom and Seung Hee Suh. © by Houghton Mifflin Company; page 168, "Beauty and the Beast of Advertising," by Jean Kilbourne, from *Media & Values* (Winter, 1989), the Center for Media Literacy, pp. 8-10. Reprinted by permission from the Center for Media Literacy; page 171, "Out, Out—" by Robert Frost, from *The Poetry of Robert Frost* edited by Edward Connery Latham. Copyright ©1975 by Henry Holt & Co., LLC, Publisher, New York; page 172, "The Telephone Call," by Fleur Adcock, *Poems 1960-2000* (Bloodaxe Books, 2000). Reprinted by permission; page 173, "The Story of the Hour," by Kate Chopin.

Chapter 8   Page 190, "A Veteran Remembers," by Howard Zinn from *The Boston Globe,* November 11, 1999 issue. Reprinted by permission from Howard Zinn; page 191, "Poor Man's Gourmand," by Russel Baker. Copyright 1975 © by The New York Times Company. Reprinted by permission; page 193, "The Pitcher," from *The Orb Weaver* by Robert Francis. ©1960 by Robert Francis, Wesleyan University Press, reprinted by permission of the University Press of New England; page 194, "Moving Camp Too Far," from *A Snake in her Mouth: Poems 1974-1996* by Nila Northsun. Copyright ©1996 by Nila Northsun. Reprinted by permission from West End Press; page 195, selection from *Cathedral* by Raymond Carver. Copyright ©1981 by Raymond Carver. Reprinted by permission of Alfred A. Knopf, a division of Random House, Inc.

Chapter 9   Page 210, "Concord Hymn," by Ralph Waldo Emerson; page 227, "The Discovery of What It Means to Be an American," ©1959 by James Baldwin, originally appeared in *The New York Times Book Review.* Collected in *Nobody Knows My Name* ©1961 by James Baldwin. Copyright renewed. Published by Vintage Books. Reprinted by arrangement with the James Baldwin Estate; page 231, "Conversational Ballgames," from *Polite Fictions: Why Japanese and Americans Seem Rude to Each Other* by Nancy Sakamoto and Reiko Naotsuka. Copyright ©1982 by Nancy Sakamoto and Reiko Naotsuka. Reprinted by permission from Nancy Sakamoto; page 235, "Top of the Food Chain," from *Without a Hero* by Coraghessan Boyle. Copyright © T. Coraghessan Boyle. Used by permission of Viking Penguin, a division of Penguin Putnam, Inc.; page 251, "To Err is Wrong," from *A Whack on the Side of the Head* by Roger von Oech. Copyright ©1983, 1990, 1998 by Roger von Oech. By permission of Warner Books, Inc.

Chapter 10   Page 257, "I Seen Where a Woodchuck Had Come and Went," by Timothy E. Trask. Reprinted by permission from Timothy E. Trask; page 262, "I Have a Dream," by Martin Luther King, Jr. Reprinted by arrangement with The

Index